# THE REAL ESTATE BOOK

## Forms, Letters and Clauses

# THE REAL ESTATE BOOK

FORMS, LETTERS AND CLAUSES

## The Ultimate Paper Trail


*Oliver E. Frascona, Esq., GRI*
*Katherine E. Reece, CRS, GRI*

Edited by
Joseph L. Frascona, J.D.
Jean E. Frascona, LL.B.

**Library of Congress Cataloging-in-Publication Data**

Frascona, Oliver E., 1947-
The real estate book : forms, letters, and clauses : the ultimate paper trail / Oliver E. Frascona, Katherine E. Reece ; edited by Joseph L. Frascona, Jean E. Frascona.
p. cm. — (Real estate law series)
Includes index.
ISBN 0-941937-02-X (paper) ; $49.95 (est.)
1. Real estate business—Law and legislation—United States—Forms. 2. Vendors and purchasers—United States—Forms. 3. Real estate business—Records and correspondence. I. Reece, Katherine E., 1951- . II. Frascona, Joseph Lohengrin. III. Frascona, Jean Ezard. IV. Title V. Title: Ultimate paper trail. VI. Series
KF2042.R4F7 1995
346.7304'37—dc20
[347.306437] 94-25141
CIP

Real Estate Law Series

from

**Real Law Books, Inc.**
Post Office Box 3113
**Boulder, Colorado 80307-3113**
U.S.A.
Telephone 303-494-6661

Printed in the United States of America

# Dedication

This book is dedicated to the professional real estate people who assist us all in the search, acquisition, financing, and sale of real estate, one of the most precious commodities available in our free society. Acknowledgment is also made to the National Association of Realtors® which works tirelessly through the never-ending efforts of its members to preserve the rights of each of us to buy, own, use, and sell real estate. The authors are members of and greatly appreciate the efforts of the National Association of Realtors® for its continuing commitment to educate Realtors®, the public, and governments both large and small about the ever-changing aspects of private property ownership.

It is appropriate to pause to thank the real estate professionals, brokers and salespeople, executive officers, clients and friends, in and out of the real estate profession, who have encouraged this effort. It is through the unconditional support and help given by these friends and family that we have been able to complete what we feel is a comprehensive manual for the real estate professional, whether just entering the profession or having been in practice for a number of years.

To those who recognize some of the facts and wording, thank you for your prior written permission that allowed us to use your real-life experiences. If you recognize some names they were used with permission.

A special thank you to Monica Frascona and Alexander Frascona. Once again they allowed Dad to work on this project at their expense in loss of time. I love you both so much. Also, this work would not have been possible without the example set by my parents, Professor Joseph L. Frascona, Esq., Professor of Law, Retired and Jean E. Frascona, LL.B., Cambridge, England, Barrister-at-Law, who have written numerous law books together for over fifty years. Katherine, you were the breath of fresh air, the touch with someone who actually sells real estate every day, that helped to make this book all that I have dreamed it might be.

To all my special friends, who have given to me their unconditional support and encouragement to accept the challenges and rewards of new dimensions in my life. In memory of my parents, Thomas J. Reece and Alma Kathleen Reece, whose guidance over the years instilled in me both a sense of survival and the knowledge that all things are possible if you just believe in your ability to accomplish any dream. Oliver, you are the source of inspiration that propelled me to reach for the dream.

**Real** Help for **Real** People in **Real** Estate®

# Preface

Selling real estate was once a relatively simple pastime. It is now one of the most complex and litigious professions in America. The money that the average person invests in a home represents a substantial portion of the individual's net worth. Purchasing a home is one of the most important decisions that any family will make. Whereas people once bought a home and lived there for a long period, they now move around the country and the world as easily as walking to the store for a soda. The state and federal laws that govern the buying, selling and financing of real estate are voluminous and constantly changing. The public can not possibly be familiar with all aspects of even the average real estate transaction. They just want to buy or sell real estate.

Disclosure requirements, fair housing guidelines, environmental hazards, and multiple forms of third party and seller financing are just a few of the many hurdles that a "normal" transaction must overcome. Enter the real estate broker and salesperson. As if just trying to keep abreast of the rules and regulations that affect their industry were not overwhelming enough, real estate professionals, like so many other professionals, must also protect themselves against the very public they strive to serve. The rationale of the thinking of many buyers and sellers is that they are not responsible for anything, much less their own decisions! If a problem arises from the transaction, it must be the fault of someone else, i.e., the real estate professional.

As a matter of course, the real estate broker has become the drafter of a multiplicity of clauses that are required to tailor a transaction to the individual desires of the buyer and seller. The broker and salesperson need a guide where they can find the information they require to assist them. The broker needs a reference where the salespeople can obtain instruction, standard forms, clauses and similar information so that they can properly assist the public with their real estate needs. The salesperson needs a quick reference, a place to start, a form to review, the opportunity to revise something that is almost what they need if not exactly the perfect fit. We hope that this book fulfills that need.

This book is an attempt to give you, the real estate professional, an observation point from which to map your own descriptive correspondence, draft your own clauses and design and complete your own standard forms. Use it as a place to start when you need to draft a contract, addendum, form or cover letter. We hope that you will use it to achieve the high ground of excellence and reap many more successful real estate transactions. We hope that it will help you eliminate the ever-pressing sensation of needing to look backwards over your shoulder for possible disputes, confrontations, and litigation. Look forward instead to strengthening your own internal personal and office standard of practice and communication. It is in the strength of your own standard, properly imparted to those with whom you transact business, which will ultimately determine your success in dealing with people.

Creating your own "paper trail" will help you to fully inform others of the alternatives presented, tighten your contract preparation, improve your decision-making skills, and reduce your liability. Your success there, in turn, will arise from your increased ease and efficiency in stating clearly to everyone--your clients and customers, lenders, the public, suppliers, and others on whom we all rely for support and business--the pertinent facts of any transaction, the limits of your liability, and the necessary notifications and confirmations.

Although we have used the names of friends and associates, that should not be interpreted as an endorsement or disparagement. Cases in point are just that, actual cases. The names have been changed in some cases to protect us all.

## Caveat--Disclaimer

Yes, there must be one. This book would not work if we did not have one. This material is designed to give the reader as many "places to start" as possible. Although great care has been taken to ensure that the information contained is accurate, pertinent, and to the point, each situation and each intended use is different. All clauses, forms, and letters should be the work product of the reader as an individual author. While written for general use throughout the United States, the reader should seek competent local legal advice before using any of the material contained herein.

This publication is sold with the understanding that neither the authors nor the real estate or law firms of which they are members are giving legal or other professional advice nor recommending the use of these letters or other material in the form in which they appear in this book. This publication is not intended to be, and should not be used as, a substitute for legal advice.

We are also concerned that there may be a typographical error or that a particular local law or custom may contradict the contents of the material presented. Therefore, we must indicate that we make no representations as to the accuracy of the information contained herein and are not liable to anyone for its use or misuse.

We want to encourage everyone to have a personal copy that can contain their own notes and modifications accordingly. Use this publication and the material contained herein at your own risk. THERE ARE NO WARRANTIES, EXPRESS OR IMPLIED, INCLUDING FITNESS FOR A PARTICULAR PURPOSE, MADE WITH RESPECT TO THIS MATERIAL.

## The Copyright

What may you do with the clauses, forms, letters and information that are in this book? Yes, it is copyrighted material. That means that nothing in this book may be photocopied or reproduced in any manner for resale to others without the prior written consent of the authors. However, you may copy it for your own use. That is why we wrote it.

## Computer Disk and Photo Ready Forms

The forms are available in 8.5" x 11" photo ready formats. The language is exactly as shown in the book. They are designed for immediate use with or without your company logo. They were not photo reduced for the book. Each was typeset separately so the line endings and format may differ from that displayed in the book.

The forms and letters are also available on computer diskettes. This is to save hours and hours of retyping. They are exactly as written in the book. The computer diskettes are compatible with either the IBM® or MacIntosh® format.

# Introduction

In order to be helpful, the book had to have a structure. We have chosen the pattern of events in the "normal" real estate transaction, if there still is such a thing! We hope that the information and ideas contained in this book will spark your thought process and give you an idea base from which to work. From that base you can always create a polite and clear note or letter which meets your need to disclose information to your clients and customers, disclaim liability for actions that were never yours from the start, and answer questions for the record. It's simple. It's a good habit. And you will see how the use of professional correspondence not only protects you and your broker but also consistently helps you sell real estate.

As a modern real estate professional, you must work with and literally depend upon information from many different members of the public at large. You say many things to various clients, customers, subagents, agents for other parties, lenders, title companies, inspectors, appraisers, investors and other people. You often make these statements intending to encourage or induce someone to take a particular action, purchase, sell, finance, lease, appraise or otherwise deal with real property. In addition, as a cautious professional, you are becoming more and more aware of the duty being imposed upon real estate professionals by brokers, lenders, other agents, regulatory authorities, boards, legislatures, and courts to disclose ever-increasing amounts of information. Often the standard by which you might be judged is not even available for inspection until the authority actually decides the case.

Even clear, concise, consistent speech has always been susceptible to various interpretations at the time it is uttered. Later, the memory tends to remember what one wants it to remember. The golden rule of "the test of the meaning of a communication is what a person in the position of the addressee can reasonably understand it to mean" is being stretched to the limit. The court system, the regulators, the legislatures at all levels, in an effort to protect us all from even ourselves, are increasing the amount of regulation to be imposed on the business of providing access to shelter, the most basic of all brokerage businesses.

Carefully drafted contracts now potentially require many different clauses. Some clauses are used and others are considered and discarded in the process of selection and refinement of the modern real estate contract. The use of a "forms" or "clauses" collection is a must. To draft from scratch is too time consuming and leaves open the possibility that something was not thought of.

Standard forms must be identified, refined and printed so that the standard aspects of the transaction are presented and consented to in a uniform manner. This protects the public as well as the broker and salesperson. Cover letters, clarifying nearly all information presented and the extent of the broker's and agent's roles, are becoming a must. In the face of such potential liability, there is no need for the real estate professional to simply give up and write letters that will discourage the reader when the skillful use of the cover letter can also be a professional selling tool.

There are still buyers and sellers who want to and will consummate transactions through the brokerage network. In fact, it is the very complexity that we all abhor that is entrenching the real estate broker as a necessity in modern life. Just ten years ago real estate transactions were far simpler. All loans were thirty-years fixed; governments did not have planned unit developments (PUD's); down-zoning was unknown; the approval process took three to four weeks; land available for development was plentiful; the air was clean; water, electricity and natural gas were everywhere. Not so today.

The real estate professional is looked upon by many as an equal to the legal profession. People expect the real estate professional to have access to standard forms and to be able to draft contracts of a much more complex nature than in the past. While we continually encourage people to "see an attorney" we also recognize that many attorneys do not regularly deal in real estate. They have to rely on the draft from the real estate professional.

The skillful creation of a "paper trail" that imparts a feeling of respect for the real estate professional in the eyes of the reader, that fully informs and assists in reinforcing the sale, and presents vital information in a hard-to-dispute form is the core of this work. It is our desire that you take heart from this book and become confident from its use so that you, too, can draft contracts, forms and letters which will accomplish all this in your own situations.

Comments and sample forms, clauses and letters are just that: samples. You should rethink your actual content and not rely solely on the forms we are presenting. Although each case is a little different, try to develop your own standard forms, clauses, letters and habits so that you always handle a similar situation in the same manner. Careful, planned consistency is the best defense. Establish yourself as a consistent professional.

Recognizing that both sexes are actively represented in the real estate profession, we have tried to write so that the need to use a particular gender is eliminated. When that is not possible, we have used various genders at random. The use of any particular gender is to save the constant use of his/her, he/she.

We have included different variations of the same standard form. Mix and match as you fell appropriate. We wanted to provide several finished options for the reader.

*Please read the sample clauses, forms and cover letters in the book before you use them. Do not assume that everything is perfectly the way you want it. Read it.*

Real estate must be fun. Enjoy your life. If you are not having fun change professions. There is no instant replay. Remember, you are real estate.

Oliver E. Frascona | Katherine E. Reece

# TABLE OF CONTENTS

## Chapter Three
## The Buyer Relationship

**Chapter Five**
**The Contract**

**Chapter Seven**
**Closing Matters**

# Chapter One
# The Basics
### *Guidelines for the Entire Office*

## *Pledge of Allegiance to the Broker*

I pledge allegiance to the broker of my office.

I recognize that I am the agent of that broker.

I understand that my broker is probably personally liable for my actions and inactions in the real estate business.

I will conduct my personal life so as to augment the professional standing of my real estate company and associates.

I will ask questions when I do not know what to do.

I will continue to learn and advance my knowledge and professionalism.

I will endeavor to deal honestly with everyone.

I will keep my broker informed about every aspect of the transactions in which I am involved.

I will purchase property for my own account only after talking with my broker and obtaining my broker's written permission.

I will ask my broker before I obligate myself or the company.

I will keep accurate and timely records of all aspects of every transaction in which I am involved.

I will deal in securities or property management only with the prior written permission of my broker.

I will conduct all my business as though it were to be reviewed by the Real Estate Commission on a daily basis.

## *Pledge of Allegiance to the Salesperson*

I will trust my salespeople and support their efforts.

I will develop an office policy and continue to update it to reflect the changes in the profession.

I will develop and provide standard forms for the use of my salespeople.

I will continue to further my education so that I can convey accurate and precise information to my salespeople.

I will provide and maintain an office environment that is conducive to generating real estate business.

I will recruit and retain salespeople who adhere to the principles outlined in this pledge.

I will provide assistance and supervision at all times and be available when my salespeople need me.

I will encourage my salespeople to pursue and continue their professional education.

I will set an example in my business practices that embodies the spirit of National Association of Realtor® Code of Ethics and the law.

I will be responsible for training my salespeople in all aspects of the real estate transaction.

I will conduct all my business as though it were to be reviewed by the Real Estate Commission on a daily basis.

## *Pledge of Allegiance to Members of the Public*

I pledge to safeguard to the best of my abilities the trust that is placed in me to assist you with your housing needs.

I promise that I will provide you with all the necessary information available that is pertinent to your individual real estate transaction.

I promise that I will allow you to make the decisions that affect your real estate needs.

I am committed to the spirit and letter of the law to provide everyone with equal access to housing.

I will encourage you to avail yourself of professional attorneys, accountants, surveyors, appraisers, contractors, inspectors and others that are more skilled in their areas of expertise than I am.

I will not let my personal relationship with others deter me from cooperating with them to accomplish your transaction.

I will not let my desire to profit from the transaction alter the course that you have selected.

I will tell you when I do not know the answer to your questions.

I will accept compensation only from sources that I have first disclosed to you.

I will continue to stay abreast of those areas where it is reasonable to expect information from a real estate professional.

## *Rules of the Road for the Office*

We will never:

> Enter into oral agreements where only a written agreement would constitute a binding agreement between parties.
>
> Intentionally misrepresent any aspect of a real estate transaction.
>
> Serve as the attorney-in-fact for anyone.
>
> Act in an agency capacity for anyone other than as provided in our agreement with that party
>
> Accept a position as an escrow agent.
>
> Commingle anyone's funds.
>
> Guarantee the performance of any party.

## The Real Estate Broker in Litigation

**Seller and Broker Beware.** The old days of "buyer beware" are gone. In their place has come an increasing attempt by the courts to "protect" the consumer from everyone including, on occasion, himself. In this age of consumerism, everyone dealing with the public is the subject of increased scrutiny. Doctors, lawyers, manufacturers, distributors, retailers and real estate brokers all deal with and provide vital services to the public. The real estate broker is poised in a unique position as the purveyor of one of our most basic needs: shelter. In addition, over the last decade the real estate profession has been successful in its effort to enhance the image of real estate brokers. The public and the courts have accepted real estate salespeople as professionals, are treating them as such, and are holding them to expectations of top professional practices.

**No Inflation and Greater Complexity.** These are the two final nails in the unprepared broker's coffin. First, there is no consistent inflationary blanket to cover the mistakes of the past. Instead of just selling the home that may have been a mistake, everyone is having to live with them. Second, the world of real estate has become increasingly more complicated. The analysis of the available financing from institutions almost requires a degree in mathematics and the proficient use of a sophisticated calculator, not to mention a crystal ball for each new tax code revision. There is some merit of truth in the theory that tax code revisions are just an ongoing part of the so called "CPA Full Employment and Guaranteed Retirement Act."

Being secure about the type and extent of any financing that may be carried by the seller and being able to anticipate the potential remedies of the various parties in the event of default require a law degree with a specialty in real estate law. The overlapping rules, including all the association, local, county, state and federal statutes and regulations, are increasing at a rate faster than anyone can even read. These often-conflicting requirements place brokers in the middle of the political arena and leave them vulnerable to lawsuits from all sides.

**The Demands Upon The Modern Professional Broker.** The sale and acquisition of real estate has become so complex that an untrained person, even one who is a professional in another field, is no longer able to navigate the safe route to a properly closed transaction without a real estate professional as a guide. Into this world steps the real estate professional and her broker with the broker being liable not only for everything that she herself does but also for the actions or inactions of her agents.

In an attempt to protect the public often as not from itself, the court is placing more and more responsibilities on the broker and pulling the fiduciary duty knot tighter and tighter. Brokers are increasingly being held responsible for their actions, inactions, contract drafting, and other responsibilities related to a real estate transaction. They must learn now how to generate sophisticated paperwork to document the extent of their efforts to a court who is listening to a plaintiff's every word and looking for a mistake, a misrepresentation, an omission, or a way to establish an agency arrangement not previously thought to exist, or a way to provide the basis for assigning liability to both the salesperson and the broker.

**Personal Liability.** In many states, the broker is held personally liable for everything, regardless of any corporate entity which may exist. Damages from litigation, not to mention the attorney's fees, can run into tens of thousands of dollars, ruining years of work and an otherwise promising and profitable career. It is time to learn from the policies and practices of the large professional companies in other fields of endeavor by creating a professional paper trail.

**Disclaimers.** Disclaimers or disclosures are here to stay in every business. They have become a fact of life. Think about the information that doctors give their patients before surgery, auto mechanics give you and us before they work on your car, instructors give their students before they attempt to teach.

**Disclosure.** The broker is now viewed as the source for the information that should be given to the buying and selling public. Documented disclosure is a fixture. Disclosure given with a certain style or flair will enable the broker to present the information in a manner that will assist the public and enhance the broker's reputation. But first you must know what is required. Then you must document what you did so that everyone will remember.

## Clients and Customers as Plaintiffs

**The Uniform Care and Feeding of Plaintiffs.** Real estate professionals are, by nature, a helpful and trusting group of individuals that spend a small concentrated amount of time with strangers and start to treat them like lifelong friends. Treat all clients and customers as if they were going to be plaintiffs. Just because you have bought lunch or dinner for several days or shown someone houses and are now on a first name basis, do not let your guard down. Regard the other person as if he were an FBI agent or government tester. Your treatment of everyone should stand up to the closest scrutiny. Would you like to hear what you have just told someone played back on a tape recording in a court? Would you like to have your daily routine manner of conducting your real estate activities reported in the local newspaper? If the answer is no, maybe you should not say it or do it. This is not to say that you need to be anything other than a uniform, courteous, polite and detail-oriented professional.

**Sources of Plaintiffs.** Although through the subagency system you may be included in some litigation merely from being the listing broker and allowing subagency, most of the plaintiffs from whom you will be obligated to defend yourself will come from your own list of client, customer, and real estate affiliate contacts. Consider the list of people who may be responsible for your losing your license and livelihood and *think.* Look over your customer, client, and affiliate lists for people with the following characteristics-invariably they make great potential plaintiffs:

## *Profile of a Potential Plaintiff*

Someone who starts a conversation with "you can trust me."

Someone who envies the material possessions of others.

Someone who feels that the world is not fair to them.

Someone who tells you about the poor conduct of another real estate professional, lawyer, doctor or lender. You may be next in line.

Someone who confides in you. Quite frankly, you do not need to know secrets because you cannot tell them to anyone. They can only contaminate your mind and thought process and ultimately interfere with good business judgment and practice.

Someone who "feels" that they have not been told the truth.

Someone who "feels" cheated in this transaction or in life in general. Complainers are Plaintiffs.

Someone in a position of apparent authority--a loan officer, an attorney, another broker--who suggests that some action or statement is either correct or incorrect in direct contradiction to what you know to be true.

Someone who wants to "get away" with something, wants to avoid paying a legally just obligation, or who thinks there is a way to "get around" the rules, especially loan qualification procedures and financial disclosure requirements.

More often than not plaintiffs fall into two categories. First, plaintiffs often turn out to be people that you thought were close friends. Ask yourself: Is this because they expected more than you normally deliver, or because you used a standard of practice for friends different from the one you use with your regular clients? With whom would you cancel an appointment first--a new client or an old friend? Second, it should come as no surprise to you that plaintiffs often arise from those people you probably felt were potential trouble. It is rare for a complaint to come from an average customer or client. When in doubt treat friends like strangers and try not to treat strangers like friends.

## *Myths about Disclaimers*

Disclaimers have to be stuffy and dry to be effective.

Disclaimers, if actually read by the addressee, will kill the deal. "No one will buy this property if I have to tell them all that."

Oral disclaimers are just as good as written ones.

The buyers and sellers I deal with are my friends; I do not need a disclaimer for them.

Someone else said it; and even if I know it is false, the fact that someone else made the statement is enough to get me off the hook.

Only attorneys can or should write appropriate and adequate disclaimers.

Even though the company policy prescribes the use of this form, I can just change a few words, and it will do the same job.

Buyers do not need disclaimers.

I can always give the disclaimer after the showing, after the contract is signed or even at the closing. It will be just as effective.

No one really cares about or reads a disclaimer.

An adequate disclaimer will cover any mistake I might make regardless of the severity.

Disclaimers are like indemnification agreements.

I do not need a disclaimer because our company has errors and omissions insurance.

Disclaimers are like an insurance policy. They always provide ample protection.

## The Work Habit

**Friend or Foe?** Are you your own best friend or worst enemy? The manner in which you regularly conduct your business is admissible evidence to demonstrate that there is a pattern of practice--whether it be good or bad--relevant to discrimination, price fixing, negligence, or competency. It is like having good manners. If you have them, they work when you do not think about them. A pattern of good conduct can show a court, judge and jury that you are a careful and consistent professional. Once that has been established, you can win a case using the procedures you always use day to day in the conduct of your business as demonstrated in other cases.

**Pattern of Practice.** On the other hand, the most frequently utilized strategy of the opposition is to establish a pattern of practice that tends to discredit the witness. This will compromise your position even if in this particular transaction you actually did do and say the things that you claim. No protection system will work unless you establish a pattern of conduct, a reputation and a history of doing things correctly. Believe it or not, professionals who draft comprehensive cover letters are respected by their clients and customers and receive the coveted referral. Their perception of such conduct is one of professionalism and attention to detail. This coveted reputation is better than "he is a real tough person". It becomes, "she is a real stickler and a professional. She will have all her paperwork in order. Suing her is a waste of time." No one wants to start, pay for, work on, or take a losing suit to court. Fifty percent of all lawyers lose. The difference between those who successfully litigate a case is often based solely in aligning oneself with a winning case.

**The First Trial.** The first place your case will be tried is in the office of the other lawyer. He will never admit defeat to you in front of his client. However, after you leave you want him to make specific comments to his client. "Did you see how organized they were and the paperwork they had", or "I believe they are telling the truth. They were so professional." The opposing counsel will realize that you probably did send the documents you said you sent, that you did explain to his client the areas that you said you explained and that there is a good possibility that his client is lying. No civil attorney, except possibly the government, wants a client he knows, or fears, is lying. The retainer demanded by opposing counsel after such a meeting, formerly $1,000, is now $3,000.

## Company Protection Policies

**Office Manual.** Establishing a manual containing specific procedures to be followed in each transaction, as well as routine and formal mechanical treatment of all the company's clients and customers, is the best first line of defense. A manual allows the agents to concentrate on selling real estate rather than on worrying about the need for and the exact wording of disclaimers, informational letters, and contract clauses. It is immediately accessible when the need arises. All well-drafted manuals should be capable of becoming reading material for even the most discriminating individuals, such as regulators, opposing counsel, clients, customers and the Real Estate Commission.

**Brochure.** One or more company brochures which include a list of the services offered, the fees charged (if appropriate), and a series of checklists for the client, customer, agent, and the company is quite valuable. It is a good way to explain to everyone in a uniform and consistent manner which services are and are not available, what is expected of each party to a proposed transaction, and the amount to be charged for each respective service. This is especially useful in discouraging unwanted property management which can be listed as a separate item with its own cost analysis. A set of well drafted company policy statements or brochures with good content and type styles can be a great protection device, ensure uniformity of information being conveyed and serve notice of established company policies. The use of comprehensive checklists for all stages of any transaction removes the sense of uncertainty as to what tasks need to be completed. Having these expectations in writing greatly reduces the level of stress experienced by both the salesperson in the field and the broker. Then it is no longer necessary to rely on memory for all the required steps in a transaction.

**Standard Forms.** Standard forms are the only answer. Attorneys have used them for years and are consistently developing new ones. This is not because they are lazy or stupid. Quite the contrary, they realize that the thought process that went into the last problem can be utilized on the next similar problem and duplicated without having to rethink and plan for the problems previously presented and solved.

**Standard Practices.** Company wide standardization of practice and procedure is an absolute must. This can be accomplished by creating a complete program that includes the use of only those forms and clauses that have been approved by the state, if applicable, and by the company. The use of a series of approved cover letters for each stage of a transaction should be coupled with a schedule for their step-by-step distribution.

When a transaction does not fit the standard, it must receive broker attention. Discouraging the on-the-spot modification of standard forms and procedures for the unusual transaction is imperative. It is these transactions that have the highest degree of risk. This way the broker knows that each client and customer is getting the standard information, the required disclosures, and the same set of instructions. In addition, the agent does not have to allow herself to be pressured into making a decision that might not be in anyone's best interests. It removes the need to improvise and allows everyone to concentrate on the listing, sale, and closing of real estate transactions that will not result in future problems.

## *Early Disaster Recognition*

Be alert. Watch for the unusual in the usual.

Above all be consistent. Treat everyone and every transaction in the same manner. No special deals.

If it seems too good to be true, it probably is. When things do not seem correct or you do not feel comfortable, talk with your broker or your attorney immediately. Things have a way of moving quickly when they are going the wrong way.

Have a personal attorney available whom you respect, who is above reproach and with whom you can talk when you feel the need.

As soon as the deal starts to look funny, get away from it and make your departure known. If you are leaving a formal meeting, be sure that your departure is noted in the minutes. In other circumstances remember those people who in turn will remember the timing of your departure.

Make your notes as contemporaneously as possible and retain them. Note what occurs in each transaction and at all meetings. Write letters to your broker, or as a broker, to your salespersons. Document your position and policy in writing, not just by oral conferences. Should you elect to resign, a letter of resignation stating the reasons for your action is important.

If the communication is with a client or a customer, an unrelated witness who is not a relative or associate is invaluable.

Tape recordings are very useful. It is unfortunate, but the tape recorder tends to keep honest people's memories in sync. It has literally saved the reputation and fortune of many salespeople.

Be true to yourself. You know when things are wrong. You will remember what happened and worry about the potential repercussions long after the money has been spent.

Remember the government, local, state and federal has a lot more resources that we do. Even if you win, you loose when you tangle with them.

If someone says "its the principle of the matter" it is usually the money that really matters.

## The Referral

You will live or die by your referrals. Be sure that whomever you recommend conducts business in the same professional manner and with the same ethical standards that exemplifies your business practices. There is never a need to refer a person to anyone if the association will not be to your direct benefit. If the customer is pleased with your referral, you will get a little emotional pat on the back some of the time and maybe a thank you. If there is any problem, the customer will attempt to hold you responsible; and you will suffer the financial and emotional consequences of the customer's displeasure.

## Tips, Tricks, and Traps

**Abbreviations.** If at all possible, do not abbreviate anything. Spell it out. Who is the Alex in the statement "Alex and Monica Frascona"? Is this Alex Frascona? It could be Alexander the Great or Alex Hunter. Did you assume that they were married? They are brother and sister. The absence of abbreviations is a sign of professionalism, reduces the need to make assumptions, and avoids misunderstandings.

**Certified Mail vs. Regular Mail.** If it is important enough to send by certified or registered mail, you should *also* send it by regular mail. There is a lattice of different regulations for each state. Some subject matters require one form of mail and some allow for the other. In addition, there are a number of cases that indicate that simply sending a letter by certified or registered mail is not sufficient to constitute delivery or notice, especially if the addressee does not claim the letter. A better procedure is to send two identical copies of the letter, one certified or registered and the other by way of regular mail. You may wish to indicate on the original, prior to photocopying, "*Original Sent Certified Mail*" and "*Copy Sent Regular Mail.*" If this is your established practice when you send certified or registered mail, it will be seen as proof that, in fact, that is what you did for the matter in question.

**Checks and Endorsements.** Remember that you become liable for the ultimate payment of the check when you endorse one that is made payable to you. If it is going from you to someone else, endorse it with these words "*without recourse*". When the check includes language that purports to release the payee you need to remember that endorsements are subject to change. The bank will still cash the check unless you add the words: "*modification or alteration of this restrictive endorsement makes this check void.*"

**Confirmation.** A good alternative to a letter that requires an affirmative act--such as the signature of the reader which is often difficult to obtain--is the confirming letter. The confirming letter shifts the burden of action to the reader. This is a very convenient method for confirming the content and timeliness of an oral statement. In addition, it firmly places the responsibility to act on the reader if the content does not match his or her understanding of what was said.

Many people who will not take the step of signing the disclosure statement, will also not take the time and effort to deny the facts as outlined in a confirming letter. By simply stating "This is to confirm our discussion of last Tuesday wherein I indicated..." you have not only provided good service but established a favorable legal standing if questioned. It helps keep the good deals good and brings the bad, time-wasting or dangerous ones to the forefront.

**Cooperating Salespersons.** Your association and cooperation with other real estate professionals will enhance the rapid sale of your listings. Build a reputation of being fair but consistent in your representation of your client. Always look for ways to create a winning situation for both parties to the contract. Always be complimentary about the efforts of the cooperating Realtor® while at the same time protecting your client's interests. By creating and adhering to a standard of practice that is honest and predictable, cooperating agents will be eager to show and sell your listings. Remember that in representing the Seller you are agreeing to do all that is necessary to sell his home. "Listing stuff" may actually mean showing the home to the buyer for the cooperating salesperson when schedules do not permit otherwise as well as doing other tasks that may be considered the other salesperson's job. A letter of thanks and addition of the cooperating Realtor® to your exclusive Realtor® database for future listing announcements will encourage the salesperson to inquire about your listings first when he has another buyer.

**Copies.** Copies, policy, and habit are the added plums that give your testimony the credibility that is needed to place the burden of proof on the person who failed to respond. Never let yourself get caught in the position of not responding if such a tactic is used on you. Many people simply do not want to respond if they know the answer is not what they have indicated over the phone or that it will cause the recipient to question the response. People simply try to do what they like to do and leave the unpleasant work for later. This is sudden death when you are utilizing the silent response letter arrangement.

Writing a letter to one addressee but drafting it knowing that it will be read by those indicated as having received copies is a useful tactic. Copies to your clients or customers of third party letters serve to inform your client or customer of the progress being made and make them aware of the content of the letter as efficiently as if the letters had been addressed to them.

An indication on the letter of who is to receive copies can be a good record of where copies of the letter were actually sent. You can even include the addresses to which a copy was sent if you wish. This puts the reader on notice that you are letting others know of the activities described in the letter. It can discourage people from contesting the fact that they received the mailing and the truth of its contents. It is also a courtesy since the letter is no longer private. Think of the time-saving advantages of telling everyone exactly the same information at the same time.

Make a habit of including this common notation at the bottom of your letters. Example:

cc: Oliver E. Frascona, Esq.
4750 Table Mesa Drive
Boulder, CO 80303

Hon. William Armstrong, U.S. Senator

Please note that most elected officials take their mail seriously. Only include them when you actually send a copy to such an individual and then only when the copy has a specific purpose. Sending miscellaneous mail to such offices is a lot like crying wolf.

**Copies--Blind.** There are occasions when you do not want to indicate who received a copy. In such instances you would omit the copy information, but always remember to note on your copy the people who actually received a copy.

**Dates.** Regardless of what you write it on, always date all correspondence. It is a good habit to date and initial, or make a mark known only to you, in the lower left or right hand corner of everything you draft, approve or review. The rules vary from state to state. However, unless specified otherwise, references to dates are generally to calendar days. If you want to avoid any possible misunderstandings, specify "calendar", "business" or "banking" days.

**Drafts.** Try hard never to let your first draft be the final draft. Doing the first draft in pencil will force you to rewrite the letter or the contract at least once. You will always do a better job the second time. Another useful tool is a rubber stamp marked "DRAFT for DISCUSSION PURPOSES ONLY."

The enemy is misunderstanding. Clear and concise documents go a long way to eliminating rather than fostering any potential misunderstanding. Try it for a while and see if your second or third drafts create a better final product.

**Exhibits.** The proper wording is "*The attached Exhibit A-Legal Description, consisting of ___ pages, is incorporated herein and hereby made a part of this document by this reference.*" Even if you do not use all of that, try to give each exhibit a title as well as a letter. There can be a lot of legal descriptions marked "Exhibit A" when a stack of documents is dropped. Another useful trick is to number each client or transaction and place that number on all documents that affect the transaction. If in doubt you can use the street address.

**Facsimile.** Are faxes legal? How many times have we heard that? A fax is just a copy, nothing more or less. Think of a fax machine as a copy machine where the input tray and the output tray are located far apart. We are beginning to see instances where people have removed or altered the phone number that comes with the fax to mislead people into thinking that the fax originated from a different location. Yes, some recipients are changing the time that is set into the receiving machine in an attempt to convince someone in a multiple contract situation that the subsequent contracts arrived before the first. And we still see a lot of people with "selective" memory about having received the fax in the first place.

There is no substitute for notes and copies of transmissions. In addition, with the advent of overnight mail there is no reason not to get the signed original in the mail, or as a minimum original signatures in counterpart when the parties to the transaction or in different geographical locations. Yes, lots of people conduct the entire transaction with faxes and do not insist on the original. We must be held to a high standard.

When sending or receiving a facsimile, always remember your agency status, if any. Insist that the cooperating agent be ready to personally receive the transmittal and always insist that no one send offers to you without your prior knowledge. Even with cover letters that indicate "the information that follows is confidential and only intended for the recipient", there is no guarantee that others will not review the material. The irony of most fax machines is that the order of transmission is reversed and the cover sheet ends up on the bottom of all the pages sent so that any hope of confidentiality is lost.

**Formality.** Everyone wants to be treated like the corporate executive. People perceive that such individuals always get formal letters. More importantly, the court will place a greater significance on a formal letter than on an informal one, especially if disclosure is the issue. Compliment the reader. Treat him like an ambassador. Formal letters can be written so that they read in an easy manner. They need not be stiff.

**Frequency.** When in doubt write a letter. It is hard to imagine sending too many letters. Contact is the first step to contentment, and it establishes care and concern. Most people just want to know what is going on so that they can adjust their plans accordingly. Communication is almost always the key. Lack of communication is one of the three most often listed causes of litigation.

**Letterhead.** Always write all your letters on letterhead if possible, and always keep a copy for your file. Like a business card, letterhead exudes credibility and makes a statement about you. Yes, it is perfectly acceptable to use handwriting on letterhead on occasion. It is definitely a personal touch. You may also try the typed letter with a personal note at the bottom. This gives the impression that you cared enough to personalize the letter with a note rather than just signing the letter.

**Margins and Spacing.** These little things accomplish a lot. Ragged right margins are more friendly and less formal. They tend to get more attention and are read more frequently. In addition, they give a personal touch to a standard letter.

Right-justified margins are more standoffish and receive less scrutiny. Right-justified margins are useful to indicate that your office is modern, organized, has a word processor or other automated document-preparation capability, and a standard procedure for completing your professional tasks. That they also tend to attract less scrutiny may or may not be beneficial, depending on your message.

**Mechanics.** No one will ever know what you know. Nor will they be able to open your head and look inside. Most of us will be judged by our paperwork and personality. There is never an excuse for poor grammar or punctuation. They leave the reader with a sense that the author is not a professional.

White out is not only an invitation to modification, but it is personally unacceptable. White out on colored paper gives a very poor impression to the client or customer. If someone cannot prepare a crisp, clean letter, how will they do with contract documents and the important things such as deeds, notes, and the like?

**Memorandum of Previous Oral Conversation.** This is a very useful tool utilized by many attorneys when the cow is not only out of the barn but is hamburger, and you need to cover the tracks. You start your communication with the words, "This is a memorandum of our previous oral conversation of Friday, June 28th, 1910," and follow with the body of what you indicated in that previous oral conversation. This serves to document your disclosure, not as to the date of the memorandum, but as to the date the conversation took place. This is not always a fail-safe system because the other party may refuse to sign, may deny the fact of the previous conversation and/or may even controvert it which could put you in a more difficult position than had you not tried this tactic. Use it only when the outcome is known.

**Notaries and Witnesses.** It is possible that if you are merely present during a transaction, no matter how much you disavow your role, someone will hold you responsible for something. Therefore, as a notary never allow anyone to sign whose identity you have not verified and who does not sign in your presence. The number of forged notary signatures, a form of state-approved witness with a seal, would destroy your faith in people.

**Case in Point.** *A notary testified, under oath, that she saw Nancy sign a document she had notarized. There was no doubt in her mind that Nancy and Fred had appeared before her personally and were the signatories. She could even pick out Nancy now from the present group, standing next to Fred. Imagine her surprise when she was informed that the lady standing next to Fred was really named Roberta, his girl friend, and not Nancy, Fred's wife.*

The story got even better when it was learned that the individual who had signed Nancy's name was a man, not Roberta, not Nancy, and not present. Once you have been with a stranger for a few days, you too might be tempted to notarize her signature. Require the proper identification with every signature.

**Originals.** Any document that has an original signature is an original document. There is no substitute for an original. Let the other people have copies. If everyone wants an original, make duplicate originals (several identical copies all with original signatures). If there are numerous changes to a document, make the changes, photocopy the altered original, and sign the photocopies as originals. You must retain a copy of every letter sent and every signed document that passes through your hands. The good record keepers are hard to discredit. Be one of them.

**Personal Touch.** If you utilize a word processor, try to make the variables in a letter more than just the name and address of the reader. Include little facts about the transaction or the property to make the form letter as personal to the reader as possible. *Do not change the standard boiler plate language established by your office*. It is there for your protection, as well as for the protection of the firm and the broker.

**Printed, Typed and Handwritten.** The highest priority is the handwritten remarks. Next comes the typed terms and conditions and finally the printed form. Remember that a printed form could be a photocopy.

For forms, the printed form is the best. For communication, a typed letter or statement is easier to read and more professional. However, a handwritten note or message is faster and may convey personal versus delegated attention to the matter. It is better to get a written response on letterhead sent immediately rather than waiting for the time or spending it in an effort to complete a perfect draft. Be careful to reread what you wrote before you send it. The next revisions will be before the jury.

**Re:** This designator on the letter means "regarding" or "in regard to" and indicates the subject of the content of the correspondence. A general reference or no reference at all attracts less attention to the particular matter than a specific reference. Specific references are useful for many letters when you want to be sure the reader's attention is focused on the issue. Alert your readers to the main subject right away and establish the reference for rapid identification when you see the letter later on by leading off your letters with a specific "Re:" line just above the salutation. If you want the letter to receive less significance, eliminate the "Re:" entirely or make it vague and uninviting.

**REALTOR®.** This is a registered mark belonging to the National Association of Realtors® (N.A.R.) which may be used by its members in the fashion designated by N.A.R. It should always be followed by the ® symbol. Realtors® should avoid its use generically in speech, in contracts, in the proper name of their company, or as a synonym for a person who is a real estate licensee, even if such licensee is a member of N.A.R. If you have additional questions or are concerned about the proper use of the mark, an extensive guide dealing with the use of the Realtor® mark is available from N.A.R.

**Receipts.** A fast and efficient system to ensure that you can describe the document received by the recipient is to have a self-inking rubber stamp made that looks something like the example below. Simply make a copy of the document, stamp it, and get the signature of the recipient. It's a fast, accurate, and efficient system that does not require a lot of thought. It is also convenient when you are trusting someone else who might not be aware of the importance or the description of the particular document or who does not know what to write on a receipt. Red, with large letters, seems to be the most useful.

*The undersigned hereby receipts for the original of this document, consisting of ___ pages, on the date indicated.*

_____________________________ ____________

*Recipient* *Date*

**Sample Closing Lines**. When you finish a letter, keep in mind the many ways to end it. The following are some sample closing lines. They vary from the simple to the firm and almost offensive. The last thing you say should be congratulatory, polite, and nice. Always end correspondence with something that is not controversial. Use these separately or combine as needed. Add your own favorites.

**Examples:**

*Please forgive the formality of this letter.* It is important for me to document, for everyone concerned, the information [advice is not a good word to use unless you mean it and are willing to stand by it] I have given you and the decisions that you have made. It may seem fastidious, but it is our office policy and helps keep my broker, the Real Estate Commission, and our malpractice carrier happy.

*It is my understanding* that you completely understand the transaction outlined by both this letter and our previous correspondence; and, after considering all the alternatives as well as the potential risks involved, *you have elected* to proceed along the course outlined herein.

*The transaction which you contemplate* and which has been outlined in this letter is one that has serious tax, financial, and legal consequences. Please understand that neither I nor anyone associated with this office is recommending that you complete the transaction in the manner you have elected. *We simply are not responsible* for anything that occurs as a result of your decision.

*Again, I would* advise you to seek competent legal, accounting, and tax advice before entering into this transaction as you have outlined it.

*As I indicated to you earlier*, the decision to present the terms you have proposed in the contract and the decision to acquire the property indicated above are your decisions alone. I must send you this letter to verify that you are acting on your own judgment and without any encouragement or advice from me or this office. I know you want to complete the transaction *as you have outlined it,* and I wish you the best of luck.

The property is simply beautiful, and I know both you and Monica will enjoy living in The Meadows. If we can be of service in assisting you in locating other property in the future, *please do not hesitate to inquire.* I have enjoyed showing you property and *admire your ability to make your own decisions.*

*Congratulations on your* acquisition of another piece of real estate. I wish you the best of luck. Thank you for selecting me and this firm to show you property.

*I admire your grasp of the complex issues* presented and the business risks involved. Congratulations upon your decision to propose and complete this transaction as you have outlined.

*As I have indicated to you all along,* and as I know you understand, this letter confirms the fact that you, and you alone, have decided to propose and to complete this transaction with the terms you have outlined. Neither I, nor the office with whom I am affiliated, nor the broker for the office can be in any way responsible for the outcome of the transaction. I admire your drive and grasp of the issues and wish you the best of luck.

**Silent Response.** The silent response cover letter is a useful tool to establish a duty on the part of the recipient either to respond or to accept the consequences. Although not as good as the required response cover letter, it is far better than no letter at all. Coupled with a conversation log which incorporates the name of the party with whom you are talking as well as the date, time and content of the conversation, plus the limited use of certified mail, the silent response letter can put you in a very defensible position. It not only documents the content of the conversation but also demonstrates the degree of care utilized to bring the information to the client or customer.

**Structure.** Start every communication, especially a letter, with something pleasant that compliments the reader or makes him feel at ease. Put your reader in the right frame of mind for the content of the letter.

The body of the letter should be polite and tactful but always explicit, especially when a disclaimer is being conveyed. Mix several ideas in a single letter to equalize the content between disclaimer and information. A long letter is a good place to include a lot of serious disclaimers you do not want someone to dwell upon since it will probably never get the reader's full attention and yet will cover the notification process. Several separate letters serve to keep the reader informed but each will receive closer scrutiny. This is a good way to convey good news or routine information. When you want to be sure they read it, keep it short.

The closing should always be polite and offer your assistance: "If there is anything I can do to assist you, please do not hesitate to let me know." "Thank you for your cooperation and assistance in this matter." "We are happy to be your agents." "It is always a pleasure to have you as a client." Even if the content of the letter is difficult, always make the closing pleasant.

**Telephone Trust.** The telephone is used to such an extent that we never even know with whom we speak or how to verify the information or quotations upon which we rely. Lenders, title companies, inspection services, surveyors, taxing authorities, homeowners associations, ditch and water companies, governmental authorities and similar entities provide us with information that we accept, pass on to our clients and customers and fail to verify or commit to memory. Too often the information changes and the memory of the person to whom we have spoken and upon whom we have relied now fades as time and pressure are applied. A letter to the party confirming the information received or quoted will prompt instant recall.

**Term Definition.** A convenient way to define a term for later use is to enclose it in parenthesis with quotation marks after the first use of the word; i.e., the real property ("Property"). Thereafter, you can simply refer to it as the Property. This helps your letter be precise without being wordy and gives it that professional appearance.

# Chapter Two
# Listing the Seller's Real Estate
***Finding, Listing, Representing, Working With and Retaining Sellers***

## *General Rules of the Road*

**Be the Expert** -- Everyone knows you know real estate

**Be the Source** -- If anyone needs to know something about real estate they call you

**Be the Professional** -- "He is always working" is the reputation you desire

**Be Recognizable** -- When they see your name or picture they know you are "the real estate person". Your business card, stationary, flyers, postcards--all promotional material-- must have your picture.

**Be Outgoing** -- Tell everyone you are in real estate. Do not expect them to remember you, you remember them.

**Be There Always** -- People list with the last person who talked to them about real estate.

**Be the Photographer** -- Take and send pictures all the time. Pictures of your listings, pictures of yourself, pictures of your sellers outside their home. People love pictures.

## Searching for the Seller

Where should you look for sellers? Everywhere. Everyone who owns real estate will want to sell it sooner or later. As a new or seasoned real estate licensee, you will always be in constant need of sellers. The secret is to set up sources that continue to produce listings. Often the experienced person will indicate that they follow one source to obtain listings. The very successful people follow many sources.

If this is your "farm" area, geographical or otherwise, you need to maintain communication with the prospective sellers at all times. Personal cover letters spaced at reasonable intervals is one of the best ways to accomplish this. While there are several ways to maintain contact, we will address the "information is more than I can stand" method. It was said well in an old commercial, "when E. F. Hutton talks......"

**Sphere of Influence.** There are many sources of listings. Sellers can be found everywhere. As a beginning real estate salesperson look to your family, friends, and all those people with whom you do business. Never overlook anyone. Set up a database of contacts from your sphere of influence immediately to let everyone know you are in the business. Enclose your business card with all your bill payments and by all means give your card to everyone whom you meet or with whom you talk. Yes, that means the gas station attendant, the waitress along with the tip, and the person who does work for you around the house. A business card is the least expensive form of advertisement you will ever fund.

Letters to your sphere of influence should be sent every 45-60 days. These include those people from whom you receive services either personal or professional on a routine basis. This includes your banker, manicurist, barber, tire salesperson, department store clerk, grocery store owner, dry cleaner, social club associations, dentists, physicians and many more.

**Geographical Farm.** Sellers may be solicited from a geographical "farm" area. The contact with these individuals must be consistent so that the owners recognize you as the authority on real estate in their area. Include information about the market in the neighborhood as well as mail that shows your activity in other additional areas. These sellers may be "moving up" to a different style home or to a neighborhood in a different location. If you include all your "Just Listed" and "Just Sold" announcements you will be viewed as a full-time real estate person who takes his job seriously. The best results will be realized if you combine your mail-outs with a "warm" telephone call to establish rapport with people that you know through your correspondence.

Be unique in your selection of printed material to send to your farm area. If your competition is doing newsletters, do letters or postcards instead. If they do small postcards, then send oversized ones. Alternate colors on flyers or stay with black and white. If everyone is sending Christmas cards, then send an "after the holidays and beginning of the New Year" greeting. Coordinate the theme of your mailings with special events, holidays, how you do business and always *ask for their business.*

Some people do not like canvassing the neighborhood and others do. For those that do, here are some ideas. If you are on a limited budget and need to get started or get started again, get out and let people see you in your farm area. If you are well known, people are impressed that you stop to say hello in your farm area. It is not some place that is away from you but a part of you. Nothing substitutes for showing up in the neighborhood to see people that you know. They will see you always dressed in business attire and always working. They will be impressed that you stopped your busy day to deliver something in the neighborhood. As an ice breaker for the new area, bring something useful or fun. You can coordinate gifts with a special day or event such as home baked cookies, pumpkins near halloween, flags near memorial day or fourth of July, or pies near Thanksgiving.

**Referrals.** Once you have established yourself by a number of successful transactions you will find that a larger percentage of your business will be derived from past clients and customers and referrals. This is the most satisfying place to be! Always ask for referrals when you close a transaction, when you correspond with your client database, and in any conversation that involves real estate. Let your clients and customers know you are in the business long term and appreciate their future business as well as the business of their friends and business associates. They will forget to refer people to you unless you ask.

**For Sale By Owner (FSBO).** What better place to find a motivated seller than one who has listed the property himself? If he does not begin with an urgent desire to sell his home, he will soon have one as he becomes more aware of the intricacies associated with finalizing a successful real estate transaction. With buyer agency becoming more of the norm, it is important to know the inventory of FSBO's in your real estate market whether you plan to solicit the listing or not. You may find that an introduction based on the honest attempt to gain information about their home so that you may add it to your personal database of available properties for potential buyers will open the doors to more communication.

A series of letters that provide both information useful to the seller as well as emphasizing the need for a professional who is in the business full time will soon impress upon the seller that he can not hope to accomplish the same results by his merely holding an Open House and placing a sign in the yard.

**Expired Listings**. This seller is either frustrated and anxious for results or perhaps was never motivated to sell in the first place. The key to getting your foot in the door here is timing. For those who wish to corner this market, you must be on the Multiple Listing computer daily with an immediate call to the seller as soon as the listing shows it has expired. The reasons for the home not selling may not be the fault of the previous listing broker so it is important to determine the motivation of the seller. You do not want to be in the same situation as the previous broker with money spent on marketing and no sale.

## Letter - Potential Client

Mr. Pat Potential
Mrs. Pam Potential
420 Anywhere Avenue
Your Town, CO 00000

Dear Mr. and Mrs. Potential:

I just wanted to say thank you once again for the exceptional service I received from you (*or your establishment*). It is always a pleasure doing business with you. Without a doubt you are a professional. The service and quality you provide is consistent and exceptional.

It occurs to me that we might be able to assist each other. As you know I am a real estate professional. In my daily business of meeting people both new to our area as well as those who have lived here for some time, I find myself routinely referring clients to businesses. I have always been happy to refer people to you. It gives me pleasure to be able to assist my clients in establishing their own network of services where they will be satisfied. This enhances my relationship and rapport with them.

In your daily work you come into contact with a number of people who may wish to buy or sell real estate or who just have questions about real estate in general. When that happens, I would appreciate your recommending that they talk to me and let me know of their interest. You can rest assured that I will do my very best to justify the trust and confidence that you place in me. My goal is for those people to return to you thanking you for the referral.

For your convenience I am enclosing several of my business cards. Please give them to those individuals that you feel could use real estate assistance.

Sincerely,
The Orcas Island Company

by: Katherine E. Reece
Realtor®, CRS, GRI

**Letter - Sphere of Influence**

Mr. Frank Friendly
Mrs. Frances Friendly
420 Boy Scout Lane
Boys Town, CO 00000

Dear Frank and Frances:

You and I are both active members in the Boulder Girl Scouts. It is difficult at times to believe we have time for any other activity, but I thought I would give you an idea of what I do with the rest of my life!

I am a real estate broker who assists people with perhaps the largest investment of their lifetime--their personal home. Or it may be the purchase or sale of their second home, vacation home or investment property. If people have a specific real estate concern it is my job to provide them with the information they need to make the right decisions for their individual situation.

I am now at a point where I am able to select the people with whom I work. My first choice is to work with people I know and with whom I share similar interests and values. This makes the process for buying and selling real estate more enjoyable and satisfying for everybody. I have found time and time again that when the right people are working together, success happens!

From time to time I'd like to be able to drop you a note to help you stay informed about the market and to remind you that I am in the real estate business. If there is anything that I can do to assist you with your work, please let me know. I come into contact with a large number of people on a daily basis and would be happy to send them your way if you wish.

Sincerely,
The Orcas Island Company

by: Katherine E. Reece
Realtor®, CRS, GRI

## Letter - Geographical Farm

Mr. Pat Potential
Mrs. Pam Potential
420 Anywhere Avenue
Your Town, CO 00000

Dear Mr. and Mrs. Potential:

Allow me to introduce myself. I am Kathy Reece with The Orcas Island Company During the upcoming months you will be hearing from me about the real estate market in general and as it pertains to your home. I specialize in marketing homes in this area.

One of the most important aspects of marketing a home for a seller is exposure. I like to let the neighborhood know when a home comes on the market. Often someone right here knows of a friend or associate that might like to live in this area. In addition to local exposure we market homes throughout the state and nationally.

Below is a partial list of properties that have sold recently and the price at which they closed.

(*Include a list of homes for the neighborhood*)

I look forward to meeting you personally when I am in the neighborhood next time. If you have any present plans for selling your home or know someone that might like to live here please let me know. Feel free to call me at the office or my home at any time. Real estate is a seven day a week profession. I have enclosed a business card for your convenience so that you can request information about the various services that I provide.

Thank you for your time.

Sincerely,
The Orcas Island Company

by: Katherine E. Reece
Realtor®, CRS, GRI

*Please disregard this letter if your home is currently on the market*

### Letter - Referral

Mr. Roger Referral
Mrs. Ruth Referral
420 Reference Lane
Their Town, CO 00000

Dear Rogg and Ruthie:

Congratulations on your new home! It has been my pleasure to assist you in finding your new home and monitoring the closing all the way to the end. Even the best paved road has a few bumps, and I know you felt that way a few times along the route. I appreciate your cooperation and perseverance.

I know you are happy to be settling into your new home. I will miss working with you. I need to find someone new to help find a new house. I would love to work with one of your friends or business associates who is looking for a new home. Please keep me in mind when someone mentions real estate. I have enclosed a few business cards. Just hand them out when you get the opportunity.

Thank you again for letting me help you with your real estate needs. You made good decisions and that made my job a lot easier.

Sincerely,
The Orcas Island Company

by: Katherine E. Reece
Realtor®, CRS, GRI

**Letter - For Sale by Owner**

Mr. Sam Seller
Mrs. Sandy Seller
4750 Table Mesa Drive
Boulder, CO 80303

Re: 4750 Table Mesa Drive

Dear Mr. and Mrs. Seller:

Congratulations! I see that you have placed your home on the market for sale. Selling real estate is an exciting and challenging endeavor. For your sake, I hope that your real estate experience is brief and successful. However, if you do decide at any time to turn the marketing of your home over to an expert, I hope that you will consider the advantages of allowing my firm, The Orcas Island Company, to do the job.

Selling homes is my profession. Not only is this my full time job, but more often than not I am working overtime through evenings and weekends to get the job done. Every day I assist people with getting *the price that they select in the shortest amount of time with the least amount of difficulty.*

Won't you let me help you? There is no obligation. I would be happy to schedule an appointment so that I may show how I work and share with you everything you'll need to monitor in order to secure a successful sale. All I ask is that you consider me in the event that you decide you need help.

Sincerely,
The Orcas Island Company

by: Katherine E. Reece
Realtor®, CRS, GRI

### Letter - For Sale by Owner #2

Mr. Sam Seller
Mrs. Sandy Seller
4750 Table Mesa Drive
Boulder, CO 80303

Re: 4750 Table Mesa Drive

Dear Mr. and Mrs. Seller:

Mr. and Mrs. Seller, please know that I wish you well in your attempts to sell your home by yourself. However, you have been at this for a while now and the time toward your initial goal is getting shorter. May I suggest that you allow me to step in and help you.

Based on my first impression of your home I am certain that The Orcas Island Company can effectively market your home. Part of marketing any home is creating a competitive demand for exactly what you are selling. I do this for a living every day and do not invest my time in lost causes. I believe in your home and in getting it sold. Once you have reviewed the specific marketing plan for your individual home, I am certain you will be anxious to get started.

I certainly understand your desire to save money (i.e., the commission) but I wonder if your overall costs in mortgage payments and extended time on the market may not be more detrimental to your net proceeds. It is not a question of what professional marketing costs you, but more a question of how much I can put in your pocket. It is not uncommon for *Professional Real Estate Marketing* techniques to quickly bring firm offers for considerably more than you have been offered privately. You see, the buyers also expect to save the same commission.

You may have found that negotiating with potential buyers on your own home can be somewhat uncomfortable. Buyers and other agents tend to feel more comfortable with me because they know that once the sale is over and you are long gone, I'll still be here if they have a question or problem. Other agents are eager to show my listings because they can be assured of adequate disclosure and a smooth transaction.

Tell me what you need. I would be happy to furnish you with a list of references from people I have represented as well as professionals with whom I have worked. Please do not hesitate to call me. My card is enclosed for your convenience.

Sincerely,
The Orcas Island Company

by: Katherine E. Reece
Realtor®, CRS, GRI

### Letter - For Sale by Owner #3

Mr. Sam Seller
Mrs. Sandy Seller
4750 Table Mesa Drive
Boulder, CO 80303

Re: 4750 Table Mesa Drive

Dear Mr. and Mrs. Seller:

Congratulations! I see that you have placed your home on the market for sale. Selling real estate is an exciting and challenging endeavor. If there is anything that I can do to assist you, do not hesitate to call me.

I am a professional real estate salesperson and know how much there is to be done to get a home ready for a potential buyer. To help you get started I have enclosed some information that might help you prepare for the potential buyers.

First is an MLS information sheet. While you may not have access to the Multiple Listing Service, this sheet will let you know the kinds of information other sellers are making available to buyers through the Realtor® system. In addition, I have enclosed a Sellers Property Disclosure Statement which informs the potential buyer about the physical condition of the home. Most buyers expect to receive this information to assist them in deciding which home to purchase. Finally, I have enclosed a copy of the contract that our office uses so that you can prepare to fill in the necessary blanks. I have not included our clauses and addenda as they were developed for us by our attorneys and are for our use only.

Selling homes is my profession. Every day I assist people with getting *the price that they select* in *the shortest amount of time* with *the least amount of difficulty*. It is the way in which I feed my family each and every day. I am committed to finding buyers for sellers and sellers for buyers. Not only is this my full time job, but more often than not I am working overtime through evenings and weekends to get the job done. Please feel free to call me at any time. This is not an 8:00 a.m. to 5:00 p.m. job. Yes, Saturdays and Sundays are fine although I usually am conducting a client's open house part of the day each Sunday.

Sincerely,
The Orcas Island Company

by: Katherine E. Reece
Realtor®, CRS, GRI

## Letter - Expired Listing

Mr. Sam Seller
Mrs. Sandy Seller
4750 Table Mesa Drive
Boulder, CO 80303

Re: 4750 Table Mesa Drive

Dear Mr. and Mrs. Seller:

I have watched your property through the Multiple Listing Service and note that the listing you currently have has expired. Please consider me and this firm to be the real estate agents who can effectively market and sell your home.

While working with prospective buyers, I have previewed and included your home on my inventory for showing appointments. I would like the opportunity to meet with you to share my insights on marketing your home as well as to express the objections that buyers had when viewing your home. Please keep in mind that while your home is not the right home for every buyer, there are ways to stage a home for marketing that will enhance it's special features.

Selling homes is my profession. Every day I assist people with getting *the price that they select* in *the shortest amount of time* with *the least amount of difficulty*. It is the way in which I feed my family each and every day. I am committed to finding buyers for sellers and sellers for buyers. Not only is this my full time job, but more often than not I am working overtime through evenings and weekends to get the job done. I believe in Open Houses, community advertising, specialty advertising and "target marketing" to the group of potential buyers that will be able to afford your home.

Enclosed is my personal reference list of satisfied sellers and buyers for your perusal. You will notice many of your neighbors have successfully sold or bought homes with my assistance. Please feel free to call any of the families listed. They will be happy to give you candid answers to any questions you may have.

My real estate office sells real estate. We have agents who carry an inventory of listings as well as several buyer agents working almost exclusively with buyers. While this puts us in the middle of real estate transactions, we *sell* houses. We are always looking for qualified buyers.

I will call you to set an appointment so that we may discuss the advantages of listing your home with The Orcas Island Company Please do not hesitate to call me. My card is enclosed for your convenience. I hope to see you soon.

Sincerely,
The Orcas Island Company

by: Katherine E. Reece
Realtor®, CRS, GRI

P.S. Here is a recent picture that I took of your home. I think that it came out quite nicely. I will have it duplicated and ready for mailing to my initial target market by the time I see you.

**The "Captive Seller".** Often the real estate licensee thinks that the seller will list with a "captive" broker, one that has a prior relationship with the seller. The rules for keeping the captive seller and taking the captive seller are the same. Follow the general rules of the road at the beginning of the chapter.

Remember, sellers are looking for professionalism. They want a professional broker to represent them in the sale of their property. The way to keep your "close personal friends" your "captive sellers" is to keep in constant professional contact, not just social contact. *Treat close friends like strangers and work hard for their listing. Treat strangers, other people's close personal friends, professionally.*

Have you ever watched a "For Sale" sign go up on a "good friend's" house? That seller listed with someone else for a variety of reasons. Cards and letters are fine, but not enough. You should also endeavor to include in your letters information about real estate and the market. Be the reliable source of information on interest rate figures, loan descriptions, the escrow process, how to stage a home for optimum exposure, repairs or improvements that will maximize the seller's net profits and experts they can contact for questions beyond your expertise or liability. The more complex and expansive the information the better the impression will be. Mix in the complex information with the simple so that the seller is confident beyond any doubt that *you* are the *expert* in the real estate market and the *only source* for information that they need.

The format of your correspondence may be on letterhead in a sealed envelop with a commemorative stamp or on a bulk rate stamped postage card. Just send it! For some a variety of styles works best and for others having a consistent piece of mail identifies the individual to the seller. As a minimum place your name and/or picture on the addressee side of the envelope or postcard so that the seller always notes the correspondence is from you whether it is read or not.

Never take anything for granted. Send pictures of the properties that you have for sale. Send pictures of yourself. Send pictures of the sold property that you or someone in your office has sold. Show them that you are "doing real estate".

Never let them see you sweat and never let them see you casual. Even if you are in a pickup truck, act as if you are looking at ranches. People will tell you that you "work too much" and need to "slow down", but they will list with you because you "are in the business everyday".

**Property Management.** Offering to manage property can be a lucrative source of sellers. If you do not wish to manage rental property, you might consider a referral arrangement with property managers who do not like to list and sell property but like to manage it.

The key is the property management contract. Is it a given that you will get the listing? Some people think so. It is not a given. The property management contract should have a clause addressing the potential sale during the management period and provide for a listing opportunity after the management contract expires.

**Caution.** *There is a potential anti-trust violation with "tying"--a contract for the sale of one product on the condition or contingency that another product will be sold. Each product should be sold or offered separately without such a condition or contingency.*

The commission structure should have one fee if there is a package including the subsequent listing and another if the fee covers just management. In other words, you can have a fee for management and a fee for listing and a third fee for both. Each must be commercially reasonable. The owner will select the third option because they like you and not just for the amount that you charge.

**Rule.** *Breach of a fiduciary duty forfeits the commission regardless of loss.*

Not only would it be improper, but it would be a breach of a fiduciary duty to attempt to procure a commission from the sale of property during the property management period if listing or selling the property were not a part of the property management contract. When you enter into the property management contract, insert a clause that protects the managing broker.

**Clause.**

1. The broker, as partial consideration for managing the property, reserves the right to list the property for a period of ____ months after the termination of the property management agreement pursuant to the terms of the attached listing contract.

-or-

1. During the term of this property management agreement, owner shall be obligated to pay broker a commission upon any sale of the Property. Such commission arrangement shall be as set forth on the attached listing agreement.

## Broker Liability

The broker, being responsible for the entire world and, very often, for several well-meaning salespersons, is concerned that the new potential seller understand several principles at the start of what could be a lasting relationship. In most states the listing is the property of the broker, and the broker is personally liable not only for his own actions and inactions but also for that of the salespersons whose licenses hang under the broker's license.

To that end, the broker wants to make sure that the potential client understands several legal principles and the procedures followed by the broker's firm. Most importantly, the broker desires to limit the apparent authority of the salesperson in the client's eye by defining the extent of such authority early in the relationship.

A nice cover letter from the broker before the initial contact by the agent or immediately thereafter can accomplish these objectives. If you have a firm brochure or printed statement that can accompany this letter, the letter should include a specific reference to the brochure and the pertinent disclaimer clause or the firm policy statement. Include in your brochure a statement that the broker is the only person that can bind the company by entering into guaranteed sales, establishing commissions, etc., so that it is there for all to see.

## The Farm Letter of Introduction

As the salesperson goes out into the field in search of a listing, it would be helpful if he had a letter of introduction to the owner. Specific wording which designates the limitations of the salesperson's ability to bind the company can be included so that a pattern is established early in the agency relationship. A simple short letter will do. A series of letters could incorporate many additional topics.

This letter of introduction must be one page or less. Try to make the paragraphs short and simple. Start each paragraph with a sentence that immediately grabs the reader's attention. This is the most important line of the paragraph. Use bold type if necessary. If the reader is just skimming the content he will read the bold or italics portion no matter what. However, be cautious about overusing bold and italics or else it will loose its significance and the letter will look too much like a furniture advertisement!

Read and reread your introductory letters. They can be improved over and over again. Watch for redundant statements. Try to make them as personal as possible without sounding generic. Make them as specific as you can to the target market area.

Once the salesperson has made the contact, follow up with an initial letter from the broker, the salesperson or another salesperson in the office. Talk about the seller's property if there is a potential listing. Otherwise be thankful and appreciative for their time and leave the door open for future contact and business.

Do you believe it will be hard to get your broker to write a letter? Type the letters on the word processor. Insert the new potential seller's name, modify the letter to talk about the specific house and print them ready for the broker's signature. You can mail them. It works. Brokers, sign the letters for your salespeople. Make them a standard letter that they can modify to suit a particular area or project.

**Tip.** *Letters are good for the broker also. They limit the liability of the broker for actions of the salesperson. They eliminate stress upon the salesperson when confronted by the seller about commissions, guaranteed sales, etc.*

**Style.** *This is your first letter to this couple. The inside address should have both first names and both last names. Some spouses resent being considered an appendage and want their own recognition. The start of the letter should not say Sam and Sandy because we do not know them that well yet.*

*Leave a professional impression. It will last longer than the content of the letter. Follow up with a personal contact as soon as possible.*

**Commercial/Industrial.** *Do not be fooled. A letter of introduction here is critical. The commercial salesperson/broker needs to overcome the affinity between the potential seller and his/her friends. Introductory letters or references are the key. The more personal the letter the better. Collect letters of introduction from past clients and keep them on file. Letters addressed "To Whom it May Concern" will come in handy in the future.*

*Remember to mention agency. Most commercial sellers and buyers think of the salesperson that is working with them as "their agent". Mention it often. Also mention your "In-Company Sale Policy" when you can. Your competition may have no concept of how a proper In-Company Sale Policy operates.*

**Exchange.** *If the property is not owner occupied, a tax deferred exchange under Section 1031 of the Internal Revenue Code must be mentioned to the owner of the property. What a great source of business. The results may be not one sale but two and maybe a lot more.*

### Letter - Introduction of Salesperson to Owner

Mr. Samuel Seller and Mrs. Sandra Seller
4750 Table Mesa Drive
Boulder, CO 80303

Re: 4750 Table Mesa Drive, Boulder

Dear Mr. and Mrs. Seller:

This is to introduce Katherine "Kathy" Reece. She is a salesperson with The Orcas Island Company Kathy has been in real estate for many years and knows the market well. I am very lucky to have her as a member of this office. I have attached a copy of her personal brochure for your review.

Kathy is looking for those individuals that might be interested in a complimentary market evaluation or comparative market analysis to determine if it makes sense to sell at this time. When she comes to your home, if you are interested please let her know. If not, thank you for your time. In any event, I am sure that you will enjoy meeting Kathy. She knows this area of town quite well.

The Orcas Island Company offers services to buyers as buyer agents and to sellers as seller agents. Since we sell a large number of our listings ourselves, ask Kathy about our "In-Company Sale" policy.

I supervise each listing and sale personally. In order to grant our salespeople more time for real estate, all contracts that bind The Orcas Island Company are signed by me as broker.

Most Sincerely,
The Orcas Island Company

by: Oliver E. Frascona, Broker

**Letter - Tax Deferred Exchange Commercial Solicitation**

Mr. Samuel Seller, President
The IBM Corporation
4750 Table Mesa Drive
Boulder, CO 80303

Re: 1640 Townsend, Montrose

Dear Mr. Seller:

Allow me to introduce myself. I am Oliver Frascona, broker of The Orcas Island Company We specialize in commercial real estate and investments. One of my salespeople, Kathy Reece is looking for properties that may be ready to come on the market.

Kathy Reece has ten years of experience in the real estate business. I have attached her personal brochure for your review. She has decided to actively search for new listings in this market area as we are not able to meet all of our buyers' demands for commercial real estate. We need more listings.

Kathy will be stopping by to meet you when she is in your area this week. I think you would enjoy meeting her if you have a moment. In the event you are unavailable at that time, she will leave a copy of our company brochure which gives a synopsis of the services we offer to our commercial clients as well as a biographical sketch of her real estate career. We can appreciate your busy schedule. Therefore, if time does not permit you to talk with Kathy and you desire to have Kathy evaluate your property, please call her directly at (303) 494-3000 ext. 63 for a complimentary market evaluation.

You may wish to examine the benefits of a tax free or tax deferred exchange. Ask Kathy to explain the mechanics that may allow you to sell your present property, then select a replacement property and close on it in the future with little or no tax effect. Does this sound too good to be true? It is called a 1031 Tax Deferred Exchange. These are rapidly becoming standard in the commercial real estate industry.

Thank you for taking a minute to read this letter.

Most Sincerely,
The Orcas Island Company

by: Oliver E. Frascona, Broker

**Letter - Introduction of Salesperson to Owner #2**

Mr. Samuel Seller
Mrs. Sandra Seller
4750 Table Mesa Drive
Boulder, CO 80303

Re: 4750 Table Mesa Drive, Boulder

Dear Mr. and Mrs. Seller:

This is to introduce Katherine "Kathy" Reece. She is a salesperson with The Orcas Island Company Kathy has been in real estate for ten years and knows the market well. I have attached a copy of her personal brochure for your review. I consider myself very fortunate to have her as a member of this office.

Kathy is looking for those individuals that might be interested in a complimentary market evaluation or comparative market analysis to determine if it makes sense to sell at this time. When she comes to your home, please let her know if you are interested. If not, thank you for your time. In any event, I am certain that you will enjoy meeting Kathy. She knows this area of town quite well.

The Orcas Island Company offers services to buyers as buyer agents and to sellers as seller agents. Since we sell a large number of our listings ourselves, ask Kathy about our "In-Company Sale" policy. In addition, we have a fully staffed tax deferred exchange department. Tax deferred exchanges allow people with rental property or raw ground to sell, close, select a new property and buy it with a tax expense that may be zero.

I supervise each listing and sale personally. This allows our salespeople more time for real estate. All contracts that bind The Orcas Island Company are signed by me as the broker. Thank you for taking the time to read this letter. The Orcas Island Company looks forward to meeting your real estate needs.

Most Sincerely,
The Orcas Island Company

by: Oliver E. Frascona, Broker

**Letter - Introduction Broker Follow Up**

Mr. Samuel Seller and Mrs. Sandra Seller
4750 Table Mesa Drive
Boulder, CO 80303

Re: 4750 Table Mesa Drive, Boulder

Dear Mr. and Mrs. Seller:

Thank you taking the time to meet and talk with Katherine Reece the other day. She came back with rave reviews about your home. I can hardly wait for the office preview. I know that some of the salespeople around here are already talking about your property to others.

Should you decide to sell and select The Orcas Island Company and Kathy to assist you, we will work hard to ensure that the marketing and sale efforts produce results. As the broker I am personally responsible for each transaction and take each one very seriously. If there is anything I can do to assist you in the listing stage, please feel free to call me at my office or home number. My business card is enclosed for your convenience.

I look forward to meeting you when we have our company preview. Again, thank you for taking the time to talk to Kathy.

Most Sincerely,
The Orcas Island Company

by: Oliver E. Frascona, Broker

## Letter - After Contact/Broker Associate

Mr. Samuel Seller and Mrs. Sandra Seller
4750 Table Mesa Drive
Boulder, CO 80303

Re: 4750 Table Mesa Drive, Boulder

Dear Mr. and Mrs. Seller:

Thank you taking the time to meet and talk with Kathy Reece the other day. She came back with rave reviews about your home. I can hardly wait for the office preview. Kathy has been telling us all about the large fenced yard and the wonderful flowers that are everywhere. The office is already talking about your home. People are trying to think of customers and clients that might be interested if we are selected to market it.

Your home sounds wonderful. I look forward to meeting you when we have our company preview. I work with a lot of buyers. This sounds like a property that I would be happy to introduce to some of them.

Most Sincerely,
The Orcas Island Company

by: Claudia Kennedy, Broker Associate

**Letter - After Initial Contact/Broker**

Mr. Samuel Seller and Mrs. Sandra Seller
4750 Table Mesa Drive
Boulder, CO 80303

Re: 4750 Table Mesa Drive, Boulder

Dear Mr. and Mrs. Seller:

Thank you taking the time to meet and talk with Kathy Reece the other day. We realize that you are not interested in selling your house at this time. However, it was nice of you to allow Kathy to see the interior of your home.

We are a full service real estate company and will be here in the future if you should have any questions about real estate. It has become so complicated and seems to be getting more so every day. Selling or buying a home is one of the largest transactions many people enter into in their lives.

Should you know of someone who is interested in a complimentary market evaluation of their house or is thinking about buying a home, Kathy and I would be happy to provide assistance. She is an exceptional salesperson with a long list of happy clients and customers.

Again, thank you for taking the time to talk to Kathy Reece. [*Add a personal comment here if you can think of one. A reference to a common hobby or particular event that will cement the contact.*]

Most Sincerely,
The Orcas Island Company

by: Oliver E. Frascona, Broker

# After the Initial Contact

You need to become the "source" for answers about the complex real estate business. You want to leave the seller thinking that if s/he ever has a real estate need s/he will call you. So tell them some of the things that you know.

Not all of the following items need to be addressed in the first letter, but they will serve as a checklist of items that need to be addressed sooner or later. Some are mentioned in different letters since putting them all in the first letter could be overwhelming. Different sellers may require more or fewer of these items in the first letter. As these items are discussed, the seller will start to get a feeling about the agent, the broker, the firm, and the complexities of modern real estate. This can be a very good marketing tool because the seller begins to realize that this is an area where a professional is a necessity, and that you are just the professional to employ.

Agency and Apparent Authority. Establish early the fact that the broker exists and is a party to the transaction, that only the broker binds the firm, and that the broker is available for problem-solving and consultation. Also establish early the extent of the agency relationship which is being created and reinforce it often. Itemize exactly what the broker and salesperson will do for the client, what they will not do, and what is expected of thc clicnt. Limit or eliminate the apparent authority of the salesperson to bind the broker or the firm. This can be an advantage to the broker, firm, and salesperson because the seller now knows the limit of the salesperson's authority to make certain decisions and that the salesperson can not bind the broker in most matters.

The actions or inactions of the salesperson or the broker may serve to override the information and disclaimers given at any point in time. Therefore, the constant reference to the extent of authority or lack thereof is important. You can not say it once, act in direct contradiction to the written statements, and hope to be protected.

**Tip.** *Conduct speaks louder than promises and will be the ultimate determining factor. Under promise and over deliver.*

**Agency Office Policy.** This is the written policy discussing how you will represent or assist sellers, buyers, both or neither. It outlines the procedures that your office will follow for a "normal listing" and for "dual agency" or "no-agency" listings. In some states it is a law that your office have a written agency policy. Whether it is the law in your state or not, composing an office agency policy is an opportunity to out market your competition. Having your company agency policy in brochure format in a nice readable form available for the salesperson to leave for the public to see will place you far are ahead of the game. Some sample agency policies are included in this book. Feel free to use them after making the appropriate changes to comply with your firm's objectives.

**Agency, Subagency Alternatives and Potential Dual Agency.** Describe the various alternative types of potential subagents or buyers' brokers, their relationship to the seller, the salesperson, and the broker. Review compensation of the various forms of other agents. Many people are unfamiliar with this system of agents and brokers working together. Help them understand. Their new knowledge will confirm their confidence in you and also in the extent of the professional network that is available to assist in the sale of their property.

This may even serve as a start on the protection system in the case of a seller who turns into a buyer. The first thing we all do when a seller, whose listing we have or have had, asks to see other real estate is to tell the seller that we are no longer his agent and are now acting as the subagent for all the other sellers out there. Right? Subagency is dead or dying depending upon where you are located in the country. There are not many buyers who when told that everything that they tell the broker will be told to the seller will honestly elect subagency.

**Caution.** *Giving a full and proper rendition of the subagency alternatives when the property is listed may serve to limit these future problems. But then there is no real cause for concern. After all the old seller is now a friend, and we all know that friends are "safe" and do not need the normal disclosures that mere customers and clients would receive.*

**Tip.** *The first salesperson that explains agency openly and easily to the seller will get the listing. Let the competition struggle with the concept.*

**Anti-Trust and Commissions.** Address any anti-trust commission and cooperative split problems if you feel they might be present. Clearly establish the commission policies of the firm. This will make the salesperson's job of presenting or negotiating the commission much easier and will establish that the broker has the right to split the total commission if the broker so desires. It is important for the broker to indicate to the seller early on that the broker retains the exclusive right to determine if there will be a split, the amount of such a split, and the terms upon which the broker will pay the cooperating broker.

Too frequently, after the broker has become obligated to a particular cooperating broker, the seller determines that the seller should enter into the decision-making process. Set forth the rules, if any, for such splits. We would discourage this except in the instance when the buyer uses the services of a buyer's broker at the buyer's expense, and therefore tries to modify the price offered to the seller and the commission that the broker will be entitled to receive from the seller.

"Tying" is when one product must be purchased with another product. An easy example would be if you had to buy a tooth brush to get tooth paste. In real estate it is improper to tie two products together. A broker who indicated that you had to re-list with that broker if you bought a raw lot in a subdivision would have anti-trust tying concerns. The buyer/builder should not have to use the listing services of a particular broker in order to buy the raw lot. Mandatory re-list clauses are probably not proper. Seek a written opinion from your anti-trust attorney before you embark on such a course of action.

**Brochure.** If you do not have a standard brochure or firm position statement, you might consider drafting one along the lines of the model letters in this book. A brochure is a good medium for standardizing the information that is presented to the public before you have the opportunity to correct or clarify it with a cover letter to any one prospect. Remember to limit the authority of the salesperson or agent to bind the company. Indicate that all contracts that bind the company must be signed by the broker to be enforceable.

**Comparable "Comps".** There is constant discussion about whether or not the selling salesperson should, can or must show comps. There is no need for this matter to be the subject of litigation for you some day. In order to solve the problem of potential litigation, address the use of comparables when listing the seller. It is the seller who should grant the permission to show comparables to prospective buyers. After all, the seller is the principal. Frankly, we would not advise the acceptance of a listing that did not provide for the ultimate selling salesperson, whether within the listing office or otherwise, to be able to show comparables to a prospective buyer. We feel that comps are in the same category as zoning, condition of the property and real property taxes. The buying public is probably "entitled" to see comps.

There are three types of comparable properties. First, there are those that are currently listed. Consider physically showing your seller the competition before you agree on the listing price. Second, there are those homes that are already sold's. If the data is recent and truly comparable, it is the best reflection of the probable price that will attract the buyer in a short period of time. Finally, there are listings that expired. Some people refer to these as "properties that the market rejected", and we feel that is a more correct label. It tells the seller that this price was not the right price for these properties.

**Condition of the Property.** The seller, not the broker, is going to represent the condition of the property. Most firms have an addendum to the listing contract that allows the seller to designate the current condition of the property. Adding to this a recitation of one's reliance on the seller's representations may provide an incentive to be more specific and accurate and provide the broker with additional protection. The trend is to hold the broker responsible for defects he could have discovered, even though he did not actually discover them.

**Confidential Information.** The seller must know what information he can expect to be kept confidential and what information must be disclosed. Here is a simple check list for information.

Confidential ("Seller's Personal Secrets") Information:
The seller's bottom line.
The price of the last counter proposal.
The final sales price, until the transaction is actually closed.
The fact that the seller needs to move rapidly.
That the seller is being transferred out of the area.
That the seller is sick.
Any family emergency that effects the seller's ability to negotiate.
The existence of a pending divorce.

Not Confidential:
The fact that the roof leaks.
The fact that there is water in the area basements.
Any material fact about the property--*a fact of such importance as to influence a reasonable person's conduct.*
The fact that the highway is being expanded.
The buyer's ability to qualify for the contract as proposed.
The proximity to high tension lines.

**Due-on-Transfer Clauses.** Be careful not to participate in a transfer of a property secured by an FHA or VA loan that contains due-on-transfer clauses without first obtaining the consent of the lender. "Assumable with qualification" is a due-on-transfer loan. Some people think that it is a violation of the law to participate in a transfer over an FHA or VA due-on-transfer clause. Those people work for the enforcement arm of the federal government. You do not need their business.

**Earnest Money.** He who holds the earnest money will surely be the center of attention when a dispute arises. Almost without exception, there is nothing you can or should do to distribute the money without a written release from both parties. You can not make a determination on the merits of each party's application for the funds nor determine if a default has occurred. That inability to act will put you in an awkward position. Now is the time to explain to the seller the laws relating to earnest money. Point out the contract wording in the sales contract that deals with earnest money. Explain your limits early.

Control of the earnest money may or may not pose a problem. Generally, it is a contract term, and therefore the parties can designate who will retain the earnest money. As the seller's agent, you want control of the money or the direction to designate on your seller's behalf who shall have control. Except for the good relationship you will have with your bank as the result of the funds sitting in your account there is little benefit in holding earnest money. Title companies are always willing to accept this type of position. In any event the preferred repository designated by the seller and the minimum amount that the seller requires with any offer need to be discussed.

**Tip.** *We would advise you to try to let someone else hold earnest money. Whoever holds the earnest money will certainly be a defendant in any action to obtain the earnest money.*

**Fair Housing.** Clear the air and establish the rules early with regard to The Fair Housing Law. People, especially testers, appreciate frankness and will respect you for your knowledge of the law. You are protecting the seller against potential problems as well as yourself. If there is going to be a problem here, it is better to know it very early. Do not tolerate even a tacit or "winky-winky" form of discrimination. You represent "equal access" to real estate.

**FHA Interest Proration.** There is no proration for FHA loan payoffs. Therefore, the seller will pay a full month's interest for any portion of a month that the loan is in effect. If the transaction is closing at the end of the month, the mortgage pay off funds must be received by the lender before the first business day of the following month in order to avoid another full month of interest. FHA loan payoffs do not require 30 days prior notification.

**Tip.** *When preparing for closing that results in an FHA loan payoff make sure you schedule the closing early enough so that you can make sure that the payoff gets to the lender before the end of the month.*

**Financing.** Start the seller thinking about the ever-increasing list of alternatives. Present to the seller the basic description of certain types of financing that are available that may be suggested by potential buyers. Describe the potential impact of the general forms of financing on the seller and how each of the alternatives likely to arise in this transaction will affect the salability of the property. Documenting the discussion of financing is becoming very important as financing alternatives vary in complexity and in the effect they may have on sellers in varying situations.

**Hazardous Materials.** Long considered a "commercial thing", hazardous waste is now a condition to be addressed in both residential real estate and raw land transactions. With the advent of concern about radon gas, chemical spills, buried waste materials, lead paint, asbestos and the like, it is often impossible for the broker to know what may be lurking below the surface. The only adequate form of protection is to have experts test the premises--much as is done in many parts of the country for termites--and make the report available to potential purchasers before they contract for the property. The alternative is to wait to see if the buyer will require any tests as a condition precedent to closing. However, a lot of time may pass before you know if you have a deal.

**Inspections, Engineers and Home Warranties.** The use of inspectors to limit the broker's and salesperson's liability for all sorts of potential problems, although not mandatory, is certainly a recommended practice. Acquainting the seller early on with the idea that various other professionals will be required to complete the transaction serves to indicate areas that are not within the purview of the agency relationship and not among the list of tasks that the real estate firm provides. The cost, the availability of home warranty services, and the extent of their coverage need to be explained at the outset of the relationship.

**Liability for the Premises and Open Houses.** Explain the limits of the company's liability and the need to make an inventory of property of unusual value. Give a review of the people who will seek access to the property and the measures that are in place to restrict, limit, or supervise such access. The fact that the broker will not be responsible for anything except gross negligence must be presented.

Discuss the office "Open House" policy and its beneficial use as a marketing tool. Acknowledge the quiet concern people have about having other people in their home. Strangers and neighbors who have not before had access to the home will now potentially have access and possibly become aware of personal items. Present the benefits, liabilities, and potential problems and let the client decide. Be clear that the client can always reserve the decision for a later time.

**Liability and Lock Boxes.** Present the lock box system used by your office and the possible security problems that exist with any listing that utilizes the lock box system. People will appreciate your care for their possessions. Although it may be a system with substantial problems, such as a system with one key for all boxes or one that uses boxes easily opened or destroyed by unauthorized people, it may be a marketing necessity. The decision to use a lock box must be clearly the seller's. If you have a superior system in operation for your company, this would be a good time to point out its comparative advantages. Still, however, explain the limits of the company's liability.

High technology security and customer tracking has come to the lock box industry. There are now lock boxes produced by Supra Products, Inc. of Salem, Oregon, that are fully electronic. The keys are about the size of two books of matches and allow the listing broker to track who was in the property and at what time. There is no need to do anything except let the key read the box and then let the telephone read the key. Yes, you can limit access during specified times. Yes, you can ensure that illegal access does not occur as a result of the key being in the possession of an unauthorized user. The code expires every thirty days. Authorized users must call an 800 number for an updated code which is good only for the particular key. Each box can retain almost a hundred showing appointments. This is the wave of the future.

**Mortgage Insurance Premiums (MIP).** With the advent of prepaid FHA mortgage insurance, sellers and buyers need to make some decisions about how to incorporate the mortgage insurance premiums into the transaction. Whether it should be prorated or included as a part of the purchase price--especially in a transaction that calls for an assumption of an existing policy--can mean a substantial amount of money for the seller to receive and for the buyer to part with. Adequately explaining the alternatives and effects of each selection, as well as the method of proration, is important. As the amount of the insurance premium comes closer and closer to the total commission, your portion of the commission becomes an obvious source of funds for adjustment in the event of a dispute.

**Multiple Listing Service (MLS).** *The Magic Listing Service.* Explain the broker's membership in, access to, and the operation of the Multiple Listing Service. Some people still think that the information in the MLS is confidential. We all know that is no longer true. Some people wonder if it ever was. It has never ceased to amaze us that the MLS was thought to be confidential, and yet everyone spent money to advertise the same information in various promotional brochures that are given away to the public. Also indicate that, although the information in the MLS is for brokers' use, it could be relied upon by the public and therefore must be accurate. It is the broker's desire that the listing be accurate to the last detail. Encourage the seller's review of the MLS information sheet, which is attached to some states' listing contracts, in order to establish that it accurately presents the facts about the property.

**Pricing.** The broker should never set the price. One broker used to place a deposit slip on the office wall when she obtained the listing. Her sales presentation was based on the premise *"I sell all of my listings". If you want to test the market, list with someone else. If you want to sell, list with me."* The advantage was that she wasted very little of her money on listings that did not sell.

The price that you will allow the seller to ask and still accept the listing is a very sensitive area. If you establish the price, you may be liable for its determination. You may also lead the seller to believe that you are an appraiser, and that may set you up for future liability if the market proves you wrong. Therefore, we discourage the broker or the salesperson from attempting to establish the price. If you utilize a "Comparative Market Analysis" make sure that it indicates that it is not an appraisal.

Some firms have a limit on the amount of what they feel is "blue sky," or overpricing. They are unwilling to work on listings that are priced so high that the property will probably not sell within the listing period and therefore not be worth the effort and expense. Accepting an overpriced listing, failing to service the listing or disparaging it to fellow real estate agents is asking for trouble. Try to capture the listing at a reasonable price, established by the seller, and boost the professional image of the salesperson and firm. This can be accomplished professionally by providing the seller with the information that you have available about comparable sales and current listings and letting the seller suggest the listing price. At that time you can determine if in fact it is worth your effort.

**Case in Point.** *A listing broker took Oliver out to view several "competitively priced" properties in his market area. After Oliver had seen several properties, they all seemed to "blend into one", and it was easier to establish the listing price. Later when an offer was presented Oliver already knew the market as well as the buyer and could counter with a reasonable price. Yes, the home sold. The final result was that Oliver was pleased with the price "he selected" as well as the overall efforts of his broker.*

**Tip.** *You decide at what price it makes sense to take the listing and let the seller decide if they want to list with you.*

*One method for educating the seller about the fair market value of his property is to show him other active listings that are similar to his home in the neighborhood.*

**Purchasing for Your Own Account.** The seller will never see the sale to a broker as an arm's length transaction. He will always think that the broker had superior market knowledge and took advantage of him. Buying for your own account is very risky. Some offices prohibit it. You only do it because the property is a good deal, and you know it. You know it is a good deal because you think that you can resell it at a profit later.

**Rule.** *Self dealing in general is not a good idea. Using the information gleaned while an agent of your seller, to purchase from your seller, your principal, is a breach of your fiduciary duty to the seller.*

**Tip.** *If you think that you or someone in your office might like to purchase listed property, reserve the right to buy for your own account when you list, as a term of the listing.*

**Caution.** *This is the most dangerous type of arrangement. An agent trying to deal with a client. Attorneys get disbarred for such activity.*

The suggestions in this section anticipate your using an attorney to assist the seller. Yes, that means that the attorney may destroy your proposed transaction. There is a hint! Remember the seller was a former client and relied upon you for advice. Also remember that it was your interest that made all these problems arise. If at all possible, buy it before you list it.

Once you start the listing process you are on the inside. From that point forward you must treat the potential seller/client as an actual seller/client. The fact that it is not listed yet is irrelevant. While seeking the listing you became privy to the seller's confidential information. Now you must treat this seller just like any other purchase of a company listing.

**Tip.** *When listing a particular property and reviewing the terms that are proposed for a particular buyer, Katherine tells the potential seller, "I have just become the buyer, not a listing agent. Let me write a sales contract, not a listing agreement. Take it to your attorney for approval and this property is SOLD."*

We have provided some rather stringent measures to help assuage your potential risk:

1. Help the seller with the additional legal and appraisal expenses associated with your attempts to purchase the property.
2. Take the process seriously and follow all the steps.
3. Give the seller the chance to get out any time prior to closing.
4. Provide for the seller's attorney to approve the transaction in advance.

**Jury Talk.** *"We trusted the broker to list our house. Everyone said he was the best. Little did we know that he would not sell our house so that we would have to sell it to him after all at a discount. He failed in his efforts to sell it because he wanted to buy it from us. He had us so fooled that we actually begged him to buy it. Of course he knew that we had to close on our new house or lose our deposit."*

**Radon.** More and more relocation companies are refusing to purchase properties that have not had a radon test. Many times, in order to take advantage of the company buy-out program when the buyer later sells, he will require a radon gas test because the existence of a satisfactory inspection prior to his acquiring ownership will be a requirement for later resale. The proper tests need to be encouraged and performed by recognized experts as soon as possible after the listing is signed. Indicating this to the seller before or immediately after obtaining the listing will add to your credibility as an expert, support the correct perception that marketing a home is complex, and protect you from later--sometimes years later--having to explain why you did not test the property. Such tests are generally a seller's expense; therefore, extracting the money to pay for the test or having the seller agree to pay the tester directly is important.

**Tip.** *Do not advance money for anyone.*

**REALTOR®.** Professional affiliation *is* the difference. To be a member of the National Association of REALTORS® means that the licensee has agreed to adhere to a strict Code of Ethics. A Realtor® is a dedicated professional who keeps attuned to the changes in the real estate industry, both locally and nationally. Many complete rigorous educational courses to develop their skills and knowledge and earn special certifications such as the GRI and CRS. Being a Realtor® is a commitment to the Code, to arbitration of disputes between REALTORS® and clients, to continuing education and to the protection of the public's right to own and dispose of property. It is a commitment to excellence. REALTORS® *participate* in real estate; they do not just sell it. Any correspondence to potential clients or customers or to the public at large should always contain the Realtor® logo and the advantages of having a Realtor® to guide them successfully through all phases of the transaction.

**Soils Condition.** Much as with the tests for hazardous materials, a soils test or report may alleviate a lot of problems later on. A report from a soils engineer in most states is not too expensive and should be encouraged. If any damage is evident, an inspection and a report indicating what action is recommended should be strongly encouraged. Structural damage that is a result of a soil condition will become a condition later on and possibly result in lost marketing time during a prime season. It goes without saying that the report must be given to all prospective purchasers before they are under contract.

**Structural Integrity vs. Mechanical Integrity.** Engineers are the experts with regard to the structural integrity of the dwelling. Generally, they do not pass on the physical or operating condition of the various mechanical devices located on the property. Mechanical inspections and the subsequent insurance are available from a variety of competitors. The buyer and seller often operate under the misconception, convenient or innocent, that the mechanical inspection also covers the structure. Clear recommendations indicating the talents and scope of the different classes of inspectors and their resultant coverage will limit the valid future claims of a buyer looking for either a way out of the transaction or someone to help with the monthly payments.

If your firm allows both buyer representation and seller representation, agents to purchase properties listed with the firm, or other transactions that provide potential conflicts of interest, this is the time to explain in specific detail exactly what the relationship will be in such an event. Sample dual agency forms and forms that provide for the purchase of a property for one's own account are found in this book.

**Tax Deferred Exchange.** With the codification of the rules for tax deferred exchanges, they have become a practical alternative for everyone. No longer are they available only for those who could afford expensive attorneys, these exchanges are open for all to enjoy. The difference in the tax bill is amazing. With this ease of use comes an obligation on the part of the real estate professional, residential or commercial, to know the basics of a tax deferred exchange.

> **Rule 1** -- The property must be "like kind" and that means real estate. Yes, you can trade a commercial property for a piece of vacant ground or an apartment house for a turkey farm. A homeowner who has a rental property can trade it for anything that is real estate. No, you can not trade an owner occupied residence for anything.

> **Rule 2** -- You do not have to trade "simultaneously". The taxpayer, seller, can sell the property you have listed, leaving the money in escrow and select another property that you help them buy. Whose agent are you now?

**Rule 3** -- They must target the replacement property within 45 days of the first closing date. The deadline for identifying a replacement property is calculated from the closing date, not the contract date. The property to be sold could be under contract for a few months, and there still remains 45 days to identify another property.

**Rule 4** -- They must close on the replacement property within 180 days of the first sale. Who better to help them than you?

**Rule 5** -- You are probably not a tax accountant or a tax attorney. Let that person do the tax advice and you deal with the real estate. You get paid and they run the risk of getting sued.

**Rule 6** -- Never indicate "tax free". Always refer to the potentially "tax deferred" exchange.

**Clause.**

1. Broker shall offer the property under the terms: "Seller will cooperate with a tax deferred exchange."

1. Broker has advised Seller to contact a professional of the Seller's choosing to review the prospects of a section 1031 tax deferred exchange.

1. Broker has advised the Seller that Broker is not a tax expert. Seller should seek a competent attorney or Certified Public Accountant to investigate the possibility of a tax deferred exchange under Section 1031 of the Internal revenue Code.

1. Seller may be able to defer taxes on all or part of the gain realized by the sale of this property. Broker is not the source of such advice. Seller should seek other counsel to determine if such a savings or deferral is possible.

# Company Agency Policy

## General Provisions

In order to better serve the public, our customers and clients, we have adopted the following agency policy for our business. Each salesperson needs to be familiar with and follow these procedures.

The Company is committed to providing professional service for all sellers, buyers, landlords and tenants that we elect to serve. Our primary function is to assist the public with the acquisition, disposition and leasing of real property.

This real estate brokerage consists of a licensed real estate broker, sometimes referred to as the designated broker, and licensed salespersons, including salespersons who have broker's licenses and who have elected to operate in a salesperson's capacity. In the event that we have multiple offices, locations, now or in the future, all locations are considered a single entity. Each office is not a separate company or brokerage company. They are separate branches of a single entity.

"The Company", is defined to include all licensed salespeople and the broker. By law we are all "fingers on the hand of the broker", a single entity. If we are or become a part of a franchise, the "The Company" only refers to our franchise office(s), as a single entity, and not those owned by other franchisees.

When any salesperson accepts an agency listing for a seller's house or an agency listing for a buyer, a "Company Listing", the entire Company becomes the agent of the seller or buyer. The "Broker" means the broker of record with the state regulatory agency that is in charge of the office. In a large multi-office company it shall mean the broker or managing broker for each individual office.

In the event a member of the public asks to have a copy of this policy, any salesperson may, after checking with the Broker, provide that person with a current copy.

The Company is committed to Fair Housing. Regardless of the agency capacity in which we serve, we will always work for "equal access" to all property for all people.

## Listing Seller's Real Property -- Seller Brokerage

We, The Company, have elected to represent sellers who are interested in selling or leasing their real property. In order to properly list a seller's property with The Company, the following must be completed:

I. Seller Listing Procedures.

A. Oral listings are prohibited. Seller must complete a written listing agreement utilizing The Company approved form. "Pocket" or other listings that are not in written form on The Company approved form are prohibited.

B. The "Listing Salesperson", the individual that actually obtained the potential listing, shall submit that proposed listing agreement to the Broker for final approval.

C. All listing agreements shall include The Company "In-Office" Sale Addendum and Commission Division Schedule.

D. Once a listing agreement described above is approved, a duplicate original, executed by the Broker, or the Broker's designee, shall be returned to the seller and a duplicate original shall be placed in the property file.

E. Each property shall have a separate file maintained by the Listing Salesperson on behalf of the Broker. Access to the property file is restricted to the Listing Salesperson and the Broker. No one else shall have access to or view that file without the prior approval of the Broker.

F. Listing Salespeople are authorized to solicit listings for any term that is at least ________ day(s) in length and not more than ________ day(s) in length. To solicit other terms requires the prior approval of the Broker. Listings may be extended in writing signed by both the seller and the Broker.

II. Working with Other Brokers -- Cooperation and Compensation Policy:

A. This office shall not offer nor accept subagency and no offer shall be made to compensate any potential subagent without the prior written consent of the Broker and the seller.

B. The Company encourages the "cooperating" broker and all salespeople in that cooperating broker's office(s), licensed brokers located within the geographical area designated by The Company, to show and sell all listed property. The Company will compensate all buyer agents and "Transaction Brokers", brokers that are not acting as buyer agents or seller agents but possess a valid real estate license in this state, or any other state if applicable law so provides. The exact portion, amount or percentage shall be indicated in the listing agreement and on the office information sheet.

III. Purchasing a Company Listing:

A. In general, purchasing a Company Listing is not permitted. The potential conflict of having to go from being an agent of the seller to a principal working to buy the seller's property presents problems. Salespeople are encouraged to make the "buy or not to buy for their own account" decision before they attempt to list a potential seller's property.

B. Exceptions can be made on a case by case basis only by the Broker and only upon the following minimal conditions:

1. The Listing Agreement is terminated without reservation. It can not be terminated "if the salesperson's offer is accepted"; and,

2. The seller hires an attorney of the seller's selection and The Company pays the first $__________ of that fee; and,

3. The seller hires an appraiser of the seller's selection and The Company pays the first $__________ of that fee; and,

4. The contract to purchase indicates:

*"The purchaser, who was formerly acting as a salesperson with The Company, the listing agents of the seller, is purchasing this property for his/her own account with the expectation of making a profit. This contract shall not be valid unless approved by the seller's attorney. Seller releases The Company and the buyer for any and all claims that may arise as a result of this sale as contemplated in the contract. Seller is not relying upon any representation made by The Company nor by the buyer to enter into this transaction or contract."*

IV. Purchasing a Property not Listed with The Company:

A. Salespeople are permitted to purchase for their own account property listed with other brokerage companies or property that is not listed with any company, a "for sale by owner" only upon the terms and conditions outlined herein.

B. All such purchases shall be submitted to The Company prior to entering into any contract to purchase to insure that The Company knows what the salespeople are doing in the real estate area. The Company has the right to prohibit the purchase in The Company's sole discretion. However, The Company can not acquire the property directly or indirectly for its own account after such a disapproval.

C. In all such instances all contracts shall indicate:

*"Purchaser is a licensed real estate broker or salesperson, not acting in an agency capacity, specifically not acting as an agent or subagent of the seller, purchasing this property for the purchaser's own account with the expectation of making a profit. The seller hereby acknowledges that seller shall have no cause of action against The Company as a result of this purchase. The property is not listed with The Company. There is no commission due and payable to The Company or the purchaser as a result of this contract."*

V. Guaranteed Sales -- Guaranteed Purchases

A. The Company is reluctant to enter into arrangements wherein The Company is agreeing to purchase a property listed with The Company for sale. The potential for conflicts of interest is inherent in such an arrangement. Generally, our concerns are outlined below.

1. First we are hired by the seller as their agent to sell their property and they then perceive that The Company has failed in that regard we will purchase the property. It may be that the failure of the property to sell is because the seller priced the property to high, refused to accept what looked like a reasonable offer or any number of other reasons.

2. Now The Company is placed in a position of having to deal at arms length with our principal, the seller. This position is not unlike that outlined in "Purchasing a Company Listing" above.

3. Finally, The Company must negotiate with our principal to obtain the property at a price that reflects the potential holding costs, time value of money, commissions to be paid, taxes which The Company may be liable for during the holding period. Once The Company owns the property and is trying to re-market it there is always the possibility that we sell the property for a net profit. Should that occur there is a potential that the seller will seek that profit.

B. Profit and Loss

1. In the event that The Company makes a profit within a year after the acquisition, we will commit to repay that amount to the former client, the seller.

2. In the event that The Company suffers a loss, The Company will simply bear the loss as a normal business expense.

C. Approval and Special Circumstances. The Company will only enter into Guaranteed Sales upon the following criteria:

1. Salespeople are not authorized to commit The Company to any purchases of real property at any time.

2. The Broker shall be the only authorized representative to commit to a Guaranteed Sale.

3. The Company shall utilize the Guaranteed Sale Agreement currently approved by The Company modified for this particular circumstance as is necessary.

D. Salespersons Guaranteed Sales are considered as Purchasing a Company Listing and those procedures shall apply. The Company discourages salespeople from even thinking about personally entering into such an arrangement.

## Subagency

The Company has elected not to represent sellers through the subagency system. Every salesperson shall inform a prospective buyer that The Company will not accept any offers of subagency from any source.

## Listing a Buyer -- Buyer Agency

The Company has elected to represent buyers who indicate that they want representation. Every salesperson shall inform a prospective buyer of their right to representation. In order to properly list, that is represent, a buyer, the following must be completed:

I. Buyer Listing Procedures:

A. Oral listings are prohibited. Buyer must complete a written listing agreement utilizing The Company approved form. Absent a written listing agreement, The Company shall be acting as Transaction Brokers, defined below.

B. The "Listing Salesperson" or "Buyer's Salesperson", that is the individual that actually obtained the potential listing, shall submit that "proposed" listing agreement to the Broker for final approval.

C. All listing agreements shall include The Company "In-Office" Sale Addendum.

D. Once approved, a duplicate original, executed by the Broker, or the Broker's designee, shall be returned to the buyer and a duplicate original shall be placed in the buyer's file.

E. Each buyer shall have a separate file maintained by the Listing Salesperson on behalf of the Broker. Access to the buyer file is restricted to the Listing Salesperson and the Broker. No one else shall have access to or view that file without the prior approval of the Broker.

F. Listing Salespeople are authorized to solicit listings for any term that is at least ________ day(s) in length and not more than ________ day(s) in length. To solicit other terms would require prior approval of the Broker. Listings may be extended in writing signed by both the seller and the Broker.

II. Sources of Compensation:

A. The Company policy is that the transaction (buyer and /or seller) shall be responsible for only "one" commission. A portion of the total commission is paid to the seller's broker and a portion of the total commission is paid to the buyer's broker.

B. The Listing Agreement shall reflect the commission payable to The Company as a result of representing the buyer. The Company shall use all legal means to obtain, on behalf of the buyer, the agreed upon commission. That commission shall be sought from the following sources, as provided in the listing agreement, in the following order of priority:

1. Listing Office (Broker), cooperating broker fee, a portion of the total commission payable by the seller to the listing broker, through the MLS or separate agreement between Brokers; and/or, the

2. Seller, terms specified in the sale contract; and/or, any

3. Third party indicated by buyer, such as a referral company, relative, employer; or, the

4. Buyer paid directly to The Company.

III. Sources of Property to be Presented to the Buyer:

A. All property indicated in the MLS book; and,

B. All other properties that are personally known to the individual salesperson assisting the buyer; and,

C. Any property located by the buyer.

## Assisting a Buyer without Representation—Transaction Broker

The Company has elected to allow buyers to view and buy property without compelling them to either enter into a Listing Agreement employing The Company as Buyer Agents nor having to accept the fact that The Company is acting as a subagent of the various sellers in the market. Every salesperson shall inform a prospective buyer of their right to simply see property, The Company not acting as either a Buyer Agent or a Seller's Subagent. In order to properly assist a buyer as a Transaction Broker, the following must be completed:

I. Transaction Broker Disclosure/Listing Procedures:

A. The salesperson shall provide the buyer with either a copy of the Company Agency Policy or an Agency Disclosure form approved by The Company.

B. The Disclosure shall include the Company "In-Office" Sale Addendum.

C. The salesperson shall request that the buyer sign one copy of the disclosure for our records. However, the buyer's signature shall not be required for The Company to provide assistance. The salesperson shall always make a note of the date and time of delivery to the buyer on a copy of the disclosure and retain it in the buyer file at The Company.

D. Each buyer shall have a separate file maintained by the Salesperson on behalf of the Broker. Access to the buyer file is restricted to the Salesperson and the Broker. No one else shall have access to or view that file without the prior approval of the Broker.

E. The buyer and The Company may enter into a written Transaction Broker Agreement upon such terms and conditions as are mutually agreeable between The Company and the buyer.

II. Sources of Compensation:

A. The Company policy is that the transaction shall be responsible for only "one" commission.

B. Absent agreement to the contrary, The Company shall seek compensation only from the Listing Broker. The Company needs to be compensated for their services. Therefore, The Company shall not be required to inform the buyer of, nor show, property where there is not a present expectation of receiving an adequate cooperative commission.

III. Sources of Property to be Presented to the Buyer:

A. All properties that are listed with The Company; and,

B. All property indicated in the MLS book as providing adequate compensation for The Company acting in a Transaction Broker capacity; and,

C. All other properties that are personally known to the individual salesperson assisting the buyer that provide for adequate compensation for The Company acting in a Transaction Broker capacity; and,

D. Any property located by the buyer that either provides for adequate compensation or where the buyer will adequately compensate The Company.

## "In-Company", "In-House" or "In-Office" Sales

There are two sources of properties available for a prospective buyer. Property listed with The Company and property that is not listed for sale with The Company. Property that is not listed with The Company, property listed for sale through another brokerage company and property offered for sale directly by the owner, "for sale by owners". It is important to The Company that the buyer be able to see and buy any property that is available, whether listed with The Company, listed with another brokerage company or not listed with any brokerage company.

I. Property listed with The Company -- "In-Company Sales":

A. Seller's Agent. Absent a written buyer agency agreement to the contrary, The Company shall act as an agent of the seller for all such sales.

B. Buyer Broker/Transaction Broker. In the event that the buyer has elected to be governed by the terms and conditions of a buyer listing agreement, as indicated above, then when the buyer is interested in buying a property listed with The Company, the terms and conditions of The Company "In-Office" Sale Addendum shall govern and The Company shall act as a Transaction Broker for the transaction, not representing either the buyer or the seller. The Company shall never represent the buyer for the purchase of a property listed with The Company.

C. Agent/Subagent. There shall never be any agency relationship whatever between the buyer and The Company for the acquisition of property listed with The Company.

When the buyer is interested in a property that is not listed by a seller with The Company, an "out of office sale", The Company shall act either as a buyer agent or a transaction broker.

All questions regarding the Agency Policy of The Company shall be directed to the Broker.
Effective Date:____________________

Broker:________________________________________

## Subject Matter Cover Letters

The following are sample cover letters for specific topics. Not everyone will use every letter. Some may be consolidated and some done in a series. They may be written by the broker to all listings on a once a month basis or sent by the salesperson on a listing by listing basis. Remember if you want them to read it, keep it short. If you do not want them to read it, make it long.

These letters are not only intended to provide information to the prospective seller but also to impress upon them that real estate is for professionals only. Each talks about a different aspect of a proposed transfer that is second nature to the listing broker or salesperson. However, for someone who does not deal in real estate on a daily basis ie., a potential for sale by owner, the topics addressed may amount to several good reasons to list with you.

Part of your efforts is to list the property for sale. In addition you do a lot of work after the sale to get things closed. Many prospective sellers discount those efforts. These letters emphasize all the aspects of real estate transactions. In order to save space these letters will not be reproduced in a later section. A simple revision should suffice to use them after the listing is signed or even during a pending transaction.

**Letter - Agency Alternatives (Subagency/Buyer Agency)**

Mr. Sam Seller and
Mrs. Sandy Seller
4750 Table Mesa Drive
Boulder, CO 80303

Re: 4750 Table Mesa Drive, Boulder

Dear Sam and Sandy:

It is our desire that each seller be fully aware of the agency options that are available. While Kathy either has explained or will explain them to you and give you a copy of the state mandated agency disclosure form and our company office policy, I want to take a moment to drop you a letter since this is a very important issue.

This firm lists property as agents of the seller. That means that we represent you in the sale of your property. In addition we represent buyers looking for property. A good example would be when you go out with Kathy to look for your next home. In that event we would probably be acting on your behalf as your buyer agent. Yes, there is a separate listing agreement. Kathy will probably give it to you when she lists your home as a seller's agent. In this firm we like all agreements to be written so that everyone knows what to expect from each other.

Other firms become exposed to your home as the result of our advertising in various publications, through marketing meetings and breakfasts, as a result of the Multiple Listing Service, and as a result of the efforts of all the salespeople in the firm. We need to make sure that we offer these "co-operating" firms some direction as to the types of agency offering we will acknowledge. There are essentially two choices.

First, Subagents. Subagents work with a buyer but represent you, the Seller, and owe you duties of utmost good faith, loyalty and fidelity. Unfortunately, you may be vicariously liable for the acts of these Subagents when they are acting in the scope of the agency relationship. That is why we carry malpractice insurance.

Second, Buyer Agents. Buyer Agents represent the Buyer and owe duties of utmost good faith, loyalty and fidelity to the Buyer only. Do not worry. We will not let them know any confidential information about you and your sale. We provide only the information regarding the physical condition of the property to every co-operating broker. The good news is that you are probably not vicariously liable for the acts of buyer agents. Although buyer agents work with the Buyer, we agree to pay them a portion of our commission to encourage them to show and sell your home. In a similar manner, when we are acting as your agent for the purchase of your next house, we will try to collect our fee from that seller.

In most cases the co-operative broker is much more closely aligned with the buyer anyway. It is important to be careful about the information you make available to those that you might meet at the property site. We encourage you not to meet and talk with prospective buyers as you might give them or their agent information that they could use to your detriment. This often happens when the buyer asks an innocent question such as "were you transferred?" Sometimes it is hard to answer without giving away information that should remain confidential.

In our office we have both types of agents. In fact, it may be one of our salespersons acting as a buyer agent that sells your house. In that situation we follow our "In-Company" Sale Policy. Kathy will provide you with a copy for attachment to the listing contract.

Finally, in an effort to procure as many qualified buyers as possible, we shall seek assistance from and offer compensation to brokers, licensed by any state, located outside our market area, in the form of a referral fee. While nobody seems to know, we do not consider these referring brokers as subagents of the seller. They are simply licensed brokers who are paid a referral fee.

Most Sincerely,
The Orcas Island Company

by: Oliver E. Frascona, Broker

**Letter - Agency Alternatives (No Subagency/Buyer Agency)**

Mr. Sam Seller and
Mrs. Sandy Seller
4750 Table Mesa Drive
Boulder, CO 80303

Re: 4750 Table Mesa Drive, Boulder

Dear Sam and Sandy:

It is our desire that each seller be fully aware of the agency options that are available. While Kathy either has explained or will explain them to you and give you a copy of the state mandated agency disclosure form and our company office policy, I want to take a moment to drop you a letter since this is a very important issue.

This firm lists property as agents of the seller. That means that we represent you in the sale of your property. In addition we represent buyers looking for property. A good example would be when you go out with Kathy to look for your next home. In that event we would probably be acting on your behalf as your buyer agent. Yes, there is a separate listing agreement. Kathy will probably give it to you when she lists your home as a seller's agent. In this firm we like all agreements to be written so that everyone knows what to expect from each other.

Other firms may become exposed to your home as the result of our advertising in various publications, through marketing meetings and breakfasts, as a result of the Multiple Listing Service, and as a result of the efforts of all the salespeople in the firm. We need to make sure that we offer these "co-operating" firms some direction as to the types of agency offering we will acknowledge. There are essentially two choices.

First, Subagents. Subagents work with a buyer but represent you, the Seller, and owe you duties of utmost good faith, loyalty and fidelity. Unfortunately, you may be vicariously liable for the acts of these Subagents when acting in the scope of the agency relationship. That is why we do not offer compensation and co-operation to subagents. We will always pay a referral fee, described later, to any licensed real estate broker if they procure a buyer for your property. We simply can not agree to be liable nor to subject you to the liability of a subagent that we know nothing about.

Second, Buyer Agents. Buyer Agents represent the Buyer and owe duties of utmost good faith, loyalty and fidelity to the Buyer only. Do not worry. We will not let them know any confidential information about you and your sale. We provide only the information regarding the physical condition of the property to every co-operating broker. The good news is that you are probably not vicariously liable for the acts of buyer agents. Although buyer agents work with the Buyer, we agree to pay them a portion of our commission to encourage them to show and sell your home. In a similar manner, when we are acting as your agent for the purchase of your next house we will try to collect our fee from that seller .

In most cases the co-operative broker is much more closely aligned with the buyer anyway. It is important to be careful about the information you make available to those that you might meet at the property site. We encourage you not to meet and talk with prospective buyers as you might give them or their agent information that they could use to your detriment. This often happens when the buyer asks an innocent question such as "were you transferred?" Sometimes it is hard to answer without giving away information that should remain confidential.

In our office we have both types of agents. In fact, it may be one of our salespersons acting as a buyer agent that sells your house. In that situation we follow our "In-Company" Sale Policy. Kathy will provide you with a copy for attachment to the listing contract.

Finally, in an effort to procure as many qualified buyers as possible, we shall seek assistance from and offer compensation to brokers, licensed by any state, located within or outside of our market area, in the form of a referral fee. A condition of this referral fee is an acknowledgement that the other broker and salespersons are not acting as our agent which would make them your subagents. We treat all inquiries as if they came from a buyer agent and cooperate with every person we legally can to get your property sold without subjecting this firm or you, our seller, to any additional liability.

Most Sincerely,
The Orcas Island Company

by: Oliver E. Frascona, Broker

**Letter - Broker to Potential Subagent**

Mr. Ed Schmale, Broker
Pacific United Realty
21 North Center Green
Denver, CO 80213

Re: Subagency Relationship
Smith Road Property
Hampden and Fifth Streets

Dear Ed:

Thank you for calling this office to inquire about acting as our subagents with regard to the above property. We are offering a commission equal to ____% of the total sales price of the property to the successful subagent who procures the buyer ready, willing and able to complete the transaction as proposed by the seller, our principal. This obligation to pay you such a commission and the payment of commission itself are subject to the following terms and conditions:

First, you are the agent who procures the buyer who ultimately purchases the property. To ensure that there is no confusion, the names of all prospective buyers must be submitted to this office, either before you show the property or within twenty-four hours after the scheduled showing. We intend to give those names to the seller, our client, in order to provide protection for both of us in the event that a buyer should try to circumvent our listing agreement.

Second, our obligation to pay you a commission is predicated upon our receipt of our commission in cash. Should we be forced to accept conditional payment, which we may in our sole discretion elect to do, we will not be obligated to pay you until we are paid. In addition, we shall have no obligation to institute any form of collection procedure, including litigation, to collect the commission due. Should such action be necessary, you will be expected to share, in advance and on demand, in the expense of collection, including attorney's fees for the attorney I select, or forfeit your right to any portion of the proceeds of such an effort.

Third, that you do not compromise the interests of the seller, our principal, by your actions or inactions. We require that you provide us, in a timely fashion, with any information that you possess as to the financial qualifications of the prospective buyer, his intentions, and the amount that he will ultimately be willing to offer for the property. We understand that you will use your best efforts on behalf of the seller to obtain the highest and best offer possible.

Your acceptance of this proposal is evidenced by your taking any action with regard to the real estate without first giving us a written statement to indicate that you are not accepting the proposal. You will be responsible for your own actions and inactions not consistent with the laws of agency in this state and the terms of this letter.

It is a pleasure to have you as a subagent for the potential sale of this property. Please understand that this commission split is not offered with the intention that you split any listing commissions which you may independently have originated and upon which we become your subagents in the same fashion.

Sincerely,
The Orcas Island Company

by: Katherine E. Reece
Realtor®, CRS, GRI

**Letter - Buyer Agency Relationship**

Ms. Sharon Reichman, Broker
Pacific United Realty
21 North Center Green
Denver, CO 80303

Re: Buyer Agency Relationship

Dear Sharon:

Thank you for you inquiry. This letter is to confirm the extent of cooperation and terms upon which you may show and sell property that we have listed. Subject to the terms and conditions of this letter, we will pay you a commission equal to ___% of the total sales price of any property that is sold and closed with a buyer that you procure. Such procurement, of course, must be during our listing period and any proper extensions or protection periods that may exist thereafter. This obligation to pay you such a commission, and the payment of commission itself are subject to the following terms and conditions:

First, you are the agent who procures the buyer who ultimately purchases the property. To insure that there is no confusion, the names of all prospective buyers must be submitted to this office, either before you show the property or within twenty four hours after the scheduled showing. We intend to give those names to the seller, our client, in order to provide protection for both of us in the event that a buyer should try to circumvent our listing agreement.

Second, our obligation to pay you a commission is predicated upon our receipt of our commission. Should we be forced to accept conditional payment, which we may in our sole discretion elect to do, we will not be obligated to pay you until we are paid. In addition, we shall have no obligation to institute any form of collection procedure, including litigation, to collect the commission due. Should such action be necessary, you will be expected to share, in advance and on demand, in the expense of collection, including attorney's fees for the attorney I select, or forfeit your right to any portion of the proceeds of such an effort.

Third, so that you and I do not waste our time and the time of our clients, we require that you provide us, in a timely fashion, with any information that you possess as to the financial qualifications of the purchaser for this property. We understand that you will use your best efforts on behalf of the buyer to obtain the best offer possible.

Showing our listings is all the verification that we need to the terms of this agreement. Anticipating that you will accept, let me tell you that we are glad to have you as a competitor. Please sell all the property that you can that is listed with this office. You will, of course, be responsible for your own actions and inactions. We both understand that we are free to make the same, similar, and different agreements with other potential cooperating offices without regard to the contents of this agreement upon such terms and conditions that we alone determine are adequate without regard for or notification to you.

Please understand that this is not a proposal for a reciprocal agreement, and no such agreement is sought by this letter. In the event you wish to discuss the terms under which you will allow us to act as buyer agents for property that you have listed, please let me know. You are under no obligation to pay us upon the same terms or conditions that are agreed upon here for your payment. This agreement supersedes any offer in the Magic Listing Service.

Sincerely,
The Orcas Island Company

by: Katherine E. Reece
Realtor®, CRS, GRI

**Letter - Potential Buyer's Broker**

Mr. LaVerne Davis
SanVern Realty Consultants
Boulder, CO 80303

Re: Buyer's Brokerage Arrangement

Dear LaVerne:

Thank you for your inquiry regarding our policy for dealing with potential buyers' brokers. As you know, we are very interested in marketing our seller's property to all interested buyers. We welcome the participation of buyers' brokers and, subject to the qualifications outlined in this letter, are happy to acknowledge your agency relationship with your buyers.

Upon your initial contact please advise us that you are acting as a buyer's agent. You will be paid the amount indicated in the Magic Listing System book in the event that you are the procuring cause for the ultimate sale. That agreement to pay you is not subject to any conditions. In the event that you are also receiving money from your client, please indicate that fact. There is not need to indicate the amount. That is between you and your client the same way our listing commission is between our office and the seller.

Upon initial contact we do not need to know the name of your buyer; however, you agree to provide us with that name immediately upon request should we need to disclose it to our seller to protect our rights to receive a commission during any holdover period indicated in our listing. That will protect us both should the listing expire while the buyer is still interested in the property.

Our obligation to pay a commission is predicated upon our receipt of our commission in cash. Should we be forced to accept conditional payment, which we may in our sole discretion elect to do, we will not be obligated to pay you until we are paid. In addition, we shall have no obligation to institute any form of collection procedure, including litigation to collect the commission due. Should such action be necessary, you will be expected to share, in advance and on demand, in the expense of collection, including attorney's fees for the attorney I select, or forfeit your right to any portion of the proceeds of such an effort. We reserve the right to require, as a condition precedent to payment, a statement from your principal outlining the fact that you are not receiving anything of value from that principal as a result of this transaction, i.e., that you are not also being paid by the buyer.

Your acceptance of this proposal is evidenced by your calling this office and obtaining information about a listing or scheduling a showing. We are happy to have you as a competitor and to provide you with access to the properties that we have listed. We expect you to exercise due care and at all times to safeguard the property and possessions of the sellers we represent. Please sell all the property that you can that is listed with this office. You will, of course, be responsible for your own actions and inactions. You understand that we are free to make the same, similar, and different agreements with other potential buyers' brokers and subagents, without regard to the contents of this agreement, upon such terms and conditions that we alone determine are adequate without any obligation to notify you.

Please understand that this is not a proposal for a reciprocal agreement, and no such agreement is sought by this letter. In the event you wish to discuss the terms under which you will allow us to act as buyer agents or non-agents, real estate broker, for the sale of your listings, please let me know. You are under no obligation to pay us upon the same terms or conditions that are agreed upon here for your payment.

Sincerely,
The Orcas Island Company

by: Katherine E. Reece
Realtor®, CRS, GRI

**Letter - Anti-Trust**

Mr. Sam Seller and
Mrs. Sandy Seller
4750 Table Mesa Drive
Boulder, CO 80303

Re: 4750 Table Mesa Drive, Boulder

Dear Mr. and Mrs. Seller:

You will see in our listing agreement a section which addresses the commission that our office charges and several items dealing with the commission that we offer and pay to a "co-operating" brokerage office. All commissions are payable to the broker. Some people think that "everyone charges the same fee" or that "all the fees are pretty much standard." Nothing could be further from the case.

While it may appear that a lot of the commissions charged are similar, there are no "standard" commissions. The "co-operative" commissions that our firm offers and pays to other brokerage firms are set by this firm. The Multiple Listing Service, Board or Association of REALTORS® does not establish nor set commissions or co-operative commissions. Each office independently determines what they will charge, whom they will pay and how much.

The value of our services is based on many things: the quality of service we provide, the number of listings that we feel we can properly and successfully market in a given period, the time estimated for the sale of various listings, the price ranges of listings that we hope to market, and the overall cost of doing business in today's market. If other firms price their services at a similar or equal rate, that is a result of their own analysis and is solely their concern. We feel that the level of professionalism and the degree of success that we attain for our clients justifies our commission rate.

I know that after you have had the opportunity to experience our services you will agree. The amount of commission we charge is one of the items for which I alone am responsible, and I would be glad to discuss it at length with you if you so desire.

Most Sincerely,
The Orcas Island Company

by: Oliver E. Frascona, Broker

**Letter - Pre-Listing Company Brochure**

Mr. Sam Seller and
Mrs. Sandy Seller
4750 Table Mesa Drive
Boulder, CO 80303

Re: 4750 Table Mesa Drive, Boulder

Dear Mr. and Mrs. Seller:

Please let me introduce myself. I am the licensed broker for The Orcas Island Company I have just spoken with Katherine Reece who has been describing your home in detail to me. I must say she is very excited and feels that she can market it successfully, on the terms and conditions you have established, as the agent for this office if we are selected to be your listing agent.

When you list with this company, through Kathy, you also obtain the cooperative efforts of the rest of our professionally trained agents and our entire officc staff of support personnel. I have included a brochure describing the services that we as a team provide to our clients. If you have time, please look it over since it describes all of the various services that we provide, the areas that you are responsible for, the areas that we both have no control over, some valuable information about the complexities involved in modern real estate, and why I am proud to be the responsible broker for this office. As I am sure you know, all contracts that bind the brokerage firm must be signed by me pursuant to state law.

If I can be of any assistance, please do not hesitate to give me a call anytime. Thank you.

Most Sincerely,
The Orcas Island Company

by: Oliver E. Frascona, Broker

**Letter - Due-On-Transfer**

Mr. Sam Seller and
Mrs. Sandy Seller
4750 Table Mesa Drive
Boulder, CO 80303

Re: 4750 Table Mesa Drive, Boulder

Dear Mr. and Mrs. Seller:

Once you make the decision to list your property with The Orcas Island Company, one of the first items on our agenda will be to request information on the terms of your current mortgage. Your mortgage may contain what is generally called a "due-on-sale" clause. Basically this clause gives the mortgage lender the right to call the entire loan due if you transfer the property to a buyer. Relax, this is not the end of the world.

The due-on-sale clause simply means that, should you elect to sell your home by allowing the purchaser to assume your existing mortgage, the existing mortgage lender will have to be consulted. The buyer will have to qualify to assume the loan. Should the mortgage lender determine that the buyer "qualifies", they will allow the transfer and assumption. We assist people with this type of financing problem every day. We must take the necessary steps to ensure that we have time to obtain the approval and that buyers who seek to assume your loan are indeed qualified.

Yes, you could elect to transfer the title to a buyer without notifying the mortgage lender. However, that would enable the lender to accelerate the loan and potentially force a refinancing or foreclosure. In such instances we require that the seller and buyer seek and obtain written approval from their respective attorneys prior to entering into the contract.

As with all assumptions, we can not be responsible for the ability of the buyer to make all the payments. That determination is yours. We will help you obtain a credit report and financial statement, if you so desire, to assist you with this decision. In addition, we have found that consulting your banker is one of the best ways to determine the financial capabilities of a prospective buyer. They make these decisions every day.

Most Sincerely,
The Orcas Island Company

by: Claudia Kennedy, Broker Associate

**Letter - Earnest Money**

Mr. Sam Seller and
Mrs. Sandy Seller
4750 Table Mesa Drive
Boulder, CO 80303

Re: 4750 Table Mesa Drive, Boulder

Dear Mr. and Mrs. Seller:

The policy of most of the offices in this state is that any entity selected by the parties can be the holder of the earnest money deposit. It is the policy of this firm that we, as the listing brokerage company, in the absence of direction from you to the contrary, either hold the earnest money or select the escrow agent to hold the earnest money. These funds are placed in a separate bank account segregated from our operating accounts.

Unless everyone agrees to the contrary, the earnest money is not placed in an interest-bearing account. The need to have the interest accrue to a specific social security number or federal identification number on the date the account is set up makes the routine setup and payout from such an account a nightmare. In addition the amount involved and therefore the interest which would accrue is insufficient to warrant the effort. If, however, the amount is large or the term of its retention long in duration, an interest-bearing account is an alternative we are happy to provide for either the buyer or seller. In such a circumstance it is normal that the interest accrue as additional earnest money.

Over the years this company has adopted a policy of encouraging the parties to select an escrow agent or title company to hold the earnest money deposit. This independent escrow agent will accept, retain, and disburse any funds that are associated with your real estate transactions. This procedure ensures an impartial stakeholder, reduces bookkeeping, and removes us from any dispute that may arise with regard to the disposition of any such funds in the future.

By law we are not authorized to make any determination with regard to the entitlement of anyone to any portion of the earnest money in the event of a dispute.

Most Sincerely,
The Orcas Island Company

by: Oliver E. Frascona, Broker

## Letter - Fair Housing

Mr. Sam Seller and
Mrs. Sandy Seller
4750 Table Mesa Drive
Boulder, CO 80303

Re: 4750 Table Mesa Drive, Boulder
Federal, State and Local Fair Housing

Dear Mr. and Mrs. Seller:

This firm is committed to the principles and practices of fair housing. We support equal access to the American dream, housing. We want to be sure that every individual who is financially able to qualify for your home has an opportunity to see it and attempt to purchase it. At a time when some people feel that they are excluded, for whatever reason, we want to do everything possible to provide equal access to housing for everyone.

We are proud to display the Housing and Urban Development (HUD) Equal Housing Opportunity Poster, "*We do business in accordance with the Federal, State and Local Fair Housing Law*". It is illegal to discriminate against any person because of race, creed, color, sex, religion, national origin, handicap or familial status. Some states and cities add additional categories. In order to comply fully with the letter of the law and it's spirit, we simply do not discriminate against anyone, period. We are happy to say that all of the agents in our office have signed the Affirmative Marketing Agreement previously requested of all real estate agents by the Department of Housing and Urban Development.

As real estate professionals, we are pledged to providing equal access for every potential purchaser to all locations and types of housing that are available in this area that may be selected by the potential customers or clients who inquire about housing. I know you are happy to know that we, as your agents, will show your home to anyone who shows an interest and the financial ability to afford to buy it. We make sure that every potential customer knows that your house is available and is made aware of the features that it offers. This helps protect you as a seller since the Federal, State and Local Fair Housing Law applies to all of us.

Most Sincerely,
The Orcas Island Company

by: Claudia Kennedy, Broker Associate

## Letter - FHA Interest Payoff

Mr. Sam Seller and
Mrs. Sandy Seller
4750 Table Mesa Drive
Boulder, CO 80303

Re: 4750 Table Mesa Drive, Boulder

Dear Mr. and Mrs. Seller:

Once you make the decision to list your property with The Orcas Island Company, one of the first items on our agenda will be to request information on the terms of your current mortgage. If it is an FHA mortgage, we need to be careful about the date and time of closing for your home. The FHA mortgage probably provides that in the event of a payoff an entire month of interest will be charged for any portion of the month that the loan remains outstanding. In short, you may not want to close on the last day of the month, have the final payoff credited with the lender after the first of the following month and be required to pay another full month of interest.

We work with the closing agents to ensure the proper calculation of interest due. In addition, we make sure that there is time to get the payment to the mortgage lender before another month's interest is added on. In the event we are forced to close on or near the last day of the month through no fault of yours, we endeavor to provide in the contract that the buyer will pay the interest for the following month. We also make sure that the closing agent mails overnight the payoff to the lender to try to save you a month's interest.

While this is not always possible, I will attempt to arrange the transaction so as to save you as much interest as possible.

Most Sincerely,
The Orcas Island Company

by: Claudia Kennedy, Broker Associate

**Letter - Hazardous Waste and Inspections**

Mr. Sam Seller and
Mrs. Sandy Seller
4750 Table Mesa Drive
Boulder, CO 80303

Re: 4750 Table Mesa Drive, Boulder

Dear Mr. and Mrs. Seller:

We are all aware of the potential for contamination. Radon, lead paint and asbestos can exist in every home. More serious waste problems crop up at the most inopportune times. If we are selected to market your home, one of the first things that we do is discuss with you any possibility that a hazardous situation exists in your home. Such things as close proximity to high tension lines, a power plant, or waste disposal site can discourage a potential buyer.

While most people are inclined to inspect and review a property thoroughly after making an offer, some cautious buyers will want to have the property inspected for the presence of radon gas and other hazardous materials and to verify the condition of the soil prior to being obligated to purchase. Today many lenders and relocation companies make such verifications a must for their participation in a transaction.

Most importantly, a potential purchaser will probably inquire about and subsequently require that a test be conducted prior to his final purchase of your home. All this takes time when you can least afford it, that is, after the buyer has bound your home with a signed contract but before the closing has occurred. This is a critical period when you will want to have as few problems as possible.

The solution that we recommend is to have every home that we list tested as soon as possible for the condition of the soil and the presence and extent of radon gas and other hazardous materials. In this way, we can have the test results available for potential purchasers who can review them *prior* to making their decision to purchase. Hopefully we can then eliminate the need for the contract to be conditional upon the results of a subsequent test.

A list of firms that provide these services is enclosed. Please discuss your options, make a selection and order the tests. I would be glad to assist the tester of your choice by meeting her at the property during the day as I realize that you are both quite busy. In fact, after you make the selection and give me a budget of how much you wish to spend, I would be glad to arrange for the test on your behalf.

I can see no reason why both tests should not be simply a matter of course. Having them ready might just be the factor that helps that buyer decide on your home. Buyers, once they see what they want, usually are in a hurry to move in. The inspections would eliminate one more delay.

I work with the various inspectors and agencies to make sure that the inspections that you select are completed. This frees you to live your life and lets me stay on top of the sale of your home.

Most Sincerely,
The Orcas Island Company

by: Claudia Kennedy, Broker Associate

## Letter - Hazardous Waste and Inspections Commercial

Mr. Sam Seller and
Mrs. Sandy Seller
4750 Table Mesa Drive
Boulder, CO 80303

Re: 4750 Table Mesa Drive, Boulder

Dear Mr. and Mrs. Seller:

Commercial real estate is often affected by hazardous waste. No potential buyer wishes to acquire a location that has existing waste or the potential of waste without knowing these facts as part of the initial disclosure. Therefore, one of the first things that we do when we get a listing is to encourage the seller to obtain or update a phase one audit.

While most people are inclined to inspect and review a property thoroughly after making an offer, buyers will also want to have the property inspected for the presence of radon gas and other hazardous materials and to verify the condition of the soil prior to being obligated to purchase. Today many lenders make such verifications a must for their participation in a transaction.

If there is a problem we want to know early. One of our objectives is that you complete the sale without any lingering fears of later repercussions from the ultimate buyer, someone that you most probably do not even know yet. We like to have the phase one audit and engineering results available for potential purchasers who can review them *prior* to making their decision to purchase. Hopefully we can then eliminate the need for the contract to be conditional upon the results of a subsequent test.

I know you want to complete this sale with a minimum of delay and potential problems. Therefore, I am willing to do whatever you direct to expedite the process and to coordinate the people you choose to make the necessary repairs and inspections.

Most Sincerely,
The Orcas Island Company

by: Claudia Kennedy, Broker Associate

## Letter - Lock Boxes

Mr. Sam Seller
Mrs. Sandy Seller
4750 Table Mesa Drive
Boulder, CO 80303

Re: 4750 Table Mesa Drive

Dear Sam and Sandy:

The lock box is one of the most valuable marketing tools available today. This electronic system allows those that are participants but not the public at large accessibility to your home. It also allows us to track the date and time of each entry. People can see your home easily, and we can maintain accurate records detailing each person who saw your home.

These key safes contain a key to your home which can be accessed by other members of the Multiple Listing Service. Once the listing has been finalized, we can review the Lock Box Authorization Form. You can make the decision as to whether or not you want to take advantage of this sophisticated security and entry system.

Most Sincerely,
The Orcas Island Company

by: Claudia Kennedy, Broker Associate

## Letter - Mortgage Insurance (MIP) FHA/Conventional

Mr. Sam and Mrs. Sandy Seller
4750 Table Mesa Drive
Boulder, CO 80303

Re: 4750 Table Mesa Drive, Boulder

Dear Sam and Sandy:

When I explain mortgage insurance policy to my customers, I always feel it would be nice to have a little explanation in written form to review since it has become a significant amount of money and the alternatives are not always clear to brokers, lawyers, closing agents, let alone sellers and buyers. This is a little overview for you to keep handy throughout your listing with me. If you want to discuss it at any time just let me know, and I will try to explain it further.

Private mortgage insurance consists of a small initial premium and monthly premiums that are reflected in the interest rate of the loan. There are no prorations upon sale and no refunds. It is a simple system.

FHA mortgage insurance consists of two premiums. One is calculated as a percentage of your loan balance and collected each month. There is nothing that we can do about that. The other is collected in advance and runs for a term longer than a year. There is a possibility that you might get a credit for the amount of your unused premium.

The general rule for items that have been prepaid by the seller is that the buyer purchases the unused portion of such expenses since the buyer will enjoy the benefits of the unused portion of the contract. Fire insurance is a typical example. The buyer either buys the balance of the seller's fire insurance policy, since the new buyer will be covered as the owner for the remainder of the term, or the buyer obtains his own insurance and the seller is allowed to cancel his policy and receive a refund from the insurance company.

Mortgage insurance, absent an agreement to the contrary, should be treated in the same manner. The problem that occurs with FHA mortgage insurance is two-fold. First, unlike most expenses, this is not an annual policy; it is a multi-year policy fully paid in advance. The proration, that is, the division between the buyer and the seller of the unused portion of the prepaid premium, would substantially increase the amount of money that a buyer would need, and the amount that the seller would receive, upon the closing of the transaction.

Second, the prepaid premium is not easily prorated. The computation tables that are available from the Department of Housing and Urban Development essentially load more of the premium into the first years of the life of the policy. This means that in the event of cancellation the amount available for a refund diminishes rapidly with each passing year. Essentially the proration is calculated as if the buyer, who would be the owner of the mortgage insurance policy, cashed it in for a refund on the date of closing. The amount the buyer would receive is the amount that would be allocated to the seller at the closing.

As I have indicated previously, in the event there is an offer that entails the assumption of your FHA loan, it is often not possible for the buyer to also bear the burden of the proration. Therefore, the buyer may ask that the prepaid insurance not be prorated. Not an equitable proposition. I shall continue to indicate that the FHA insurance must be prorated in addition to the listed price of your home. Much like our discussion of assumptions, this presents a decision that ultimately must be made by you when you receive an offer to purchase.

Thank you for letting me take the time to review this complex little area. Feel free to call if you want to talk it over some more.

Most Sincerely,
The Orcas Island Company

by: Oliver E. Frascona, Broker

**Letter - Multiple Listing Service**

Mr. Sam Seller and
Mrs. Sandy Seller
4750 Table Mesa Drive
Boulder, CO 80303

Re: 4750 Table Mesa Drive, Boulder

Dear Sam and Sandy:

Yes, we are members of the Multiple Listing Service or "MLS". We can place your property listing in the Multiple Listing Book and Multiple Listing Computer for review by numerous other licensed salespeople. Before we do this, we will submit to you the information as it will appear in the MLS so that you can review it to ensure its accuracy.

It's an extra step; but no one knows your home better than you do, and we want to be sure that everything we publish will detail your home's available options and features as accurately as we both can make them. Although the MLS includes a statement indicating that it is for the exclusive use of member brokers and that the information contained therein is not to be strictly relied upon, we want our listings to be as accurate as possible.

Some people request that their property not be exposed to the MLS. We do not encourage such a practice. By not allowing us to market your home through the MLS, you severely limit our ability to expose your property to a multitude of potential buyers in order that we might find that one buyer who will buy your home. In addition, our competitors will think that we reserved the listing so that we could sell the property ourselves and deprive them of the opportunity to sell it to their buyers.

We realize that there are extenuating circumstances that may warrant not utilizing the MLS and would be happy to discuss your particular situation with you. With your informed consent and my approval, as the broker, we could make an exception to accommodate your individual marketing needs.

Most Sincerely,
The Orcas Island Company

by: Katherine E. Reece, Broker

## Letter - Purchase for Own Account

Mr. Sam Seller and
Mrs. Sandy Seller
4750 Table Mesa Drive
Boulder, CO 80303

Re: 4750 Table Mesa Drive, Boulder

Dear Mr. and Mrs. Seller:

We are in the business of selling real estate for our sellers. Should a salesperson desire to buy property for their own account, they are encouraged to do so prior to the listing being taken. We want to be either a buyer or your agent, but not both. As a general rule, this firm does not allow agents to purchase any property that we have listed. Exceptions are made in unusual situations. All such sales require the prior written approval of the broker.

If this is of interest to you, we can provide you with the standard form that we use in such situations. First, there will have to be a paragraph inserted in the listing agreement that outlines our procedures. Second, when the property is placed under contract, you will have to obtain the written consent of your attorney to the proposed transaction.

*We realize that we are missing a unique opportunity to be involved in litigation, but nevertheless wish to try to limit from the outset what is by definition a bad situation.*

We look forward to having your home in our inventory of available homes. It is always a pleasure to have a well-kept and well-maintained home such as yours in our inventory of available listings.

Most Sincerely,
The Orcas Island Company

by: Oliver E. Frascona, Broker

## Letter - REALTOR® Professional Affiliation

Mr. Sam Seller and
Mrs. Sandy Seller
4750 Table Mesa Drive
Boulder, CO 80303

Re: 4750 Table Mesa Drive, Boulder

Dear Sam and Sandy:

Not every real estate licensee is a REALTOR®. Once someone obtains a real estate brokers or salespersons license, he or she may apply for membership in the board or association of Realtors®. We think that Realtors® are striving to be the best that they can be.

We are proud to be members of the National Association of Realtors® through our affiliation with our Board or Association of Realtors®. This means that we adhere to the Code of Ethics and participate in the various educational opportunities that are available to members of the board. I have included a copy of the Code of Ethics for your perusal.

Being a Realtor® means we are concerned with the state of real estate in our area. We support the private ownership of real estate and the ability to convey it. If you would like more information about the Realtor® organization please let me know.

Most Sincerely,
The Orcas Island Company

by: Claudia Kennedy, Broker Associate

### Letter - Tax Deferred Exchange

Mr. Sam Seller and
Mrs. Sandy Seller
4750 Table Mesa Drive
Boulder, CO 80303

Re: Tax Deferred Exchanges under
Section 1031 of the Internal Revenue Code

Dear Mr. and Mrs. Seller:

If the property you are selling is your personal residence, then this letter is not applicable. However, should the property you are selling be other than your personal residence or should you own other property that you are thinking of selling, this letter will provide you with some very interesting information. There is no way to eliminate taxes. There *is* a way to potentially defer taxes into the future. That is called a tax deferred exchange.

This is not intended to substitute for advice from your accountant or attorney. It is only intended to give you some insight into the potential savings that are available to everyone through the use of this Internal Revenue Service Code section. If after you read this letter you are interested, please give me a call and we can set up a time to review it in more detail. A brief explanation follows:

You must be dealing with "like kind" property. That means real estate. Apartments, single family houses, farms, ranches, industrial buildings, warehouses, raw land are all examples of like kind property. You can trade any one for the other. In fact you can trade one for many or many for one.

Difficult? Not in the least. First, you sell your property in the normal fashion. We will provide you with the clause that can be inserted into your contract. It will not affect your sale in the least and not put any additional demands upon the buyer. In fact the sale occurs just like normal.

A qualifying intermediary such as a title company, friend, broker or attorney holds the proceeds of sale. It is important to select someone for that position who knows what they are doing and whom you can trust. We can assist you with that selection should you desire.

Then you have 45 days to indicate to the qualifying intermediary up to three properties that you think you might like to own. There are provisions for designating more than three properties, but we do not have enough room here for them. Yes, you might already have them under contract.

Finally, you have to close them within 180 days of the initial tax deferred closing. That is all. We will be glad to examine the effect and potential savings that you may be able to obtain. If you are thinking about selling one property and buying another, this may be an alternative you may wish to consider.

Tax deferred exchanges are fun, easy and can save you a substantial amount of money now. We are happy to assist you without practicing law or accounting. We charge no additional fees. It is just another service to our sellers.

Most Sincerely,
The Orcas Island Company

by: Oliver E. Frascona, Broker

## Transaction Broker Alternative

In order to demonstrate that in fact a seller can list a property with a broker without entering into an agency relationship, we have included a copy of a generally accepted Exclusive Right-to-Sell (Transaction Broker) Listing Contract. This form demonstrates that the basic services the seller desires can be accomplished without creating an agency relationship. This is the form of choice for the authors when they list their personal real estate for sale with a brokerage company. Utilizing a transaction broker has the distinct advantage of eliminating vicarious liability. The seller is not liable for the actions or inactions of the broker and all the salespeople in the broker's office.

Yes, you still need to be a licensed salesperson working for a licensed broker. Yes, you still have a long list of duties to the seller and the buyer. Yes, you should annex a form indicating the services that you provide to the buyer and the seller.

## Exclusive Right-to-Sell (Transaction Broker) Listing Contract

______________________, 19_____

____________________________________________________________________ ("Seller") hereby irrevocably appoint(s) ____________________________________ ("Broker") as Seller's exclusive broker for the purposes and under the terms specified herein, and the parties agree:

1. **Purpose.** The purpose of this contract ("Listing Contract") is to engage the efforts of Broker to accomplish the sale of the real property legally described as:

   also known as:_____________________________________________

   together with such items of personal property indicated herein (collectively, the "Property").

2. **Broker's Services.** Broker is not an agent or advocate of Seller or buyer.
   a. Broker shall exercise reasonable skill and care for Seller including, but not limited to:
      i. Presenting all offers to and from the Seller in a timely manner regardless of whether the Property is subject to a contract for sale;
      ii. Advising the Seller and the buyer to obtain expert advice as to material matters about which the Broker knows but the specifics of which are beyond the expertise of the Broker;
      iii. Accounting in a timely manner for all money and property received;
      iv. Keeping the Seller and the buyer fully informed regarding the transaction;
      v. Assisting the Seller and the buyer in complying with the terms and conditions of any contract for sale including closing the transaction;
      vi. Disclosing to the Seller adverse material facts actually known by the Broker; and
      vii. Informing the Seller and the buyer that, in their respective capacities, they shall not be vicariously liable for the acts of the Broker.
   b. Broker shall not disclose the following information without the informed consent of the Seller:
      i. That the Seller is willing to accept less than the asking price for the Property;
      ii. What the motivating factors are for the Seller to sell the Property;
      iii. That the Seller will agree to financing terms other than those offered;
      vi. Any material information about the Seller unless the disclosure is required by law or failure to disclose such information would constitute fraud or dishonest dealing; or

v. Any facts or suspicions regarding circumstances which may psychologically impact or stigmatize any real property pursuant to state law.

c. Broker shall disclose to any prospective buyer all adverse material facts actually known by Broker including but not limited to adverse material facts pertaining to the title to the Property that will remain after delivery of deed and the physical condition of the Property, any material defects in the Property, and any environmental hazards affecting the Property which are required by law to be disclosed.

3. **Sale.** "Sale of the Property" or "Sale" means the voluntary transfer or exchange of any interest in the Property or the voluntary creation of the right to acquire any interest in the Property (including a contract or lease).

4. **Effect of this Listing Contract.** By this appointment, Seller agrees to conduct all negotiations for the Sale of the Property only through Broker, and to refer to Broker all inquiries received in any form from real estate brokers, salespersons, prospective buyers, tenants or any other source during the time this Listing Contract is in effect. Seller authorizes Broker to disclose any facts about the Property. In addition, Seller agrees that any Broker compensation which is conditioned upon the Sale of the Property shall be earned by Broker as set forth herein without any discount or allowance for any efforts made by Seller or by any other person in connection with the Sale of the Property.

5. **The Listing Period.** Broker's authority under this Listing Contract shall begin on ____________________, 19_____ and shall continue through midnight on ____________________, 19_____ ("Listing Period").

6. **Price and Terms.** Price: U.S. $ __________. Terms:

   Minimum amount of earnest money deposit U.S. $ __________ in the form of ☐personal check ☐corporate check ☐promissory note ☐cash ☐___________.

7. **Deposits.** Broker is authorized to accept earnest money deposits pursuant to a proposed Sale contract. Broker is authorized to deliver the earnest money deposit to the closing or escrow agent, if any, at or before the closing of the Sale contract.

8. **Price to Include.** The purchase price includes the following items if owned by Seller:

   (a) if attached to the Property on the date of the agreement for Sale: lighting, heating, plumbing, ventilating, and air conditioning fixtures, TV antennas, water softeners, smoke/fire/burglar alarms, security devices, inside telephone wiring and connecting blocks/jacks, plants, mirrors, floor coverings, intercom systems, built-in kitchen appliances, sprinkler systems and controls, built-in vacuum systems (including accessories), and garage door openers including _____ remote controls;

(b) if on the Property whether attached or not on the date of this Listing Contract: storm windows, storm doors, window and porch shades, awnings, blinds, screens, curtain rods, drapery rods, fireplace inserts, fireplace screens, fireplace grates, heating stoves, storage sheds, all keys; and

(c)

The above described items ("Inclusions") shall be conveyed by Seller to buyer by bill of sale at closing, all in their present condition, ordinary wear and tear excepted, conveyed free and clear of all taxes, liens and encumbrances unless assumed by buyer . The following attached fixtures are excluded from the Sale:

9. **Title and Encumbrances.** Seller represents to Broker that title to the Property is solely in Seller's name. Seller shall deliver to Broker true copies of all relevant title materials, lease(s) and survey(s) in Seller's possession and shall disclose to Broker all easements, liens and other encumbrances, if any, on the Property, of which Seller has knowledge. Seller authorizes the holder of any obligation secured by an encumbrance on the Property to disclose to Broker the amount owing on said encumbrance and the terms thereof.

   In case of Sale, Seller agrees to convey, by a __________ deed, only that title Seller has in the Property. All monetary encumbrances (such as mortgages, deeds of trust, liens, financing statements) shall be paid by Seller and released except as Seller and buyer may otherwise agree. Existing monetary encumbrances are as follows:

   The Property is subject to the following leases and tenancies:

   If the Property has been or will be assessed for local improvements installed at the time of signing a Sale contract, Seller will be responsible for payment of same unless otherwise agreed. Broker may terminate this Listing Contract upon written notice to Seller that title is not satisfactory to Broker.

10. **Evidence of Title.** Seller agrees to furnish buyer, at Seller's expense, Seller's choice of a commitment for, and a policy of, title insurance or an abstract of title to the Property certified to a current date in the amount specified by any Sale contract.

11. **Prorations.** General taxes for the year of closing, based on the taxes for the calendar year immediately preceding closing, rents, water and sewer charges, homeowner's association dues, and interest on continuing loan(s), if any, and ______________________________ shall be prorated to date of closing.

FHA or private mortgage insurance premium ☐ shall ☐ shall not be apportioned to the date of closing. Any such amount shall be apportioned as follows:______________________________________________________.

12. **Possession.** Possession of the Property shall be delivered to buyer as follows:

subject to leases and tenancies as described herein.

13. **Material Defects - Broker Disclosures - Inspection.** Seller agrees that any defects of a material nature (including, but not limited to, structural defects; soil conditions; violations of health, zoning or building laws; nonconforming uses and zoning variances) actually known by Broker must be disclosed by Broker to any prospective buyer . The Seller agrees that any buyer may have the Property and Inclusions inspected and that Broker may encourage such inspections.

    Seller agrees to provide buyer with a Seller's Property Disclosure form completed to the best of Seller's current, actual knowledge.

14. **Commission to Broker.**
    a. **Commission.** In consideration of the services to be performed by Broker, Seller agrees to pay Broker in U.S. dollars as follows:
        1. **Sale Commission.**
            i. _____ (%) of the gross sales price, or

               ________________________________________
            ii. **Lease Commission.**
               _____ (%) of the gross rent under the lease, or

               ________________________________________
        2. **When Earned.** Such commission shall be earned upon the happening of any of the following:
            a. Any Sale of the Property within the Listing Period by Seller, by Broker or by any other person;
            b. Broker finding a buyer who is ready, willing and able to complete the transaction as specified herein by Seller; or
            c. Any Sale of the Property within _____ calendar days subsequent to the expiration of the Listing Period ("Holdover Period") to anyone with whom Broker negotiated and whose name was submitted, in writing, to Seller by Broker during the Listing Period (including any extensions thereof).
        3. **When Applicable and Payable.** The commission obligation shall apply to a Sale made during the Listing Period or made during any extension of such original or extended term. The commission described in subsection (a)(1) shall be payable at the time of the closing of the Sale as contemplated by subsection (b)(1) or (b)(3), or upon fulfillment of subsection (b)(2) where either the offer made by such buyer is defeated by Seller or by the refusal or neglect of Seller to consummate the Sale as agreed upon.

4. **Lease and Lease Option Commissions.** If the transaction consists of a lease or a lease and right to purchase the Property, the commission relating to the lease shall be as provided in subsection (a)(2), payable as follows:

b. **Limitations on Broker's Compensation.** Broker shall not accept compensation from the buyer, the buyer's agent, or any entity participating in or providing services for the Sale without the written consent of Seller.

15. **Other Brokers, Assistance -- Multiple Listing Service.**

a. Broker shall seek assistance from and offer compensation to the following brokers outside of the listing company (Check all that apply.)

☐ Brokers Representing the buyer ("Buyer Agents"). (Buyer Agents representing the buyer owe duties of utmost good faith, loyalty and fidelity to buyer only. Seller is not vicariously liable for the acts of Buyer Agents.) Broker will offer compensation to Buyer Agents as follows:
_____ (%) of the gross sales price, or ____________________

☐ Brokers assisting the buyer in the transaction but not acting as agents ("Transaction-Brokers"). (Transaction-Brokers must exercise reasonable skill and care for the parties. Seller is not vicariously liable for the acts of Transaction-Brokers.) Broker will offer compensation to Transaction-Brokers as follows:
_____ (%) of the gross sales price, or ____________________

b. Broker ☐ will ☐ will not submit the Property to a multiple listing service. Reason property not submitted to MLS:____________________
____________________

16. **Forfeiture of Payments.** In the event of a forfeiture of payments made by a buyer, the sums received shall be divided between Broker and Seller, one-half thereof to Broker, but not to exceed the commission agreed upon herein, and the balance to Seller.

17. **Cost of Services; Reimbursement.** Broker shall bear all expenses incurred by Broker, if any, to market the Property and to compensate cooperating brokers, if any. Broker will not obtain or order any other products or services unless Seller agrees in writing to pay for them promptly when due. Unless otherwise agreed, Broker shall not be obligated to advance funds for the benefit of Seller in order to complete a closing. Seller shall reimburse Broker for payments made by Broker for such other products or services authorized by Seller.

18. **Maintenance of the Property**. Seller agrees Broker shall not be responsible for maintenance of the Property nor shall Broker be liable for damage of any kind occurring to the Property, unless such damage shall be caused by the negligence of Broker.

19. **Other Sellers.** Seller acknowledges that Broker may have agreements with other sellers to market and sell their properties.

20. **Nondiscrimination.** The parties agree not to discriminate unlawfully against any prospective buyer because of the race, creed, color, sex, marital status, national origin, familial status, physical or mental handicap, religion or ancestry of such person.

21. **Recommendation of Legal Counsel and Attorney Fees.** By signing this document, Seller acknowledges that Broker has advised that this document has important legal consequences and has recommended consultation with legal and tax or other counsel, before signing this contract. In case of arbitration or litigation between Seller and Broker in their respective capacities, the parties agree that costs and reasonable attorney fees shall be awarded to the prevailing party.

22. **Copies and Modification.** This Listing Contract is executed in multiple copies and Seller acknowledges receipt of a copy of this Listing Contract signed by Broker. No subsequent modification of any of the terms of this Listing agreement shall be valid, binding upon the parties, or enforceable unless made in writing and signed by the parties. This Listing Contract constitutes the entire agreement between the parties relating to the subject hereof, and any prior agreements pertaining thereto, whether oral or written, have been merged and integrated into this Listing Contract.

23. **Counterparts.** If more than one person is named as a Seller herein, this Listing Contract may be executed by each Seller, individually, and when each Seller has executed a copy of this Listing Contract, such copies taken together shall be deemed to be a full and complete contract between the parties.

23. **Additional Provisions.**

Accepted:

Seller: Seller:

______________________________ date ______________________________ date

Real Estate Broker:

______________________________

by date

# After the Listing is Signed

Now that you have the seller's acknowledgement on the listing agreement the work has really begun. Communication is even more important now by both telephone and written correspondence. Send a confirmation letter of any communication discussed by telephone and keep an accurate and concise telephone log. A good practice to follow is written market updates to the seller on a previously agreed upon basis. *Sellers have no concept of the time you actually spend on their transaction but expect that you should spend every waking moment working for them regardless of the number of listings you service.* After all, their listing is the most important.

**The Seller's Checklist.** When you are busy with multiple transactions, checklists become imperative to a smoothly running day. It is much simpler to follow a checklist for routine tasks so that you do not have to reinvent the wheel for the same process each time. If you employ an administrative assistant the checklist becomes even more critical to ensure that you are indeed "cloned" in your approach to procedures. You can arrive at your listing appointments confident in knowing that all the forms are properly completed with the necessary information and that all are indeed there! Being organized and prepared will give the immediate impression of being a professional in the real estate field.

**Continued Correspondence.** Send the seller a letter or postcard describing what you are doing to sell their home no matter how routine the procedure may seem to you--entering into the Multiple Listing Service, sending announcements to their neighbors, sending flyers to cooperating Realtors®, calling buyers' agents, distributing flyers at your local Realtor® meetings. Reconfirm the office policy on key issues such as inspections, lock boxes, agency, disclosures and all other aspects of marketing the seller's home in your continuous correspondence. Stay in touch.

These letters can be more personal. "Dear Sam and Sandy" is more appropriate now. Standard letters or postcards can be used to suggest items not selected. It is sometimes difficult to tell a seller to "clean " the house. Oftentimes, by just seeing the item listed on the standard form, the seller will get the idea without the need to check the box.

Another idea is to provide the seller an extensive checklist for preparing the home for sale with the idea that, of course, not all items will apply to him. You will find that he will have a tendency to make certain all are complete.

**Tip.** *Walk through the home with the seller with "buyer's eyes". Ask him to note any changes he feels he should make to the home in order to sell it. Emphasize that you are on his team, but as the professional chosen to market his home, you will note any objections you would anticipate a potential buyer would have. Decide at the onset how the*

> *seller will address any such objections to the condition of the home. Katherine has used a tape recorder effectively for the walk through with a written list provided to the seller. By doing this you have already "paved the way" to discussion of any objections to the home.*

**Market Updates.** No matter how many times you tell a client or customer, either Seller or Buyer, a specific piece of information regarding his transaction, he will tend to have "selective memory" when the occasion fits. In the client's defense it is impossible to remember the volumes of information not to mention the content of all the forms he has signed in today's real estate transaction. Remember that is why he hired a real estate professional in the first place.

The practice of using a written update to keep the client informed and happy just makes common sense. Not only does it keep her informed of items which have been accomplished and eliminate confusion of what needs to be done but gives her a realistic impression of all that you are doing on her behalf to sell the property. Seldom will you receive a call demanding to know why the home has not sold or implying you are not doing your job. The last paragraph of the update should always request the client to call you within a specific period of time if she has questions. This places the burden on the client to speak up now with any suggestions or changes she wishes to make. If none is proposed, you at least have a record of having made suggestions yourself. This again helps to establish that standard of practice common to all your transactions if your client should become a plaintiff.

Do not hesitate to be as detailed as possible with daily entries. There will be a tendency not to include those items you consider routine to any transaction. They may be routine to you but to your client it shows that you are doing something for them every day. It will show that your are "working all the time" for them. They may even call to apologize to you for their house not selling when you are working so hard for them and offer the price reduction themselves! It has happened.

## Listing Checklist

Date:__________________

Name:______________________________ RES Phone: __________________

Address:_____________________________ OFF Phone: __________________

______________________________________

Title Company:_________________________ File No: ______________________

Contact:______________________________ Phone: _______________________

### LISTING PROCEDURE

____1. Mail broker introduction letter
____2. Assemble listing presentation packet
____3. Visit the seller
____4. Mail follow up letter to seller
____5. Mail selected subject matter letters
____6. Actual listing presentation date:__________
____7. When listing documents are signed by Seller:
  a. Broker's signature on Listing Agreement
  b. Enter into the MLS computer
  c. Write MLS# on property profile sheet
  d. Deliver copy of MLS sheet to seller with confirming letter
____8. Mail selected after listing letters
____9. Notify seller about home warranty
____10. Assemble office showing instructions
____11. Mortgage information request letter mailed to lender ___________
____12. If condo or town home, request association documents, covenants, etc.
____13. Target market
  a. Assemble showsheet draft and make package for property
  b. Take pictures and send one to seller
  c. Mail photos to market area (down 50%)
  d. Photo plus picture to shopping center boards
____14. Assemble neighborhood "just listed" letter and mail
____15. Assemble Realtor® network "new on market" letter
____16. Make open house appointment with seller
____17. Hang the lock box and obtain the seller consent form
____18. Schedule broker's open (letter of confirmation to seller)
____19. Make proforma Marketing Update Sheet master

**WHEN LISTING SELLS**

_____1. Original of contract to file
_____2. Original of contract to title company
_____3. Prepare and deliver escrow instructions
_____4. Prepare letter designating tasks to be completed
  a. Mail to seller
  b. Mail to buyer (via other broker)
_____5. Prepare performance deadlines sheet
_____5. Revise listing status in MLS
_____6. Revise status in floor book
_____7. Begin to assemble appraisal package for appraiser
_____8. Designate and start to mail the letters that will flow through the pre-closing period
_____9. Mail lender selection letter

**WHEN LOAN IS APPROVED**

_____1. Mail loan confirmation letter
_____2. Confirm loan status with lender and title company
_____3. Make a project checklist to delegate outstanding tasks

**WHEN TRANSACTION CLOSES and RECORDS**

_____1. Purge office file, prepare MLS sold change form
_____2. Enter MLS status change
_____3. Give office file to accountant
_____4. Complete 4x5 index card for client database
_____5. Input into personal farm database
_____6. Send note and gift to client
_____7. Send follow up letters to all parties
_____7. Ask for referral to new client!

## Marketing Update

for
Mr. Sam Seller
Mrs. Sandra Seller
4750 Table Mesa Drive
Boulder, Colorado

Today's Date:____________________ Date of Last Report:________________

Reporting Period:________________

Listing Date:____________________ Days on the Market:________________

Original List Price: $______________ Current List Price: $______________

ACTIVITY

_______ Showings from other offices
_______ Showings from our office
_______ Open houses
_______ Written proposals received

Comments from other salespeople/buyers:

________________________________________________________________
________________________________________________________________
________________________________________________________________

My Comments:

[Add your personal comments about the progress of the marketing. Include any future appointment dates such as inspections, performance deadlines on contracts, escrow or loan progress concerns that you want the client to remember. Offer suggestions here for any change in marketing strategy such as improving the property condition, offering additional incentives to potential buyers or price reductions. Be upbeat, but honest about any difficulties encountered in the marketing or escrow process.]

Please call me with 48 hours of receipt of this report if you have any questions, specific needs, comments or suggestions concerning the sale/marketing process of your home. I shall continue my work and dedication as we progress towards a completed sale of your home. Thank you.

Most Sincerely,
The Orcas Island Company

by Katherine E. Reece
Realtor®, CRS, GRI

## Showing Report Form

### *SHOWING REPORT*

**To**: ______________________________________________

**Property**
**Address**:__________________________________________

Your home was shown on the date(s) indicated below. Included are some of the comments that our office received. I thought that you might like to see them.

**Date(s)**
**Shown**:___________________________________________

**Comments**:

☐ Exterior needs to be painted
☐ Carpets need to be cleaned
☐ House seemed cluttered
☐ Garage seemed cluttered
☐ Interior needs to be painted
☐ Animals made showing difficult
☐ Children made showing difficult
☐ Tenants made showing difficult
☐ It would have been easier to show without the owners being present
☐____________________________________________________
☐____________________________________________________

I checked some suggestions that might assist us in showing your home in the future. Review them when you have a minute and I will give you a call.

**Suggestions to enhance future showings**:

☐ Consider offering incentives so tenants would cooperate with showings
☐ Consider paying "points" to a new lender to assist a buyer with a loan
☐ Remove or store some items so that your home looks even larger
☐ Leave fresh baked bread in the oven before showings
☐ Leave a fire in the fireplace
☐ Place potpourri in your home
☐____________________________________________________
☐____________________________________________________
☐ Please call me at ____________________ when it is convenient

Salesperson:_______________________________ Date: __________

**Thank you for selecting us to market your home**

**Letter - After Listing is Signed (Broker)**

Mr. Sam Seller
Mrs. Sandra Seller
4750 Table Mesa Drive
Boulder, CO 80303

Re: 4750 Table Mesa Drive, Boulder

Dear Sam and Sandy:

Kathy and I and all the members of this firm are happy and proud to have been selected to market your home. Kathy has been an agent with this company for many years and has assisted many people in both marketing their existing property and in selecting new real estate. As I am sure she indicated to you, all contractual obligations of The Orcas Island Company to be effective under the law, must be formally approved by me as the licensed broker. This allows agents to concentrate on the marketing of your home, leaving the obligations of this firm to the broker.

I am happy to inform you that I, as the broker of The Orcas Island Company, have just accepted and countersigned your proposed Listing Agreement, including the Seller's Property Disclosure Addendum, as submitted by Katherine Reece. A copy of the fully executed Listing Agreement is enclosed for your records. Welcome to our list of clients.

Kathy has been describing your home, including your beautiful master bedroom, extensive well-cared-for garden and oversized garage with a shop area, in detail to everyone in the office as she prepares us for our office tour. I look forward to seeing your home personally on the tour.

Please feel free to contact me at any time should you wish to discuss your relationship with this company. I am always happy to discuss any aspect of your real estate needs or your relationship with this company or real estate in general.

Most sincerely,
The Orcas Island Company

by: Oliver E. Frascona, Broker

**Letter - After Listing is Signed (Salesperson)**

Mr. Sam Seller
Mrs. Sandy Seller
4750 Table Mesa Drive
Boulder, Colorado 80303

Re: 4750 Table Mesa Drive

Dear Sam and Sandy:

I want to thank you for selecting me and The Orcas Island Company to market your home. I will be working hard to get your home SOLD upon the terms you have selected in the shortest amount of time possible.

I will begin to market your home through the Multiple Listing Service (MLS) as soon as I have your approval of the "MLS Information Sheet". The listing information will then be entered in the MLS computer and any Realtor® from any member company can access that information twenty-four hours every day. In addition, everyone knows they can reach me at home, on my cellular phone or by digital pager if they need assistance.

I have delivered information about your property to each salesperson in the office. Additionally, I will be talking about your listing at our upcoming office meeting and other Realtor® events.

Sam and Sandy, I know that selling real estate can sometimes be overwhelming. If you have any questions, comments or criticisms, please give me a call. I believe the marketing of your home is a team effort, and open communication is the best way to solve any problems that may arise.

Sincerely,
The Orcas Island Company

by: Katherine E. Reece
Realtor®, CRS, GRI

## Letter - Listing Price Verification

Mr. Sam Seller
Mrs. Sandy Seller
4750 Table Mesa Drive
Boulder, CO 80303

Re: 4750 Table Mesa Drive

Dear Sam and Sandy:

As I indicated when we listed your home, we want to be sure that you arrive at a price that reflects your understanding of the market. That has been done, and we congratulate you on pricing the property within a range that allowed us to accept the listing. Of course, no one knows the final sales price and terms.

As I indicated when we listed your home, the Competitive Market Analysis is yours to keep. It showed you those homes that we were able to locate that were similar to yours that had either sold, been rejected by the market or were still available as competition. Those are the same comparable properties that we indicated we would provide to an interested buyer when they inquire about the relative value of your home. Buyers must go through the same process that you experienced as they try to determine the price of your home.

I am so glad that I am a Realtor® and not an appraiser. As a Realtor® I can provide the data regrading relative value to the public and let the buyer and seller determine the price they feel is correct. Then once the contract is signed, we can all see if the appraiser agrees with the parties. We simply can not set nor be responsible for the price of real estate. We decide if the price determined by the seller is close enough to the market in our minds to warrant marketing the property at the selected price.

Most sincerely,
American Real Estate Service

by: Tina B. Daniel, Broker-Owner
Realtor®, CRS, GRI

## Letter - Listing MLS Information Verification

Mr. Sam Seller
Mrs. Sandy Seller
4750 Table Mesa Drive
Boulder, CO 80303

Re: 4750 Table Mesa Drive

Dear Sam and Sandy:

As I indicated when we listed your home, we want to submit your home to the Multiple Listing Service as soon as possible. Enclosed is the Multiple Listing Service data input form that I have completed for your home. Please review it as soon as possible.

If you desire to change or correct anything, let me know immediately. We are eager to represent your home accurately. Unless there are a number of changes, a phone call will do the job nicely. I know you are busy. If I do not hear to the contrary by Friday, I will assume that everything is correct and will submit the listing to the MLS in its present form.

Most sincerely,
The Orcas Island Company

by: Katherine E. Reece
Realtor®, CRS, GRI

**Letter - Copy of Showsheet**

Mr. Sam Seller
Mrs. Sandy Seller
4750 Table Mesa Drive
Boulder, CO 80303

Re: 4750 Table Mesa Drive

Dear Sam and Sandy:

Enclosed for your records is a copy of the feature showsheet which has been mailed to all the real estate brokers who routinely have buyers for homes such as your home. This helps to keep your home first in salespersons' minds when they meet buyers and helps to trigger their remembrance of your home for those clients looking for homes now.

Of course, this exposure is in addition to that already received from the Multiple Listing Service. This is just one of the extra things I do to ensure that your home is exposed to the largest number of salespersons and potential buyers.

Should you have any questions or suggestions, please do not hesitate to call me. It is the team approach that will help us both toward a mutually beneficial business relationship.

Sincerely,
The Orcas Island Company

by: Katherine E. Reece
Realtor®, CRS, GRI

## Letter - Just Listed Neighbor's Home

Mr. Noisy Neighbor
Mrs. Nosey Neighbor
4760 Table Mesa Drive
Boulder, Colorado 80303

Re: 4750 Table Mesa Drive

Dear Noisy and Nosey:

Your neighbors at 4750 Table Mesa Drive have just listed their home with my company, The Orcas Island Company I will be doing my best to market the home to obtain a successful sale in the shortest amount of time.

I would like to ask for your assistance. If you know of any friends or neighbors who may be renting at this time or business associates who may have expressed an interest in living in your neighborhood, please have them contact me. I have enclosed a brochure on the home for your information.

We will be having our first Open House this Sunday, September 10, between the hours of two and five in the afternoon. I do hope you will stop by to see how lovely and well maintained your neighbors have kept their home.

If you have any questions about the property, please do not hesitate to call me. My card is enclosed for your convenience.

Sincerely,
The Orcas Island Company

Katherine E. Reece
Realtor®, CRS, GRI

**Just Listed in Your Neighborhood**

**The Orcas Island Company**

# JUST LISTED
# IN
# YOUR NEIGHBORHOOD

Your neighbors Sam and Sally Seller have just listed their nice home at 4750 Table Mesa Drive with me and my company. We will be doing everything we can to market that home in the shortest possible time.

You can help. If you have friends, relatives or business associates who have either expressed an interest in living in this neighborhood or whom you believe would enjoy living here, please let me know.

Our first open house is:________________________________

Please fell free to stop in and bring interested friends.

I am always available should you have questions about Sam and Sandy's house or real estate in general. Financing rates are always moving. If you have thought of refinancing, I would be glad to give you the names of the lenders that we use for our clients.

**Katherine E. Reece, Realtor®, CRS, GRI**

Home:__________ Office:__________ Mobile:__________

## Letter - Hazardous Waste and Soils Condition

Mr. Sam Seller
Mrs. Sandy Seller
4750 Table Mesa Drive
Boulder, CO 80303

Re: 4750 Table Mesa Drive

Dear Sam and Sandy:

As we discussed when I presented our company's policies prior to your selecting our firm and me to represent you, there are many outside factors that need to be determined or confirmed so that buyers can make informed decisions about what it is that they are buying. One of our objectives is that you complete the sale of you home without any lingering fears of later repercussions from the ultimate buyer, someone that you most probably do not even know yet.

While most people are inclined to inspect and review a property thoroughly before making an offer, some cautious buyers will want to have the property inspected for the presence of radon gas and other hazardous materials and to verify the condition of the soil prior to being obligated to purchase. Today many lenders and relocation companies make such verifications a must for their participation in a transaction.

As I indicated, the information that I have been reading suggests that all homes have some radon gas present. The key issue is to determine the amount. In addition, the composition of the soil on which the house is built concerns many buyers. In this area, bentonite, an expanding clay soil, is common. The key is to determine the composition of the soil, the extent to which it is composed of bentonite, whether or not the soil is a factor that needs to be addressed, and the extent of any hazardous substances, such a radon gas.

Most important, a potential purchaser will probably inquire about and subsequently require that a test be conducted prior to his final purchase of your home. All this takes time when you can least afford it, that is, after the buyer has bound your home with a signed contract but before the closing has occurred. This is a critical period when I like to have as few problems as possible.

The solution that we recommend is to have every home that we list tested as soon as possible for the condition of the soil and the presence and extent of radon gas and other hazardous materials. In this way, we can have the test results available for potential purchasers who can review them *prior* to making their decision to purchase and therefore hopefully eliminate the need for the contract to be conditional upon the results of a subsequent test.

A list of firms that provide these services is enclosed. Please talk it over, make a selection and order the tests. I would be glad to assist the tester of your choice by meeting her at the property during the day as I realize that you are both quite busy. In fact, after you make the selection and give me a budget of how much you wish to spend, I would be glad to arrange for the test on your behalf.

I can see no reason why both tests should not be simply a matter of course. Having them ready might just be the factor that helps that buyer decide on your home. Buyers, once they see what they want, usually are in a hurry to move in. The inspections would eliminate one more delay.

As I mentioned on my initial meeting with you, there are a number of areas that would tend to indicate to a potential purchaser that the property has some form of structural defect. Once this is known to me, I have to point out the presence of such a defect. Having an engineer's report to show that the repairs you have elected to perform will totally take care of the potential problem, or that you have already performed the repairs satisfactorily to eliminate the problem, will help market what otherwise could be a slower moving property.

When you have made your selection, just indicate it on the bottom of this letter and drop it back to my office. I have enclosed a stamped self-addressed envelope for your convenience. Thank you for selecting me as your agent. I am proud to have your home in my inventory of listings and to represent you as your real estate agent. I know you want to complete this sale with a minimum of delay and potential problems. Therefore I am willing to do whatever you direct to expedite that and to coordinate the people you choose to make the necessary repairs and inspections.

Sincerely,
The Orcas Island Company

by: Katherine E. Reece, Realtor®

Enclosure: List of Radon Inspectors
List of Soils Engineers

cc: Oliver E. Frascona, Broker

## Letter - Structural and Mechanical Inspections and Home Warranty

Mr. Sam Seller
Mrs. Sandy Seller
4750 Table Mesa Drive
Boulder, CO 80303

Re: 4750 Table Mesa Drive

Dear Sam and Sandy:

The acquisition of a home is the largest purchase the average person will attempt in a lifetime. Real estate transactions are becoming more and more complex. Most people are convinced that the cautious buyer will make inquiry into thestructural condition and mechanical condition of all prospective properties. To avoid making what might be interpreted by some as "the mistake of a lifetime," many buyers are reviewing reports that indicate the structural and mechanical integrity of properties they are considering buying.

Having the requested information available when a prospective buyer inquires allows us a better chance of capturing a sale while other sellers are still trying to determine whether they will allow an inspection and at whose expense. While other sellers are unsure about who will select the various inspectors and the timing of the inspections, we will have the results available. This requires making a decision with regard to the type of inspection, the extent to which it will be performed, who will be selected to perform it within your budget. Should any defects come to light, we will have the opportunity to make corrections or obtain adequate insurance before the discovery of some minor defect destroys a potential sale.

### Structural Inspection -- Engineer's Report

While we can use a friend or builder, engineers have the greatest impact upon a prospective buyer. Engineers are licensed by the state. I am not and never want to be an engineer. As with all professions, the degree of expertise varies from individual to individual. If you have someone that you feel confident about, I would recommend you contact her soon. Most engineers will write a report indicating their opinion with regard to the structural integrity of the home in general. These professionals generally do not indicate the condition or life expectancy of the mechanical systems in your home. Although this can be expensive, it also is very useful to demonstrate to a prospective purchaser that an engineer has inspected the home. This will discourage the buyer from obtaining a separate inspection, thus potentially saving time and expense.

## Mechanical Inspection -- Home Warranty Companies

There are a number of companies offering a service which generally includes an inspection of the mechanical systems and appliances located in a home. The report will indicate whether they are in good working order and, should repair be necessary, what is suggested. In addition, many of these companies offer an insurance policy that protects the insured, usually the buyer, against failure of the indicated components within the terms of the policy. This may seem expensive; however, it is part of the marketing package included with a new home. New homes are definitely part of our competition.

There are numerous competitors in the marketplace for this kind of service. Although I cannot be responsible for the several individuals and companies listed on the attached sheet, I do know that they have been utilized in the past by other home owners. Each should be happy to provide you with a list of past clients to assist you in making your decision. Prior to making your decision you will want to review each policy carefully as well as consider the reputation of each company.

Our firm acts as an agent for the attached Home Warranty company. We feel confident that their policy is one of the best in the market place. To date buyers have indicated that they have received excellent and prompt service. A copy of their policy is attached for your review. Please feel free to select any home warranty provider. Our list of providers and recommendations is to be considered as a service to you and not as an endorsement or guarantee of the services they provide.

I will be happy to work with the professionals you select to provide access to your home in the event it is necessary to schedule their visit at a time when you will not be present. If you wish, after your selection and negotiation of the fee with the inspector, I will be glad to arrange for the actual timing of the inspection. Unless you indicate to the contrary, I will remain at your home until the inspection is complete.

Sincerely,
The Orcas Island Company

by: Katherine E. Reece, Realtor®

cc: Oliver E. Frascona, Broker

## Direction to Obtain Inspections

You are hereby instructed to contact and employ on my behalf the following entities that I have selected, within the cost guidelines indicated, to accomplish their respective inspections. Please inform each to provide you with a written report as soon as possible after their job is completed. Where indicated on this form, I want an estimate prior to employment. Please request that the proper entity provide us with an estimate of the premium for a Home Warranty Policy for a one-year period.

| Entity: | | Phone: |
|---|---|---|
| Min Fee: $ | Max Fee: $ | Estimate First: (yes) (no) |

| Entity: | | Phone: |
|---|---|---|
| Min Fee: $ | Max Fee: $ | Estimate First: (yes) (no) |

| Entity: | | Phone: |
|---|---|---|
| Min Fee: $ | Max Fee: $ | Estimate First: (yes) (no) |

| Entity: | | Phone: |
|---|---|---|
| Min Fee: $ | Max Fee: $ | Estimate First: (yes) (no) |

| Entity: | | Phone: |
|---|---|---|
| Min Fee: $ | Max Fee: $ | Estimate First: (yes) (no) |

I hereby authorize and direct you to present the results of all inspections to any and all prospective buyers. This will help to eliminate any potential liability either of us might incur. Please indicate to each inspector that he should send the statement for his services directly to me for payment. Thank you for your efforts on my behalf.

_______________________ _____________
Seller Date

_______________________ _____________
Seller Date

**Letter - Confirming Action**

Mr. Sam Seller
Mrs. Sandy Seller
4750 Table Mesa Drive
Boulder, CO 80303

Re: 4750 Table Mesa Drive
Inspection Selection

Dear Sam and Sandy:

It was nice to get your call today. This is just a note to tell you that I was able to contact the inspector. He agreed to complete the engineer's report within the next two weeks for a fee not to exceed $150. In addition, I also contacted Radon Gas Associates and requested that they come over next Thursday to perform the test for the flat fee of $125.00 to which you agreed.

I compliment you on your selection of these experts for the inspections. I am happy that I was able to obtain their services within the budget you set. I do not want to spend any more of your money than absolutely necessary. Both specialists indicated that they would bill you directly at the end of the job.

One more step to a well-planned sale. It never ceases to amaze me what it takes to properly market a property in these complicated times. If you have any questions please give me a call. It is a pleasure to act as your listing agent. I hope that your wife is feeling better.

Sincerely,
The Orcas Island Company

by: Katherine E. Reece
Realtor®, CRS, GRI

cc: Oliver E. Frascona, Broker

## Liability for the Premises

**The Key.** The seller usually gives the agent a key to the house. This starts a series of delegations of the right to enter the property. The number of reported thefts and other problems grow as agents become more involved in the servicing of many different listings and touring houses with various buyers. The mere fact that a person has obtained a real estate license and possibly joined a board or multiple listing service is unfortunately no indication of the reputation, degree of care, integrity, or ability of that agent. More importantly, the customers of some brokers, unknown to those agents, use this showing procedure as an opportunity to case vacant houses and view possible entry systems or to set up open windows or doors for accomplices. There are even some subagents that let the purchaser have the key to view the property.

You need not concern your client with all these particulars. However, maintain an awareness yourself so that you will always remember to assist your client in understanding his or her side of the responsibility inherent in letting others into the home. *Be clear and be safe.*

**Other Selling Licensees.** Automatically assume that you need a higher degree of concern and care for any showing request other than your own. This should be paramount in the listing broker's mind, and the decision to allow an unaccompanied showing should be examined closely. The broker is becoming responsible for the manner in which he protects the property of his client, the seller. Ask yourself: "Could I demonstrate a high degree of care in court? To whom did I give the key or the lock box combination? Was it to someone I did not even know?"

**Personal Unlocking Service.** There is absolutely no substitute for opening the home for each prospective purchaser, whether or not accompanied by any other form of agent. The practice of personally opening the home for each showing appointment is rare and difficult when coordinating a convenient time for all parties, but may be appropriate for unknown selling licensees. This does not suggest interfering with the relationship between the prospective purchaser and the agent showing that prospective purchaser the home.

There is an absolute duty to take care of the house when you get the key and a responsibility to ensure that others who acquire entry to the house and/or use of the key be scrutinized carefully. Remember: It is very easy to make a duplicate key.

**Tip.** *Decide how much of the risk you can reasonably accept and let your client know your limits. You decide how you do business and let them decide if they want to do business with you.*

**Expensive Items and Limit of Liability.** The seller is someone that you know very little about and who may have an insurance claim in mind for items that were never on the property. Establish the extent of liability and the degree of care that is expected. In addition, ask the seller to make an inventory of expensive items. Simply and politely state that the firm is not responsible for furs, jewelry, gun collections and the like. Recommend that the seller temporarily store these items elsewhere during the marketing of the home.

**The Lock Box.** Lock boxes can vary from the rudimentary, single key and uniform key to the electronic recording key safe. While some people are still using a single key system, the pressure upon the entity responsible for the operation of the system is mounting to provide a more security oriented system. Yes, there are many keys outstanding and unaccounted for. Yes, HUD does utilize such a system. Remember they are the government and they generally deal with vacant houses.

Next is the combination box system. Supra Products, Inc. (SPI) manufactured many of these boxes which came with the combination of S-P-I. To this date, there are hundreds of boxes on houses that still use that code. The careful Realtor® has since changed the combination and continues to change the combination on these boxes. The problems with this old technology are well known. The box can be picked or drilled.

The state of the art are electronic lock boxes. These recording safes actually retain the date, time and identity of each person that accesses the box. The information is instantly available through the key for security and marketing purposes. Run by a computer, access is regulated and keys expire every thirty days. While there is still room for unauthorized entry it is greatly reduced.

Great care should be taken in the selection of a system and in giving access to the key, combination or electronic recording. Not even the cover letter will protect you from the negligence of your own agents nor that of the plethora of others waiting to see or preview the house for whatever reason.

There are many that think that the entity responsible for operating the lock box system has a duty to implement an electronic or other state of the art system. The criteria are reasonable cost, availability and ease of implementation in order to provide reduced liability to the consumer. In sort, you may not be able to defend the position that "it was not the broker". You may be forced to try to indicate why you did not maintain a state of the art system for home security and entry tracking.

Nothing protects you from gross negligence, such as the giving out of the lock box combination to unknown persons assumed to be real estate agents, or the dissemination of the information over the car phone. It goes without saying that no one should allow anyone to know the access code or to "borrow" the key or the electronic key pad. Neither the firm nor the agent should have a standard combination. Be demonstrably cautious. Never use the same combination for more than one property at any given point in time. Change the combination between listings and certainly see that the combination is changed at least monthly, if not weekly. A lock box authorization or release form is a must.

**Case in Point.** *The owner of a condominium in a large complex allows the agent to put the key to the entire building in a lock box placed on the main entry. There is a theft, and the broker is held responsible for encouraging the thief by the placement of the lock box, indicating that a vacant unit in the building is for sale. To make matters worse, the agent also placed a lock box on the unit entry door. This was a nice way of pointing to the unit that was for sale and, in the mind of at least one hearing panel member, of making the unit vulnerable. That was held to be negligence since there was a theft in the unit for sale and in two other units in the building in a single day.*

*Interestingly enough, there was no accurate record of the individuals who had access to the combination nor of those who had shown the property in the preceding two weeks. The few names that were available proved to include one person that was not a member of any board, held no license, and had no operable local phone number.*

*The listed unit was robbed without the use of force. It is so easy when you have the combination. I wonder what a court would have decided. The broker was very happy to write a few checks.*

**Periodic Inventory.** If there are a lot of valuable items left in a listed home, a periodic inventory by the seller and/or agent may help to eliminate the allegations of negligence or theft that may arise in such situations. Some people, after claiming that they were robbed while the property was listed, have been extremely lucky in their post-theft, post-settlement with some insurance company to be able to locate items almost identical to those that were stolen. There is no need to be a victim of such practices.

**Letter - Post Listing General Lock Box**

Mr. Sam Seller
Mrs. Sandy Seller
4750 Table Mesa Drive
Boulder, CO 80303

Re: 4750 Table Mesa Drive

Dear Sam and Sandy:

As I indicated, one of the available marketing tools to allow fast access to other cooperating and in-house salespersons is to place a lock box on your door. This is a key safe that contains a key to your home and is accessed by other members of the Multiple Listing Service. Please read the Lock Box Authorization Form, sign and return it to me if you wish to utilize this system.

I look forward to previewing your home with the entire office staff in the next few days when your home is scheduled as part of our weekly office tour. It is so nice to have my name on your property listing. If you have any questions, please feel free to call me or my broker at any time.

Sincerely,
The Orcas Island Company

by: Katherine E. Reece
Realtor®, CRS, GRI

## Lock Box Authorization Form

We, the undersigned owner(s) of the following described real estate, hereby authorize you, subject to the conditions indicated below, to place a lock box on our property. In addition, we understand that you will not be responsible or liable to us for the unauthorized use of the lock box or the key located therein, as long as you are in compliance with the terms of this agreement. We understand that potential cooperating licensed salespeople will enter our property through the use of the lock box. While we understand that you will try to limit such access, we realize that there is no way that you can be responsible for unauthorized access through the lock box. We thank you for your suggestion that we inventory our household possessions.

Property Address: ________________________________________

Type of Lock Box: ________________________________________

Special Conditions: ______________________________________

__________________________________________________________

__________________________________________________________

Access to be given to (*please initial all that apply*):

Appraisers: ______________ Inspectors: ______________

Other: ___________________________________________________

Owner: Owner:

__________________________ __________________________

Dated: ____________________ Dated: ____________________

**Letter - Post Listing Combination Lock Box**

Mr. Sam Seller
Mrs. Sandy Seller
4750 Table Mesa Drive
Boulder, CO 80303

Re: 4750 Table Mesa Drive

Dear Sam and Sandy:

There are several methods for showing your home. Our preferred method is for any salesperson from our office or another office to have an opportunity to talk with me prior to any showings. The salespeople in our office are constantly encouraged to talk to the listing salesperson prior to a showing. There are many instances where this is simply not possible.

If you desire, we will place a lock box on your home. This presents special risks for the unauthorized entry to your home and requires your written authorization prior to its placement. The advantage of having a key placed in the lock box is that other salespeople can view the home after making a telephone appointment without the need to travel to several offices to obtain keys and then repeat the journey after each series of showings. In a metro area such as ours the distance between offices can be great. By providing more accessibility for showings to potential cooperating agents, you will ultimately receive more showings and exposure for your home.

In spite of all our efforts, we feel that it is always in your best interest to place valuable jewelry, coins, currency, and other easily-removable items in your safety deposit box at your bank or to store these items, as well as expensive tools and furs and the like, at another location. We simply can not and will not be responsible for such items. If you have any large items of value, other than your ordinary furniture, such as expensive televisions, computers, video equipment and the like, we encourage you to mark these items with your social security number and to provide us with an inventory and relative value statement. We have included a simple form given us by the insurance agency to assist you in taking such an inventory.

Most sincerely,
The Orcas Island Company

by: Oliver E. Frascona, Broker

## Letter - Post Listing Combination Lock Box #2

Mr. Sam Seller
Mrs. Sandy Seller
4750 Table Mesa Drive
Boulder, CO 80303

Re: 4750 Table Mesa Drive

Dear Sam and Sandy:

There are several methods for showing your home. Our preferred method is for any salesperson from our office or another office to have an opportunity to talk with me prior to any showings. The salespeople in our office are constantly encouraged to talk to the listing salesperson prior to a showing. There are many instances when this is simply not possible.

In order to facilitate all possible showings, we can provide a lock box or key safe for your property. This device is attached to the property and contains the key to your home. When the proper combination is entered the key is released. In order to provide more security we change the combination frequently and do not use the same combination for all our listings. Nevertheless, there is risk associated with such a box. The combination could become known to a prospective purchaser or others.

In spite of all our efforts, we feel that it is always in your best interest to place valuable jewelry, coins, currency, and other easily-removable items in your safety deposit box at your bank or to store these items, as well as expensive tools and furs and the like, at another location. We simply cannot and will not be responsible for such items. If you have any large items of value, other than your ordinary furniture, such as expensive televisions, computers, video equipment and the like, we encourage you to mark these items with your social security number and to provide us with an inventory and relative value statement. We have included a simple form given us by the insurance agency to assist you in taking such an inventory.

Thank you again for listing your home with our agency. We are happy to be marketing your property for you.

Sincerely,
The Orcas Island Company

by: Katherine E. Reece
Realtor®, CRS, GRI

cc: Oliver E. Frascona, Broker

## Combination Lock Box Authorization Form

We, the undersigned owner(s) of the following referenced property, hereby authorize you, subject to the conditions indicated below, to place a lock box on our door. We fully understand that the combination will be set by you and changed by you at intervals you determine. In addition, we understand that you will not be responsible or liable to us for the unauthorized use of the lock box or the key located therein, so long as you are in compliance with the terms of this agreement.

We understand that potential cooperating licensed salespeople will contact you and request the combination which you are authorized to provide to them so that they can view our property without your presence. We realize that there is a risk that the combination will be discovered by parties with interests adverse to ours and that it may encourage people to consider this property for illegal entry. While we understand that you will try to limit such access, we realize that there is no way that you can be responsible for unauthorized access through the lock box. We thank you for your suggestion that we inventory our household possessions.

Property Address: ______________________________________

Type of Lock Box: ______________________________________

Special Conditions: ____________________________________

________________________________________________________

________________________________________________________

Access to be given to (*please initial all that apply*):

Appraisers: ______________ Inspectors: ______________

Other: _________________________________________________

Owner: Owner:

__________________________ __________________________

Dated: ____________________ Dated: ____________________

**Letter - Electronic Lock Box/Key Safe**

Mr. Sam Seller
Mrs. Sandy Seller
4750 Table Mesa Drive
Boulder, CO 80303

Re: 4750 Table Mesa Drive

Dear Sam and Sandy:

There are several methods for showing your home. Our preferred method is for any salesperson from our office or another office to have an opportunity to talk with me prior to any showings. The salespeople in our office are constantly encouraged to talk to the listing salesperson prior to a showing. There are many instances when this is simply not possible.

In order to facilitate all possible showings, we can provide an electronic lock box or key safe for your property. This device is attached to the property and contains the key to your home. It is accessed by an electronic card that is issued to each member of the Multiple Listing Service. The box will register which key accessed the box and indicate the time and date of the entry. In addition, I can set the box so that it will not allow access before or after certain hours and on special occasions. When the electronic key is placed in the box, the key to your home is released. While we feel that this is the best available system, there is still room for illegal or unauthorized entry. We simply can not be responsible for that risk.

For any showing made by appointment through our office, we contact the other salesperson for a report once the showing has been completed. We access the box periodically to determine who is showing the property and contact them for feedback in the event showings are made without an appointment.

In spite of all our efforts, we feel that it is always in your best interest to place valuable jewelry, coins, currency, and other easily-removable items in your safety deposit box at your bank or to store these items, as well as expensive tools and furs and the like, at another location. We simply cannot and will not be responsible for such items. If you have any large items of value, other than your ordinary furniture, such as expensive televisions, computers, video equipment and the like, we encourage you to mark these items with your social security number and to provide us with an inventory and relative value statement. We have included a simple form given us by the insurance agency to assist you in taking such an inventory.

Sincerely,
The Orcas Island Company
by: Katherine E. Reece
Realtor®, CRS, GRI

**Letter - Electronic Lock Box/Key Safe #2**

Mr. Sam Seller
Mrs. Sandy Seller
4750 Table Mesa Drive
Boulder, CO 80303

Re: 4750 Table Mesa Drive

Dear Sam and Sandy:

There are several methods for showing your home. Our preferred method is for any salesperson from our office or another office to have an opportunity to talk with me prior to any showings. The salespeople in our office are constantly encouraged to talk to the listing salesperson prior to a showing. There are many instances where this is simply not possible.

We utilize the electronic key safe that I demonstrated when we first listed your home. This system allows me to immediately determine which salesperson has accessed your home as well as the exact time of entry. This helps me provide more security and allows me to track potential buyers immediately. Valuable marketing information can be obtained from the potential buyer and any objections to the home can be relayed to you so that we can market your home effectively.

Although it is impossible to personally know all of the possible salespeople that might show your home, we will not let anyone unknown to us show your home unaccompanied. We have informed all other prospective salespeople that we reserve the right to accompany anyone who displays an interest in viewing your home.

In spite of all our efforts, we feel that it is always in your best interest to place valuable jewelry, coins, currency, and other easily-removable items in your safety deposit box at your bank or to store these items, as well as expensive tools and furs and the like, at another location. We simply can not and will not be responsible for such items. Nor can we be responsible for the unauthorized access to the property through the key safe system. If you have any large items of value, other than your ordinary furniture, such as expensive televisions, computers, video equipment and the like, we encourage you to mark these items with your social security number and to provide us with an inventory and relative value statement. We have included a simple form given us by the insurance agency to assist you in taking such an inventory.

Thank you again for listing your home with our firm. We are happy to be marketing your property for you.

Most sincerely,
The Orcas Island Company
by: Oliver E. Frascona, Broker

## Electronic Recording Key Safe (Lock Box) Authorization Form

We, the undersigned owner(s) of the following described real estate, hereby authorize you, subject to the conditions indicated below, to place an electronic recording key safe (lock box) on our door. We understand that the box will record each entry. We also understand that many individuals have electronic keys to the box. In addition, we understand that you will not be responsible or liable to us for the unauthorized use of the key safe or the key located therein, so long as you are in compliance with the terms of this agreement.

We understand that potential cooperating licensed salespeople will contact you and request permission to show the property without your presence. While we understand that you will try to limit such access, we realize that there is no way that you can be responsible for unauthorized access through the key safe. We have indicated the times that we do not want any access in the special conditions section. Please program the key safe accordingly. We thank you for your suggestion that we inventory our household possessions.

Property Address: ______________________________

Type of Key Safe: ______________________________

Special Conditions: ______________________________

______________________________________________

______________________________________________

Access to be given to (*please initial all that apply*):

Appraisers: ______________ Inspectors: ______________

Other: ______________________________________

Owner: Owner:

______________________ ______________________

Dated: __________________ Dated: __________________

**Letter - Open House**

Mr. Sam Seller
Mrs. Sandy Seller
4750 Table Mesa Drive
Boulder, CO 80303

Re: 4750 Table Mesa Drive

Dear Sam and Sandy:

With a house that is as nice as yours or that has a location such as yours, we have found that having it open to the public on a Saturday, Sunday or evening gives people an opportunity to look through your home in a relaxed atmosphere. Warm bread in the oven, a fire in the fireplace or cut flowers can enhance the sense that your home is perfect for them.

We would have an agent on the premises at all times and would encourage you to take the day off and go somewhere else so that the house is available for inspection by interested persons. This allows the home to look larger and more spacious than it would if we were all there and also reduces the intimidation factor when a prospective purchaser enters.

I will be contacting you to schedule some tentative times so that I can plan an advertising strategy in advance to try to maximize the number of prospects we can anticipate.

Sincerely,
The Orcas Island Company

by: Katherine E. Reece
Realtor®, CRS, GRI

## Open House Request/Authorization Form

Property
Address:________________________________________________________

Please consider this as our request for your office to hold our house "open to the public". We understand that you will provide equal access to everyone regardless of their potential membership in a "protected class" as defined by the laws, rules and regulations of the federal, state and local governments.

We understand that there is a risk that the public, when viewing our home, may damage it or steal some of our property. To prevent or reduce our potential loss, we have obtained insurance on our possessions in an amount we feel is appropriate and/or removed and stored those items about which we are concerned. We know that it is impossible for you to be physically present with everyone when more than one person is walking through our home. Therefore we will not hold you responsible for any loss occasioned by having our house open to the public.

We understand that you will notify us within __________ days in advance of the open house date to verify the exact date and time for the open house. We agree to have the house clean and prepared to show to the public. In addition, if we have pets we will remove our pets from the property during the open house period.

Our special requests follow:

____________________________________________________________

____________________________________________________________

____________________________________________________________

Thank you.

Date:____________________

Owner(s):

____________________________________________________________

## Property Management

**By Design.** Property management seems to flow from two distinct sources. First, the arrangement is set up by design. The owner and the agent enter into a comprehensive agreement dealing with the rights, duties, and obligations of both the owner and the agent. These vary from simple rent collection and mortgage payment application, to full rental and management authority, including the right to offer, negotiate and lease the premises, bring eviction actions, contract and pay for repairs, and generally deal with the real property.

**By Default.** Second, a property management arrangement simply happens. This occurs when the real estate professional, while in the course of her normal listing duties, is called upon to be the agent for the owner in a capacity not anticipated or delineated in the original listing agreement. The agent then unwittingly becomes a more comprehensive agent for the owner for leasing, repair, maintenance, eviction, and so forth without the proper agreement. The result is that the owner denies the relationship when it suits him and the agent and broker are left with expenses, tenant suits, and other problems without any assistance from the owner. See to it early that your duties are made clear so that you will not be victimized by either an owner's exaggerated expectations or by your own desire to be helpful.

**Confirmation of the Tenancy.** If you should decide to accept the job of property manager, we would suggest a nice little letter to each tenant to verify the current status of that particular tenant's tenancy. This will serve to verify any information you were fortunate enough to have received from the landlord and establish a rapport with the tenants. This type of letter can also be useful at the start of a new year just so that the tenant does not start to feel he is the owner.

**Eviction.** There are those that need excitement in the world, and eviction is the place to get it. If you are going to act as the agent for the eviction of a tenant, we would recommend a series of cover letters to confirm each step in the procedure and to request instructions often. When the counterclaim comes it will be nice to be able to hide under the agency cloak. To be entitled to that protection, you must have been acting within the scope of your agency. Yes, that means more than a standard listing agreement.

**Equity Skimming.** While you would never participate in an equity skimming scheme, it is a good idea to be familiar with the meaning of the term. In this situation, the owner, intending from the outset to make money and not payments, acquires a property with the intent to rent it and keep the rent paid by the tenants. Such a person pays the utility companies and often any association fees but neglects to pay the taxes or mortgage payments. It is important to note that intent is a key element in this definition in many states.

Equity skimming is not a term that would generally apply to the owner of a single property who, after owning it for some time, finds that s/he can no longer subsidize the rent to make all the required payments. Often the real estate broker is collecting the rental amounts and turning the rent over to the owner.

To avoid even the appearance of impropriety in such circumstances, we suggest that the broker cease to manage any property that he/she knows is in such a situation. The owner or someone else can handle the rental payments. Maintain the listing but cease managing the property.

**Tenant Mentality.** Tenants are important people in real estate. It is the tenant and his all-important rental payments that drive the income property market. The good tenants can mean a lot and deserve an owner's best. But recognize that many tenants are red flags. These others fit part of our plaintiff profile. They do not generally have a lot of assets, wish they owned a house, are jealous of the owner and his real estate agent, have little down-side risk in litigation, and very often no ability to stick around after you win the suit, let alone pay the amount of the judgment against them. It is next to impossible to recover from a tenant, in court, what it has cost to play.

**Tip.** *Yes, your principles are important. But just as with the other kind of principal, they need to be placed where they will compound interest, not compound problems.*

If, for whatever reason, you must function as a manager, get a written agreement and get paid separately and adequately for it.

**Protection.** As the broker and/or agent you are interested in protecting yourself from the perils and pitfalls of becoming a volunteer management agent. At the same time you want to keep the listing and assist the owner as much as necessary so that the property can be marketed. At first this may seem impossible, but it is really quite easy. All that is required is that you define the relationship as it exists and as it may evolve.

**Caution.** *It is important to note that property management is not covered by many of the professional liability insurers. This is because of the extreme exposure and loss that occurs in this field when it is practiced by the inexperienced real estate agent, generally without any documentation as to the extent of the agent's authority. A quick review of your policy might be helpful.*

**Tenancy Agreements.** The tendency to suggest or use a lease agreement that was used in the last deal or is a standard form can be very strong. Resist the urge. Have the owner select and designate a form. Do not proffer your form; that is practicing law and not necessary to accomplish the objective. Leases, even in the most mundane residential transaction, are very complex and often devoid of what might later prove to be important clauses.

**Timing.** As with all notices and agreements, agreement before the fact is the preferred route. In this case, however, the memorandum of previous oral conversation or agreement is a useful bootstrapping tool. If you sense that any of your relationships might be cloudy on this matter, fire off some memoranda of your previous oral agreements or conversations immediately.

**Payment.** You work hard enough to earn your normal commission. Charge a fee for the additional management services you may be induced to perform. Fees are a good way to either eliminate the request for management or to open the door for a satisfactory comprehensive management agreement.

**Withdrawal.** Any management agreement--in addition to a multitude of other agreements not to be discussed in this book--should contain a provision allowing you to withdraw, turn the damage deposits over to the owner, with tenant confirmation of course, and stop managing the property when you have had enough.

## Letter - Verification of the Terms of the Tenancy/Owner

Mr. Robert S. Caplan
Mrs. Laurian Greening
750 Prospect Lane
Colorado Springs, CO 80903

Re: Unit 203 B

Dear Mr. Caplan and Mrs. Greening:

Another year has ended, and it is time to get everything ready for the accountant and the dreaded tax return. I hope that last year was all that you hoped it would be, and that next year meets your expectations.

Each year the accountant requests that I verify the terms of each tenancy. Please take a minute to confirm for the accountant that you are the tenants in the property indicated above and are occupying this property under a rental arrangement that does not include any option to purchase.

| | |
|---|---|
| Family: | Robert, Laurian, Monica and Adam |
| Pets: | No pets are allowed |
| Tenancy: | Month to month |
| Monthly rent: | $450.00 |
| Deposit: | $400.00 |
| Rent due on: | The 1st of each month in advance |
| Late on the: | 15th |
| Late Charge: | $50.00 |
| Rent paid through: | December |

Thank you for your efforts. It makes the accounting so much easier.

Most sincerely,
The Orcas Island Company
Agents for the Owner of the Property

by: Oliver E. Frascona, Broker

Approved:
(Only one approval is needed. Any tenant may approve for all tenants.)

____________________ or ____________________

Robert S. Caplan Laurian Greening

*Please return one copy in the enclosed stamped self addressed envelope.*

## Letter - Verification of the Terms of the Tenancy

Mr. Robert S. Caplan
Mrs. Laurian Greening
750 Prospect Lane
Colorado Springs, CO 80903

Re: Unit 203 B

Dear Mr. Caplan and Mrs. Greening:

Please allow me to introduce myself as the as the new property manager for the owner of this building. I enjoy assisting people with their living needs and want you to know that I am available during normal working hours at the above office. Please feel free to contact me there for the payment of rent and other business related to the building. I too have a family and have promised my wife that I will not work after 5:00 P.M. unless it is an emergency. I know you will understand that in an emergency I would want you by all means to contact me at home at 494-6661.

My records indicate that the following is a correct status report of your account:

Your family consists of: Robert, Laurian, Monica and Adam
Pets: No pets are allowed
Tenancy: Month to month
Monthly rent: $450.00
Deposit: $400.00
Rent is due on: the 1st of each month
Late on the: 15th
Late Charge: $50.00
Rent is paid: In advance
Rent paid through: March

If any one of the above terms is incorrect, please call me and send me a written letter indicating what you feel is in error. You must do both. If it is easier, just make a notation on this letter and sign your name. If I do not hear from you within five days from the date of this letter to the contrary, I will understand that this is the correct information.

Most sincerely,
The Orcas Island Company

by: Oliver E. Frascona, Broker

cc: Alexander J. Frascona, Owner

**Letter - *Just for Fun* -- Verification of the Terms of the Tenancy**

Mr. Robert S. Caplan
Mrs. Laurian Greening
750 Prospect Lane
Colorado Springs, CO 80903

Re: Unit 203 B

Dear Mr. Caplan and Mrs. Greening:

Let me introduce myself. In order to obtain the listing for the sale of the building where you are now a tenant, I have grudgingly decided to manage the property. Please refrain from making statements that would hinder the sale of the property as I am showing it at odd hours of the day and night. The only reason that I am taking this job is that I hope it will help me retain the listing on the property.

I have heard that you are a difficult tenant, and I intend to run a tight ship. If you even think about causing trouble, I will have to file a legal action for the owner. No, I do not want to be bothered at home in the evenings or on the weekend. Just call the office if you need to talk to me.

Yes, there will be other agents showing the property that have no clue about its features. Just keep a low profile and do not make disparaging statements about the property. There are no leaks. There is no problem with the heat. The electric wiring is not aluminum as some think.

I know that you think that the property is located in close proximity to a nuclear waste site that is yet to be identified, but you need not share that belief with the prospective buyers. You might even think that if you give each buyer enough trouble you will be allowed to stay here. Wrong, you will be evicted immediately.

Finally, as an inducement for you to cooperate I will pay you $500.00 if the property is sold within the first month of my listing or $250.00 if it sells in the second month. You will be given thirty days prior notice of any contract so that you can arrange for a new place to live. If things work out ok, I will even act as your agent to locate a home for you to buy or rent.

Most sincerely,
The Orcas Island Company

by: Oliver E. Frascona, Broker

cc: Alexander J. Frascona, Owner

**Letter - Property Management**

Mr. Sam Seller
Mrs. Sandy Seller
4750 Table Mesa Drive
Boulder, CO 80303

Re: 4750 Table Mesa Drive

Dear Sam and Sandy:

Thank you for telling me that you will be moving out by the end of the month. I had hoped that your home would sell by this time. I know that you intend to rent the property for a few months on a month-to-month basis, and thought I should explain the firm's position with regard to our property management services.

Property that is occupied by people other than the owner often raises concern about the extent of management that the owner may expect from us as a listing office. Property management is not covered in our listing contract. Therefore, we do not render any property management services without the express prior written approval of both our broker and the owner. We have long felt that the listing of a property for sale and the management of real estate are very different tasks and should be covered separately. We have two levels of service available.

First, our limited service. Under this plan, we do not take an active role in the management of the property. We limit ourselves to responding to your instructions, preferably in letter form, requesting us to accomplish certain specific tasks. Such items include: the collecting of rents, paying specific payments, arranging for work to be done or confirming that the work has in fact been performed, showing the property to prospective tenants, cooperating with the attorney of your selection--in the event eviction becomes necessary--and generally working on a case-by-case basis with no duty to manage the property, except as indicated.

We are not responsible for policing the property or the tenants. We do not initiate action nor are we responsible for "management" of the property. We do not execute leases on your behalf nor do we commence any litigation regarding the property or any tenant on your behalf or in your name. We feel that these items are best done by your attorney. Our fee is $______ per hour spent while following your instructions.

Second is our full-service management service. This is the subject of our Management Agreement, a copy of which is enclosed for your review. We would be happy to provide you with full-service management. Before we can accept the responsibility of full-service management, this agreement needs to be completed, signed both by you as owner and by the broker, and returned to this office with the indicated retainer deposit.

As you can see, the full-service management agreement provides that we will use our best efforts to lease, maintain, supervise, and care for your property on your behalf. This involves much more than simply collecting the rents. Therefore, it is the subject of a separate, comprehensive, agreement.

To confirm the limited service please send us a letter or simply make a note on the bottom of this letter and return it. To engage in the full service system execute the Management Agreement and return it. Unless we receive your written selection of the method of service that you desire, we will assume that we are not responsible for the management and maintenance of the property under either system. Should you later direct us to perform certain tasks, we will assume that we are operating under the provisions outlined above under the first option.

If I can be of any further assistance, please do not hesitate to let me know. We are proud to have your property listed for sale with this office and feel that we can complete the marketing of your real estate with or without regard to our being party to the property's management.

Most sincerely,
The Orcas Island Company

by: Katherine E. Reece, Realtor®

cc: Oliver E. Frascona, Broker

**Letter - Property Management Referral**

Mr. Sam Seller
Mrs. Sandy Seller
4750 Table Mesa Drive
Boulder, CO 80303

Re: 4750 Table Mesa Drive

Dear Sam and Sandy:

Thank you for telling me that you will be moving out by the end of the month. I had hoped that your home would sell by this time. I know that you intend to rent the property for a few months on a month-to-month basis, and thought I should explain the firm's position with regard to our property management services.

As I indicated to you earlier, neither this firm nor any of the salespeople are allowed to engage in the property management business. Our broker feels that we are in the business of representing sellers and in the professional marketing of our clients' homes for sale as well as representing buyers interested in the purchase of real estate, and not in the management of real property. It can be very time-consuming and can distract us from our primary goal. I wish I could help you, but it is simply not possible.

Often a friend or neighbor is adequate for the isolated short-term case of property management. If that does not appeal to you, there are a lot of people whose exclusive business is property management Although I can not be responsible for the several individuals and companies listed on the attached sheet, I do know that they have been utilized in the past by other home owners. Each should be happy to provide you with a list of past clients to assist you in making your decision.

I will assist your property manager any way that I can. By working together we can help each other and effectuate the rental and sale of your property.

Sincerely,
The Orcas Island Company

by: Katherine E. Reece
Realtor®, CRS, GRI

cc: Oliver E. Frascona, Broker
Monica Jean Frascona, Owner

## Letter - Property Management Equity Skimming

Mr. Sam Seller
Mrs. Sandy Seller
4750 Table Mesa Drive
Boulder, CO 80303

Re: 4750 Table Mesas Drive

Dear Sam and Sandy:

We are happy to have your property listed for sale. While collecting the rents and turning them over to you promptly, we have noticed that the mortgage payments on the property are not being made in a timely manner. While you are welcome to do as you wish with your rental receipts, we do not wish to be involved with the collection of rent that does not go to maintain the mortgage.

We will continue to list your property for sale and endeavor to obtain a buyer before the property goes into foreclosure. However, we can not continue to collect the rental amounts that come due. It might be a good idea to collect them yourself or have a friend or other professional collect them for you. Our fear stems from the concept of "equity skimming".

In this situation, the owner, *intending from the outset* to make money and not payments, acquires a property with the intent to rent it and keep the rent paid by the tenants. Such a person does not pay the taxes or the mortgage payments. As a result the property goes into foreclosure.

In your case we do not have any idea what your intent is, but we do not think that you acquired the property with the intent of letting it go to foreclosure. Equity skimming is not a term that would generally apply to the owner of a single property who, after owning it for some time, finds that he can no longer subsidize the rent to make all the required payments.

To avoid even the appearance of impropriety in circumstances where we, in our own discretion, feel that such is the case, we will not release any money to the owner unless we are satisfied that it is being applied to the payment of the utilities, association dues, the mortgage and the like, and that all such payments are being made in full. To avoid this potential problem we will not be collecting the rent anymore. I am sure that you understand our position.

Most sincerely,
The Orcas Island Company

by: Oliver E. Frascona, Broker

## Seller Financial Status

**Liens and Loans.** As early as possible you need to ascertain the liquidity of the property you are trying to sell. You are going to make commitments to cooperating brokers for a portion of the commission. Let's find out early if there is enough equity to pay the commission. Many people do not tell their broker that they are behind in their loan payments, the property is in foreclosure or that there are tax or judgment liens against the property.

**Owners and Encumbrances Report.** Referenced by many names across the country, this is a report similar to a preliminary commitment from a title company that indicates the defects, encumbrances and clouds on the title. Smart brokers are ordering "to be determined" title insurance commitments to verify the information often verbally conveyed in an owners and encumbrances report. Get the seller to pay the fee if you can.

**Loan Status.** Regardless of how certain you are that the property will not be sold by way of an assumption, it happens. You need to know the status of the existing loan. Information on the underlying mortgage on the seller's property should be obtained as soon as possible to determine if there is any chance the loan may be in default. Having a home go into foreclosure is often very personal and embarrassing to the seller. They may not provide that information initially in hopes that the home will sell before anyone knows. It is critical to know in which stage of foreclosure the seller may be involved.

***Tip.*** *Resist the temptation to advance the funds yourself to obtain this information. In addition, never, we mean never, take the sellers' word for their loan balance.*

In some instances you can verify the loan balance by telephone with the loan number. Other times just looking at the latest mortgage receipt stub, if one is available, is sufficient. Many people have "troubled" real estate, and they have a hard time acknowledging that fact internally let alone disclosing it to a stranger. Be sensitive and professional but insist on ordering a payoff and an assumption statement. You just never know which you might need.

The best system is to write a letter to the lender asking for the appropriate information. A sample follows. You can modify it to suite your needs. The key elements are the loan number and that the information can be delivered, faxed or sent to the broker or salesperson.

Do it early. The pressure may mount as the problem becomes more evident. Get the information as early as you can.

**Caution.** *Many times the lending institution will offer to "cooperate" with the home owner to give him time to sell or reduce his payments while the home is on the market. At the same time the lender is discovering the location and financial capability of the borrower, your seller. Should things not work out, the lender will have all the information they need to pursue the seller. Consult with the attorney for the seller before you give out information to the lender.*

It will also become critical for you as the seller's agent to carefully monitor the contract performance deadlines so that obligations in a foreclosure sale may be met. Be careful--remember whom you represent. Disclosing that the property is in foreclosure is rarely in the seller's best interest. Do not do this without the seller's prior *informed* consent.

Other information gleaned from the mortgage information will assist you in offering the correct financing terms. Will the loan be "due-on-sale" if sold by way of seller financing or by an installment land contract? Is there a possibility of an assumption without notifying the lender? Maybe an assumption with or without substitution of liability?

**Caution.** *A transfer that violates the lender's due-on-sale clause could cause serious trouble for everyone. If one party contemplates a transfer that violates the due-on-sale clause, make sure the buyer, seller and you have an attorney to guide you through the proposed transaction.*

**Caution.** *FHA and VA loans that contain a "due-on-sale" or "due-on-transfer" clause are a more serious problem. Consult with an attorney first. Never attempt to transfer the title to a property that contains an FHA or VA due-on-sale clause. It may be illegal.*

Does the lender require that the new buyer qualify with an assumption and will the interest rate change with an assumption? Having a ready answer to these questions will enhance your ability to assist any new buyer or their agent with the proper financing terms and arrangements.

**Letter - Existing Lender for Loan Status**

Mr. and/or Ms. Bobby Fisher
Seal Mortgage and Loan
250 Anywhere Street
Next Door, CO 00000

Re: Loan Number:
Borrower:

Dear Sir or Madam:

We have just listed our house for sale with the real estate company indicated on this letterhead and, in particular, with the salesperson whose card is attached. Please consider this as our request that you immediately send to our real estate firm an assumption statement and a payoff statement indicating the balances that are current for our loan.

In the future we have authorized our real estate salesperson, indicated below, to contact you directly to facilitate either the transfer and assumption of the loan or the payoff of the loan. Please offer them you cooperation. Should you wish to contact us we can be reached at:

Mr. Sam Seller
Mrs. Sandy Seller
4750 Table Mesa Drive
Boulder, CO 80303

Telephone: (303) 494-6661

Thank you for your consideration. We have enclosed our check to your order in the amount of $______________ for your preparation fee.

Salesperson:______________________________

Sincerely,

____________________________________
Sam Seller

____________________________________
Sandy Seller

cc: The Orcas Island Company
Katherine E. Reece, Realtor®, CRS, GRI

## Letter - Existing Lender for Loan Status #2

BancBoston Mortgage Corp.
P. O. Box 0000000
Boston, MA 02241

Re: Your loan number:________________
Borrowers: Sam and Sandy Seller
Property: 4750 Table Mesa Drive, Boulder, CO 80303-5575

Dear Sirs:

Enclosed you will find a mortgage information release form signed by the above referenced owners for the property indicated.

Please provide me with the following information at your earliest convenience.

Current mortgage balance
Current interest rate
Type and class of mortgage
Assumption terms and conditions
Prepayment penalty

I have enclosed a check to your order in the amount of $_________ and would ask that you forward an assumption and payoff statement. I have enclosed a self addressed, stamped envelope for your convenience.

Sincerely,
The Orcas Island Company

by: Katherine E. Reece
Realtor®, CRS, GRI

# OWNER'S AUTHORIZATION AND REQUEST FOR LOAN INFORMATION AND VERIFICATION

To: ________________________________

Mortgage Company Name

________________________________

Mortgage Company address

________________________________

City, State, Zip

Re: (Property Address)

________________________________

________________________________

________________________________

Please release to the indicated real estate company all information regarding my/our loan with your company.

Sincerely,

________________________________

Sam Seller

________________________________

Sandy Seller

cc: The Orcas Island Company
Katherine E. Reece, Realtor®, CRS, GRI

## Termination of a Listing and Post Listing Period Protection

**Termination.** The listing period may terminate for various reasons. First, the listing expires. Second, the seller cancels the listing. There are a series of cases that seem to indicate that since the listing agreement is a consensual agency relationship between the principal and the agent, it is terminable at will by the principal, the seller. This does not imply that the broker is not entitled to some compensation; only that the listing can be cancelled. Third, the broker could decide that he does not want the listing anymore. It is much more difficult for the agent to cancel than the principal. Seek local counsel before consenting to the attempted termination of any listing agreement by the seller. Here is a sample holdover clause to be included in the listing agreement to protect the broker.

**Clause.**

1. Commission shall be earned upon the occurrence of any of the following:

   a. Sale of the Property within the Listing Period by any person; or,

   b. Broker finding a buyer who is ready, willing and able to complete the transaction as specified herein by Seller; or,

   c. Sale of the Property within _____ calendar days subsequent to the expiration of the Listing Period to anyone with whom Broker negotiated and whose name was submitted to the Seller by Broker during the Listing Period.

There is a lot of discussion about how long the protection period should be in the contract. As long as you can get. Do not tolerate clauses that purport to extinguish the holdover rights if the property is relisted with another broker.

**Tip.** *Delete such clauses similar to the one indicated below in italics before you present the proposed listing agreement to the seller.*

**Clause.**

1. Commission shall be earned upon the occurrence of any of the following:

   a. Sale of the Property within the Listing Period by any person; or,

   b. Broker finding a buyer who is ready, willing and able to complete the transaction as specified herein by Seller; or,

c. Sale of the Property within _____ calendar days subsequent to the expiration of the Listing Period to anyone with whom Broker negotiated and whose name was submitted to the Seller by Broker during the Listing Period. *Provided, however, that Seller shall owe no commission to Broker under this subsection if a commission is earned by another licensed real estate broker acting pursuant to an exclusive right-to-sell listing contract or an exclusive agency listing contract entered into during this period.*

In order to protect yourself under the terms of the Listing Agreement, you must disclose to the seller the names of all persons with whom you have negotiated (talked about the property) for the sale of the property during the listing period. Note that a showing is not a requirement, only negotiations. Contrary to some opinions, the presentation of a contract from a prospective purchaser during the listing period does satisfy this requirement. The disclosure of the list of possible buyers must also be made during the listing period. Written disclosures are all that we are concerned with here since a seller is unlikely to acknowledge an oral disclosure if there is litigation.

**Subagent Advantage.** Of course if you still utilize subagents, they are working for you, the listing broker, and they owe the full range of fiduciary duties to you. Subagents are required to tell their principal, the listing broker, the name, address and phone numbers of all interested buyers. That might bother some selling agents, but then they would not be subagents. They would be buyer brokers. The listing broker might have a cause of action against the subagent for breach of a fiduciary duty resulting in loss of a commission if the subagent refuses to divulge such information to the listing broker.

**Cooperating Selling Agents.** The difficult task is to protect yourself with regard to the negotiations conducted with prospective purchasers by your cooperating selling agents because they will generally not have disclosed the names of their customers to you. This is where an accurate and concise record of showings and interest in the property will allow you to contact those cooperating agents and politely request that they provide you with the needed information.

**Potential Post Listing Seller FSBO.** Try to impress upon the seller the complexity of the sale of real estate today so that the seller will feel that he truly does need your services even if a potential buyer were to approach him the day after the expiration of the listing. The letter to the seller should attempt to emphasize some facet of the transaction with which you feel he is most uncomfortable such as sources of new financing, the need to accept a home in trade or a guaranteed sale, the need for a home warranty program or other service that he cannot get from the local attorney who probably has no idea how to market a home properly anyway. That attorney will be your competition once the buyer is located.

**Procuring Cause.** You may have a noncontractual claim for a commission if you can show you were the "procuring cause" of an ultimate sale. Do not place too much faith in this or any other "equitable" remedies. The limited success of those claims has generally been in the absence of a listing contract. When there is a contract, the court will look to it for the agreement of the parties.

**Lien for Commission.** Under current law in most states neither the broker nor the salesperson has any right to file any document that effectively places a lien upon the property. Brokers do not have a security interest in the seller's property to secure the payment of their commissions. Wish you had one? Well, here is the clause. It is doubtful that too many sellers will sign it. Do not be afraid to ask for it in a commercial or ranch transaction where you will expend a lot of money for a long period of time.

**Termination Time Limit.** Once the listing is terminated, you may still be obligated to retain the personal information about the seller that you obtained while an agent. That is to say, after the listing has terminated if you become a buyer agent or are "working with" a buyer you may still have to keep the seller's personal secrets secret. Here is a potential clause to try to alleviate that situation. Good luck.

**Clause.**

1. Seller hereby grants broker a security interest in the Property to the extent of the broker's commission.

2. Upon termination of this listing agreement, broker shall not be an agent of seller. Broker shall be released from any and all fiduciary duties and may represent any buyer attempting to purchase seller's property without any obligation to keep confidential any of the seller's previously confidential information.

**Relisting Broker.** If you are the subsequent listing broker who is listing after an expired or terminated listing, you should ask to examine the previous listing agreement. You need to determine, if in fact, there are buyers that are covered by a holdover period. This practice of protection for a buyer obtained during a listing period is common in many states. The mere fact that a buyer was shown the home through the listing broker's marketing efforts entitles the broker to a commission on the sale to any prospect whose name was properly given to the seller during the term of the listing.

**Showing Data**

**Seller's Name:**______________________________ **Address:**______________________

| DAY | DATE & TIME | AGENT NAME | COMPANY | PHONE NUMBER | COMMENTS |
|---|---|---|---|---|---|
| | | | | | |
| | | | | | |
| | | | | | |
| | | | | | |
| | | | | | |
| | | | | | |
| | | | | | |
| | | | | | |
| | | | | | |
| | | | | | |
| | | | | | |
| | | | | | |
| | | | | | |
| | | | | | |
| | | | | | |
| | | | | | |
| | | | | | |
| | | | | | |

### Letter - List of Buyers on Termination of a Listing - Subagents

Mr. Tina B. Daniel, Broker
American Real Estate Service
915 East Race
Searcy, CO 80303

Re: 4750 Table Mesa Drive

Dear Tina:

Our records indicate that you scheduled and completed a showing of the above referenced property as our subagents. Please provide me with the names of the purchasers that viewed the property so that we can deliver those names to the seller. This will protect both offices in the event the buyer buys the property after the expiration of the listing period. While I hope that your buyers purchase the property during the listing period, one can never be too careful.

I understand that you may be reluctant to provide us with that information for fear that we might attempt to sell your buyers this or another property. I can assure you that we will not attempt to solicit your customers. We want you to show us the same courtesy when we have shown property that you have listed. The important issue is that we are both compensated if the buyer buys the property.

If you want to discuss this matter with me personally, please call me. If you wish, you can fax the information back on the bottom of this letter. Any comments that would help market the property would be appreciated. You can be candid.

| Date: | Buyer's Name: |
|---|---|
| __________ | ________________________________________ |
| __________ | ________________________________________ |
| __________ | ________________________________________ |

I look forward to working with you in the future, appreciate you as a cooperating broker and further appreciate your association with us and your attempts to market this property.

Most sincerely,
The Orcas Island Company

by: Oliver E. Frascona, Broker

## Letter - List of Buyers on Termination of a Listing -- Subagents #2

Mr. Tina B. Daniel, Broker
American Real Estate Service
915 East Race
Searcy, CO 80303

Re: 4750 Table Mesa Drive

Dear Tina:

Our records indicate that you recently showed this property. While I think that the sellers will renew their listing with this office, I like to try to protect all of the brokers who have acted as our subagents during the listing period. Should your buyer ultimately purchase the property and, with or without the knowledge and assistance of the seller, attempt to avoid paying us our commission, I want to be ready. In order to avoid such a result, I need to indicate to the seller the names of those individuals with whom you may have negotiated or have shown the property as well as the dates of your negotiations and/or showings.

I understand that you may be reluctant to provide us with that information for fear that we will then try to sell this property or other listings to those individuals you have indicated to us are interested in buying this property. I promise you that we will not attempt to solicit your customers in any fashion. There is simply no reason for us both to lose the right to an earned commission if these buyers buy.

Time is short and your cooperation is greatly appreciated. Thank you for your assistance. In the event you ever need the same assistance from this office upon the expiration of one of your listings, please do not hesitate to ask and we will comply promptly. We are competitors, but there is no need to allow a seller to profit from our failure to protect ourselves as the standard listing provides.

I look forward to working with you in the future, appreciate you as a cooperating broker and further appreciate your association with us and your attempts to market this property.

Most sincerely,
The Orcas Island Company

by: Oliver E. Frascona, Broker

## Letter - List of Buyers on Termination of a Listing/General

Mr. Tina B. Daniel, Broker
American Real Estate Service
915 East Race
Searcy, CO 80303

Re: 4750 Table Mesa Drive

Dear Tina:

Thank you for showing this property. Our listing agreement with the seller provides that in the event a buyer who was shown the property during the listing period buys the property after the listing expires, we will still be owed a commission. Of course, we cooperate with your brokerage office by splitting the commission as indicated in the MLS system. All that we need to do is provide the seller with the names of the buyers who have seen the property.

I understand that you may be reluctant to provide us with that information for fear that we might attempt to sell your buyers this or another property. I promise you that we will not attempt to solicit your clients or customers. We extend to you the same courtesy we would expect when we have shown property that you have listed. The important issue is that we both get paid if the buyer buys the property.

If you want to discuss this matter with me personally, please call me. If you wish you can fax the information back on the bottom of this letter. Any comments that would help market the property would be appreciated. You can be candid.

Date: Buyer's Name:

__________ ______________________________________________

__________ ______________________________________________

I look forward to working with you in the future, appreciate you as a cooperating broker and further appreciate your association with us and your attempts to market this property.

Most sincerely,
The Orcas Island Company

by: Oliver E. Frascona, Broker

**Letter - Expiration of the Listing Period -- Seller**

Mr. Sam Seller
Mrs. Sandy Seller
4750 Table Mesa Drive
Boulder, CO 80303

Re: 4750 Table Mesa Drive

Dear Sam and Sandy:

In spite of all of our marketing efforts, our listing period is about to expire. It has been a pleasure to serve as your agents. We have been happy to receive so many nice compliments from the numerous cooperating brokers who have had the opportunity to show your home. Your efforts to accommodate our attempts and your willingness to always have your house ready for last minute showings have certainly been helpful. We all want to commend you on your efforts.

Try as we have, we seem to have been unable to locate a buyer who is ready, willing, and able to complete the purchase of your home as proposed in your instructions in the listing agreement. I will be contacting you to encourage you to extend your listing with this firm. We are all very eager to locate a suitable buyer for you. We know your home better than anyone else and have invested quite a lot of time and money in the marketing of your home.

The following is a list of the persons with whom we, or those brokers to whom we offered cooperation and compensation, have been negotiating and who have not yet made an acceptable offer to purchase your home. Should any of these individuals purchase your home during the post listing period indicated in the listing agreement, they would be considered to have been located and procured through our efforts. We therefore would be entitled to payment of the indicated commission.

As always, the sale of your home on terms acceptable to you is our primary concern. We hope that some of these people do in fact purchase your home within the allotted time since it will accomplish your goals and help us to recover the expenses we have incurred in our efforts to market your home. Since these parties are "protected buyers" we will be glad to assist you with the sale. Just contact us when you need our assistance.

Prospective purchasers obtained directly through this office:

Mr. William G. "Bill" Henderson
Mr. and Mrs. Randall Kemp

Mr. Gary J. Caswell

In addition, the following cooperating brokers have shown the property and have negotiated with their buyers:

Claudia Kennedy and other salespeople at Kennedy Properties, Inc.
Linda Peterson at Peterson Properties, Ltd.
Ms. Monica Jean Frascona of the MJF Corporation

Thank you for allowing us the opportunity to market your home. I trust you will relist with Kathy when she meets with you. If there is anything I can do to assist you or clarify our position, please do not hesitate to call me.

Most sincerely,
The Orcas Island Company

by: Oliver E. Frascona, Broker

**Letter - Expiration of the Listing Period -- Seller #2**

Mr. Sam Seller
Mrs. Sandy Seller
4750 Table Mesa Drive
Boulder, CO 80303

Re: 4750 Table Mesa Drive

Dear Sam and Sandy:

The initial term of your listing with our office will soon expire. Enclosed is a listing extension form extending the listing for an additional period of time. Often the basis for the ultimate decision to purchase begins with the introduction to the property by one of our agents or a cooperating salesperson, but there is simply not enough time to bring the buyer to the final decision prior to the expiration of the listing.

Should any of these buyers contact you personally, please give me a call immediately so that I can complete the sale in a professional manner. With real estate being as complicated as it is today, there is a lot more to be done than just drafting a contract for sale. A continuation of our services will ensure that you as the seller is properly represented and the buyer is made aware of all of the disclosures that the law now requires as well as the different sources of financing that are available.

I have prepared a new listing form for the MLS containing the information about your property. Sometimes a "reintroduction" will encourage someone to make the decision to buy. A copy is enclosed. In addition I have included the comparable sales in your area. This might be a good time to consider offering terms more in line with those offered for the properties that have sold. I will call you tomorrow to discuss the entire relisting process.

It has been a pleasure to serve as your agent. We have been happy to receive so many nice compliments from the numerous cooperating brokers who have had the opportunity to show your home. Your efforts to accommodate our attempts and your willingness to always have your house ready for last minute showings have certainly been helpful. We all want to commend you on your efforts.

Here is a list of the persons with whom we, or those brokers to whom we offered cooperation and compensation, have been negotiating and who have not yet made an acceptable offer to purchase your home. Should any of these individuals purchase your home during the post listing period indicated in the listing agreement, they would be considered to have been located and procured through our efforts. We therefore would be entitled to payment of the indicated commission.

As always, the sale of your home on terms acceptable to you is our primary concern. We hope that one of these people does in fact purchase your home within the allotted time since it will accomplish your goals and help us to recover the expenses we have incurred in our efforts to market your home. Since these parties are "protected buyers" we will be glad to assist you with the sale. Just contact us when you need our assistance.

Prospective purchasers obtained directly through this office:

Mr. William G. "Bill" Henderson
Mr. and Mrs. Randall Kemp
Mr. Gary J. Caswell

In addition,the following cooperating brokers have shown the property and have negotiated with their buyers:

Claudia Kennedy and other salespeople at Kennedy Properties, Inc.
Linda Peterson at Peterson Properties, Ltd.
Ms. Monica Jean Frascona of the MJF Corporation

Thank you for allowing us the opportunity to market your home. I trust you will relist with Kathy when she meets with you. If there is anything I can do to assist you or clarify our position, please do not hesitate to call me.

Most sincerely,
The Orcas Island Company

by: Oliver E. Frascona, Broker

## Listing Agreement Clauses and Addenda

The listing agreement sets the stage for the entire relationship with the seller. We have compiled several clauses and some explanation of those clauses to assist you with the preparation of the listing agreement. As usual, try to determine not only what will transpire but also who will be in charge of making decisions. The seller may want you to think that you are in charge but the seller is always in charge. This is an agency requirement and good business judgment.

**Tip.** *People are always trying to get someone else to make decisions for them. The decisions will be made to the seller's liking. All that remains is to determine whom the seller can blame or sue in the future.*

It is much better to include a clause that would cover any future possible issue even though it may not seem applicable at the time of the listing. It is much more difficult to negotiate an agreement with the seller as an issue arises later in the listing period. Some brokers believe it is better to "leave well enough alone in the beginning" and just deal with things as they come up. Contrary to that belief, it is much better for all parties to have established criteria for potential issues. When they do arise, you will then be able to go merrily along without conflict or misunderstanding.

**Clause Regarding Use of Professionals.**

1. This form has important legal consequences and the parties should consult legal and tax or other counsel before signing.

-or-

1. Brokers and salespeople are not licensed to practice law. They can not give legal advise. You are advised to seek such legal, tax, environmental, and other counsel as you determine appropriate.

-or-

1. The real estate contract may have significant legal remedies. The broker and salesperson can not give you legal, tax or other advice. You are advised to obtain the advice that you deem appropriate.

-or-

1. Do not rely upon the salesperson or broker assisting you. They are not licensed to practice law or accounting. Consult with competent legal, tax or other counsel before signing.

2. The property may qualify for a tax deferred exchange under Section 1031 of the Internal Revenue Code. We recommend that you seek tax or legal counsel to assist you with such an exchange.

-or-

2. Broker shall offer the property "Seller will cooperate with a tax deferred exchange."

-or-

2. Broker has advised Seller to contact a professional of the Seller's choosing to review the prospects of a section 1031 tax deferred exchange.

3. If you are over 55 years of age, you may qualify for beneficial tax treatment on the sale of your personal residence. There are several rules with which you will need to comply. We advise you to seek competent tax advice.

4. If you sell this home and have occupied it as an owner, you may be able to avoid paying some or all of the tax on your gain, if any, by purchasing a replacement home that meets the guidelines of the Internal Revenue Service. We encourage you to seek competent tax advice regarding this matter.

**Clause Regarding the Physical Condition of the Property.**

1. Seller hereby authorizes broker to indicate to all prospective buyers "the property is located within 50 miles of a nuclear weapons facility."

-or-

1. Seller hereby authorizes broker to indicate to all prospective buyers "the property is within a line of sight to high tension power lines."

-or-

1. Seller hereby authorizes broker to indicate to all prospective buyers "the property next door is being utilized as a shelter for paroled criminals."

-or-

1. Seller hereby authorizes broker to indicate to buyers "seller and broker strongly encourage you to have the home inspected."

It would be improper to indicate that the house next door was anything other than another house if the occupants were protected by the federal or state fair housing laws. Remember, the law covers such things as group homes for the handicapped or mentally challenged.

### Clause Regarding Title Status.

1. Seller authorizes and instructs broker to obtain a title commitment to determine the status of the title to the seller's property. Broker shall order and obtain the commitment from a company that will not charge unless the property is sold.

-or-

1. Seller authorizes broker to obtain a title insurance commitment at seller's expense.

2. Broker is authorized to contact all lien holders and obtain payoff statements for all liens upon the property.

3. Seller shall provide "extended coverage" title insurance.

-or-

3. Seller shall comply with the reasonable requirements of the title insurance company and pay the premium to obtain form 130 endorsement.

### Clause Regarding Prepaid FHA Mortgage Insurance Premiums.

1. Prepaid FHA mortgage insurance premiums shall be prorated to the date of delivery of deed using the schedule attached to this Listing Agreement.

-or-

1. Prepaid FHA mortgage insurance premiums shall be prorated to the date of delivery of deed using the schedule provided to the closing agent by HUD.

-or-

1. The unused portion of any prepaid FHA mortgage insurance premiums will be purchased by the buyer at closing. The amount will be determined utilizing a form provided by HUD for such prorations.

### Clause Regarding FHA Mortgage Interest.

Seller is hereby made aware that FHA mortgage interest is not prorated for the month of the loan payoff. Seller will owe a full month's interest if the loan is in effect for one day of the following month. There is no guarantee that the loan payoff will reach the lender prior to the end of the month. This may cause the seller to be responsible for an additional month's interest.

### Clause Regarding Hazard Insurance.

1. Broker has advised the seller that his existing hazard insurance policy may not cover the period of time between the closing and delivery of deed and the actual surrender of possession by the seller. The seller is advised to seek the counsel of his insurance agent and obtain a written assurance satisfactory to the seller as to the extent of his coverage on and after closing.

-or-

1. Seller is hereby advised that in the event he allows someone other than himself to occupy the property, either during the pendency of the listing or after the sale has closed, the existing hazard insurance policy may not cover the premises or the possessions of the seller or the occupant.

-or-

1. Seller is advised that in the event the seller remains in the property after closing the seller's homeowner's policy may not cover the property nor his contents as the insurance company may deem the former seller to be a tenant and not insured under a "homeowner's" policy.

### Clause Regarding Liability Upon Assumption.

1. The seller, in the absence of a written release signed by the lender to the contrary, will remain liable for the repayment of the loan on the property in the event the seller allows it to be assumed. In the event of an assumption and subsequent default by the buyer, the **seller will not be able to reacquire the property.**

2. The broker, her agents, subagents and employees are not liable for any event that occurs after the delivery of the deed, including, but not limited to, a failure on the part of the buyer or subsequent buyers to make any payments after assuming the mortgage or after a subsequent transfer without an assumption. We are not responsible for the actions of the buyer after the property is transferred.

3. Owner acknowledges that, although a purchaser may assume the existing note and mortgage, the owner shall remain personally liable for the ultimate repayment of the loan.

### Clause Regarding Reservation of the Right to Purchase Property for Own Account.

1. Broker reserves the right to purchase the seller's property at the listed price or such price as seller may accept at any time during the term of the listing. This reservation shall apply to all the salespeople in broker's office. Seller

waives any claim for a conflict of interest regarding such sale. Seller agrees that neither the broker nor any salesperson assisted seller in the determination of the listing price. In the event a salesperson purchases the property, the following procedures shall be followed:

a. The seller and broker shall terminate the listing agreement for the subject property; and,

b. The broker or a salesperson in the broker's office ("salesperson") will submit an offer to purchase the seller's property; and,

c. The price may, at the discretion of the salesperson, be reduced by any commission due as a result of the listing agreement; and,

d. The offer shall be conditional upon the seller's attorney reviewing and approving in writing the offer prior to it becoming a contract; and,

e. The salesperson shall contribute $__________ to the seller's actual attorney fees at closing; and,

f. The seller shall be entitled to rescind the contract of sale at any time prior to closing and the salesperson shall immediately make the contract terminated; and,

g. Seller may be required by salesperson to obtain an independent appraisal of the property. In such an event salesperson shall pay $______ toward seller's expense for the appraisal at closing.

**Clause Regarding Determination of the Listing Price.**

Seller has considered the Competitive Market Analysis which indicates the price of other similar properties that have sold, are listed or were rejected by the market, provided by Broker in the determination by Seller of the listing price. Broker is not responsible for determination of the listing price.

**Clause Regarding Comparable Properties.**

1. I hereby authorize you to provide data about comparable listed, sold and rejected properties available through the MLS or otherwise to prospective buyers in order to assist them in valuing my property.

-or-

1. It is ok with me for you to show comps to a potential buyer even if they undermine the listed price of my property.

## ADDENDUM TO LISTING CONTRACT
### (Purchase by Licensee)

This addendum is hereby made a part of the Listing Contract between the indicated Seller and the Real Estate Broker ("Broker") dated ________________, 19 ____ concerning the Seller's real estate ("Property") located at: ______________________

______________________________________________

1. Broker and Seller agree that Broker and Broker's salespeople ("Buyer Salesperson") have the right to purchase the Property for their own account.

2. The parties acknowledge that this creates a potential conflict of interest. Broker shall use the Broker's best efforts to obtain a buyer not associated with Broker upon the terms and conditions outlined by seller.

3. Seller has consulted with an attorney of seller's selection prior to the execution of this listing agreement. The signature of that attorney approving this addendum as to form is evidenced below.

4. In the event Buyer Salesperson decides to attempt to purchase the property the Broker and Seller will first negotiate the termination of this listing agreement. Seller is under no obligation to terminate the listing and allow Buyer to purchase the property.

5. Subsequently the Buyer Salesperson will submit an offer. This offer will not be effective unless approved by Seller's attorney in writing as to form. Buyer Salesperson shall pay Seller, upon the transfer of title, the sum of $300.00 as a contribution to the Seller's legal fees.

6. Buyer Salesperson will suggest that the Seller obtain an independent appraisal prior to accepting Buyer Salesperson's offer. Buyer Salesperson will contribute $300.00 to the cost of such an appraisal upon transfer of title.

7. Any such offer shall contain language that allows the seller to accept another contract and terminate this contract at any time prior to the date and time indicated for the transfer of deed and closing.

In the event of a conflict between these terms and those in the body of the Listing Contract, the terms on this Addendum shall prevail.

| | |
|---|---|
| ______________________________ | ______________________________ |
| Seller date | Seller date |
| Real Estate Broker: | Approved as to form: |
| ______________________________ | ______________________________ |
| by date | Attorney for seller date |

### Clause Regarding a Broker Guaranteed Sale.

Seller and broker have agreed that broker will purchase the property under the terms of a separate Guaranteed Sale Agreement.

### Clause Regarding Schedule of Rents and Deposits.

The owner warrants that the attached schedule of rents and deposits is a true and correct representation of the rents and deposits actually collected and currently due. In addition, the owner represents that each individual listed as a tenant is actually occupying the property according to the terms indicated. Owner shall transfer all deposits and prorate all rents as of the date of delivery of deed. There are no incentives or rent preferences in effect that would alter or amend the rental information contained on the attached list.

### Clause Regarding Commission Rates.

1. Compensation charged by real estate brokers is not set by law. Such charges are established by each real estate broker.

-or-

1. There are no standard commissions. Each broker establishes his own fee structure.

-or-

1. No entity is allowed to set or establish commission or fee structures. Each broker determines the fees that he will charge and the amounts that he will offer to cooperating brokers.

-or-

1. Commissions charged by real estate brokers are not set by the state, the board or association of Realtors® nor by law or agreement. These fees are established by each real estate broker independently.

### Cooperative Commissions.

**Rule.** *Breach of a fiduciary duty forfeits the commission regardless of loss.*

Even if we got the house sold, we could lose the entire commission if we breached our fiduciary duty--the duty to tell the seller what we were doing on the seller's behalf.

**Tip.** *Tell the seller how you do business, and let the seller determine if he wants to do business with you.*

There are many potential relationships between the listing broker and the selling broker and between the selling broker and the buyer. It is imperative that the listing broker address, in the listing agreement, the various options offered by the broker's company. Indicate who will be paid and how much. With what type of selling brokers will we work?

Adequate treatment should avoid the broker hearing some of these statements for the first time at the same time they are heard by the jury.

**Jury Talk.** *"They did not work on my property very hard. They refused to cooperate with other brokers. They kept my property a secret in their office hoping to sell it themselves instead of exposing it to all the brokers in their market area."*

*"They only offered other brokers _____%, and that was not enough."*

*"I never knew that I was liable for these other brokers, these subagents. They should have told me when I listed the property that I would be liable for all the brokers in my area."*

*"When I heard that they were not cooperating with buyer brokers, I was furious. Those are the people that have buyers. Why would we not work with them to get my house sold?"*

**Clauses and Addenda for Cooperative Commissions.** The following sample addenda and clauses address the commission options facing the listing broker. It is suggested that the seller consent to the cooperative commission schedule. They are basic and intended to be reviewed by the reader and a selection made. The paragraphs with the same number are alternative paragraphs.

There are several different addenda from which to choose. We have tried to provide different forms that contain the terms for each alternate way of doing business. Read them carefully and then select the one that best suits your current needs. They will be right here when you decide to change the way you do things.

## ADDENDUM TO LISTING CONTRACT
### (Cooperative Compensation and Commission Structure)

This addendum is hereby made a part of the Listing Contract between the indicated Seller and Real Estate Broker ("Broker") dated ____________________, 19 ______ concerning the Seller's real estate ("Property") located at: ______________________

______________________________________________________________________

1. **Cooperating Commission.** Broker shall seek assistance from, and offer ______ % of the gross selling price to, all brokers licensed by this state, located within the market area of Broker, whose licenses are with a company other than the Broker's company. This offer shall include Subagents and Buyer Agents.

2. **Referral Fees -- Buyers.** Broker, in an effort to procure as many qualified buyers as possible, shall seek assistance from, and offer compensation to, brokers, licensed by any state, located outside Broker's market area in the form of a referral fee. Depending upon the referring licensee, Broker shall pay a referral fee equal to but not less than _______% nor more than ______% of that portion of the total commission (percentage of the gross selling price) indicated above for the licensee assisting the buyer.

In the event of a conflict between these terms and those in the body of the Listing Contract, the terms on this Addendum shall prevail.

| | |
|---|---|
| ______________________________ | ______________________________ |
| Seller      date | Seller      date |

Real Estate Broker:

______________________________

by      date

## ADDENDUM TO LISTING CONTRACT
### (Cooperative Compensation and Commission Structure)

This addendum is hereby made a part of the Listing Contract between the indicated Seller and Real Estate Broker ("Broker") dated ____________________, 19 ______ concerning the Seller's real estate ("Property") located at: ____________________

____________________________________________________________

1. **Cooperating Commission**. Broker shall seek assistance from, and offer ______ % of the gross selling price to, all brokers (subagents, buyer agents or otherwise) licensed by this state, located within the market area of Broker, whose licenses are with a company other than the Broker's company.

2. **Referral Fees -- Buyers**. Broker, in an effort to procure as many qualified buyers as possible, shall seek assistance from, and offer compensation to, brokers, licensed by any state, located outside Broker's market area in the form of a referral fee. Depending upon the referring licensee, Broker is authorized to pay other brokers a portion of Broker's total commission, determined by Broker in Broker's sole discretion, for the referral of prospective buyers for Seller's property.

In the event of a conflict between these terms and those in the body of the Listing Contract, the terms on this Addendum shall prevail.

______________________________ ______________________________
Seller date Seller date

Real Estate Broker:

______________________________
by date

# ADDENDUM TO LISTING CONTRACT
## (Cooperative Compensation and Commission Structure)

This addendum is hereby made a part of the Listing Contract between the indicated Seller and Real Estate Broker ("Broker") dated ____________________, 19 ______ concerning the Seller's real estate ("Property") located at: ____________________

____________________________________________________________

1. **Cooperating Commission**. Broker shall seek assistance from, and offer ______ % of the gross selling price to, all brokers licensed by this state, located within the market area of Broker, whose licenses are with a company other than the Broker's company. This offer shall include Subagents and Buyer Agents.

-or-

1. **Cooperating Commission**. Broker shall seek assistance from, and offer ______ % of the gross selling price to, all brokers (subagents, buyer agents or others) licensed by this state, located within the market area of Broker, whose licenses are with a company other than the Broker's company.

-or-

1. **Cooperating Commission**. Broker shall seek assistance from, and offer ______ % of the gross selling price to, all brokers licensed by this state, except brokers attempting to act as subagents, located within the market area of Broker, whose licenses are with a company other than the Broker's company. Subagents work with a buyer but represent the Seller and owe duties of utmost good faith, loyalty and fidelity to Seller only. Seller may be vicariously liable for the acts of subagents when acting in the scope of the agency relationship. Buyer agents representing the buyer owe duties of utmost good faith, loyalty and fidelity to buyer only. Seller is probably not vicariously liable for the acts of buyer agents.

2. **Referral Fees -- Buyers**. Broker, in an effort to procure as many qualified buyers as possible, shall seek assistance from and offer compensation to brokers, licensed by any state, located outside Broker's market area in the form of a referral fee. Depending upon the referring licensee, Broker shall pay a referral fee equal to but not less than _______% nor more than ______% of that portion of the total commission (percentage of the gross selling price) indicated above for the licensee assisting the buyer.

-or-

2. **Referral Fees -- Buyers**. Broker, in an effort to procure as many qualified buyers as possible, shall seek assistance from and offer compensation to brokers, licensed by any state, located outside Broker's market area in the form of a referral fee. Depending upon the referring licensee, Broker is

authorized to pay other brokers a portion of Broker's total commission, determined by Broker in Broker's sole discretion, for the referral of prospective buyers for Seller's property.

-or-

2. **Referral Fees -- General**. Broker, in an effort to cooperate with as many other brokers as possible, is authorized to pay other brokers a portion of Broker's total commission, determined by Broker in Broker's sole discretion, for the referral of Seller or prospective buyers for Seller's property.

In the event of a conflict between these terms and those in the body of the Listing Contract, the terms on this Addendum shall prevail.

_________________________________ _________________________________
Seller date Seller date

Real Estate Broker:

_________________________________
by date

# COMMISSION DIVISION ADDENDUM TO LISTING CONTRACT
## (Cooperative Compensation and Commission Structure)

This addendum is hereby made a part of the Listing Contract between the indicated Seller and Real Estate Broker ("Broker") dated ____________________, 19 ______ concerning the Seller's real estate ("Property") located at: ______________________

______________________________________________________________________

1. Broker shall seek assistance from and offer the indicated compensation as a percentage of the gross selling price, to the following brokers licensed by this state, located within the market area of Broker, whose licenses are with a company other than the Broker's company.

☐ (a) ______ % to other brokers representing Seller ("**Subagents**"). Subagents work with a buyer but represent the Seller and owe duties of utmost good faith, loyalty and fidelity to Seller only. Seller may be vicariously liable for the acts of Subagents when acting in the scope of the agency relationship.

☐ (b) ______ % to brokers representing the buyer ("**Buyer Agents**"). Buyer Agents representing the buyer owe duties of utmost good faith, loyalty and fidelity to buyer only. Seller is probably not vicariously liable for the acts of Buyer Agents.

2. Broker, in an effort to cooperate with as many other brokers as possible, is authorized to pay other brokers a portion of Broker's total commission, determined by Broker in Broker's sole discretion, for the referral to Broker of prospective buyers for Seller's property.

In the event of a conflict between these terms and those in the body of the Listing Contract, the terms on this Addendum shall prevail.

| ______________________________ | ______________________________ |
|---|---|
| Seller date | Seller date |

Real Estate Broker:

______________________________

by date

# COMMISSION DIVISION ADDENDUM TO LISTING CONTRACT
## (Cooperative Compensation and Commission Structure)

This addendum is hereby made a part of the Listing Contract dated __________________, 19 ____ between the indicated Seller and Real Estate Broker ("Broker") concerning the Seller's real estate ("Property") located at:
______________________________________________________________________

1. Broker shall seek assistance from and offer the indicated compensation, as a percentage of the gross selling price, to the following brokers licensed by this state, located within the market area of Broker, whose licenses are with a company other than the Broker's company.

☐ (a) ______ % to other brokers representing Seller ("**Subagents**"). Subagents work with a buyer but represent the Seller and owe duties of utmost good faith, loyalty and fidelity to Seller only. Seller may be vicariously liable for the acts of Subagents when acting in the scope of the agency relationship.

☐ (b) ______ % to brokers representing the buyer ("**Buyer Agents**"). Buyer Agents representing the buyer owe duties of utmost good faith, loyalty and fidelity to buyer only. Seller is probably not vicariously liable for the acts of Buyer Agents.

☐ (c) ______ % to other licensed brokers assisting the buyer in the transaction but not acting as agents of either the buyer or seller. Such licensees must exercise reasonable skill and care for the parties. Seller is probably not vicariously liable for the acts of these brokers.

2. Broker, in an effort to cooperate with as many other brokers as possible, is authorized to pay other brokers a portion of Broker's total commission, determined by Broker in Broker's sole discretion, for the referral to Broker of prospective buyers for Seller's property.

In the event of a conflict between these terms and those in the body of the Listing Contract, the terms on this Addendum shall prevail.

| ______________________________ | ______________________________ |
|---|---|
| Seller date | Seller date |

Real Estate Broker:

______________________________
by date

## COMMISSION DIVISION ADDENDUM TO LISTING CONTRACT
### (Cooperative Compensation and Commission Structure)

1. Broker shall seek assistance from and offer the indicated compensation, as a percentage of the gross selling price, to the following brokers licensed by this state, located within the market area of Broker, whose licenses are with a company other than the Broker's company.

☐ (a) ______ % to other brokers representing Seller ("**Subagents**"). Subagents work with a buyer but represent the Seller and owe duties of utmost good faith, loyalty and fidelity to Seller only. Seller may be vicariously liable for the acts of Subagents when acting in the scope of the agency relationship.

☐ (b) ______ % to brokers representing the buyer ("**Buyer Agents**"). Buyer Agents representing the buyer owe duties of utmost good faith, loyalty and fidelity to buyer only. Seller is probably not vicariously liable for the acts of Buyer Agents.

☐ (c) ______ % to other licensed brokers assisting the buyer in the transaction but not acting as agents of either the buyer or seller.

Seller recognizes that there may be some brokers licensed by the state, that are not acting as buyer agents and whom the seller does not want as subagents because of the potential vicarious lability. Seller hereby authorizes Broker to co-operate with every conceivable other broker licensed by this state to accomplish the sale of the property without incurring vicarious liability. Such Broker should, but may not, exercise reasonable skill and care for both buyer and seller. Seller is probably not vicariously liable for the acts of these licensed brokers.

2. Broker, in an effort to cooperate with as many other brokers as possible, is authorized to pay other brokers a portion of Broker's total commission, determined by Broker in Broker's sole discretion, for the referral to Broker of prospective buyers for Seller's property.

In the event of a conflict between these terms and those in the body of the Listing Contract, the terms on this Addendum shall prevail.

______________________________ ______________________________
Seller date Seller date

Real Estate Broker:

______________________________
by date

## COMMISSION DIVISION ADDENDUM TO LISTING CONTRACT
### (Cooperative Compensation and Commission Structure)

1. Broker shall seek assistance from and offer the indicated compensation, as a percentage of the gross selling price, to the following brokers licensed by this state, located within the market area of Broker, whose licenses are with a company other than the Broker's company.

☐ (a) ______ % to other brokers representing Seller ("**Subagents**"). Subagents work with a buyer but represent the Seller and owe duties of utmost good faith, loyalty and fidelity to Seller only. Seller may be vicariously liable for the acts of Subagents when acting in the scope of the agency relationship.

☐ (b) ______ % to brokers representing the buyer ("**Buyer Agents**"). Buyer Agents representing the buyer owe duties of utmost good faith, loyalty and fidelity to buyer only. Seller is probably not vicariously liable for the acts of Buyer Agents.

☐ (c) ______ % to brokers assisting the buyer in the transaction but not acting as agents of either the buyer or the seller ("**Transaction Brokers**"). Transaction Brokers should exercise reasonable skill and care for the parties. Seller is probably not vicariously liable for the acts of Transaction-Brokers.

2. Broker, in an effort to cooperate with as many other brokers as possible, is authorized to pay other brokers a portion of Broker's total commission, determined by Broker in Broker's sole discretion, for the referral to Broker of prospective buyers for Seller's property.

In the event of a conflict between these terms and those in the body of the Listing Contract, the terms on this Addendum shall prevail.

______________________________ ______________________________
Seller date Seller date

Real Estate Broker:

______________________________
by date

# Chapter Three
# The Buyer Relationship
*Doing What Comes Naturally*

## *The Nature of Buyers*

1. Buyers are the ones who will own the property after the closing.

2. A large percentage of buyers think that you are their agent even if you are not. They say things like "my Realtor®" or sometimes "my Rcalator" when referring to the salesperson assisting them.

3. The law is moving quickly to protect buyers by requiring a myriad of disclosures regarding all aspects of a real estate transaction.

4. The informed buyer is the buyer of the future. Buyers do not always know what they want. Give them information.

5. Buyers will be around after the sale and will remember who helped them acquire this new piece of real estate. You may have represented the seller, the buyer, neither or both. The buyer is the one who will probably start the suit.

6. Buyers who are dissatisfied with their new acquisition will be searching for a way to extricate themselves from the transaction. It is the buyer against whom you must protect yourself.

7. Sellers, lacking a seller-financing situation, will generally take their money and be gone, sometimes out of state. As a practical matter the seller may not be available to help with the post closing problems. They often do not remember the key points that were so easy to express only months before. They become afflicted with "selective memory".

8. Buyer representation is a modern concern, both for the industry and for the court system. Whether or not your company allows such a system, and there are many arguments for and against offering it as an alternative, it must either be explained to the buyer or you must indicate clearly that you are the seller's agent.

9. Everyone must understand the concept of buyer agency and be prepared to explain it and deal with it in some fashion.

## *Pledge of Service to the Buyer*

I will provide you with all the information that I have in my possession regarding any home that you may select.

I will search all Multiple Listing Services of which I am a member for property such as you designate.

I will provide you with all information that I have concerning the physical condition of any property that you select.

I will provide you with the agency disclosure forms and explain the options available to you including the manner in which we sell our own listings in plain language.

I will allow you to make the decisions that affect your real estate needs. I will not make decisions for you even if you ask me to.

I am committed to the spirit and letter of the law to provide everyone with equal access to housing.

I will encourage you to avail yourself of professional attorneys, accountants, surveyors, appraisers, contractors, inspectors and others that are more skilled in their areas of expertise than I am.

I will encourage you to have each property inspected prior to, or as a part of, your contract to buy.

I will not inspect any property for you. I am not a property inspector.

I will not let my personal relationship with others deter me from cooperating with them to accomplish your transaction.

I will keep you informed about the changing financing market so that you can make an intelligent selection of a lender to assist you with financing.

I will tell you when I do not know the answers to your questions.

I will accept compensation only from sources that I have first disclosed to you.

I will continue to stay current in those areas where it is reasonable to expect information from a real estate professional.

I will treat you honestly at all times.

## *Passive Defense Techniques.*

1. In a lawsuit, it is always nice to have someone who has the ability to pay. Attorneys call this the "deep pocket" theory. Be the poorest in the group.

2. Wealth is a personal thing. There is no need to explain to potential plaintiffs that you have a lot of money. Do not say "I did 10 million last year" if you can help it.

3. The perception that you are not much of an adversary, are poorly organized, do not pay attention to details, do not keep good records, or have something to hide may encourage someone to include you in litigation.

4. Law suits are a spectator sport. Be prepared to demonstrate through your paperwork that you have disclosed properly and treated the buyer in the appropriate manner.

5. Try not to discuss other transactions that you have completed in order to indicate that a risky transaction will work. The more you describe other transactions, the more you may have the opportunity to defend a tenuous perception of what happened.

6. Display the image of an organized, detail-oriented, highly professional agent who *always* follows the rules and is above reproach. No one likes a well organized individual as a defendant. She is too credible.

7. Be someone your kids can respect. Be someone who does not make a derogatory comment about others.

8. Always try to limit the amount of unimportant information you give to a buyer, client, or other potential plaintiff. Stick to the facts about the property.

9. Limit your liability by explaining alternatives, rules, local sources of information, the extent of your abilities and agency status in written form from the beginning.

10. Use cover letters to confirm actions taken by yourself and others.

11. Do the right thing. Do not be swayed because the information seems important. Is it confidential? Did you promise someone that you would not tell? Do you have a fiduciary duty to the buyer?

12. Unless you are a buyer's agent, you have no duty to the buyer other than honesty. Honesty does not mean telling the seller's personal secrets.

## *Myths about Buyer Agency*

*You can not look in the Magic Listing System for property.* Sellers put their listings in the MLS because they were looking for buyers. You have buyers.

*Buyers must pay their agents to be legal.* Anyone can pay anyone in most states. People have the right to contract as they please. People can agree on paying points. Why not agree on paying the brokers?

*Banks will not recognize a buyer agent.* Banks do not care. They want to loan money to the buyer. FHA and VA may present some unusual problems. If you charge a reasonable fee and disclose it in the beginning, problems are limited.

*No one understands it.* The buyer understands it very well. He wants someone who is on his side, not the seller's side. Many buyers always thought that they had this.

*You can't show and sell your own listings.* Of course you can. Yes, it requires defining in advance what you will and will not do. Remember, the seller wants to sell the house. That is why he hired you as the listing broker. Most sellers think that you will sell the home yourself when they list with you. Most sellers turned buyers will want to see your listings also. Explain the rules in advance so that they can enjoy the game.

## *Myths about Transaction (Real Estate) Broker*

*You can not look in the Magic Listing System for property.* Sellers put their listings in the MLS because they were looking for buyers. You have buyers. You are not a seller's agent or buyer's agent. You simply are a broker selling the house. You are neutral, just like a stock broker. Disclose information about the property and not about the people.

*Buyers must pay the broker to be legal.* Anyone can pay anyone in most states. All that is required is a real estate broker's license. People are free to hire a licensed broker to assist them with a real estate transaction. People can agree on paying points. Why not agree on paying the brokers?

*Banks will not recognize a transaction broker.* Banks do not care. They want to loan money to the buyer. FHA and VA may present some unusual problems. If you charge a reasonable fee and disclose it in the beginning, problems are limited. Act like a broker and you will get paid like a broker.

*No one understands it.* That is the first thing people think. Brokerage is easier than agency to understand. You discuss the real estate and not the people. It is an option for the people who do not know you well enough to accept you as their agents but want to see and buy real estate. They simply do not want an agent. The buyer understands it very well. He wants someone who is neutral.

*You can't show and sell your own listings.* Of course you can. Yes, it requires defining in advance what you will and will not do. Remember, the seller wants to sell the house. That is why he hired you as the listing broker. Most sellers think that you will sell it yourself when they list with you. Most sellers turned buyers will want to see your listings also. Explain the rules in advance so that they can enjoy the game.

*It is illegal.* Check your state laws. While some states specifically endorse it, others specifically say that you can not do it. Most do not have an opinion. They license people as brokers and salespersons and have never thought about agency or non agency. What is a referral fee?

## *What to Tell, What to Keep Secret.*

| | **Buyer Clients** | **Buyers (Non Clients)** |
|---|---|---|
| Facts about the property | Yes | Yes |
| Personal facts about the seller | Yes | No |
| Motivation for seller to sell | Yes | No |
| Seller sickness or death | Yes | No |
| The terms of previous offers to buy | Yes | No |
| Terms of counter offers that failed | Yes | No |
| What price to offer | No | No |
| What price to counter | No | No |
| Which form to use | No | No |
| Which inspector to use | No | No |
| Which lender is the "best" | No | No |

## Finding and Working With a Buyer

**Searching for the Buyer**. Where do buyers come from? Everywhere! If you think back to prospecting for sellers, you will note that all the sources for buyers are identical with those for sellers. The sphere of influence, geographical farm, referrals from satisfied past and present clients or customers, and property management tenants have an overflowing pool of buyers just waiting for professional assistance to find the right home.

Don't overlook the For Sale By Owner, "FSBO". The owner of the "For Sale By Owner" may initially be unwilling to pay a real estate fee to someone working with a buyer on the sale of his property. Remember this is the same person who will be searching for professional assistance when he begins his search for a replacement home and will be less hesitant to allow the seller to authorize a commission split with the salesperson on his buyer team. It is likely that a professional real estate licensee will sell the FSBO and the commission will be included in the price regardless of who is perceived to pay it. The salesperson must be careful to disclose his relationship to everyone. It always amazes us that someone who was working with a buyer would try for a "one party" listing as a seller's agent.

Where there is a seller, there will be a buyer. Do not forget to ask the sellers that you represent if you can assist them in the purchase of their next home. They will be looking for a new home the instant that you sell their property. Let's hope that they want you to continue as their Realtor®. Some agents think that they own these sellers and are aghast when they find that "their seller" has gone out and bought a new property without them. Can you think of a easier way to acquire a new buyer than when you are listing a seller? Even if they are moving to a different location, you can obtain a fee by referring them to another broker. Keep in contact with the seller who moves to a different location, even out of state. Katherine has received a number of buyer referrals from a seller who knows a business associate or friend moving to the area he has left.

Always be on the alert and listening for the opportunities to assist a first time buyer, the buyer who is "moving up" and also needs to sell his present home and buyers looking for investment properties. That might mean another property to sell and one or more to help them purchase. Buyers looking for second homes and vacation homes represent a growing market. Maybe they could pool their resources with another couple. Where there is a buyer, there will be a seller in the future. When you approach your real estate business as a long term endeavor, you will be there for the same individuals as buyer or sellers for all their real estate transactions. If you pattern each transaction with the idea that you want repeat business, you will indirectly conduct your daily activities in the professional manner to ensure that end.

"Farm" for buyers the same way you do for sellers. In fact, any and all correspondence should include references to buying or selling real estate if you are assisting the public with both types of transactions. Talk about real estate by telling stories about a couple or individual that you helped purchase a property. Never put the buyer down or make light of his attributes. Set the stage so that the transaction is productive for the buyer because of your skills. Leave the people thinking "if I ever want to buy, that is the person that I should call." Everyone should know that you are working with buyers, as well as sellers, in real estate.

**Broker referrals.** Networking with brokers within your local association or board as well as intrastate, interstate, and even internationally will supply a steady stream of referrals for relocating clients. Many of the large franchise companies furnish a relocation network of referrals within their structure. If you are not a member of this type of real estate firm, you can start your own network database. Keep all those cards you collect at Realtor® events whether local, state, or national.

Get to know the people to whom you contemplate sending a referral. Remember, that person is not only a direct reflection on you, but is the only way of holding on to the buyers you send to them and the only way you will get paid. No matter how loyal the client may have been to you, loyalty will not overcome the lack of service on the other end. When you are the recipient of another broker's client, keep in contact with the broker with regular updates.

Utilize the benefits of your professional designations. The Certified Residential Specialist, CRS, directory offers you the assurance of networking with other Realtors® who see the importance of specialized continuing education. These individuals have invested in attaining a higher level of professionalism and will conduct their business accordingly. They also complete more of their transactions and make more money than the average salesperson. You are referring your buyer to a professional who will make you look good.

**Buyer Contact Card** Date of Initial Contact: ____________________

Name:____________________________________________________________

Address:__________________________________________________________

City, State, Zip:_______________________________________________ __________

Phone: Work____________ Home______________Car___________Other___________

Source of Buyer: ___Open House ___Advertisements ___Walk in ___Referral

Buyer is a
Tenant:______ Current Rent:______________ Lease Expires:__________________

Buyer is an
Owner:_______ Value:_____________ House Listed with:_____________________

Buyer's Price Range:_________________________________

Has been looking for ______ months Occupancy Date:_______________________

Gave Disclosures: ___Agency ___In-Co Sale ___Fair Housing

Notes:____________________________________________________________

**Motivation of the Buyer and Qualification.** Before you ever allow a buyer in your car to see properties, you must first determine the urgency of her desire to buy and if, in fact, she has any money to do so. Urgency alone does not make a buyer. One of the most difficult things to tell someone who really wants to own her home is that there just is not any way she can currently qualify to make her dream a reality. Of course, that presupposes that you have investigated all the possibilities available to include family assistance with loan qualification or the down payment, co-signors or co-mortgagors. Nothing compares to the sense of accomplishment felt when you can help a struggling buyer realize her dream through creative efforts and financing. On the other hand, if the impossibility of buying a home is approached with honesty and with empathy, the buyer will return to you when her financial situation and qualification improve.

During the initial interview be certain to determine if the buyers sitting across from you are the final decision makers. The ultimate decision of which home to select may rest with another family member or third party especially if that entity will be responsible for a portion or all of the down payment or qualification. Establish the parameters that the buyer desires in his home. These include the location or neighborhood, the desired price range and monthly mortgage payment, age of home, style of home (single or multi-level), importance of proximity of schools, entertainment, shopping malls, transportation, and any special needs if the buyer is handicapped.

Selecting the right people to work with will make you money every time. Some salespeople work with whomever comes to town. A few minutes of questions at the initial interview lets the buyer know that you are a professional salesperson who only works with qualified people. They will *want* to become your buyer. They will want the best.

**Determine Your Agency Status.** Prior to the buyer revealing any confidential information, you must verify what your relationship will be with that buyer. Explain verbally to the buyer the services you can provide as a buyer agent, subagent, or neutral real estate broker. Discuss the fees relative to each and the methods for payment for your fees or commission. Once the buyer determines the degree of representation he wishes to have, acknowledge the agreement with a written employment contract. Do not be afraid to charge people for your services. You are worth it.

Agency is not the issue. You will make a selection as we will discuss later. What is important is that you understand the basic functions assigned to, or associated with working with, the buyer. Regardless of your status, the buyer is expecting you to provide service before the contract, during the contract and after it is signed. Know the basic duties and follow a checklist.

**Signing the Agreement.** Once you have decided that these people are worth your effort, you need to sign a contract with them that details your services and how you will be paid. Remember these factors that apply to all buyers:

The buyer wants to buy a home. That is why he is talking to you.

You do this for a living. This is not a hobby.

Someone has to pay you for your services. That is how you pay your bills.

Indicate some of the services that you provide.

Professionals talk about their fees just as you do.

No one wants to pay you if they can help it.

The buyer will help you get paid if you ask him.

The buyer will insist that you get paid once you explain the facts of life to them.

Your commission is part of thc transaction.

Written agreements cement your relationship, impose loyalty from the buyer and define the parameters under which you will work.

Ask for the order. Then sign up the buyer!

The duration of the agreement can be a key element in obtaining the buyer's consent. If it is a seller whose home you already have listed, you have rapport. That seller turned buyer will sign whatever you place in front of him.

If the buyer is not well known to you, he will be more reluctant to sign a long term agreement. Do not be hesitant to ask for a few days or a week instead of a long term listing. Maybe he will not be the right person with whom you will want to spend valuable time. Protect yourself for the property that you do show him, but leave the listing short and the buyer will be more agreeable to sign. He does not know you either. After a few days with you, he will be happy to extend. You will see extension clauses in some of our forms.

**Inventory of Homes to Show.** Once you clearly have parameters for the buyer's desired home, search your inventory of homes. Don't neglect to check recent expired listings, the newspaper advertisements, For Sale by Owners and other Realtors® for homes expected to come on the market in addition to researching the current listings in the Magic Listing Service. Your research can extend to letters or door knocking in areas where the buyer has expressed an interest to live. If you have a written agreement, you know your method of payment has been covered even if you show a FSBO. Remember to indicate in your agreement exactly the extent of the inventory you are willing to research in order to try to locate the desired home.

**Prepare the Offer.** Your technical expertise must be thorough when drafting and preparing an offer for the buyer. Provide the buyer with a detailed market analysis for the neighborhood where he has selected the home so that he can make an informed decision on pricing. You will also need to be knowledgeable of market trends for the area. Are new developments anticipated that may flood the inventory? Are there plans for road widening projects or are other city and county assessments imminent? Do not rely on the information provided by the listing agent in ascertaining whether you have given full disclosure of material facts to your buyer. Once the price and terms have been determined, review all other aspects of the contract with the buyer. Review the necessity for inspections and the significance of any contingencies included in the contract. When the contract and addenda are completed, reviewed and approved by the buyer, attach a copy of the lender's pre-qualification letter and a cover letter of introduction before presenting the offer to the listing agent or seller. A sample cover letter can be found in the following chapter on contracts.

**Home Warranty.** Sometimes a salesperson may inadvertently provide an opportunity for the buyer to litigate. The only way to ensure that all parties understand what is offered, rejected or waived is to provide a written form. This also applies to the cost and availability of a home warranty program. If you get a commission on the sale of a home warranty policy, inform them of that fact. If there are several companies that offer the service, provide a list just as you would with any other service provider.

**Case in Point.** *Out of town buyers are referred to the salesperson by their son-in-law, your close personal friend. Everyone looks at the home which obviously needs a lot of work. The salesperson tells them about home warranties. They decide not to buy one. The contract is written and includes an inspection clause. The buyers have the home inspected and verify the defects. The buyers are fully aware of the defects and decide to purchase the home anyway at a price that reflects the work to be done. The defects are clearly disclosed in written form. Everything seems great. After closing the buyers testify that they were sure that the salesperson "guaranteed the home" and agreed to do whatever it took to make it "right" for them. They indicate that the salesperson said he would "take care of everything". Now they feel that such a statement meant fix the property. They indicate that they were never told about a home warranty!*

**Once the Offer is Accepted.** A continuation of the research begun prior to writing the offer may be necessary to remove contingencies and conditions. Offer to be present for all inspections and assist with scheduling the appointments. Insist on the buyer being present so that the information he receives is firsthand and not misrepresented by subsequent explanations. It is important to monitor impending deadlines for contingencies which must be performed by the buyer or from which the buyer will benefit. Offer to accompany the buyer when applying for a loan or supply the buyer with a list of items that are necessary for the lender's file. Prepare a package for the appraiser to consist of a comparative market analysis, special features of the home and neighborhood statistics if the listing agent does not. Be prepared to meet with the appraiser. Monitor the escrow, title and mortgage processes to ensure a timely closing.

**Closing.** Even the smoothest transaction can fall to pieces in the end. The emotions of both the buyer and seller are the most frayed at this stage. Many facets of the transaction must come together in the final hour. Remind the buyer of the necessity for a cashier's check to close, if applicable in your state. The hazard insurance binder must be in the lender's file. Review the closing documents including the settlement statement for any errors on names, addresses, or prorations. *Don't forget to ask for the referral!*

**Insurance.** Remember, if your buyer is moving in early or letting the seller remain on the property after closing there may not be the proper insurance coverage. The "homeowner's" policy in most states covers the homeowner only. People who move in early or stay after closing are tenants and not covered by the "homeowner's" policy. If you are helping the buyer, remember to make sure that her property is insured. She will remember the service and send you potential buyers as a result.

**The New Owner Has Possession.** And you have been paid! Now the buyer has hopefully become a long term client and a source of constant referrals. It is a good idea to send or deliver a housewarming gift once the buyer has had an opportunity to settle in their new surroundings. Contact after the closing can be maintained by a reminder to re-key the home, place important documents in a safe place, and by supplying a mortgage amortization schedule. Be sure you place them in your client database and stay in contact!

## Checklists

Professional airline pilots who have flown thousands of hours never memorize any of the checklists. They must use a checklist. They are required to read it and check it each time before, during and after each flight. There is a reason. If there is a checklist and it is followed, the chance of failure is greatly reduced. Nothing takes the place of a good checklist outlining the tasks to be performed and the division of labor. Define at every possible juncture what is expected of everyone and most people will either comply with their appointed tasks or alter the checklist. Either way you are happy. A checklist of and for your own actions is a good example of a precise standard method of operation, a good defense, and a superb credibility builder.

A 3 x 5 card, a standard form, a rolodex card, or a computer entry system can be used to track all stages of working with the buyer. Personal attention to detail is the only solution to a smooth closing with no after closing blues. Here is a sample buyer checklist. Make your own. Put it in the work processor and add to it each time you think of an additional item that you need to report or accomplish.

## Buyer Checklist

Date:__________________

Name:________________________________________ RES Phone: ____________

Address:______________________________________ OFF Phone: ____________

____________________________________________________________________

Title Company:________________________________ File No: ________________

Contact:______________________________________ Phone: ________________

Mortgage Company:_____________________________ File No: ________________

Contact:______________________________________ Phone: ________________

**LISTING PROCEDURE**

____1. Mail broker introduction letter
____2. Assemble buyer listing agreement packet
____3. Appointment with the buyer
  a. Motivation _____Hot____Warm____"Lookey-Lou"
  b. Determine agency status
  c. Written buyer listing agreement
  b. Pre-qualify the buyer
  c. Commitment to appoint with a lender
    Items for lender checklist
  d. Determine property parameters
    Price________________________
    Age_________
    Square footage_________
    Bedrooms/Baths_________
    Schools__________________________________
  d. Set appointment to show properties
____4. When listing documents are signed by buyer:
  a. Broker's signature on Listing Agreement
  b. Copy for the buyer with everyone's signature
____5. Mail follow up letter to buyer
____6. Mail selected subject matter letters
____7. Confirm mortgage qualification with lender
____8. Obtain written letter of pre-qualification

**SHOWING PROCEDURE**

____1. Prepare show inventory
  a. Research MLS actives and expireds
  b. Call Realtor® network for new listings
  c. Research newspaper advertisements
  d. Contact FSBO owners
____2. Preview homes without buyer
____3. Select homes that meet the buyer criteria
____4. Set appointments for showing buyer
____5. Showing day:
  Allow adequate time
  Allow with breaks for rest and meals
  Schedule the properties in the correct order for a sale

**WRITING THE OFFER**

____1. Collect all data for price and terms
____2. Review contract and addenda with buyer in detail
____3. Attach lender pre-qualification letter
____4. Attach cover letter explaining and selling the offer

**WHEN THE OFFER IS ACCEPTED**

____1. Original of contract to file
____2. Original of contract to title company
____3. Prepare and deliver escrow instructions
____4. Prepare letter designating tasks to be completed
  a. Mail to buyer
  b. Mail to seller (via other broker)
____5. Prepare performance deadlines sheet
____6. Begin to assemble appraisal package for appraiser
____7. Designate and start to mail letters that will flow through the pre-closing period
____9. Mail lender selection letter
____10. Schedule inspection appointments
____11. Accompany buyer to inspections

**WHEN LOAN IS APPROVED**

____1. Mail loan confirmation letter
____2. Confirm loan status with lender and title company
____3. Make a project checklist to get through closing
____4. Verify that inspection report was received
____5. Congratulatory letter for inspection (offer home warranty)

**WHEN TRANSACTION CLOSES and RECORDS**

____1. Purge office file, prepare MLS sold change form
____2. Give office file to accountant
____3. Complete 4x5 index card for client database
____4. Input into personal farm database
____5. Send note and gift to client
____6. Send follow up letters to all parties
____7. Ask for referral to new client!
____8. Deposit your check

## Loan Application Checklist

1. Relocation paperwork
    a. Military
        i. Orders
        ii. Current leave and earnings statement
    b. Corporate relocation package
    c. Home guarantee information for relocation buyer
2. Check book for appraisal and credit report
3. Work address and telephone number
4. Deposit verification information for each account
    Bank name
    Bank address
    Bank phone number
    Account number
    Latest bank statement
5. Credit card and loan information
    Creditor name
    Creditor address
    Creditor account number
    Nature of debt
    Balance
    Payment schedule
6. Addresses for last three years
7. Tax returns for past two years (be ready to sign them)
8. Personal financial statement or list of major assets and values
    Cars, Boats, Trucks, Vacation homes, etc
9. VA loans -- Certificate of Eligibility
10. Copy of lease or rental agreement
11. Copy of sale contract on existing property
12. Copy of closing statement and deed for previous houses that still have you on the loan
13. Identification showing social security number

## The Use of Professionals

**Delegation.** There is no need to be all things to all people. If there is someone else who can preform the required task, their services need to be recommended and encouraged. Should the buyer be reluctant, a cover letter is an appropriate way to indicate the importance of your suggestion. You may say, "You realize that I have got to give you a letter indicating that I thought you should seek an independent appraisal or a structural inspection prior to signing the contract." By this time they are ready for that statement. Follow it up with a letter.

**The Referral.** The salesperson exposes herself to great danger with the consistent recommendation of a friend or associate. You will not only look bad if there is ever a problem, but you may have placed yourself in a lose-lose position. If you are going to recommend the services of a professional, mentioning that other clients have seemed satisfied or have told you that they were pleased with the service might be a tactful way to indicate that one person is in fact better than the other. Offer a list of at least three separate individuals compiled from your known resources, the yellow pages, a circular put out by the certificating organization, or a professional publication.

Referrals are a good way to lose a customer and rarely make any money. Agents live with a referral long after the transaction is closed and the money spent.

**Complexity.** The status of the modern real estate transaction today simply does not lend itself to the general broker who is an expert in everything. The buyer will buy without your having to obligate yourself. Let the buyer decide on the expert and employ the expert personally. Do not arrange for, or contract for, the expert.

**Opinions.** Too often salespersons give title insurance opinions by saying something like, "Sure the title is OK. Those are just standard exceptions." You might hear a new agent or an agent helping a good friend say, "This is the best loan available," or "Tom Richmond at Richmond Mortgage is the best; whatever he says is what you should do," feeling compelled to have an opinion or the need to "keep the deal together."

Inflation is never as much as anyone wants when he is thinking of selling and always too high when he is thinking of buying. Neither you nor a buyer can simply sell a mistake. The parties are going to rely on your statements. Should your statements prove to be in error, you will be responsible and so will the broker. The use of standard letters can help clear the air and explain in specific detail the duties you have and have not assumed. This will help to limit the liability of everyone including your broker. Stay out of the glib opinion business and just offer responsible service.

## Letter - Buyer's Use of Professionals

Mr. and Mrs. Jonathan A. Goodman
Apartment 610 A
12th and Main Street
Denver, CO 80303

Re: 909 First Street

Dear Mr. and Mrs. Goodman:

As you know, our firm is comprised of professional real estate people whose job it is to assist sellers and buyers with their real estate needs. I will be happy to help you locate a house that you feel not only suits your needs but which also fits your budget.

Once that is done, we encourage the selection and use of the services of other professionals to satisfy the requirements indicated in the contract. Your satisfaction is important, and you will certainly want to avail yourself of the assurances you desire. We are not in the lending, title insurance, termite inspection, structural inspection, radon testing or home warranty businesses; nor are we in the business of providing legal or accounting services. Being real estate agents is a full time job in itself.

Although we all have received recommendations from previous clients and customers regarding their selections and favorites and have a list of our own friends, we cannot recommend any one firm or person whom we think will fill your needs. That selection is a personal one, left up to you. To provide you with a place to start however, I will provide you with a list of people who have been utilized by other buyers in the past or who have done work for us. Of course I can not accept responsibility for the work product of any of these firms or individuals. The decision to utilize one or more of the firms or individuals on the list is your personal decision.

I hope the list will be helpful in making your choice. If I can be of any further assistance, please do not hesitate to let me know. But first, we have to find the right house.

Sincerely,
The Orcas Island Company

by: Katherine E. Reece
Realtor®, CRS, GRI

**Letter - Buyer--Professionals--Older Home**

Mr. and Mrs. Jonathan A. Goodman
Apartment 610 A
12th and Main Street
Denver, CO 80303

Re: 909 First Street

Dear Jon and Mimi:

Congratulations on your decision to make an offer to purchase this particular property. I am pleased that you were able to locate an older home you feel is affordable and that you think you will enjoy. As you know, with all older homes, there are a number of areas that may require special attention. We recommend that in addition to obtaining the normal radon gas, septic system and water quality tests you requested, you also consult a structural engineer and a termite inspector. These are terms you included in the contract, and you will need to get started as soon as possible after the offer is accepted since there is often a delay between the time a test is requested and the time the results are obtained.

I want to try to stay within the dates outlined in your contract so that there is no chance that you will lose the property. In addition, your prompt attention will allow us to indicate to our sellers the status of the contract so that they can make decisions on other proposals, which they may elect to accept as alternative contracts if and when they arrive.

The contract indicates that you must give written notice of any dissatisfaction directly to the seller, with a copy delivered to the seller's agent prior to noon on Wednesday the 12th or the condition, requiring a satisfactory inspection, will be deemed to have been satisfied. You need to retain an inspector as soon as possible to allow for enough time to complete the inspection. I am ready to help you.

Our firm is comprised of professional real estate people who are familiar with properties in this area. Please know that we are not soil engineers nor structural engineers. Therefore, we cannot be responsible for the physical condition of the property nor the soil it rests upon. The services of other professionals are required to satisfy these questions in your mind as well as the other requirements indicated in the contract and to provide you with the assurances you desire. Transactions today are complex and require the talents of lending institutions, title insurance companies, termite inspectors, radon testers, and sometimes home warranty underwriters, not to mention the services of a lawyer or accountant.

We encourage you to seek and select the counsel of the experts of your choice in order to ensure that you are satisfied with all of the complex aspects of the purchase of your new home. Please understand that we can not accept responsibility for the work product of any of these firms or individuals. I too must rely on professionals when I acquire real property because the talents they possess are just not within my area of expertise. If I can be of any further assistance please do not hesitate to let me know.

Sincerely,
The Orcas Island Company

by: Katherine E. Reece
Realtor®, CRS, GRI

## Agency Selection Alternatives

**Company Agency Policy.** Each company must have a company agency policy. This document should set forth the position statement for the *entire* company. We feel that it should be a document that can be delivered to a prospective buyer or seller to inform them about all aspects of the company agency selections. While it will not suffice for agency disclosure, it will ensure that all members of the public are getting the same information.

**Entire Company.** Salespeople are agents of the broker, period. They are treated as an entity--one company. All listings are with the broker. The first step is to get the entire company together and solicit their understanding about how they currently do business. If you can formulate a policy that incorporates as much of the current practice as possible, it will make the transition easier. *Everyone must follow the same policy. There can be no exceptions.*

After receiving input, the managers should meet away from the office distractions and agree on the policy that they will follow. Try out various scenarios and determine if the policy truly covers all aspects of your market. Do not be overly influenced by the actions of other offices. Everyone must have a policy that works for their office.

**Company Form.** If you are looking for a good place to implement company forms, we can think of no better area than agency. Develop a set of company agency forms. Have them printed and require compliance.

**Training.** At each sales meeting have a new set of salespeople do some role playing as buyers, sellers and salespeople. Do not be critical. Emphasize the strong points. Encourage participation right down to the words to be said to the buyer. Do not interrupt. As the broker, you must let the salespeople try, fail and try again. Remember, if it is not in the meeting, the role playing will be real life. Once said in public, the script can not be rewritten. Your salespeople will ask you how to do each presentation so be ready with the proper answers. You can role play with them. If they do not know a system, they will quickly emulate yours. Make sure that you know the options cold.

**Subagents.** The listing office, *the entire office, broker and salespeople*, is an entity working as an agent of the seller. The selling office, *the entire office, broker and salespeople*, as an entity, acts as the agent of the listing office thus becoming the subagent of the seller. Subagents owe their duties of fidelity, loyalty, confidentiality, etc., to the listing office and the seller.

The salesperson who is selling the real estate is often incorrectly referred to as a subagent. While commonly accepted, the fact is that this selling salesperson is actually an agent of his/her broker and that broker, and all the salespeople in that Broker's office as a unit, are the subagents of the seller. Subagency was invented in the late 60's and is not part of the body of law often referred to as the "common law." If it seems a little awkward, it is.

Subagents are on the seller's "side" and not the side of the buyer. Subagents must disclose this fact clearly to all buyers. This disclosure has never been done by a majority of the real estate salespeople. It was very difficult to accomplish. It is hard for the authors and many judges and jurors to imagine a buyer who, after being told "*everything that you tell me, I will promptly tell the seller*" would be anxious to utilize a subagent. The conclusion is that a reasonable person would not make that election; therefore, the disclosure was not made or was made improperly.

Katherine E. Reece comes from Hawaii which has not required subagency for over a decade. The buyer has a buyer's agent and the seller has a seller's agent. Oliver E. Frascona comes from Colorado where subagency has also ceased to exist. Sellers have agents and buyers have agents. Should a member of the public not want an agent, the real estate broker and salesperson can act as a real estate broker and salesperson and not as agents. Yes, there are duties for these "transaction brokers" which are similar to those that were owed to a customer in olden days. These duties are similar to agency duties in many respects.

Some states still cling to the concept of subagency. Large offices nationwide can no longer tolcrate the potential liability for the acts of other offices and have abandoned subagency. Eventually, the concept will not exist. Few salespeople actually tell the buyer "*whatever you tell me, throughout this entire transaction, I will tell the seller.*" Few tell their seller, now turned buyer, looking for a new home, "*I used to be your agent but now I am an agent for sellers that I do not know. I will be telling them all that I know about you*". The buying public wants someone who is at least not on the seller's team. *The courts are having a field day with brokers who are failing to inform the customer of the nature of the relationship that exists between buyer and broker.*

**Exclusive Buyer Agents.** There are entire offices that do not take listings. They only represent buyers. If you were listing a property, would you want your broker to contact these offices and see if they had a buyer for your home? The fact that these offices do not take listings suggests that this form of business is not for everyone. Exclusive buyer agency does have its place in the market. These offices will always be able to indicate that they have no conflict of interest because they never act as "dual agents".

**Buyer Agency Option.** These are offices that offer the option of buyer agency if the buyer so desires. They recognize that the buyer may want representation, or at least be able to have a salesperson that is neutral. They have decided that their salespeople can represent either the buyer or the seller and sometimes both under some circumstances, with the proper advance written disclosure.

**Buyer Agency Optional or Mandatory.** There are some people you "should" represent, some you "must" represent, some you "might" represent and some you will "wish you had" represented. The following people should have a buyer agent (think about it):

> **You are the Buyer.** When you are buying a property for your own account, are you your own agent? No, you *are* the buyer. Hopefully, you are not buying one of your company's listings. Although you are the principal, many people will refer to you and regard you as a buyer's agent. Transaction Broker will not work here either. You are the buyer. Of course, you could never be a subagent of the seller.
>
> **Relatives Near and Far.** Parents, brothers and sisters, brothers-in-law, uncles, aunts, children and spouses. These are all people with whom you enjoy a special blood relationship. Transaction Broker does not apply here. No, you are on the buyer's team here whether you like it or not. You are not a subagent of the seller, period.
>
> **Buddies and Business Associates.** The person with whom you play golf each Saturday, the pastor of your church, the banker that knows all your financial dealings and you hers, the roommate from college and the partner at work or the other owner in the boat. These are people that are close to you. You should probably be a buyer agent. Yes, these could be transaction broker relationships. You would not be an agent of the seller and would not represent the buyer either. You could just sell them some real estate. Yes, you would keep the personal secrets of both sides to yourself. Just talk real estate, not people.
>
> **Sellers Ready to Buy.** If you do not think that you are "their" Realtor®, ask them. They consider you as their real estate person. That was the plan, remember?
>
> **Relocation Referrals.** These companies have made it very clear that they want their buyers to have agency representation. Maybe you could convince them that you would be neutral. Seller subagency is just not what they want.

**Non Agency Options.** A growing number of areas are trying to offer the buyer another option. Some call it transaction broker, facilitator, or just real estate broker. Regardless of the title, it is a system to provide professional services to the buying public without forcing them to accept the seller's subagent or employ their own agent. Suppose the buyer does not want you to act for the seller and is unwilling to have you as a buyer agent. Why do you think the buyer would do that? Buyers are vicariously liable in many states for the actions of their agent. That is a basic agency principle.

You will note that all of the functions indicated above apply to anyone "working with" the buyer regardless of the existence or lack of an agency relationship. We will address the differences.

As with any relationship, the salesperson has several duties that relate to the transaction. The buyer now has someone who is interested in creating a win/win transaction. The salesperson provides all the information necessary to her client to make informed decisions on each aspect of the sale. The key here is to provide information but leave the final decision to the buyer. The salesperson must be willing to investigate all resources to include the building department, tax office, any pertinent public records, and local schools in the area to gain information on the material facts of the property. A comprehensive evaluation of the comparable listings and sales in the neighborhood should be supplied to the buyer so that he can determine the price he wishes to offer. The salesperson should have the technical expertise to prepare the applicable documentation for securing the purchase. A good salesperson not only gets the offer accepted, but is able to see the transaction through to closing. The salesperson must keep the identity or other personal information of the buyer confidential. Finally, the broker must be competent in accounting for all funds.

**"In-Company" and "Out of Company" Sales.** With buyer agency comes the need to address the "In-Company" or "In-House" Sale, the sale of a company listing, and the "Out of Company" or "Cooperative" Sale rules. These are two very different relationships. The public does not want to be bothered; yet they have expectations that need to be addressed. The buyer must know the difference between buying one of your listings and buying a property listed with another firm.

**Fees.** The salesperson and the buyer must know what the agreements are regarding the fee that the salesperson expects to be paid for his/her services. This is an uncomfortable situation. We have included some forms that will help. *There is no substitute for a written contract with the buyer.* None. The salesperson and broker need to know that they will be paid for their efforts.

**Cooperative Commission.** *Real Estate is a team sport.* The days of differentiating between what a listing broker pays subagents, buyer agents, transaction brokers, real estate brokers and confused salespeople are over. Cooperative commission is exactly that. It is a commission for the cooperating real estate office. Do not let agency get in the way. Everyone will be a buyer agent or a seller agent at some point in time. Cooperate with each other so that you will always get paid when you are on the other side. Some Multiple Listing Services have made the jump to the future and eliminated any indication of agency in their services. They have also eliminated subagents. They refer to the selling office as the selling office or the cooperating office. The commission that is offered and paid is for the cooperating office, period.

**MLS Cooperation Provision.** *The use or placement of listings in the Multiple Listing Service shall not create any agency relationship between offices. Any agency* *relationship between offices shall be established outside of the Multiple Listing Service. Listing offices, in order to place a listing in the Magic Multiple Listing Service, shall offer the selling office a cooperating fee.*

MLS services that have opted to operate without references to agency have just one box for the compensation to be paid to the cooperating broker. Think about it. It is good for the seller and good for the salespeople. Everyone knows that if they procure the buyer, they can get the cooperative commission when the property closes. Careful, it is simple.

Imagine a system where there were no agency distinctions in the MLS. Think how easy it would be to list a buyer and say, *"If the property is in the MLS, I will be paid through the listing broker. It is only when we find a FSBO that you need to realize that you may have to pay me for my work."*

**Alternative Definition.** Start by defining the alternatives, if there are any, and the expectations of the buyer who is a customer or client. Do this prior to any services being rendered so that everyone will have the same expectations of the extent of the services that are to be administered. That way everyone will know when the agent has met those standards. Four objectives are at hand:

First, explain in advance either the extent of the options that are available or, in the event there are no options, the extent of the relationship between the buyer as a customer and the broker, salesperson, other agents and sellers. This must be done early, before the buyer starts to think of the agent as "my real estate person."

Second, if there are options available that include other relationships beyond the traditional seller subagency, explain the different types and the compensation alternatives, if any, which are intrinsic to each form offered by the company. This is in addition to any state-required or approved forms. The requirement imposed by the state to use their form is not necessarily for broker protection nor is it as extensive a document as a cautious buyer's broker would require, but it does serve the state's purpose of informing the buyer of the relationship in some detail.

Third, and most important to the broker and salesperson, limit the apparent authority of the agent.

Fourth, describe the services that will be provided. Care needs to be taken here to describe not only what you will do, the extent of the service, but also those things for which you will not be responsible.

Finally, sign up the buyer on a written buyer agency contract and go sell them a house.

Various forms follow. They include cooperative compensation verification forms, forms that reject subagency and Buyer Agency Agreements. Each is a little different. Read them carefully. Select the one that best suits your needs.

## Rejection of Subagency

Specific Properties

I, the undersigned, as the authorized agent for the indicated broker, hereby reject the offer of subagency made through the Multiple Listing Service with regard to the following listed properties:

621 Pine Street
75 Manhattan Drive
420 Ponderosa Drive

From this point forward I will be acting as the agent for a buyer and will not be acting as the agent or subagent of either the seller or your firm.

It is our understanding that:

____ I will be compensated by my client without contribution from either you or the seller.

____ You will compensate me by paying me the sum of ___% of the final selling price, immediately upon the closing of any transaction involving one of my clients (buyers) purchasing any or all of the above properties.

____ You will guarantee the payment by your seller of an amount equal to ____% of the listing price on the date of this communication, regardless of the ultimate selling price, payable upon the closing of any transaction wherein one of my buyers purchases any or all of the above properties.

Based on our understanding I am proceeding to show the indicated properties to my clients. If you feel that this does not accurately reflect our agreement, please call my office immediately and send me a formal rejection. Otherwise please sign below and return this form to my office. I look forward to finding the buyer for one or all of the indicated properties and completing a sale.

Most sincerely,
The Orcas Island Company

by: Oliver E. Frascona, Broker

Please indicate your acceptance of the terms herein by signing below:

Approved: Date:

______________________________ ____________________

Listing Broker or Salesperson

## Rejection of Subagency

Specific Properties

I, the undersigned, as the authorized agent for the indicated broker, hereby reject the offer of subagency made through the Multiple Listing Service with regard to the following listed properties:

621 Pine Street
75 Manhattan Drive
420 Ponderosa Drive

From this point forward I will be acting as the agent for a buyer and will not be acting as the agent or subagent of either the seller or your firm.

It is our understanding that:

____ I will be compensated by my client without contribution from either you or the seller.

____ You will compensate me by paying me the sum of ___% of the final selling price, immediately upon the closing of any transaction involving one of my clients (buyers) purchasing any or all of the above properties.

Based on our understanding I am proceeding to show the indicated properties to my clients. If you feel that this does not accurately reflect our agreement, please call my office immediately and send me a formal rejection.

It is hard to imagine that the seller does not want you to cooperate with me. My client has instructed me to show them the indicated properties in any case. Contracts for these properties will include a clause indicating that the seller will pay our commission. You can explain why you feel the transaction should bear your entire commission and mine also.

Most sincerely,
The Orcas Island Company

by: Oliver E. Frascona, Broker

Please indicate your acceptance of the terms herein by signing below:

Approved: Date:

_________________________________ ___________________

Listing Broker or Salesperson

## Blanket Rejection of Subagency

I, the undersigned, as the authorized agent for the indicated broker, hereby reject the offer of subagency made through the Multiple Listing Service with regard to any property listed by your firm.

From this point forward I will be acting as the agent for a buyer and will not be acting as the agent or subagent of either the seller or your firm.

It is our understanding that:

> ____ I will be compensated separately by my client without contribution from either you or the seller.
>
> ____ You will compensate me by paying me the sum of ___% of the final selling price, immediately upon the closing of any transaction involving one of my clients (buyers) purchasing any property you have listed.
>
> ____ You will compensate me by paying me the percentage of the final selling price indicated in the MLS system for subagents, immediately upon the closing of any transaction involving one of my clients (buyers) purchasing any property you have listed.
>
> ____ You will guarantee the payment by your seller of an amount equal to ____% of the listing price on the date of this communication, regardless of the ultimate selling price, payable upon the closing of any transaction wherein one of my buyers purchases any property you have listed.

Based on our understanding I am proceeding to show your listings.

Most sincerely,
The Orcas Island Company

by: Oliver E. Frascona, Broker

Please indicate your acceptance of the terms herein by signing below:

Approved: Date:

______________________________ ________________

Listing Broker or Salesperson

## Rejection of Subagency

Transaction or Real Estate Broker

I, the undersigned, as the authorized agent for the indicated broker, hereby reject the offer of subagency made through the Multiple Listing Service with regard to the following listed properties:

621 Pine Street
75 Manhattan Drive
420 Ponderosa Drive

From this point forward I will be acting as licensed real estate salesperson acting on behalf of my broker who is also licensed in this state. We will be assisting the buyer with his real estate needs.

It is our understanding that:

____ The broker of my office will be compensated by the buyer directly without contribution from either you or the seller.

____ Your firm will compensate my broker by paying this firm the sum of ___% of the final selling price, immediately upon the closing of any transaction involving one of the buyers with whom we are working purchasing any or all of the above properties.

Based on our understanding, I am proceeding to show the indicated properties to buyers we are working with. If you feel that this does not accurately reflect our agreement, please call my office immediately and send me a formal rejection. Otherwise please sign below and return this form to my office. I look forward to finding the buyer for one or all of the indicated properties and completing a sale.

Most sincerely,
The Orcas Island Company

by: Oliver E. Frascona, Broker

Please indicate your acceptance of the terms herein by signing below:

Approved: Date:

________________________________ ____________________

Listing Broker or Salesperson

## Agency and Compensation Card/Fax

### *Agency and Compensation Card--FAX*

Date of telephone agreement:______/______/______

Property Address:________________________________________________

**Listing Office:**________________________________________________

Salesperson:______________________________

**Selling Office:**________________________________________________

Salesperson:______________________________ Phone:____________

**Selling Office is, for the sale of this property, acting as:**

☐Agents of the Purchaser ☐Subagents of the Seller
☐Transaction (Real Estate) Brokers ☐Other:____________________

This confirms our agency and compensation agreement. The Listing Office and Selling Office agree that the Listing Office shall pay to the Selling Office, as a result of the sale (closing) of this property to a successful purchaser procured by Selling Office, upon closing,

☐ as the Selling Office's sole compensation, or
☐ in addition to any compensation paid by the purchaser to the Selling Office,

☐______% of the final sales price ☐fixed fee of $__________.____

☐Other:____________________

Approved:
Listing Office Selling Office

by :________________________ by :________________________

**Thank you for your assistance**

Please fax your agreement.

**Letter - *Just for Fun* -- Buyer's Broker Rejecting Subagency**

Mr. Larry Listing Broker
Seller's Realty and Insurance
23 West Coop Lane
Commission City, WA 80000

Re: No. 7 Benthaven Way

Dear Larry:

Thank you for taking the time to talk with me today about the above referenced property. As I indicated to you, I am rejecting your kind offer of subagency with regard to this property. In this particular instance I am operating as a buyer's broker and do not want to have any fiduciary duty to either you or the seller.

I was initially rather confused when you indicated that your seller was not interested in my showing the property if they could not be liable for me as a subagent. Now that the liability issue is cleared up, and we both realize that one benefit of buyer agency is that the seller, your client, and you are not responsible for me, I feel more confident that we can work together. Some listing offices have indicated that we were not to show the seller's property. I suppose they were afraid that we might sell it. That would certainly not please the seller. Maybe they felt that if the buyer had representation the sides would be too equal.

I am happy that you did not take such an announcement too seriously and were still able to confide in me the secrets that the seller had confided in you. The indication that the seller would take a lesser price will be very advantageous in my representation of the purchaser and will probably expedite a fast sale. I appreciate your comment that the sellers are moving out of the area due to a company transfer. That coupled with your statement that they have only a month until the company guarantee kicks in should give us time to take advantage of them.

Thank you for arranging the showing for tomorrow. I will expect a constant flow of confidential information. It is always a pleasure to work with you in a real estate transaction.

Most sincerely,
The Orcas Island Company

by: Oliver E. Frascona, Broker

## Letter - Fair Housing

Mr. Bill Buyer and
Mrs. Betty Buyer
Apartment 610 A
12th and Main Street
Tenant City, CO 00001

Re: Fair Housing

Dear Mr. and Mrs. Buyer:

Let me be the first to welcome you to Ownersville, Colorado, and to our office. We have a small cadre of professional agents and support staff who have been doing business at this location for fourteen months. Satisfied clients and customers are our primary concern.

Real estate is the American Dream. My company wants to make sure that all buyers know that they have equal access to all the real estate in our market area. We are anxious to show you property that suits your needs.

We are proud to adhere to the Department of Housing and Urban Development's Fair Housing Standards. We want you to realize that you are free to, and in fact we encourage you to, make an offer on any house that you select. The only factors limiting your selection are: the amount of money you have available to spend for a down payment, the amount that you can or will borrow, and the size of the monthly payments that you desire.

Neighborhood mix or makeup are impossible for us to determine. Please do not ask us to try to give you an estimate of the makeup of any neighborhood. We simply can not do that, even if knew. Things are changing so fast in today's market that it is impossible for us to know the make-up of any neighborhood. This is a totally open market with equal access to everyone. I am sure that you will be able to select a home that meets your needs from a wide variety of available homes either listed with our firm or through the Multiple Listing Service.

We are happy to show you and your family as many homes as you desire in any part of the city and surrounding county. We will provide you with the information at our disposal to aid you in determining the right new home for you to acquire. The different available locations vary from the urban-city-center to the rural county locations. Only you can decide which home is located in the area you desire, is best suited to your physical needs, and meets the financial requirements you determine are within your budget.

If you are ever unable to reach me or just want to talk to the broker for this company, please feel free to contact Oliver E. Frascona either in the office, (303) 494-3000, or at his home, (303) 494-6661. Oliver is a well-respected broker and I am proud to work for him. I am sure that he and I will be able to assist you in your selection of a new home in this area.

Thank you for selecting me to assist you with your real estate needs. Searching for the housing is fun. Helping people find housing is like a treasure hunt. Let's get started.

Sincerely,
The Orcas Island Company

by: Katherine E. Reece
Realtor®, CRS, GRI

**Letter - Rules of the Road for the Buyer - Subagency**

Mr. Bill Buyer and
Mrs. Betty Buyer
Apartment 610 A
12th and Main Street
Tenant City, CO 00001

Re: Buyer Agency Services for Purchasers

Dear Mr. and Mrs. Buyer:

Let me be the first to welcome you to Ownersville, Colorado, and to our office. We have a small cadre of professional agents and support staff who have been doing business at this location for fourteen months. Satisfied clients and customers are our primary concern.

Each state has its own set of laws, rules, and regulations concerning real estate in general, and real estate salespersons, brokers, lenders, title companies and other real estate affiliates specifically. I sometimes wonder how so many different systems could evolve.

In this state, the state licenses a broker for each office, and all contracts or agreements that bind the company must be signed by the broker to be effective. Salespeople are licensed under the broker and act as agents of the broker. I am happy to work for Oliver E. Frascona, the licensed broker for The Orcas Island Company

It is important to us that you understand all the aspects of a potential real estate transaction. In addition to the state mandated disclosure forms we want to address the agency issue first.

Our company acts as agents for, and represents, many owners who have listed their properties with us for sale. In addition, as members of the Multiple Listing Service, we have access to and can show you literally hundreds of additional properties encompassing all the properties listed by other member brokers.

As one of the licensed agents here, I work hard to assist buyers with their real estate needs, and I am sure that I will be able to provide you with the information you request concerning almost all of the aspects of the local real estate market, including sources of available financing, so that you will be able to make an informed selection of a new home. Regardless of which real estate company has listed the home you select, we will always disclose to you all that we know about the physical condition of the property and its proximity to schools, shopping, transportation. In addition, we will promptly inform you regarding proximity to any potential hazards such as high tension lines, nuclear weapons plants, waste disposal sites and land fills.

We are proud to adhere to the Department of Housing and Urban Development's Fair Housing Standards. We want you to realize that you are free to, and in fact we encourage you to, make an offer on any house that you select. The only factors limiting your selection are: the amount of money you have available to spend for a down payment, the amount that you can or will borrow, and the size of the monthly payments that you desire.

Neighborhood mix or makeup are impossible for us to determine. This is a totally open market with equal access to everyone. I am sure that you will be able to select a home that meets your needs from a wide variety of available homes either listed with our firm or through the Multiple Listing Service.

We are happy to show you and your family as many homes as you desire in any part of the city and surrounding county. We will provide you with the information at our disposal to aid you in determining the right new home for you to acquire. The different available locations vary from the urban-city-center to the rural country locations. Only you can decide which home is located in the area you desire, is best suited to your physical needs, and meets the financial requirements you determine are within your budget.

In this state, there are a few different options available to buyers for the acquisition of our services. It is our company policy to act as sellers' agents or subagents on all property that we show you. That means that we work for the seller all the time on properties that we have listed and on properties listed with other brokers. We never work as your agents. You need to be aware that we must tell the seller everything that we learn from or about you. This applies even if you ask that we keep information confidential.

If you are ever unable to reach me or just want to talk to the broker for this company, please feel free to contact Oliver E. Frascona either in the office, (303) 494-3000, or at his home, (303) 494-6661. Oliver is a well-respected broker and I am proud to work for him. I am sure that he and I will be able to assist you in your selection of a new home in this area.

Sincerely,
The Orcas Island Company

by: Katherine E. Reece
Realtor®, CRS, GRI

**Letter - Rules of the Road for the Buyer - Exclusive Buyer Agency**

Mr. Bill Buyer and
Mrs. Betty Buyer
Apartment 610 A
12th and Main Street
Tenant City, CO 00001

Re: Buyer Agency Services for Purchasers

Dear Mr. and Mrs. Buyer:

Let me be the first to welcome you to Ownersville, Colorado, and to our office. We have a small cadre of professional agents and support staff who have been doing business at this location for fourteen months. Satisfied clients and customers are our primary concern.

Each state has its own set of laws, rules, and regulations concerning real estate in general, and real estate salespersons, brokers, lenders, title companies and other real estate affiliates specifically. I sometimes wonder how so many different systems could evolve.

In this state, the state licenses a broker for each office, and all contracts or agreements that bind the company must be signed by the broker to be effective. Salespeople are licensed under the broker and act as agents of the broker. I am happy to work for Oliver E. Frascona, the licensed broker for The Orcas Island Company

It is important to us that you understand all the aspects of a potential real estate transaction. In addition to the state mandated disclosure forms we want to address the agency issue first.

Our company does not act as agents for, nor represent, any homeowners who have their properties for sale. We do not take listings. We will never have a conflict of interest between a seller and buyer. We are members of the Multiple Listing Service. We have access to and can show you literally hundreds of properties encompassing all the properties listed by other member brokers. Since listing agents are looking for buyers, they are generally glad to know that we have a qualified buyer as a client who wants to see the home that they have for sale.

As one of the licensed agents here, I work hard to assist buyers with their real estate needs. I am sure that I will be able to provide you with the information you request concerning almost all of the aspects of the local real estate market, including sources of available financing, so that you will be able to make an informed selection of a new home. Regardless of which real estate company has listed the home you select, we will always disclose to you all that we know about the physical condition of the property and its proximity to schools, shopping, transportation. In addition, we will promptly inform you regarding proximity to any potential hazards such as high tension lines, nuclear weapons plants, waste disposal sites and land fills.

We are proud to adhere to the Department of Housing and Urban Development's Fair Housing Standards. We want you to realize that you are free to, and in fact we encourage you to, make an offer on any house that you select. The only factors limiting your selection are: the amount of money you have available to spend for a down payment, the amount that you can or will borrow, and the size of the monthly payments that you desire.

Neighborhood mix or makeup are impossible for us to determine. This is a totally open market with equal access to everyone. I am sure that you will be able to select a home that meets your needs from a wide variety of available homes either listed with our firm or through the Multiple Listing Service.

We are happy to show you and your family as many homes as you desire in any part of the city and surrounding county and provide you with the information at our disposal to aid you in determining the right new home for you to acquire. The different available locations vary from the urban-city-center to the rural country locations. Only you can decide which home is located in the area you desire, is best suited to your physical needs, and meets the financial requirements you determine are within your budget.

In this state, there are a few different options available to buyers for the acquisition of our services. It is our company policy to act as exclusive buyers' agents on all property that we show you. We will keep everything we learn about you confidential.

If you are ever unable to reach me or just want to talk to the broker for this company, please feel free to contact Oliver E. Frascona either in the office, (303) 494-3000, or at his home, (303) 494-6661. Oliver is a well-respected broker and I am proud to work for him. I am sure that he and I will be able to assist you in your selection of a new home in this area.

Sincerely,
The Orcas Island Company

by: Katherine E. Reece
Realtor®, CRS, GRI

## Letter - Rules of the Road for the Buyer - Buyer Agency Option

Mr. Bill Buyer and
Mrs. Betty Buyer
Apartment 610 A
12th and Main Street
Tenant City, CO 00001

Re: Buyer Agency Services for Purchasers

Dear Mr. and Mrs. Buyer:

Let me be the first to welcome you to Ownersville, Colorado, and to our office. We have a small cadre of professional agents and support staff who have been doing business at this location for fourteen months. Satisfied clients and customers are our primary concern.

Each state has its own set of laws, rules, and regulations concerning real estate in general, and real estate salespersons, brokers, lenders, title companies and other real estate affiliates specifically. I sometimes wonder how so many different systems could evolve.

In this state, the state licenses a broker for each office, and all contracts or agreements that bind the company must be signed by the broker to be effective. Salespeople are licensed under the broker and act as agents of the broker. I am happy to work for Oliver E. Frascona, the licensed broker for The Orcas Island Company

It is important to us that you understand all the aspects of a potential real estate transaction. In addition to the state mandated disclosure forms we want to address the agency issue first.

Our company acts as agents for, and represents, many owners who have listed their properties with us for sale. In addition, as members of the Multiple Listing Service, we have access to and can show you literally hundreds of additional properties encompassing all the properties listed by other member brokers.

As one of the licensed agents here, I work hard to assist buyers with their real estate needs. I am sure that I will be able to provide you with the information you request concerning almost all of the aspects of the local real estate market, including sources of available financing, so that you will be able to make an informed selection of a new home. Regardless of which real estate company has listed the home you select, we will always disclose to you all that we know about the physical condition of the property and its proximity to schools, shopping, transportation. In addition, we will promptly inform you regarding proximity to any potential hazards such as high tension lines, nuclear weapons plants, waste disposal sites and land fills.

We are proud to adhere to the Department of Housing and Urban Development's Fair Housing Standards. We want you to realize that you are free to, and in fact we encourage you to, make an offer on any house that you select. The only factors limiting your selection are: the amount of money you have available to spend for a down payment, the amount that you can or will borrow, and the size of the monthly payments that you desire.

Neighborhood mix or makeup are impossible for us to determine. This is a totally open market with equal access to everyone. I am sure that you will be able to select a home that meets your needs from a wide variety of available homes either listed with our firm or through the Multiple Listing Service.

We are happy to show you and your family as many homes as you desire in any part of the city and surrounding county and provide you with the information at our disposal to aid you in determining the right new home for you to acquire. The different available locations vary from the urban-city-center to the rural country locations. Only you can decide which home is located in the area you desire, is best suited to your physical needs, and meets the financial requirements you determine are within your budget.

In this state, there are a few different options available to buyers for the acquisition of our services. It is our company policy to act as buyers' agents when showing property that is not listed with our office and dual agents for the sale of property that we have listed. A full explanation of our "In-Company" Sale policy is attached. It will become a part of your listing agreement with us. Please review it and ask any questions that you may have.

If you are ever unable to reach me or just want to talk to the designated broker of this company, please feel free to contact Oliver E. Frascona either in the office, (303) 494-3000, or at his home, (303) 494-6661. Oliver is a well-respected broker and I am proud to work for him. I am sure that he and I will be able to assist you in your selection of a new home in this area.

Sincerely,
The Orcas Island Company

by: Katherine E. Reece
Realtor®, CRS, GRI

**Letter - Rules of the Road for the Buyer - Transaction Broker**

Mr. Bill Buyer and
Mrs. Betty Buyer
Apartment 610 A
12th and Main Street
Tenant City, CO 00001

Re: Real Estate Services for Purchasers

Dear Mr. and Mrs. Buyer:

Let me be the first to welcome you to Ownersville, Colorado, and to our office. We have a small cadre of professional agents and support staff who have been doing business at this location for fourteen months. Satisfied clients and customers are our primary concern.

Each state has its own set of laws, rules, and regulations concerning real estate in general, and real estate salespersons, brokers, lenders, title companies and other real estate affiliates specifically. I sometimes wonder how so many different systems could evolve.

In this state, the state licenses a broker for each office, and all contracts or agreements that bind the company must be signed by the broker to be effective. Salespeople are licensed under the broker and act as agents of the broker. I am happy to work for Oliver E. Frascona, the licensed broker for The Orcas Island Company

It is important to us that you understand all the aspects of a potential real estate transaction. In addition to the state mandated disclosure forms we want to address the agency issue first. This is very important to us since we sell a large number of properties that we have listed.

Our company acts as agents for, and represents, many owners who have listed their properties with us for sale. In the event an offer comes from another office we act as the seller's agents. However, when we work with a buyer that wants to buy a property we act as real estate brokers or Transaction Brokers, neutral brokers.

If you are interested in property that we have listed, we will be neutral. We will tell you everything that we know about the property and the surrounding area, but we will not disclose the seller's personal confidential secrets such as how much the seller will accept or his motivation for selling. We keep similar information regarding your interests confidential also. We never tell the seller how fast you need to buy, how much money you have or your motivation to buy. Your personal confidential secrets are safe with us.

In addition, as members of the Multiple Listing Service, we have access to and can show you literally hundreds of additional properties encompassing all the properties listed by other member brokers. When you look at property that is listed with another company we will either be your agent or act in a neutral capacity. We never become subagents of the seller. The decision is up to you. We will tell you everything that we know about the property and the surrounding area. In any event we never tell the seller how fast you need to buy, how much money you have or your motivation to buy. Your personal confidential secrets are safe with us.

As one of the licensed agents here, I work hard to assist buyers with their real estate needs. I am sure that I will be able to provide you with the information you request concerning almost all aspects of the local real estate market, including sources of available financing, so that you will be able to make an informed selection of a new home. We will be happy to provide you with all the information we can obtain regarding proximity to schools, shopping and transportation. In addition, we will promptly inform you regarding proximity to any potential hazards such as high tension lines, nuclear weapons plants, waste disposal sites and land fills.

We are proud to adhere to the Department of Housing and Urban Development's Fair Housing Standards. We want you to realize that you are free to, and in fact we encourage you to, make an offer on any house that you select. The only factors limiting your selection are: the amount of money you have available to spend for a down payment, the amount that you can or will borrow, and the size of the monthly payments that you desire.

Neighborhood mix or makeup are impossible for us to determine. This is a totally open market with equal access to everyone. I am sure that you will be able to select a home that meets your needs from a wide variety of available homes either listed with our firm or through the Multiple Listing Service.

We are happy to show you and your family as many homes as you desire in any part of the city and surrounding county and provide you with the information at our disposal to aid you in determining the right new home for you to acquire. The different available locations vary from the urban-city-center to the rural county locations. Only you can decide which home is located in the area you desire, is best suited to your physical needs, and meets the financial requirements you determine are within your budget.

If you are ever unable to reach me or just want to talk to the designated broker of this company, please feel free to contact Oliver E. Frascona either in the office, (303) 494-3000, or at his home, (303) 494-6661. Oliver is a well-respected broker and I am proud to work for him. I am sure that he and I will be able to assist you in your selection of a new home in this area.

Sincerely,
The Orcas Island Company

by: Katherine E. Reece
Realtor®, CRS, GRI

## Buyer Agency Agreement

_________________,19______

_______________________________________________________________________ ("Buyer")

appoints _________________________________________________________ ("Broker") as Buyer's exclusive agent for the purpose of assisting Buyer in the acquisition of interests in real property ("Property") as indicated in Section 2, under the terms specified herein.

1. **Effect of Exclusive Buyer Agency Agreement.** Buyer shall conduct all negotiations for Property through Broker, and indicate to Broker all properties Buyer is interested in during the time this Agreement is in effect. Buyer agrees that any Broker compensation which is conditioned upon the acquisition by Buyer of Property, whether by lease or purchase (collectively "purchase"), shall be earned by Broker whenever such interests are acquired by Buyer directly or indirectly pursuant to the terms of this Agreement.

2. **Property.** The Property shall substantially meet the following requirements or be otherwise acceptable to Buyer, i.e., Buyer enters into a contract to buy such Property:

3. **Duration of Agency Agreement.** Broker's authority as Buyer's agent shall begin _________________, 19____, and shall continue until the earlier of the transfer of title to the Property to the Buyer or _________________________, 19_____.

4. **Broker's Representations and Services.** Broker shall provide Buyer with information regarding property listed in the Multiple Listing Service ("MLS") and additional property of which the salesperson assisting the Buyer has actual knowledge. Broker shall attempt to procure a prospective seller's acceptance of any offer to purchase a prospective seller's property and to assist in the completion of the transaction.

5. **Costs of Services or Products.** Unless otherwise agreed, in writing, Broker shall not obtain or order products or services, e.g., surveys, soil tests, radon tests, title reports, property inspections. Broker shall not be obligated to advance funds for the Buyer.

6. **Compensation of Broker.** In consideration of the services to be performed by Broker, Buyer shall pay Broker a fee(s), payable upon closing of the transaction(s), subject to the provisions of Section 7, equal to _________% of either the purchase price or the initial listed price on the first contact with the Property by the Buyer, whichever is the lesser price. Broker is hereby instructed to seek the fee, on behalf of the Buyer, in order of priority: from the Listing Broker, if any, from the Seller as Buyer may direct, and from any third parties as Buyer directs. The fee is conditioned upon the purchase of Property or, the purchase by Buyer of Property not in compliance with the requirements specified in Section 2, as may be selected by Buyer. The fee shall apply to Property contracted for during the original term of this Agreement or any extension(s) and shall also apply to Property contracted for within ______days after this Agreement expires or is terminated, if the Property was shown or specifically presented to the Buyer by Broker during the term or any extension(s) of this Agreement. Assignment of Buyer's rights under this Agreement or assignment of Buyer's rights in Property does not operate to defeat Broker's right to the fee.

7. **Failure to Close.** If a seller fails to close through no fault of the Buyer, the fee provided shall be waived. If Buyer is at fault, such fee shall not be waived, but shall be due and payable immediately.

8. **Disclosure of Broker's Role.** At the time of initial contact Broker shall inform all prospective sellers or their agents with whom Broker negotiates pursuant to this Agreement that Broker is acting on behalf of the Buyer.

9. **Disclosures.** Broker ___**does** ___**does not** have Buyer's permission to disclose Buyer's identity to third parties without prior written consent of Buyer. Broker agrees not to disclose information obtained in confidence from Buyer except as authorized in writing by Buyer or as required by law.

10. **Conflicting Interests.** In the event Broker has an ownership interest in any property Buyer selects, said fact shall be immediately disclosed to Buyer. Broker may show any property to other prospective competing buyers. Broker may assist Buyer in the purchase of property listed for sale by a seller with Broker pursuant to the terms of the separate agreement attached hereto.

11. **Fair Housing.** The parties agree not to discriminate against any prospective seller on the basis of the race, creed, color, sex, national origin, familial status, handicap, religion or as may be provided by local, state or federal law or regulation.

12. **Attorneys' Fees.** In case of litigation or arbitration concerning this Agreement, the parties agree that costs and reasonable attorneys' fees shall be awarded to the prevailing party.

13. **Modification.** This Agreement constitutes the entire agreement between the parties and any prior agreements, whether oral or written, have been merged and integrated into this Agreement. No modification of any of the terms of this Agreement shall be valid, binding upon the parties, or enforceable unless in writing and signed by the parties.

14. **Counterparts and Copies.** If more than one person is named as a Buyer herein, this Agreement may be executed by each Buyer, individually, and when so executed, such copies taken together shall be deemed to be a full and complete Agreement between the parties. Buyer acknowledges receipt of a copy of this Agreement signed by the Broker.

15. **Additional Provisions.**

| Buyer | date | Buyer | date |
|---|---|---|---|

Broker:

by date

## Buyer Agency Listing Agreement

(Exclusive Right)

_______________________, 19_____

_________________________________________________________("Buyer")

appoints_________________________________________________("Broker") as Buyer's exclusive agent for the purpose of assisting Buyer to acquire interests in real property as indicated in Section 2 ("Property") and under the terms specified herein.

1. **Effect of Exclusive Buyer Agency Agreement.** By appointing Broker as Buyer's exclusive agent, Buyer agrees to conduct all negotiations for Property through Broker, and indicate to Broker all properties Buyer is interested in during the time this Agreement is in effect. Buyer agrees that any Broker compensation which is conditioned upon the acquisition by Buyer of interests in real property, whether by lease or purchase (collectively "purchase"), will be earned by Broker whenever such interests are acquired by Buyer directly or indirectly, pursuant to the terms of this Agreement, without any discount or allowance for any efforts made by Buyer or by any other person in connection with the acquisition of such interests by Buyer.

2. **Property.** The Property shall substantially meet the following requirements, or be otherwise acceptable to Buyer:

3. **Duration of Agency.** Broker's authority as Buyer's exclusive agent shall begin ___________________________, 19____, and shall continue until the earlier of ___________________________, 19_____, or completion of the acquisition of the Property.

4. **Broker's Representations and Services.** Broker will use reasonable efforts to locate desired Property, to procure acceptance of any offer to purchase Property and to assist in the completion of the transaction. Broker may from time to time make submissions to Buyer describing and identifying properties appearing to Broker to substantially meet the criteria set forth in Section 2.

5. **Costs of Services or Products Obtained from Outside Sources.** Broker will not obtain or order products or services from outside sources unless Buyer has agreed in writing to pay for them when payment is due. (Examples: surveys, soil tests, radon tests, title reports, property inspections.) Broker shall not be obligated to advance funds for the Buyer.

6. **Compensation of Broker.** In consideration of the services to be performed by Broker, Buyer shall pay Broker as follows:

   (a) **Maximum Fee.** The total fees payable under subsections (b), (c) and (d) below shall not exceed the greater of $____________or _______% of the purchase price of the Property.

   (b) **Success Fee.** Broker shall be paid a fee equal to the greater of $_____________ or, _______% of either the purchase price or the initial listed price on the first contact with the Property by the Buyer, whichever is the lesser price. The success fee is conditioned upon the purchase of the Property or the acquisition by Buyer of Property not in compliance with the requirements specified in Section 2 but within the purview of this Agreement. This fee is payable upon closing of the transaction(s), subject to the provisions of Section 7. This fee shall apply to Property contracted for during the original term of this Agreement or any extension(s) and shall also apply to Property contracted for within _____days after this Agreement expires or is terminated if the Property was shown or presented to Buyer by Broker during the original term or any extension(s) of the term of this Agreement. Buyer is obligated to pay Broker's fee. However, Broker is authorized and instructed to request payment of Broker's fee by any of the following indicated methods:
   ☐ BY SELLER (Buyer inserts a clause in purchase agreement).
   ☐ BY LISTING BROKER
   ☐ OTHER:_______________________________________________

   (c) **Hourly Fee.** Buyer shall pay Broker at the rate of $____________ per hour for time spent by Broker pursuant to this Agreement, to be paid to Broker when billed to Buyer.

   (d) **Retainer Fee.** Buyer shall pay Broker a non-refundable retainer fee of $_______________ due and payable upon signing of this Agreement. This amount ☐**shall** ☐**shall not** be credited against the maximum fee.

   (e) **Other.** _______________________________________________

7. **Failure to Close.** If a seller fails to close with no fault on the part of Buyer, the success fee provided in Section 6(b) shall be waived. If Buyer is at fault, such success fee will not be waived, but will be due and payable immediately.

8. **Disclosure of Broker's Role.** At the time of initial contact Broker shall inform prospective sellers that Broker is acting on behalf of a Buyer.

9. **Disclosure of Buyer's Identity.** Broker ☐**does** ☐**does not** have Buyer's permission to disclose Buyer's identity to third parties without prior written consent of Buyer.

10. **Disclosure of Information.** Broker agrees not to disclose information obtained in confidence from Buyer except as authorized in writing by Buyer or as required by law.

11. **Conflicting Interests.** In the event Broker has an ownership interest in any property Buyer selects, said fact shall be immediately disclosed to Buyer. Broker may show any property to other prospective competing buyers. Broker may assist Buyer in the purchase of property listed for sale by a seller with Broker pursuant to the terms of the separate agreement attached hereto.

12. **Assignment by Buyer.** No assignment of Buyer's rights under this Agreement and no assignment of rights in Property obtained for Buyer under this Agreement shall operate to defeat any of Broker's rights.

13. **Nondiscrimination.** The parties agree not to discriminate against any prospective seller on the basis of the race, creed, color, sex, national origin, familial status, handicap, religion or as may be provided by local, state or federal law or regulation.

14. **Attorneys' Fees.** In case of litigation or arbitration concerning this Agreement, the parties agree that costs and reasonable attorneys' fees shall be awarded to the prevailing party.

15. **Modification of this Agreement.** No modification of any of the terms of this Agreement shall be valid, binding upon the parties, or enforceable unless in writing and signed by the parties.

16. **Entire Agreement.** This Agreement constitutes the entire agreement between the parties and any prior agreements, whether oral or written, have been merged and integrated into this Agreement.

17. **Counterparts.** If more than one person is named as a Buyer herein, this Agreement may be executed by each Buyer individually, and when so executed, such copies taken together shall be deemed to be a full and complete Agreement between the parties.

18. **Copy of Agreement.** Buyer acknowledges receipt of a copy of this Agreement signed by the Broker.

19. **Additional Provisions.**

______________________________ ______________________________

Buyer date Buyer date

Broker:

______________________________

by date

# Exclusive Right-To-Buy Contract (Buyer Agency)

______________________________, 19_____

_____________________________________________________________("Buyer")

appoints ______________________________________________________("Broker") as Buyer's exclusive limited agent for the purpose of representing Buyer to acquire interests in real property ("Property") as indicated below under the terms specified herein.

1. **Effect.** Broker is hereby engaged as Buyer's exclusive limited agent. Buyer shall conduct all negotiations for Property through Broker and refer to Broker all inquiries received from real estate brokers, salespersons, prospective sellers, or any other source during the time this contract is in effect. Buyer agrees that any compensation to Broker which is conditioned upon the acquisition by Buyer of interests in real property, whether by lease or purchase (collectively "Purchase"), will be earned by Broker whenever such interests are acquired by Buyer directly or indirectly, without any discount or allowance for any efforts made by Buyer or any other person in connection with the acquisition of such interests by Buyer.

2. **Purchase.** "Purchase of the Property" or "Purchase" means the voluntary acquisition of any interest in the Property or the voluntary creation of the right to acquire any interest in the Property (including a contract or lease).

3. **Property.** Broker shall search the Multiple Listing Services of which Broker is a member ("MLS") and make submissions to Buyer describing and identifying properties contained therein, and property actually known to the salesperson assisting Buyer, appearing to Broker to substantially meet the requirements on the attached Property Preference Sheet.

4. **Duration.** Broker's authority as Buyer's exclusive agent shall commence ______________________________, 19___, and shall continue until the earlier of ______________________________, 19___, or completion of the acquisition of the Property unless extended as indicated below.

5. **Broker's Services.** Broker will exercise reasonable skill and care for Buyer, and make reasonable efforts to locate property.
   (a) Broker will promote the interests of Buyer with the utmost good faith, loyalty, and fidelity, by:
      (1) seeking a price and terms which are acceptable to Buyer, except that Broker shall not be obligated to seek other properties while Buyer is a party to a contract to purchase Property;
      (2) procuring acceptance of any offer to purchase property and to assist in the completion of the transaction;
      (3) presenting all offers to and from Buyer in a timely manner, regardless of whether Buyer is already a party to a contract to purchase Property;

(4) disclosing to Buyer adverse material facts actually known to Broker;
(5) counseling Buyer as to any material benefits or risks of the transaction which are actually known to Broker;
(6) advising Buyer to obtain expert advice as to material matters about which Broker knows but the specifics of which are beyond the expertise of Broker;
(7) accounting in a timely manner for all money and property received; and
(8) informing Buyer that Buyer may be vicariously liable for the acts of Broker when Broker is acting within the scope of the agency relationship.

(b) Broker shall not disclose to the seller or any other third party, without the informed consent of Buyer:
(1) that Buyer is willing to pay more than the purchase price for Property;
(2) what Buyer's motivating factor(s) is;
(3) that Buyer will agree to financing terms other than those offered;
(4) any material information about Buyer unless disclosure is required by law or failure to disclose such information would constitute fraud or dishonest dealing; and
(5) any facts or suspicions regarding circumstances which would psychologically impact or stigmatize Property.

(c) Broker shall disclose to any prospective seller all adverse material facts actually known by Broker, including, but not limited to adverse material facts concerning Buyer's financial ability to perform the terms of the transaction and whether Buyer intends to occupy Property as a principal residence.

(d) Broker shall search the Multiple Listing Services of which Broker is a member and inform Buyer of other property actually known to the salesperson assisting Buyer that Broker feels substantially meets the criteria identified in paragraph #3 above.

(e) Broker has no duty to Buyer to conduct an independent inspection of Property for the benefit of Buyer and has no duty to independently verify the accuracy or completeness of statements made by the seller or independent inspectors.

6. **Costs of Services or Products Obtained from Outside Sources.** Broker will not obtain or order products or services from outside sources without Buyer's written authorization and unless Buyer has agreed to pay for them promptly when due. (Examples: surveys, soil tests, radon tests, title reports, property inspections.)

7. **Compensation to Broker.** In the event no one else pays Broker at or before closing, Buyer shall, in consideration of the services to be performed by Broker, be obligated to pay Broker a "Fee" as follows:

(a) **Price of the Property ("Price").** Price as used in this paragraph shall mean: ☐ the price of the property indicated in the purchase and sale contract, or ☐ the price established by the seller on the first day the property is introduced to the Buyer, or ☐ the lesser of the two, or ☐ the greater of the two.

(b) **Property Listed in MLS.** In the event the Property is listed with the MLS, Broker's Fee shall be the greater of the amount actually paid by the Listing Broker or ___________% of the Price.

(c) **Property Not Listed in MLS.** In the event the Property is not listed with the MLS, Broker's Fee shall be ___________% of the Price.

(d) **Source of Funds.** Broker is authorized and instructed to request payment of Broker's Fee, on behalf of Buyer, from the following sources: ☐ Listing Broker ☐ Seller ☐ Other _______________________.

(e) **General.** The Fee is conditioned upon the Purchase of the Property or the acquisition by Buyer of property not in compliance with the requirements specified above but within the purview of this contract. This Fee is payable upon closing of the transaction, unless the seller fails to close through no fault of Buyer, in which event no Fee shall be due. In the event the Buyer fails to close, the Fee shall be due and payable immediately. Broker shall not advance funds for Buyer. This Fee applies to Property contracted for during the original term of this contract or any extension(s) and shall also apply to Property contracted for within ________ days after this contract expires or is terminated if the Property was shown or specifically presented in writing to Buyer by Broker during the original term or any extension(s) of the term of this contract.

(f) **Retainer.** Buyer shall pay Broker a non-refundable retainer Fee of $__________ upon the signing of this contract, which amount ☐ shall ☐ shall not be credited against the Fee indicated above.

8. **Disclosure of Broker's Role.** At the earliest reasonable opportunity, Broker shall inform all prospective sellers or their brokers with whom Broker negotiates pursuant to this contract that Broker is acting as an agent on behalf of Buyer.

9. **Disclosure of Buyer's Identity.** Broker ☐ does ☐ does not have Buyer's permission to disclose Buyer's identity to third parties without the subsequent prior written consent of Buyer.

10. **In-Company Sale.** An "In-Company Sale" occurs when Buyer desires to view and/or purchase property listed with Broker where Broker is already acting as a limited agent on behalf of the seller. In such instances the attached "In-Company Sale Addendum" shall govern.

11. **Other Buyers.** Broker may show properties in which Buyer is interested to other prospective buyers without breaching any obligation, duty or responsibility to Buyer. In the event Broker is assisting multiple buyers all of whom are interested in the same property, Broker shall keep all information regarding each buyer and their proposed transaction confidential and shall not disclose any elements of any offer made by or to any buyer to any other buyer.

12. **Nondiscrimination.** The parties agree not to discriminate as provided by local, state and federal fair housing or laws, against any prospective seller. This

includes discrimination based upon race, creed, color, sex, marital status, national origin, familial status, physical or mental handicap, religion or ancestry of such person.

13. **Recommendation of Legal Counsel.** By signing this document, Buyer acknowledges that Broker has advised that this document has important legal consequences and has recommended consultation with legal and tax or other counsel, before signing this contract.

14. **Attorney's Fees.** In case of arbitration or litigation between Buyer and Broker in their respective capacities, the parties agree that costs and reasonable attorney fees shall be awarded to the prevailing party.

15. **Assignment and Modification of this Contract.** No assignment of Buyer's rights or obligations under this contract and no assignment of rights or obligations in property obtained for Buyer under this contract shall operate to defeat any of Broker's rights. No subsequent modification of any of the terms of this contract shall be valid, binding upon the parties, or enforceable unless in writing and signed by the parties.

16. **Entire Agreement.** This contract constitutes the entire agreement between the parties and any prior agreements, whether oral or written, have been merged and integrated into this contract.

17. **Counterparts.** If more than one person is named as Buyer herein, this contract may be executed by each Buyer, individually, and when so executed, such copies taken together shall be deemed to be a full and complete contract between the parties.

18. **Copy of Contract.** Buyer acknowledges receipt of a copy of this contract signed by Broker.

19. **Price Determination.** Broker shall prepare a Competitive Market Analysis, for potential properties selected by the Buyer, comprised of similar properties that have sold, are listed for sale or were rejected from the market, as reported to the MLS of which Broker is a member. This may not comprise all of the properties in the market area. Buyer is solely responsible for the determination of the contract price. Broker is not responsible for the determination of the contract price.

______________________________ ______________________________

Buyer date Buyer date

Broker:

______________________________

by date

19. **Extension.** This contract is extended and shall continue until the earlier of __________________, 19___, or completion of the acquisition of the Property.

| ______________________ | | ______________________ | |
|---|---|---|---|
| Buyer | date | Buyer | date |

Broker:

______________________

by date

# EXCLUSIVE RIGHT-TO-BUY CONTRACT
## (Short Form)

____________________, 19____

__________________________________________("Buyer")

appoints __________________________________________("Broker")
as Buyer's exclusive limited agent for the purpose of representing Buyer to acquire interests in real property ("Property") as indicated below under the terms specified herein.

1. **Effect.** Broker is hereby engaged as Buyer's exclusive limited agent. Buyer shall conduct all negotiations for Property through Broker and refer to Broker all inquiries received from any source. Compensation is based upon the acquisition by Buyer of any interest in real property ("Purchase").

2. **Property.** Broker shall search the Multiple Listing Services of which Broker is a member ("MLS") and make submissions to Buyer describing and identifying properties contained therein appearing to Broker to substantially meet the requirements on the attached Property Preference Sheet.

3. **Duration.** Broker's authority as Buyer's exclusive agent shall commence ____________________, 19___, and shall continue until the earlier of ____________________, 19___, or completion of the acquisition of the Property unless extended as indicated below.

4. **Broker's Services.** Broker will exercise reasonable skill and care for Buyer, and make reasonable efforts to locate property. Broker has no duty to Buyer to conduct an independent inspection of Property for the benefit of Buyer and has no duty to independently verify the accuracy or completeness of statements made by the seller or independent inspectors.

5. **Compensation to Broker.** In the event no one else pays Broker at or before closing, Buyer shall, in consideration of the services to be performed by Broker, be obligated to pay Broker a "Fee" as follows:
   (a) **Price of the Property ("Price").** Price as used in this paragraph shall mean: ☐ the price of the property indicated in the purchase and sale contract, or ☐ the price established by the seller on the first day the property is introduced to the Buyer, or ☐ the lesser of the two, or ☐ the greater of the two.
   (b) **Property Listed in MLS.** In the event the Property is listed with the MLS, Broker's Fee shall be the greater of the amount actually paid by the Listing Broker or __________% of the Price.
   (c) **Property Not Listed in MLS.** In the event the Property is not listed with the MLS, Broker's Fee shall be __________% of the Price.

(d) **Source of Funds.** Broker is authorized and instructed to request payment of Broker's Fee, on behalf of Buyer, from the following sources: ☐ Listing Broker ☐ Seller ☐ Other ________________________.

(e) **General.** The Fee is conditioned upon the Purchase of the Property or the acquisition by Buyer of property not in compliance with the requirements specified in paragraph # 3 above but within the purview of this contract. This Fee is payable upon closing of the transaction, unless the seller fails to close through no fault of Buyer, in which event no Fee shall be due. In the event the Buyer fails to close, the Fee shall be due and payable immediately. Broker shall not advance funds for Buyer. This Fee applies to Property contracted for during the original term of this contract or any extension(s) and shall also apply to Property contracted for within ________ days after this contract expires or is terminated if the Property was shown or specifically presented in writing to Buyer by Broker during the original term or any extension(s) of the term of this contract.

6. **In-Company Sale.** An "In-Company Sale" occurs when Buyer desires to view and/or purchase property listed with Broker where Broker is already acting as a limited agent on behalf of the seller. In such instances the attached "In-Company Sale Addendum" shall govern.

7. **Other Buyers.** Broker may show properties in which Buyer is interested to other prospective buyers without breaching any obligation, duty or responsibility to Buyer. In the event Broker is assisting multiple buyers all of whom are interested in the same property, Broker shall keep all information regarding each buyer and their proposed transaction confidential and shall not disclose any elements of any offer made by or to any buyer to any other buyer.

8. **Recommendation of Legal Counsel.** By signing this document, Buyer acknowledges that Broker has advised that this document has important legal consequences and has recommended consultation with legal and tax or other counsel, before signing this contract.

9. **Attorney's Fees.** In case of arbitration or litigation between Buyer and Broker in their respective capacities, the parties agree that costs and reasonable attorney fees shall be awarded to the prevailing party.

10. **Entire Agreement.** This contract constitutes the entire agreement between the parties and any prior agreements, whether oral or written, have been merged and integrated into this contract.

______________________________ ______________________________

Buyer date Buyer date

Broker:

______________________________

by date

11. **Extension.** This contract is extended and shall continue until the earlier of __________________, 19___, or completion of the acquisition of the Property.

____________________________________ ____________________________________

Buyer date Buyer date

Broker:

____________________________________

by date

## Your Seller is Now a Buyer

It is perceived as the best of all worlds when the seller, having listed his property with the broker, through the salesperson, now also wants to purchase a new or additional piece of property. The agent and the seller already have established a rapport and are able to speak with candor. The agent has learned not only the likes and dislikes of his seller turned buyer but also the personal confidential secrets of his seller turned buyer. The agent knows the amount of money the seller turned buyer probably has available, the relative financial worth of the various entities that his seller turned buyer may use to acquire property, the extent to which the seller turned buyer will go to attain his goals, and the overall strategy of the seller turned buyer. In short he knows how his seller turned buyer thinks.

In some parts of the country some salespeople are still attempting to convert the former seller, their client, into a customer for the buying side of the transaction. Most buyers feel that the agent with whom they are working is "*their*" agent. Imagine how the seller client feels after he has listed with the broker or agent, and is now going out to search for new acquisitions and is told that the former agent is now going to tell prospective sellers, strangers for the most part, the personal secrets of the seller turned buyer, the *former* client. We would guess that nearly one hundred percent of all sellers that are seeking to purchase real estate with their listing agents are convinced that the agent is working for them.

The seller turned buyer thinks, and properly so, that they still have *their* Realtor®. To argue any other way would be silly. Now we must deal with the eventuality that the seller turned buyer might want to see and buy another listing in the company office. There is a real problem here. We are about to sell another listing. Yes, that is the "prime directive" to get the seller's house sold.

This is the ever prevalent "In-Company" Sale. Call it dual agency if you must or refer to it as Transaction Broker if you want the title to fit the duties prescribed by the realities of the arrangement. Whatever the name, the role is that of a neutral party. Absent full disclosure, there is no doubt that the ultimate undisclosed dual agency arrangement has been created.

The agent becomes the agent of the buyer (former seller) and an agent of the new seller. Someone should have discussed this potential situation with every seller. Then when the seller turned buyer wanted to buy a company listing the new seller would be excited rather than suspicious. After all, that was the original plan, to sell the property yourself. Think about how a court or an uninitiated individual might see things. Very confusing. Someone is trying to take advantage of someone else. In fact we know that is not the case at all.

**Letter - Seller is also a Buyer - Buyer Agency/Dual Agency**

Mr. Sam Seller
Mrs. Sandy Seller
4750 Table Mesa Drive
Boulder, CO 80303

Re: 4750 Table Mesa Drive

Dear Sam and Sandy:

I have been happy to assist you as your agent with the sale of your present home. Thank you for selecting me to help you with the new property that you are to purchase. I consider myself well qualified, not only since I have had the opportunity to get to know you and to determine what you desire in your new home, but also because I am very familiar with many of the properties available in this area. I enjoy helping a buyer select their new home. As members of the Multiple Listing Service we have access not only to our inventory of listings but also to numerous properties available in this area that have been listed by the other brokers who are also members.

Unless you indicate otherwise, I will assist you as a buyer agent. That way I can continue to represent you instead of having to try to become a subagent of the various other sellers that have their homes on the market. I would have a hard time not being your agent and having to be the agent for a stranger. Our firm simply can not act as the agent for another seller who has listed their property with another office while we are working with you.

We want you to be aware of the various relationships that are available for sellers who are interested in looking at houses. Not all of them are offered by this firm.

Our choice is to act as your agents. This is buyer agency. You may remember that I indicated to you that our firm pays buyer agents who assist me with the sale of your home. Well, the shoe is on the other foot now. Other firms will pay me to help them sell their seller's listings. In general all the other firms cooperate so there is not need for you to pay us separately.

I will do everything that I can to solicit the cooperation and fee split from the listing broker. In the event that is not feasible, such as the case of a For Sale by Owner, then you can write a clause in the contract that will allow for the seller to pay me as a part of the transaction. However, in the event that I find the home that you select and no one else will pay me, I need to know that you will pay me.

Otherwise I would be working for free. I am sure we both agree that I can not do that.

Some salespeople act as subagents of the other sellers on the market. Our office does not offer that selection. I could not be someone else's agent and be required to work for them when I was helping you find a home.

There is a possibility that you will be interested in one of the properties listed with our company. We have some very nice listings. In that instance I will be acting as a dual agent. That means that I will be neutral throughout the transaction, acting simply as a real estate broker. This is really quite a simple solution. You may remember that I described it to you when we discussed your listing. It is the same relationship that would have existed if I had sold your home myself to another one of my clients.

I have attached our "In-Company" Sale Addendum. Yes, it is the same one that was attached to your listing. Now that you are the buyer we need to review it again. I will keep your personal secrets confidential and do the same for the personal secrets of the other sellers that we have listed. I will always indicate to you anything that I know about the physical condition of the property. I just can not tell the potential seller your motivation to buy, and I can not tell you the seller's motivation to sell.

Sincerely,
The Orcas Island Company

by: Katherine E. Reece
Realtor®, CRS, GRI

**Letter - Seller is also a Buyer - Buyer Agency/Transaction Broker**

Mr. Sam Seller
Mrs. Sandy Seller
4750 Table Mesa Drive
Boulder, CO 80303

Re: 4750 Table Mesa Drive

Dear Sam and Sandy:

I have been happy to assist you with the sale of your present home as your agent. Thank you for selecting me to help you with the new property that you are to purchase. I consider myself well qualified not only since I have had the opportunity to get to know you and to determine what you desire in your new home, but also because I am very familiar with many of the properties available in this area. I enjoy helping a buyer select their new home. As members of the Multiple Listing Service, we have access not only to our inventory of listings but also to numerous properties available in this area that have been listed by the other brokers who are also members.

Unless you indicate otherwise, I will assist you as a buyer agent. That way I can continue to represent you instead of having to try to become a subagent of the various other sellers that have their homes on the market. I would have a hard time not being your agent and having to be the agent for a stranger. Our firm simply can not act as the agent for another seller who has listed their property with another office while we are working with you.

We want you to be aware of the various relationships that are available for sellers who are interested in looking at houses. Not all of them are offered by this firm.

Our choice is to act as your agents. This is buyer agency. You may remember that I indicated to you that our firm pays buyer agents who assist me with the sale of your home. Well, the shoe is on the other foot now. Other firms will pay me to help them sell their seller's listings. In general all the other firms cooperate so there is not need for you to pay us separately.

I will do everything that I can to solicit the cooperation and fee split from the listing broker. In the event that is not feasible, such as the case of a For Sale by Owner, then you can write a clause in the contract that will allow for the seller to pay me as a part of the transaction. However, in the event that I find the home that you select and no one else will pay me, I need to know that you will pay me.

Otherwise I would be working for free. I am sure we both agree that I can not do that.

Some salespeople act as subagents of the other sellers on the market. Our office does not offer that selection. I could not be someone else's agent and be required to work for them when I was helping you find a home.

There is a possibility that you will be interested in one of the properties listed with our company. We have some very nice listings. In that instance I will be acting as a transaction broker or real estate broker. That means that I will be neutral throughout the transaction, acting simply as a real estate broker. This is really quite a simple solution. You may remember that I described it to you when we discussed your listing. It is the same relationship that would have existed if I had sold your home myself to another one of my clients.

I have attached our "In-Company Sale" Addendum. Yes, it is the same one that was attached to your listing. Now that you are the buyer we need to review it again. I will keep your personal secrets confidential and do the same for the personal secrets of the other sellers that we have listed. I will always indicate to you anything that I know about the physical condition of the property. I just can not tell the potential seller your motivation to buy, and I can not tell you the seller's motivation to sell.

Sincerely,
The Orcas Island Company

by: Katherine E. Reece
Realtor®, CRS, GRI

**Letter - Seller is also a Buyer - Sub Agency**

Mr. Sam Seller
Mrs. Sandy Seller
4750 Table Mesa Drive
Boulder, CO 80303

Dear Sam and Sandy:

I have been happy to assist you with the sale of your present home as your agent. Thank you for selecting me to help you with the new property that you are to purchase. I consider myself well qualified not only since I have had the opportunity to get to know you and to determine what you desire in your new home, but also because I am very familiar with many of the properties available in this area. I enjoy helping a buyer select their new home. As members of the Multiple Listing Service, we have access not only to our inventory of listings but also to numerous properties available in this area that have been listed by the other brokers who are also members.

Unless you indicate otherwise, I will assist you as an agent of either the sellers who have listed with our company or a subagent for the sellers who have listed their properties with another company. I will not be your agent. I will owe you no fiduciary duties. I owe my fiduciary duties to the other sellers. I can not tell you personal secrets regarding any seller. I can not tell you things such as why he is selling or how much I think that he will accept. Yes, I must tell all sellers everything that you have told me. I must tell them how much you have indicated you will offer or how desperate you are to move.

I can provide you with all the information that I have available regarding the physical condition of the property. I will research the items that you request. I will provide you with information and sources of information to make your decision-making as easy as possible. I will share with you the names of available lenders, title companies, inspection experts and other professionals to help you with the decisions about the condition and financing of your new home.

One advantage to this system is that you do not have to worry about paying me. You do not have any obligation to compensate me since I am paid by the other seller's agent through a cooperative split of the total commission paid to the other broker. Thank you for agreeing to let me represent other sellers and still help you select your new home. I look forward to assisting you.

Sincerely,
The Orcas Island Company

by: Katherine E. Reece
Realtor®, CRS, GRI

## Letter - Selling Price Verification

Mr. Bob Buyer
Mrs. Betty Buyer
47 Park View Lane
Boulder, CO 80303

Re: #4 Dream House Lane

Dear Bob and Betty:

Congratulations! You new home is under contract. It has been a delight to assist you with the location and purchase of your new home. As I have told you before, I need to clarify the way in which you determined the price that you finally decided to offer on this property.

A Competitive Market Analysis for this property was provided. It was comprised of properties which seemed to be similar to the property you wished to buy that I located through the Multiple Listing Service. We used current listings of properties, properties that had sold and properties that had been rejected from the market. As you know, the MLS does not represent all properties that are in these categories.

I am glad that I am a Realtor® and not an appraiser. As a Realtor® I can provide you with the data regarding the relative value as indicated, but I can not determine the ultimate value. That is a job for the appraiser. When we receive the final appraisal, we will see how close you were.

Thank you for selecting me to help you with the selection and acquisition of your new home.

Sincerely,
American Real Estate Service

by: Tina B. Daniel, Broker-Owner

# Chapter Four
# The "In-Company" Sale
***Selling Your Own Listing Without Getting Sued***

## Defining the Middle Ground

**The "In-Company" Sale.** Sometimes referred to as "double ending" or "double dipping", this is the sale that the seller anticipated when he hired you and the sale that you want to make if you can. The goal was to sell it yourself from the start.

This is also the sale that the buyer envisioned when the buyer called on your advertisement or "For Sale" sign. It is the sale that everyone hopes will happen. Our job is to prepare for it and conduct it within the rules established by the law and our company policy.

**Rule.** *Breach of a fiduciary duty forfeits the commission regardless of loss.*

In order not to breach your fiduciary duty to the seller or the buyer you must disclose to each in advance how you will handle the "In-Company" or "In-House" sale. This is neutral ground. Even if we got the house sold, we could lose the entire commission if we breached our fiduciary duty, namely the duty to tell the seller what we were doing on the seller's behalf. If the buyer thought that we were his agent we could loose as a result of a similar allegation from the buyer.

**Tip.** *The seller wants "you to sell their house" so tell the seller how you do business and let the seller determine if he wants to do business with you. You do not have to be all things to all people.*

**Tip:** *The buyer wants "you to show and sell them your listing" so tell the buyer how you do business and let the buyer determine if he wants to do business with you. You do not have to be all things to all people.*

**Broker's Role.** Establish an office policy making certain that not only do you understand and believe in it, but that your salespeople, all of them, not only understand it but can explain it. Try having each person stand up at a sales meeting and give their presentation to the seller or the buyer for all to hear. All salespeople in the office must be on the same team playing by the same rules. Allowing people alternatively to be the agent trying to list, a seller, a seller turned buyer, a buyer or one of the principals will make the description of the services offered easier to explain. Soon people will understand the basic real estate services that our office offers to everyone. Those are the services that a neutral person provides in an "In-Company" Sale.

**Salesperson's Role.** You must be able to understand and explain your office policy for the "In-Company" sale. In addition you must understand your competitor's policy and why your office policy is as good or better. Try not to run down competitors. It will come back to haunt you when your policy changes. Emphasize the positive aspects of your office policy and not the negative aspects of the policies of other companies. Practice your role. This is real estate, not a court room.

**Caution.** *State laws vary here a lot. In addition, many states do not realize that there are options that may not involve agency since it "has been done that way for so long."* **Check with your local attorney.**

**Rule.** *The manner in which your office, yes, the entire office, handles "In-Company" Sales must be disclosed and agreed to with either the buyer or the seller at the time he signs the listing contract. It is not proper to try to get their consent once you have an offer.*

## Choices for the "In-Company" Sale

There are essentially four choices for handling the "In-Company" Sale.

1. **Seller Agency.** This is frequently referred to as "single agency". You inform the seller that you will represent the seller at all times. While this sounds great to everyone, it does not adequately address the prospect that you might actually sell the house to someone with whom you are now working as a buyer agent. In addition, when the seller's house sells, he will expect you to be "his agent" to help him buy a new property. Perish the thought that he should select another of your personal listings or one in your company's inventory. Now you need to explain your "In-Company" Sale policy. Your policy will be one of the following. Or, you could refer the buyer to another broker outside of your company. Right!

2. **Dual Agency.** The agent attempts to represent two people or two groups of people with conflicting interests at the same time. You should check your state law. We need to define in advance what information will be passed

along to the other party and what will be kept secret. This is a common term with a lot of different interpretations. How can someone really be a "dual" agent, that is representing two people with conflicting interests at the same time? Of course, no one can. However, the term exists and will continue to exist. The practical application is that you provide a list of specific services to both the buyer and the seller.

3. **Transaction Broker.** Sometimes called facilitator, independent contractor or real estate broker, this is a non-agency relationship. It does the same thing as dual agency with a different title. The real estate professional is neutral and provides a list of services to both buyer and seller. We need to define in advance what information will be passed along to the other party and what will be kept secret.

4. **Designated Agency.** Sometimes this is referred to as "Split Agency". In general, it provides that in the event of an "In-Company" Sale the broker will designate two separate salespeople, one to assist the buyer and one the seller respectively. The broker will administer, but will not take sides. The broker will act like a dual agent or transaction broker, neutral. One salesperson, not the brokerage office, will represent the seller, in the traditional agency sense of the word, and the other salesperson will represent the buyer in a similar manner.

The choice must be selected by the broker and utilized for all transactions in the office. You can not have the Buyer or Seller selecting methods on a case by case basis. A method of incorporating the selected policy into the buyer or seller listing agreement and the contract for sale is to make reference in the respective contract to the "In-Company" Sale which will be handled pursuant to the terms of the attached addendum. This allows the company to change or modify the addenda without having to reprint the entire listing form.

The following clauses address the different relationships potentially available with the buyer and/or seller. Read each to determine if it anticipates the buyer and seller initially having an *agency* or a *working* relationship with the broker. A "working relationship" is something very similar to a "customer" relationship.

We recommend an addendum in a form similar to the ones we have provided. However, in the event you choose to use only a paragraph in the listing contract here are some alternatives.

**Clause--"In-Company" Sale -- Dual Agency.**

1. A broker may not act as an agent for more that one party with conflicting interests with another party to a transaction unless the broker, buyer and seller agree in advance in writing. When acting as a dual agent, the broker will

retain the confidential information related to each party and disclose only the information related to the physical condition of the property, the buyer's ability to qualify for the proposed transaction and whether or not the buyer will occupy the property. The broker will not disclose to either party: (1) that either will accept any price other than as listed or as offered, (2) the motivation of the other party, (3) any other information a party specifically instructs the broker to keep confidential unless the same is required by law or the failure to disclose would constitute fraud or dishonest dealing.

We hereby agree that your firm, broker and salespeople, may act as dual agents in a transaction wherein your initially represents both the buyer and the seller.

Only one commission, the one indicated in the listing agreement will be collected.

-or-

1. When acting as the agent for one party (either Buyer or Seller), Broker has duties and obligations which include utmost good faith, loyalty, and fidelity to that one principal. If the principal seller/buyer consents, however, Broker may act as a Dual Agent when both the Seller and Buyer initially have an *agency* relationship with the same real estate company ("In-Company" Sale). A Dual Agent is a broker engaged as a limited agent for both Seller and Buyer. Dual agency creates a conflict of interest because Broker's duties and obligations of confidentiality, full disclosure, and loyalty to one party conflict with those same duties to the other. Seller and Buyer may be vicariously liable for acts of a Dual Agent.

We hereby agree that your firm, broker and salespeople, may act as dual agents in a transaction wherein your initially represents both the buyer and the seller.

Only one commission, the one indicated in the listing agreement will be collected.

**Clause--"In-Company" Sale -- Transaction Broker.**

1. When acting as the agent for one party (either Buyer or Seller), Broker has duties and obligations which include utmost good faith, loyalty, and fidelity to that one principal. If the principal seller/buyer consents, however, Broker may act as a Transaction Broker (real estate broker) when both the Seller and Buyer initially have an *agency* relationship with the same real estate company ("In-Company" Sale). A Transaction Broker is a broker engaged, not as a limited agent for both Seller and Buyer, but to assist both Buyer and Seller without acting as the agent of either.

We hereby agree that your firm, broker and salespeople, may act as Transaction Brokers in a transaction wherein you initially represent both the buyer and the seller.

Only one commission, the one indicated in the listing agreement will be collected.

-or-

1. When acting as the agent for one party (either Buyer or Seller), Broker has duties and obligations which include utmost good faith, loyalty, and fidelity to that one principal. If the principal seller/buyer consents, however, Broker may act as a Transaction Broker (real estate broker) when both the Seller and Buyer initially have a *working or agency* relationship with the same real estate company ("In-Company" Sale). A Transaction Broker is a broker engaged, not as a limited agent for both Seller and Buyer, but to assist both Buyer and Seller without acting as the agent of either.

    We hereby agree that your firm, broker and salespeople, may act as Transaction Brokers in a transaction wherein you initially either represent or are working with the buyer and/or the seller.

    Only one commission, the one indicated in the listing agreement will be collected.

**Clause--"In-Company" Sale.**

1. A broker may not act as an agent for more that one party with conflicting interests with another party to a transaction. That creates a conflict of interest. However, we will assist both the buyer and seller, as real estate brokers, if we have your written consent in advance. When acting as a real estate broker, we will retain the confidential information which is related to each party and disclose only the information related to the physical condition of the property, the buyer's ability to qualify for the proposed transaction and whether or not the buyer will occupy the property. The broker will not disclose to either party: (1) that either will accept any price other than as listed or as offered, (2) the motivation of the other party, (3) any other information a party specifically instructs the broker to keep confidential unless the same is required by law or the failure to disclose would constitute fraud or dishonest dealing.

    We hereby agree that you and your firm, broker and salespeople, may act as real estate brokers and not dual agents in a transaction wherein you initially represented both the buyer and the seller. We understand that we are not vicariously liable for your actions and inactions. We also understand that you will keep information about us personally confidential and that you can not disclose to us the confidential personal information that you know about the buyer.

## Clause-Seller Confidential Information -- General.

1. You are authorized to indicate that this property is in foreclosure.

-or-

1. You are authorized to indicate that the "seller is desperate" and willing to consider any reasonable offer.

-or-

1. You may indicate to prospective buyers that we have been transferred and need to sell fast.

-or-

1. The fact that the seller has been transferred out of the area is well known. Seller authorizes broker to disclose that information to prospective buyers if they inquire "why are they selling".

-or-

1. The seller hereby authorizes the broker to indicate to prospective buyers that the seller's are involved in a divorce action.

## Clause-Seller Confidential Information -- Murder or Suicide:

1. Please indicate to all prospective buyers that there was a murder in this house on ______________________. Also provide them with the newspaper article attached to the listing agreement.

-or-

1. You are authorized to indicate to buyers that the property was the site of a suicide and provide them with the attached explanation that we have prepared.

## Clause--Miscellaneous "In-Company".

1. **"In-Company" Sale.** Seller hereby authorizes the Broker to show the property to buyers with whom the broker has or may have an agency relationship pursuant to the terms of the attached "In-Company" Sale Addendum.

-or-

1. **"In-Company" Sale**. Seller hereby authorizes the Broker to show the property to buyers with whom the broker has or may have a "working relationship" pursuant to the terms of the attached "In-Company" Sale Addendum.

-or-

1. **Designated Agency**. In the event one salesperson in our firm is working with the buyer and another salesperson is working with the seller, each salesperson shall operate independently of the other as if they were distinct separate agents for the buyer and seller respectively. There shall be no imputation of any knowledge or information between the salespersons and the broker.

   Only in the event that the buyer is procured by the same salesperson that listed the property will the "In-Company" Dual Agency provisions apply.

   In the event the buyer and seller are represented by a single salesperson, either the buyer or seller may request the broker to assign a separate salesperson to each of the parties, buyer and seller, for the purposes of the transaction. In that event, the original salesperson shall not be able to assist either party.

# "In-Company" Sale Addendum
# (Dual Agency)

1. **Amendment to Agency Contract.** This "In-Company" Sale Addendum is part of either an Exclusive Right to Buy Contract (Buyer Agency Contract) or a Listing Contract (Seller Agency Contract) between the broker named below and its sales agents ("Broker") and the undersigned Buyer or Seller dated ____________________________, 19______ . This Addendum will control in the event of any conflict with the contract to which it is attached.

2. **Limitation of Broker's Agency Obligations.** When acting as the agent for one party (either Buyer or Seller), Broker has duties and obligations which include utmost good faith, loyalty, and fidelity to that one principal. If the principal consents, however, Broker may act as a Dual Agent when both the Seller and Buyer have an *agency* relationship with the same real estate company ("In-Company" Sale). A Dual Agent is a broker engaged as a limited agent for both Seller and Buyer. Dual agency creates a conflict of interest because Broker's duties and obligations of confidentiality, full disclosure, and loyalty to one party conflict with those same duties to the other. Seller and Buyer may be vicariously liable for acts of a Dual Agent.

   a. If this addendum is signed by Seller, Broker will act only as the exclusive agent for Seller when the Property is shown to a prospective buyer who has a working relationship with another licensed real estate company, but will act as a Dual Agent only in an "In-Company" Sale.

   b. If this addendum is signed by Buyer, Broker will act only as the exclusive agent for Buyer when showing properties that are not listed with Broker, but will act as a Dual Agent only in an "In-Company" Sale.

**The remaining provisions of this addendum describe significant changes to the obligations of Broker when acting as a Dual Agent in an "In-Company" Sale.**

3. **Information that Must be Disclosed by a Dual Agent.**

   a. All adverse material facts actually known by Broker including but not limited to adverse material facts pertaining to the title to the Property which the Seller indicates will not be remedied prior to the transfer of deed; and,

   b. All information actually know to the broker, now or during the pre-closing period, regarding the physical condition of the property; and,

   c. Any environmental hazards affecting the Property which are required by law to be disclosed.

4. **Matters that Cannot be Disclosed by a Dual Agent.** Broker, when acting as a Dual Agent, shall not disclose to either Seller or Buyer without the prior written consent of the other party, any of the following information:

   a. That Buyer is willing to pay more than the purchase price offered for the property;

   b. That Seller is willing to accept less than the asking price for the property;

   c. The motivating factors for either party to buy or sell the property;

   d. That Seller or Buyer will agree to financing terms other than those offered;

   e. Any material information about the other party unless either:
      (1) the disclosure is required by law,
      (2) the disclosure pertains to material facts adverse to the Buyer's financial ability to perform the terms of the transaction,
      (3) the disclosure pertains to Buyer's intent to occupy the property as a principal residence, or
      (4) failure to disclose such information would constitute fraud or dishonest dealing.

5. **No Duty for Dual Agent to Investigate**. Broker, when acting as a Dual Agent, has no duty to conduct an independent inspection of the property for the benefit of Buyer and has no duty to independently verify the accuracy or completeness of statements made by Seller or independent inspectors. Broker, when acting as a Dual Agent, has no duty to conduct an independent investigation of Buyer's financial condition or to verify the accuracy or completeness of any statement made by Buyer.

6. **Commission**. Only one commission shall be payable. Buyer and Seller acknowledge that the commission paid to the Broker is reflected in the price of the property sold. Seller shall pay the Broker the commission indicated in the Exclusive Right to Sell Listing Contract. Buyer shall not be obligated to pay any additional commission to Broker.

______________________________ ______________________________
Buyer date Buyer date

Broker:

______________________________
by date

## "In-Company" Sale Addendum (Dual/Limited Agency)

This Addendum is hereby made a part of either the Seller Listing Contract or the Buyer Agency Contract or the Purchase and Sale Contract ("Contract"), between the undersigned real estate broker and its salespersons ("Broker") and the undersigned Seller and/or Buyer, ("Client"), collectively ("Parties"). In the event the terms of this Addendum conflict with, vary from, or modify the terms and provisions of the Contract, the terms of this Addendum shall control.

**Fiduciary Duties.** The Broker has fiduciary duties to the Client which include; *reasonable care* (to act in a reasonable manner), *undivided loyalty and confidentiality* (keeping the Client's confidences), *obedience and performance* (to comply with the Client's reasonable directions regarding the purchase and sale of real property), *accounting* (to disclose the status of all transactional money in broker's possession), and *full disclosure* (to transmit all relevant and material information known by the Broker to the Client regarding the other party).

**Seller-Broker Relationship.** When real property is listed for sale or lease by Seller with Broker, Broker acts initially as the agent of and owes fiduciary duties to the Seller ("Seller's Agent"). The Broker shall treat the Buyer honestly and shall disclose to the Buyer all defects of a material nature affecting the physical condition of the property actually known to the Broker. The Broker shall have no obligation to inspect the Property. The Broker can not, without the Seller's prior written consent, violate or modify the Broker's duty of undivided loyalty and confidentiality and full disclosure.

**Buyer-Broker Relationship.** When a Buyer engages the Broker to locate real property for purchase or lease, Broker shall act initially as the agent of and owes fiduciary duties to the Buyer ("Buyer's Agent"). The Broker shall treat the Seller honestly and shall not give the Seller false information concerning the financial condition of the Buyer, nor disclose the financial affairs of the Buyer without the Buyer's written consent. The Broker can not, without the Buyer's prior written consent, violate or modify the Broker's duty of undivided loyalty and confidentiality and full disclosure.

**"Out of Company" or "Cooperative" Sales.** When the Broker represents the Seller, and a buyer is procured through a brokerage office other than Broker's office, Broker shall transmit to Seller all information known to Broker regarding the transaction and the proposed buyer. When the Broker represents the Buyer and the property is listed with a brokerage office other than Broker's office, Broker shall transmit to Buyer all information known to Broker regarding the transaction and the proposed seller.

**"In-Company" Sales.** The Buyer and Seller acknowledge that the Buyer may seek to acquire a property listed with Broker, an "in-company", "in-office" or "in-house" sale. In such a transaction the Broker would owe conflicting fiduciary duties to both Buyer and Seller at the same time, an inherent conflict of interest. The Broker can not represent the interests of either party to the exclusion or detriment of the other party. In order for Broker to assist both the Buyer and Seller in such transactions, the Parties must consent in writing to allow the Broker to act as a "Dual (Limited) Agent", modifying the existing agency Contracts, Listing Contract and Buyer Agency Contract, between the Parties.

**Dual (Limited) Agency Modification.** The Parties agree that for all transactions wherein the Broker may initially act as both a Buyer's Agent and a Seller's Agent, the Buyer becoming interested in a property listed by the Seller with the Broker, Broker, except as herein indicated, shall provide *limited* representation to both the Buyer or the Seller in the same transaction. The Broker shall act as a Limited Dual Agent for both the Buyer and the Seller. The following shall be the duties, obligations and agreements between the Broker and the Buyer and Seller:

1. Broker shall exercise *reasonable care*, to act in a commercially reasonable manner, in the preparation of all documents and transmission of information. Broker shall answer all questions honestly, but shall properly refuse to answer questions that might violate a duty of confidentiality to either party.

2. Broker shall keep the former Client's confidences *confidential*, and not transmit any personal information known to the Broker regarding either party.

3. Broker shall be *obedient and perform*, complying with the reasonable directions and requests of both parties to accomplish the drafting and fulfillment of the terms of the contract for sale. Broker shall assist both parties to comply with the terms and conditions precedent to the closing of the transaction and shall keep both Buyer and Seller fully informed regarding all aspects of the transaction.

4. Broker shall provide an *accounting* to all Parties, disclosing the status of all transaction money in broker's possession.

5. Broker shall *disclose*, and transmit to all Parties the information known by the Broker regarding the physical condition of the property at all times prior to the transfer of deed.

6. Broker shall not give legal advice to anyone, including advice regarding the condition of the legal title to the property, nor as to the extent of the title insurance policy or exceptions.

7. Only one commission shall be payable. Buyer and Seller acknowledge that the commission paid to the Broker is reflected in the price of the property sold. Seller shall pay the Broker the commission indicated in the Exclusive Right to Sell Listing Contract. Buyer shall not be obligated to pay any additional commission to Broker.

8. A copy of this Addendum shall be a part of the final contract between the Buyer and Seller.

The Parties acknowledge that this Addendum can not be entered into without the knowledge and written consent of all the Parties. Each has read this Addendum and sought the advice of an attorney, if they so desired.

| | | | |
|---|---|---|---|
| Buyer | date | Buyer | date |

Broker:

| | |
|---|---|
| by | date |

# "In-Company" Sale Addendum
# (Real Estate Broker/Initial Agency Relationship)

1. **Amendment to Agency Contract.** This "In-Company" Sale Addendum is part of either an Exclusive Right to Buy Contract (Buyer Agency Contract) or a Listing Contract (Seller Agency Contract) dated _______________, 19_____ between the broker named below and its sales agents ("Broker") and the undersigned Buyer or Seller. This Addendum will control in the event of any conflict with the contract to which it is attached.

2. **Limitation of Broker's Agency Obligations.** When acting as the agent for one party (either Buyer or Seller), Broker has duties and obligations which include utmost good faith, loyalty, and fidelity to that one principal. If the principal consents, however, Broker may act as a Real Estate Broker (Non Agent) when both the Seller and Buyer have an *agency* relationship with the same real estate company ("In-Company" Sale). A Real Estate Broker (Non Agent) is a broker engaged as a limited agent for both Seller and Buyer. Real Estate Broker (Non Agent) creates a conflict of interest because Broker's duties and obligations of confidentiality, full disclosure, and loyalty to one party conflict with those same duties to the other. Seller and Buyer are *not* vicariously liable for acts of a Real Estate Broker (Non Agent).

   a. If this addendum is signed by Seller, Broker will act as the exclusive agent for Seller only when the Property is shown to a prospective buyer who has a working relationship with another licensed real estate company, but will act as a Real Estate Broker (Non Agent) only in an "In-Company" Sale.

   b. If this addendum is signed by Buyer, Broker will act only as the exclusive agent for Buyer when showing properties that are not listed with Broker, but will act as a Real Estate Broker (Non Agent) only in an "In-Company" Sale.

**The remaining provisions of this addendum describe significant changes to the obligations of Broker when acting as a Real Estate Broker (Non Agent) in an "In-Company" Sale.**

3. **Information that Must be Disclosed by a Real Estate Broker (Non Agent).**

   a. All adverse material facts actually known by Broker, including but not limited to adverse material facts pertaining to the title to the Property which Seller indicates will not be remedied prior to the transfer of deed; and,

   b. All information actually know to the Broker, now or during the pre-closing period, regarding the physical condition of the property; and,

c. Any environmental hazards affecting the Property which are required by law to be disclosed.

4. **Matters that Can Not be Disclosed by a Real Estate Broker (Non Agent).** Broker, when acting as a Dual Agent, shall not disclose the following information without the prior consent of the party concerned:

   a. That Buyer is willing to pay more than the purchase price offered for the property;

   b. That Seller is willing to accept less than the asking price for the property;

   c. What the motivating factors are for any party buying or selling the property;

   d. That Seller or Buyer will agree to financing terms other than those offered;

   e. Any material information about the other party unless either:

      (1) the disclosure is required by law,
      (2) the disclosure pertains to adverse material facts about Buyer's financial ability to perform the terms of the transaction,
      (3) the disclosure pertains to Buyer's intent to occupy the property as a principal residence, or
      (4) failure to disclose such information would constitute fraud or dishonest dealing.

5. **No Duty for Real Estate Broker (Non Agent) to Investigate**. Broker, when acting as a Real Estate Broker (Non Agent), has no duty to conduct an independent inspection of the property for the benefit of Buyer and has no duty to independently verify the accuracy or completeness of statements made by Seller or independent inspectors. Broker, when acting as a Real Estate Broker (Non Agent), has no duty to conduct an independent investigation of Buyer's financial condition or to verify the accuracy or completeness of any statement made by Buyer.

6. **Commission.** Only one commission shall be payable. Buyer and Seller acknowledge that the commission paid to the Broker is reflected in the price of the property sold. Seller shall pay the Broker the commission indicated in the Exclusive Right to Sell Listing Contract. Buyer shall not be obligated to pay any additional commission to Broker.

______________________________ ______________________________

Buyer date Buyer date

Broker:

______________________________

by date

## "In-Company" Sale Addendum (Real Estate Broker/Working Relationship)

1. **Amendment to Agency Contract.** This "In-Company" Sale Addendum is part of either an Exclusive Right to Buy Contract (Buyer Agency Contract) or a Listing Contract (Seller Agency Contract) dated _______________, 19_____ between the broker named below and its sales agents ("Broker") and the undersigned Buyer or Seller. This Addendum will control in the event of any conflict with the contract to which it is attached.

2. **Limitation of Broker's Agency Obligations.** When acting as the agent for one party (either Buyer or Seller), Broker has duties and obligations which include utmost good faith, loyalty, and fidelity to that one principal. If the principal consents, however, Broker may act as a Real Estate Broker (Non Agent) when both the Seller and Buyer have either an *agency or a working* relationship with the same real estate company ("In-Company" Sale). A Real Estate Broker (Non Agent) is a broker engaged as a limited agent for both Seller and Buyer. Real Estate Broker (Non Agent) creates a conflict of interest because Broker's duties and obligations of confidentiality, full disclosure, and loyalty to one party conflict with those same duties to the other. Seller and Buyer are *not* vicariously liable for acts of a Real Estate Broker (Non Agent).

   a. If this addendum is signed by Seller, Broker will act as the exclusive agent for Seller only when the Property is shown to a prospective buyer who has a working relationship with another licensed real estate company, but will act as a Real Estate Broker (Non Agent) only in an "In-Company" Sale.

   b. If this addendum is signed by Buyer, Broker will act only as the exclusive agent for Buyer when showing properties that are not listed with Broker, but will act as a Real Estate Broker (Non Agent) only in an "In-Company" Sale.

**The remaining provisions of this addendum describe significant changes to the obligations of Broker when acting as a Real Estate Broker (Non Agent) in an "In-Company" Sale.**

3. **Information that Must be Disclosed by a Real Estate Broker (Non Agent).**

   a. All adverse material facts actually known by Broker, including but not limited to adverse material facts pertaining to the title to the Property which Seller indicates will not be remedied prior to the transfer of deed; and,

   b. All information actually know to the Broker, now or during the pre-closing period, regarding the physical condition of the property; and,

c. Any environmental hazards affecting the Property which are required by law to be disclosed.

4. **Matters that Can Not be Disclosed by a Real Estate Broker (Non Agent).** Broker, when acting as a Dual Agent, shall not disclose the following information without the prior consent of the party concerned:

   a. That Buyer is willing to pay more than the purchase price offered for the property;

   b. That Seller is willing to accept less than the asking price for the property;

   c. What the motivating factors are for any party buying or selling the property;

   d. That Seller or Buyer will agree to financing terms other than those offered;

   e. Any material information about the other party unless either:

      (1) the disclosure is required by law,
      (2) the disclosure pertains to adverse material facts about Buyer's financial ability to perform the terms of the transaction,
      (3) the disclosure pertains to Buyer's intent to occupy the property as a principal residence, or
      (4) failure to disclose such information would constitute fraud or dishonest dealing.

5. **No Duty for Real Estate Broker (Non Agent) to Investigate**. Broker, when acting as a Real Estate Broker (Non Agent), has no duty to conduct an independent inspection of the property for the benefit of Buyer and has no duty to independently verify the accuracy or completeness of statements made by Seller or independent inspectors. Broker, when acting as a Real Estate Broker (Non Agent), has no duty to conduct an independent investigation of Buyer's financial condition or to verify the accuracy or completeness of any statement made by Buyer.

6. **Commission.** Only one commission shall be payable. Buyer and Seller acknowledge that the commission paid to the Broker is reflected in the price of the property sold. Seller shall pay the Broker the commission indicated in the Exclusive Right to Sell Listing Contract. Buyer shall not be obligated to pay any additional commission to Broker.

______________________________ ______________________________
Buyer date Buyer date

Broker:

______________________________
by date

## "In-Company" Sale Addendum (Transaction Broker/Initial Agency Relationship)

1. **Amendment to Agency Contract.** This "In-Company" Sale Addendum is part of either an Exclusive Right to Buy Contract (Buyer Agency Contract) or a Listing Contract (Seller Agency Contract) dated ______________, 19_____ between the broker named below and its sales agents ("Broker") and the undersigned Buyer or Seller. This Addendum will control in the event of any conflict with the contract to which it is attached.

2. **Limitation of Broker's Agency Obligations.** When acting as the agent for one party (either Buyer or Seller), Broker has duties and obligations which include utmost good faith, loyalty, and fidelity to that one principal. If the principal consents, however, Broker may act as a Transaction Broker when both the Seller and Buyer have an *agency* relationship with the same real estate company ("In-Company" Sale). A Transaction Broker is a broker engaged as a limited agent for both Seller and Buyer. Transaction Broker creates a conflict of interest because Broker's duties and obligations of confidentiality, full disclosure, and loyalty to one party conflict with those same duties to the other. Seller and Buyer are *not* vicariously liable for acts of a Transaction Broker).

   a. If this addendum is signed by Seller, Broker will act as the exclusive agent for Seller only when the Property is shown to a prospective buyer who has a working relationship with another licensed real estate company, but will act as a Transaction Broker only in an "In-Company" Sale.

   b. If this addendum is signed by Buyer, Broker will act only as the exclusive agent for Buyer when showing properties that are not listed with Broker, but will act as a Transaction Broker only in an "In-Company" Sale.

**The remaining provisions of this addendum describe significant changes to the obligations of Broker when acting as a Transaction Broker in an "In-Company" Sale.**

3. **Information that Must be Disclosed by a Transaction Broker.**

   a. All adverse material facts actually known by Broker, including but not limited to adverse material facts pertaining to the title to the Property which Seller indicates will not be remedied prior to the transfer of deed; and,

   b. All information actually know to the Broker, now or during the pre-closing period, regarding the physical condition of the property; and,

c. Any environmental hazards affecting the Property which are required by law to be disclosed.

4. **Matters that Can Not be Disclosed by a Transaction Broker.** Broker, when acting as a Dual Agent, shall not disclose the following information without the prior consent of the party concerned:

a. That Buyer is willing to pay more than the purchase price offered for the property;

b. That Seller is willing to accept less than the asking price for the property;

c. What the motivating factors are for any party buying or selling the property;

d. That Seller or Buyer will agree to financing terms other than those offered;

e. Any material information about the other party unless either:

(1) the disclosure is required by law,
(2) the disclosure pertains to adverse material facts about Buyer's financial ability to perform the terms of the transaction,
(3) the disclosure pertains to Buyer's intent to occupy the property as a principal residence, or
(4) failure to disclose such information would constitute fraud or dishonest dealing.

5. **No Duty for Transaction Broker to Investigate**. Broker, when acting as a Transaction Broker, has no duty to conduct an independent inspection of the property for the benefit of Buyer and has no duty to independently verify the accuracy or completeness of statements made by Seller or independent inspectors. Broker, when acting as a Transaction Broker, has no duty to conduct an independent investigation of Buyer's financial condition or to verify the accuracy or completeness of any statement made by Buyer.

6. **Commission.** Only one commission shall be payable. Buyer and Seller acknowledge that the commission paid to the Broker is reflected in the price of the property sold. Seller shall pay the Broker the commission indicated in the Exclusive Right to Sell Listing Contract. Buyer shall not be obligated to pay any additional commission to Broker.

______________________________ ______________________________

Buyer date Buyer date

Broker:

______________________________

by date

## "In-Company" Sale Addendum (Transaction Broker/Initial Agency Relationship)

1. **Amendment to Agency Contract.** This "In-Company" Sale Addendum is part of either an Exclusive Right to Buy Contract (Buyer Agency Contract) or a Listing Contract (Seller Agency Contract) dated ________________, 19_____ between the broker named below and its sales agents ("Broker") and the undersigned Buyer or Seller. This Addendum will control in the event of any conflict with the contract to which it is attached.

2. **Limitation of Broker's Agency Obligations.** When acting as the agent for one party (either Buyer or Seller), Broker has duties and obligations which include utmost good faith, loyalty, and fidelity to that one principal. If the principal consents, however, Broker may act as a Transaction Broker when both the Seller and Buyer have initially have either an *agency or a working* relationship with the same real estate company ("In-Company" Sale). A Transaction Broker is a broker engaged as a limited agent for both Seller and Buyer. Transaction Broker creates a conflict of interest because Broker's duties and obligations of confidentiality, full disclosure, and loyalty to one party conflict with those same duties to the other. Seller and Buyer are *not* vicariously liable for acts of a Transaction Broker).

    a. If this addendum is signed by Seller, Broker will act as the exclusive agent for Seller only when the Property is shown to a prospective buyer who has a working relationship with another licensed real estate company, but will act as a Transaction Broker only in an "In-Company" Sale.

    b. If this addendum is signed by Buyer, Broker will act only as the exclusive agent for Buyer when showing properties that are not listed with Broker, but will act as a Transaction Broker only in an "In-Company" Sale.

**The remaining provisions of this addendum describe significant changes to the obligations of Broker when acting as a Transaction Broker in an "In-Company" Sale.**

3. **Information that Must be Disclosed by a Transaction Broker.**

    a. All adverse material facts actually known by Broker, including but not limited to adverse material facts pertaining to the title to the Property which Seller indicates will not be remedied prior to the transfer of deed; and,

    b. All information actually know to the Broker, now or during the pre-closing period, regarding the physical condition of the property; and,

c. Any environmental hazards affecting the Property which are required by law to be disclosed.

4. **Matters that Can Not be Disclosed by a Transaction Broker.** Broker, when acting as a Dual Agent, shall not disclose the following information without the prior consent of the party concerned:

   a. That Buyer is willing to pay more than the purchase price offered for the property;

   b. That Seller is willing to accept less than the asking price for the property;

   c. What the motivating factors are for any party buying or selling the property;

   d. That Seller or Buyer will agree to financing terms other than those offered;

   e. Any material information about the other party unless either:

      (1) the disclosure is required by law,
      (2) the disclosure pertains to adverse material facts about Buyer's financial ability to perform the terms of the transaction,
      (3) the disclosure pertains to Buyer's intent to occupy the property as a principal residence, or
      (4) failure to disclose such information would constitute fraud or dishonest dealing.

5. **No Duty for Transaction Broker to Investigate**. Broker, when acting as a Transaction Broker, has no duty to conduct an independent inspection of the property for the benefit of Buyer and has no duty to independently verify the accuracy or completeness of statements made by Seller or independent inspectors. Broker, when acting as a Transaction Broker, has no duty to conduct an independent investigation of Buyer's financial condition or to verify the accuracy or completeness of any statement made by Buyer.

6. **Commission.** Only one commission shall be payable. Buyer and Seller acknowledge that the commission paid to the Broker is reflected in the price of the property sold. Seller shall pay the Broker the commission indicated in the Exclusive Right to Sell Listing Contract. Buyer shall not be obligated to pay any additional commission to Broker.

| | | | |
|---|---|---|---|
| Buyer | date | Buyer | date |

Broker:

| | |
|---|---|
| by | date |

## "In-Company" Sale Addendum

(Transaction Broker)

The following procedures for "In-Company Sales" are hereby made a part of the:
☐**Seller Listing Contract** ☐**Buyer Agency Contract** ☐**Purchase and Sale Contract**
dated ___________________________19____. The undersigned real estate broker and its sales agents ("Broker") and the Seller and/or the Buyer, collectively, ("Parties"), hereby acknowledge the following:

### Understanding

1. Seller engaged Broker to market Seller's property to any prospective buyer, including buyers who have initially established an agency relationship with Broker. Buyer wants to see any property which meets Buyer's needs, including property listed by Broker. In the event the Buyer becomes interested in a property listed with Broker, Seller and Buyer then desire to engage Broker to assist them both in the transaction.

2. The Broker, when acting as an agent, has fiduciary duties to only one principal, Seller or Buyer; these include: reasonable care, obedience and performance, accounting for funds received, undivided loyalty, confidentiality, and full disclosure.

3. The Broker can not act as an agent for both Buyer and Seller in the same transaction at the same time without creating a potential conflict of interest since the Broker's fiduciary duties of confidentiality, full disclosure, and loyalty to one party would conflict with those same duties to the other party.

4. The Broker can, however, act as a licensed real estate broker ("Transaction Broker"), namely a broker who assists both Parties throughout the purchase and sale transaction and not as an agent for either the Seller or the Buyer. To so act requires the prior written consent of all Parties.

### Agreement

The Parties agree that for all transactions in which Broker may initially act as a buyer's agent or a seller's agent, and the Buyer becoming interested in viewing a property listed by Seller with the Broker ("In-Company Sale"), the law of agency shall not apply, and in such event, the Buyer and/or the Seller and Broker hereby modify Broker's duties to allow Broker to act as a Transaction Broker. Buyer and Seller hereby consent to and waive any and all objections to Broker acting as a Transaction Broker. In such transactions the Parties agree that the duties, obligations and agreements between the Broker and the Buyer and/or the Seller are as follows:

5. Broker shall assist but not represent either or both Parties, independently or through attorney(s), with: the preparation of the purchase and sale contract ("Contract"); completion of and compliance with the terms and conditions of the Contract; and the closing and settlement of the transaction, keeping both Buyer and Seller fully informed regarding all aspects of the transaction.

6. Broker shall comply with all rules and regulations of the governmental licensing authority which governs the conduct of licensees in real estate transactions and with the laws of this state.

7. Broker shall have the following duties to both Parties: reasonable care, obedience and performance, accounting for funds received, disclosure of all material facts about the physical condition of property actually known to Broker, and to treat all Parties honestly.

8. Broker shall not disclose personal information about one party to the other party, unless the disclosure is required by law, or unless failure to disclose would constitute fraud or dishonest dealing.

9. Broker shall not disclose that the Buyer will pay a price or agree to terms other than those contained in the offer, or that the Seller will accept a price or terms other than those contained in the listing.

10. Broker shall not disclose the motivation of the Buyer to buy or the Seller to sell.

11. Only one commission shall be payable. Buyer and Seller acknowledge that the commission paid to the Broker is reflected in the price of the property sold. Seller shall pay the Broker the commission indicated in the Seller Listing Contract. Buyer shall not be obligated to pay any additional commission to Broker.

12. This Addendum will control in the event of any conflict with the contract to which it is attached.

____________________________ ____________________________

Buyer date Buyer date

Broker:

____________________________

by date

## "In Company" Sale Transaction Broker Addendum

This Addendum is hereby made a part of either the Exclusive Right to Sell Listing Contract or the Exclusive Buyer Agency Contract, as the case may be ("Contract"), between the undersigned real estate broker and its salespersons ("Broker") and the undersigned Seller or Buyer, ("Client"), collectively ("Parties"). In the event the terms of this Addendum conflict with, vary from, or modify the terms and provisions of the Contract, the terms of this Addendum shall control. Seller includes landlord. Buyer includes tenant. Sale and purchase includes lease.

**Fiduciary Duties.** The Broker has fiduciary duties to the Client which include: *reasonable care* (to act in a reasonable manner), *undivided loyalty and confidentiality* (keeping the Client's confidences), *obedience and performance* (to comply with the Client's reasonable directions regarding the purchase and sale of real property), *accounting* (to disclose the status of all transactional money in broker's possession), and *full disclosure* (to transmit all relevant and material information known by the Broker to the client regarding the other party).

**Seller-Broker Relationship.** When real property is listed for sale or lease by Seller with Broker, Broker acts initially as the agent of and owes fiduciary duties to the Seller ("Seller's Agent"). The Broker shall treat the Buyer honestly and shall disclose to the Buyer all defects of a material nature affecting the physical condition of the property actually known to the Broker. The Broker shall have no obligation to inspect the Property. The Broker can not, without the Seller's prior written consent, violate or modify the Broker's duty of undivided loyalty and confidentiality and full disclosure.

**Buyer-Broker Relationship.** When a Buyer engages the Broker to locate real property for purchase or lease, Broker shall act initially as the agent of and owes fiduciary duties to the Buyer ("Buyer's Agent"). The Broker shall treat the Seller honestly and shall not give the Seller false information concerning the financial condition of the Buyer, nor disclose the financial affairs of the Buyer without the Buyer's written consent. The Broker can not, without the Buyer's prior written consent, violate or modify the Broker's duty of undivided loyalty and confidentiality and full disclosure.

**"Out of Company" Sales.** When the Broker represents the Seller, and a buyer is procured through a brokerage office other than Broker's office, Broker shall transmit to Seller all information known to Broker regarding the transaction and the proposed buyer. When the Broker represents the Buyer and the property is listed with a brokerage office other than Broker's office, Broker shall transmit to Buyer all information known to Broker regarding the transaction and the proposed seller.

**"In-Company" Sales.** The Buyer and Seller acknowledge that the Buyer may seek to acquire a property listed with Broker, an "in-office" or "in-house" sale. In such a transaction the Broker would owe conflicting fiduciary duties to both Buyer and Seller at the same time, an inherent conflict of interest. The Broker can not represent the interests of either party to the exclusion or detriment of the other party. In order for Broker to assist both the Buyer and Seller in such transactions, the Parties need to consent in writing to allow the Broker to act as a "Transaction Broker" only, and thereby modify the original agency Contract between the Parties.

**Transaction Broker Modification.** The Parties agree that for all transactions wherein the Broker may initially act as both a Buyer's Agent and a Seller's Agent, the Buyer becoming interested in a property listed by the Seller with the Broker, the law of agency shall not apply. Broker, except as herein indicated, shall cease to represent either the Buyer or the Seller as an agent in the same transaction. The Broker shall act as a Transaction Broker, a licensed real estate broker who is neither the agent of the Buyer nor of the Seller but who is charged with assisting the Parties in completing the transaction as contemplated by the Parties. The following shall be the duties, obligations and agreements between the Broker and the Buyer and Seller:

1. Broker shall exercise **reasonable care**, to act in a commercially reasonable manner, in the preparation of all documents and transmission of information. Broker shall answer all questions honestly but shall properly refuse to answer questions that might violate a duty of confidentiality to either party.

2. Broker shall keep the former Client's confidences **confidential**, and not transmit any personal information known to the Broker regarding either party.

3. Broker shall be **obedient and perform**, complying with the reasonable directions and requests of both parties to accomplish the drafting of and fulfillment of the terms of the contract for sale. Broker shall assist both parties to comply with the terms and conditions precedent to the closing of the transaction and shall keep both Buyer and Seller fully informed regarding all aspects of the transaction.

4. Broker shall provide an **accounting** to all Parties, disclosing the status of all transaction money in Broker's possession.

5. Broker shall **disclose**, and transmit to all Parties the information known by the Broker regarding the physical condition of the property.

6. Broker shall comply with all the rules and regulations of the governmental licensing agency which governs the conduct of licensees in real estate transactions and with the laws of this state.

7. Broker shall not give legal advice to anyone, including advice regarding the condition of the legal title to the property, nor as to the extent of the title insurance Policy or exceptions.

8. Only one commission shall be payable. Buyer and Seller acknowledge that the commission paid to the Broker is reflected in the price of the property sold. Seller shall pay the Broker the commission indicated in the Exclusive Right to Sell Listing Contract. Buyer shall not be obligated to pay any additional commission to Broker.

9. A copy of this Addendum shall be a part of the final contract between the Buyer and Seller for the purchase, sale or lease of a property that comes within the purview of this Addendum.

The Parties acknowledge that this Addendum can not be entered into without the knowledge and written consent of both the Parties. Each has read this Addendum and sought the advice of an attorney, if they so desired.

______________________________ ______________________________

Buyer date Buyer date

Broker:

______________________________

by date

## Dual (*Limited*) Agency Addendum

This Addendum is hereby made a part of: ☐ **Seller Listing Contract** ☐ **Buyer Agency Contract** ☐ **Purchase and Sale Contract** ("Contract"), between the undersigned real estate broker and its salespersons ("Broker") and the undersigned Seller and/or Buyer, ("Client"), collectively ("Parties"). In the event the terms of this Addendum conflict with, vary from, or modify the terms and provisions of the Contract, the terms of this Addendum shall control. Seller includes landlord. Buyer includes tenant. Sale and purchase includes lease.

**Fiduciary Duties.** The Broker has fiduciary duties to the Client which include; *reasonable care* (to act in a reasonable manner), *undivided loyalty and confidentiality* (keeping the Client's confidences), *obedience and performance* (to comply with the Client's reasonable directions regarding the purchase and sale of real property), *accounting* (to disclose the status of all transactional money in broker's possession), and *full disclosure* (to transmit all relevant and material information known by the Broker to the Client regarding the other party).

**Seller-Broker Relationship.** When real property is listed for sale or lease by Seller with Broker, Broker acts initially as the agent of and owes fiduciary duties to the Seller ("Seller's Agent"). The Broker shall treat the Buyer honestly and shall disclose to the Buyer all defects of a material nature affecting the physical condition of the property actually known to the Broker. The Broker shall have no obligation to inspect the Property. The Broker can not, without the Seller's prior written consent, violate or modify the Broker's duty of undivided loyalty and confidentiality and full disclosure.

**Buyer-Broker Relationship.** When a Buyer engages the Broker to locate real property for purchase or lease, Broker shall act initially as the agent of and owes fiduciary duties to the Buyer ("Buyer's Agent"). The Broker shall treat the Seller honestly and shall not give the Seller false information concerning the financial condition of the Buyer, nor disclose the financial affairs of the Buyer without the Buyer's written consent. The Broker can not, without the Buyer's prior written consent, violate or modify the Broker's duty of undivided loyalty and confidentiality and full disclosure.

**"Out of Company" or "Cooperative" Sales.** When the Broker represents the Seller, and a buyer is procured through a brokerage office other than Broker's office, Broker shall transmit to Seller all information known to Broker regarding the transaction and the proposed buyer. When the Broker represents the Buyer and the property is listed with a brokerage office other than Broker's office, Broker shall transmit to Buyer all information known to Broker regarding the transaction and the proposed seller.

**"In-Company" Sales.** The Buyer and Seller acknowledge that the Buyer may seek to acquire a property listed with Broker, an "in-company", "in-office" or "in-house" sale. In such a transaction the Broker would owe conflicting fiduciary duties to both Buyer and Seller at the same time, an inherent conflict of interest. The Broker can not represent the interests of either party to the exclusion or detriment of the other party. In order for Broker to assist both the Buyer and Seller in such transactions, the Parties must consent in writing to allow the Broker to act as a "Dual (Limited) Agent", modifying the existing agency Contracts, Listing Contract and Buyer Agency Contract, between the Parties.

**Dual (Limited) Agency Modification.** The Parties agree that for all transactions wherein the Broker may initially act as both a Buyer's Agent and a Seller's Agent, the Buyer becoming interested in a property listed by the Seller with the Broker, Broker, except as herein indicated, shall provide *limited* representation to both the Buyer or the Seller in the same transaction. The Broker shall act as a Limited Dual Agent for both the Buyer and the Seller. The following shall be the duties, obligations and agreements between the Broker and the Buyer and the Seller:

1. Broker shall exercise *reasonable care*, to act in a commercially reasonable manner, in the preparation of all documents and transmission of information. Broker shall answer all questions honestly but properly shall refuse to answer questions that might violate a duty of confidentiality to either party.

2. Broker shall keep the former Client's confidences *confidential*, and not transmit any personal information known to the Broker regarding either party.

3. Broker shall be *obedient and perform*, complying with the reasonable directions and requests of both parties to accomplish the drafting of and fulfillment of the terms of the contract for sale. Broker shall assist both parties to comply with the terms and conditions precedent to the closing of the transaction and shall keep both Buyer and Seller fully informed regarding all aspects of the transaction.

4. Broker shall provide an *accounting* to all Parties, disclosing the status of all transaction money in Broker's possession.

5. Broker shall *disclose*, and transmit to all Parties the information known by the Broker regarding the physical condition of the property.

6. Broker shall comply with all the rules and regulations of the governmental regulatory agency which governs the conduct of licensees in real estate transactions and with the laws of this state.

7. Broker shall not give legal advice to anyone, including advice regarding the condition of the legal title to the property, nor as to the extent of the title insurance Policy or exceptions.

8. Only one commission shall be payable. Buyer and Seller acknowledge that the commission paid to the Broker is reflected in the price of the property sold. Seller shall pay the Broker the commission indicated in the Exclusive Right to Sell Listing Contract. Buyer shall not be obligated to pay any additional commission to Broker.

9. A copy of this Addendum shall be a part of the final contract between the Buyer and Seller.

The Parties acknowledge that this Addendum can not be entered into without the knowledge and written consent of all of the Parties. Each has read this Addendum and sought the advice of an attorney, if they so desired.

_______________________________ _______________________________

Buyer date Buyer date

Broker:

_______________________________

by date

## Dual (*Limited*) Agency Addendum

(For use with "In-Company" Sales Only)

This Dual (*Limited*) Agency Addendum is hereby made part of either a ☐ **Exclusive Right to Sell Listing Contract (Seller)** or a ☐ **Exclusive Buyer Agency Contract** between the broker named below and its sales agents ("Broker") and the undersigned buyer and/or seller ("Principal"), or a ☐ **Purchase and Sale Contract** between the seller and the buyer, dated ________________________ 19____.

**The undersigned Principal(s) acknowledge that:**

1. Buyer is interested in viewing any property which Buyer feels might suit Buyer's needs, including property listed by Seller with Broker.

2. Seller is interested in marketing Seller's property to any prospective buyer, including buyers who have an agency relationship with Broker.

3. The Broker acting for a single Principal, Seller or Buyer, owes that Principal a duty of undivided loyalty, confidentiality, and full disclosure.

4. Dual (*Limited*) Agency, when the Broker owes duties of undivided loyalty, confidentiality, and full disclosure to both the Buyer and Seller, creates a conflict of interest.

5. The Broker can act as a Dual (*Limited*) Agent of both Principals, the Seller and the Buyer, in the same transaction only upon the prior written consent of Broker, Buyer and Seller.

**Principal(s) and Broker hereby agree:**

1. Principal(s) hereby consents or ratifies Principal's previous consent (re-affirm by signing again when made an exhibit to the sale contract) to this modification to provide that Broker's duties are modified so that Broker may act as a Dual (*Limited*) Agent and hereby waives all objections to Broker acting as a Dual (*Limited*) Agent for a transaction for the sale of Seller's property wherein Broker initially represented Seller and Buyer.

2. Once Broker becomes a Dual (*Limited*) Agent, and so informs both Principals, Broker shall not disclose to either Seller or Buyer, without the prior written consent of the other, any of the following information:

   a. Material information regarding the other party, unless disclosure is required by law, or unless failure to disclose would constitute fraud or dishonest dealing.

   b. That the Buyer will pay a price or agree to terms other than those contained in the proposed offer to purchase, or that Seller will accept a price or terms other than those contained in the listing agreement.

c. The motivation of the Buyer to buy or the Seller to sell.

d. Information protected by any applicable "Fair Housing" laws and regulations and information which "psychologically impacts" the property.

3. The Broker shall disclose all information regarding the physical condition of the property actually known to Broker. Broker is not obligated to inspect the property.

4. Broker shall be entitled to one commission, which the Parties agree is reflected in the purchase price, indicated in the Exclusive Right To Sell Listing Agreement.

5. This Addendum shall control in the event of any conflict with the contract to which it is attached.

______________________________ ______________________________

Buyer date Buyer date

Broker:

______________________________

by date

# Designated Agency Addendum

(Listing Agreement, Sale Agreement, Buyer Agency Agreement)

This Addendum is hereby made part of either the Seller Listing Contract, the Buyer Agency Contract or the Purchase and Sale Contract between the below indicated parties dated ________________________19____.

[*Check only one box and initial below the box*]

☐ **Designated "Split" Agency.** In the event the Buyer and Seller are working with or represented by the Broker through *separate* Salespersons, for the sale of a listed property the parties hereby agree that:

______ ______ ______ ______ ______ ______

1. The selling Salesperson represents the buyer exclusively; and,
2. The listing Salesperson represents the seller exclusively; and,
3. The Broker shall be a Dual Agent, defined below; and,
4. Seller shall pay the commission indicated in the listing agreement; and,
5. Buyer shall not pay an additional commission; and,
6. Broker and Salespersons shall share in the commission; and,
7. No knowledge shall be imputed to the Broker.

☐ **Dual Agency.** In the event the Buyer and Seller are working with or represented by the Broker through *the same* Salesperson, for the sale of a listed property the parties hereby agree that:

______ ______ ______ ______ ______ ______

1. A conflict of interest exists because the parties, interests and desires may be different; and,
2. Broker and Salesperson shall act as Dual Agents of both the Seller and the Buyer; and,
3. Dual Agents *shall not*:
   a. Disclose any price or terms other than those indicated by the Buyer or Seller;
   b. Disclose the motivating factors of either Buyer or Seller; nor the price that the Seller is willing to accept;
   c. Disclose any confidential information about a party;
   d. Advocate or promote the interests of a party;
   e. Give advice to any party to the detriment of the other party;
   f. Disclose any material information about a party unless:
      i) the disclosure is required by law,
      ii) the disclosure pertains to adverse material facts about the Buyer's ability to perform the terms of the transaction or occupy the property,
      iii) failure to disclose would constitute fraud or dishonest dealing.
   g. Impute knowledge to the Broker.
4. Dual Agents shall:
   a. Disclose all material facts actually known to the Broker or Salesperson pertaining to the physical condition, including environmental hazards, of the property; and,
   b. Assist the parties with the preparation of the contract; and,
   c. Assist the parties with financing and closing of the transaction.

☐ **No Agency/Transaction Broker.** In the event the Buyer and/or Seller is working with, or is represented by the Broker through *any* Salesperson, for the sale of a property *listed with or not listed with* the Broker and both parties elect not to have an agency relationship, the Parties hereby agree that:

_____ _____ _____ _____ _____ _____

1. A potential conflict of interest may exist because the Parties interests and desires may be different; and,
2. Broker and Salesperson shall *not act as agents of either* the Seller or the Buyer; and,
3. Broker and Salesperson (Non Agents) *shall not*:
   a. Disclose any price or terms other than those indicated by the Buyer or Seller;
   b. Disclose the motivating factors of either Buyer or Seller; nor the price that the Seller is willing to accept or the Buyer willing to offer;
   c. Disclose any confidential information about a party;
   d. Advocate or promote the interests of a party;
   e. Give advice to any party to the detriment of the other party;
   f. Disclose any material information about a party unless:
      i) the disclosure is required by law,
      ii) the disclosure pertains about adverse material facts about the buyer's ability to perform the terms of the transaction or occupy the property,
      iii) failure to disclose would constitute fraud or dishonest dealing.
   g. Impute knowledge to the Broker.
4. Broker and Salesperson (Non Agents) *shall*:
   a. Disclose all material facts actually known to the Broker or Salesperson pertaining to the physical condition, including environmental hazards, of the property; and,
   b. Assist the parties with the preparation of the contract; and,
   c. Assist the parties with financing and closing of the transaction.

_______________________________ _______________________________

Buyer date Seller date

_______________________________ _______________________________

Buyer date Seller date

Broker:

_______________________________

by date

_______________________________ _______________________________

Salesperson date Salesperson date

## Designated "Split" Agency Contract Addendum

(Listing Agreement, Sale Agreement, Buyer Agency Agreement)

This Addendum is hereby made part of either the Seller Listing Contract, the Buyer Agency Contract or the Purchase and Sale Contract between the below indicated parties dated ________________________19____.

[*Check only one box and initial below the box*]

☐ **Designated "Split" Agency.** In the event the Buyer and Seller are working with or represented by the Broker through *separate* Salespersons, for the sale of a listed property the parties hereby agree that:

_____ _____ _____ _____ _____ _____

1. The selling Salesperson represents the buyer exclusively;
2. The listing Salesperson represents the seller exclusively;
3. The Broker shall be a Dual Agent, defined below;
4. Seller shall pay the commission indicated in the listing agreement;
5. Buyer shall not pay an additional commission;
6. Broker and Salespersons shall share in the commission;
7. No knowledge shall be imputed to the Broker.

☐ **Dual Agency.** In the event the Buyer and Seller are working with or are represented by the Broker through *the same* Salesperson, for the sale of a listed property the parties hereby agree that:

_____ _____ _____ _____ _____ _____

1. A conflict of interest exists because the parties' interests and desires may be different; and,
2. Broker and Salesperson shall act as Dual Agents of both the Seller and the Buyer; and,
3. Dual Agents *shall not*:
   a. Disclose any price or terms other than those indicated by the Buyer or Seller;
   b. Disclose the motivating factors of either Buyer or Seller; nor the price that the Seller is willing to accept;
   c. Disclose any confidential information about a party;
   d. Advocate or promote the interests of a party;
   e. Give advice to any party to the detriment of the other party;
   f. Disclose any material information about a party unless:
      i) the disclosure is required by law,
      ii) the disclosure pertains to adverse material facts about the Buyer's ability to perform the terms of the transaction or occupy the property,
      iii) failure to disclose would constitute fraud or dishonest dealing,
   g. Impute knowledge to the Broker.
4. Dual Agents shall:
   a. Disclose all material facts actually known to the Broker or Salesperson pertaining to the physical condition, including environmental hazards, of the property; and,
   b. Assist the parties with the preparation of the contract; and,
   c. Assist the parties with financing and closing of the transaction.

☐ **No Agency/Transaction Broker.** In the event the Buyer and/or Seller is working with or is represented by the Broker through *any* Salesperson, for the sale of a property *listed with or not listed with* the Broker and both parties elect not to have an agency relationship, the parties hereby agree that:

______ ______ ______ ______ ______ ______

1. A potential conflict of interest may exist because the parties' interests and desires may be different; and,
2. Broker and Salesperson shall *not act as agents of either* the Seller or the Buyer; and,
3. Broker and Salesperson (Non Agents) *shall not*:
   a. Disclose any price or terms other than those indicated by the Buyer or Seller;
   b. Disclose the motivating factors of either Buyer or Seller; nor the price that the Seller is willing to accept;
   c. Disclose any confidential information about a party;
   d. Advocate or promote the interests of a party;
   e. Give advice to any party to the detriment of the other party;
   f. Disclose and material information about a party unless:
      i) the disclosure is required by law,
      ii) the disclosure pertains to adverse material facts about the Buyer's ability to perform the terms of the transaction or occupy the property,
      iii) failure to disclose would constitute fraud or dishonest dealing.
   g. Impute knowledge to the Broker.
4. Broker and Salesperson (Non Agents) *shall*:
   a. Disclose all material facts actually know to the Broker or Salesperson pertaining to the physical condition, including environmental hazards, of the property; and,
   b. Assist the parties with the preparation of the contract; and,
   c. Assist the parties with financing and closing of the transaction.

**No Duty for Dual Agent or Transaction Broker to Investigate**. Broker and Salesperson(s) have no duty to: conduct an independent inspection of the property for the benefit of Buyer; independently verify the accuracy or completeness of statements made by Seller or independent inspectors; conduct an independent investigation of Buyer's financial condition or to verify the accuracy or completeness of any statement made by Buyer.

____________________________ ____________________________

Buyer date Seller date

____________________________ ____________________________

Buyer date Seller date

Broker:

____________________________

by date

____________________________ ____________________________

Salesperson date Salesperson date

**Letter - Other Brokers Rejecting Subagency**

Mr/Ms. Other Broker
Super Seller Realty
30000 Sales Boulevard
Commission, CO 99999-9999

Re: Agency Policy and Compensation Schedule for Cooperating Brokers/Offices

Dear Other Broker:

With all the confusion about agency and compensation, we have decided to write to everyone and explain what we think is very good news. It is our desire to cooperate fully with all offices and still limit both the listing broker's risk and the selling broker's risk. I hope that you are as excited about this as we are.

We want to stimulate cooperation and ensure confidence that your office is going to be compensated when you sell one of our listings. This information overrides any information provided in the MLS book.

Listings. We have determined that it is in the best interests of this firm and the sellers that we represent to offer the following compensation alternatives:

1. Cooperating Brokers and Buyer Brokers or Buyer Agents. This used to be called the "co-op" or "co-broke" sale. We want to cooperate with everyone possible. In the event that your office is licensed by the state and is not a subagent, we will pay to your office ____% of the final sales price immediately upon receipt of payment from the seller. The only requirement is that your office have a licensed broker. That is all that it takes. You do not need to be a buyer broker, buyer agent or represent anyone. In order to be paid, all you need is a broker's license.

2. Subagents. Like so many brokers across the country, we have decided that subagency is not in the best interests of the seller or this office. Therefore, we do not accept subagency and do not pay subagents. *Do not worry. If you are the procuring cause, we will pay you.* Please read the first option (#1) above.

This offer is made unilaterally on behalf of our seller clients to all brokers in the area. You do not need to agree to reciprocate to take advantage of this offer of compensation and cooperation. If you decide to treat us differently, that decision is totally up to you. We want no bilateral commission splits or provisions. We simply offer what we have decided is in the best interests of this firm and our sellers to encourage you to show and sell our listings.

Sales. When we have procured the buyer and are cooperating with your office, you are no longer potentially liable for the actions or inactions of our salespersons. On order to avoid potential conflicts of interest, we no longer are acting as subagents for sellers. We do, however, need to be compensated for working with a buyer. We indicate to our buyers and sellers that each is paying a portion of the commission which is reflected in the purchase price and is, in fact, paid by the seller to the listing broker at settlement.

1. Compensation. When we show and sell your listings, we will first be asking for compensation from your office. We will expect to be compensated in the amount that you indicate in the MLS book for subagents or buyer's agents or otherwise, whichever is the greater. We will, absent such an offering in the MLS, be contacting you on each showing to verify the commission amount. We do not collect twice, "double commissions", once from you and once from the buyer.

   We wish to leave the extent of commissions to an agreement between offices. In the unlikely event that your office and our office can not reach an agreement, which is satisfactory to compensate our office, either through the MLS or between offices, we will ask that the buyer insert a clause in the contract providing that the seller pay our commission.

2. Agency Status. We will be acting as either buyer brokers, representing the buyer, or transaction brokers, namely licensed brokers who do not represent the seller or the buyer. We will not be acting as your agents, that is as subagents of your sellers.

If you feel that the proper alternative is not addressed here, please call me immediately as we are committed to working with all brokers in the area. In order to maintain a consistent approach to all offices, this policy can be modified only by me personally and no one else in my office. If you have questions, please call me.

Most sincerely,
The Orcas Island Company

by: Oliver E. Frascona, Broker

## Letter - Other Brokers Rejecting Subagency #2

Mr/Ms. Other Broker
Super Seller Realty
30000 Sales Boulevard
Commission, CO 99999-9999

Re: Agency Policy and Compensation Schedule for Cooperating Brokers/Offices

Dear Other Broker:

With all the confusion about agency and compensation, we have decided to write to everyone and explain what we think is very good news. It is our desire to cooperate fully with all offices and still limit both the listing broker's risk and the selling broker's risk. I hope that you are as excited about this as we are.

We want to stimulate cooperation and ensure confidence that your office is going to be compensated when you sell one of our listings. This information overrides any information provided in the MLS book.

Listings. We have determined that it is in the best interests of this firm and the sellers that we represent to offer the following compensation alternatives:

1. Cooperating Broker. This used to be called the "co-op" or "co-broke" sale. We want to cooperate with everyone possible. In the event that your office is licensed by the state and is not a subagent or a buyer broker, we will pay to your office ____% of the final sales price immediately upon receipt of payment from the seller. The only requirement is that your office have a licensed broker. That is all that it takes. You do not need to be a subagent or a buyer agent or represent anyone to be compensated.

2. Buyer Broker or Buyer Agent. When your office is acting as a buyer broker or buyer agent, we pay your office ____% of the final sales price immediately upon receipt of payment from the seller.

3. Subagent. Like so many other brokers across the country, we have decided that subagency is not in the best interests of the seller or this office. Therefore, we do not accept subagency and do not pay subagents. *Do not worry. We will pay your office. Please re-read the first option (#1) above.*

This offer is made unilaterally on behalf of our seller clients to all brokers in the area. You do not need to agree to reciprocate to take advantage of this offer of compensation and cooperation. If you decide to treat us differently that is totally up to you. We want no bilateral commission splits or provisions. We simply offer what we have decided is in the best interests of this firm and our sellers to encourage you to show and sell our listings.

Sales. When we have procured the buyer and are cooperating with your office, you are no longer potentially liable for the actions or inactions of our salespersons. In order to avoid potential conflicts of interest, we no longer are acting as subagents for sellers. However, we do need to be compensated for working with a buyer. We indicate to our buyers and sellers that each is paying a portion of the commission which is reflected in the purchase price and is, in fact, paid by the seller to the listing broker at settlement.

1. Compensation. When we show and sell your listings, we will first be asking for compensation from your office. We will expect to be compensated in the amount that you indicate in the MLS book for subagents or buyers' agents or otherwise, whichever is the greater. We will, absent such an offering in the MLS, be contacting you on each showing to verify the commission amount. We do not collect twice, "double commissions", once from you and once from the buyer.

   We wish to leave the extent of commissions to an agreement between offices. In the unlikely event that your office and our office can not reach an agreement, which is satisfactory to compensate our office, either through the MLS or between offices, we will ask that the buyer insert a clause in the contract providing that the seller pay our commission.

2. Agency Status. We will be acting as either buyer brokers, representing the buyer, or transaction brokers, namely licensed brokers who do not represent the seller or the buyer. We will not be acting as your agents, that is as subagents of your sellers.

If you feel that the proper alternative is not addressed here, please call me immediately as we are committed to working with all brokers in the area. In order to maintain a consistent approach to all offices, this policy can be modified only by me personally and no one else in my office. If you have questions, please call me.

Most sincerely,
The Orcas Island Company

by: Oliver E. Frascona, Broker

## Letter - Other Brokers Rejecting Subagency Establish Buyer Agency

Mr/Ms. Other Broker
Super Seller Realty
30000 Sales Boulevard
Commission, CO 99999-9999

Re: Agency Policy and Compensation Schedule for Cooperating Brokers/Offices

Dear Other Broker:

With all the confusion about agency and compensation, we have decided to write to everyone and explain what we think is very good news. It is our desire to cooperate fully with all offices and still limit both the listing broker's risk and the selling broker's risk. I hope that you are as excited about this as we are.

We want to stimulate cooperation and ensure confidence that your office is going to be compensated paid when you sell one of our listings. This information overrides any information provided in the MLS book.

Listings. We have determined that it is in the best interests of this firm and the sellers that we represent to offer the following compensation alternatives:

1. Cooperating Broker. This used to be called the "co-op" or "co-broke" sale. We want to cooperate with everyone possible. In the event that your office is licensed by the state and is not a subagent or a buyer broker, we will pay to your office ____% of the final sales price, immediately upon receipt of payment from the seller. The only requirement is that your office have a licensed broker, nothing else. That is all that it takes. You do not need to be a subagent or a buyer agent or represent anyone in order to be paid.

2. Buyer Broker or Buyer Agent. When your office is acting as a buyer broker or buyer agent, we pay your office ____% of the final sales price immediately upon receipt of payment from the seller, .

3. Subagent. Like so many other brokers across the country, we have decided that subagency is not in the best interests of the seller or this office. Therefore, we do not accept subagency and do not pay subagents. *Do not worry. We will pay your office. Please re-read the first option (#1) above.*

This offer is made unilaterally on behalf of our seller clients to all brokers in the area. You do not need to agree to reciprocate to take advantage of this offer of compensation and cooperation. If you decide to treat us differently that is totally up to you. We want no bilateral commission splits or provisions. We simply offer what we have decided is in the best interests of this firm and our sellers to encourage you to show and sell our listings.

Sales. When we have procured the buyer and are cooperating with your office, you are no longer potentially liable for the actions or inactions of our salespersons. In order to avoid potential conflicts of interest, we no longer are acting as subagents for sellers. However, we do need to be compensated for working with a buyer. We indicate to our buyers and sellers that each is paying a portion of the commission which is reflected in the purchase price and is, in fact, paid by the seller to the listing broker at settlement.

1. Compensation. When we show and sell your listings, we will first be asking for compensation from your office. We will expect to be compensated in the amount that you indicate in the MLS book for subagents or buyers' agents or otherwise, whichever is the greater. We will, absent such an offering in the MLS, be contacting you on each showing to verify the commission amount. We do not collect twice, "double commissions", once from you and once from the buyer.

   We wish to leave the extent of commissions to an agreement between offices. In the unlikely event that your office and our office can not reach an agreement, which is satisfactory to compensate our office, either through the MLS or between offices, we will ask that the buyer insert a clause in the contract providing that the seller pay our commission.

2. Agency Status. We will be acting as buyer brokers, representing the buyer. We will not be acting as your agents, that is as subagents of your sellers.

If you feel that the proper alternative is not addressed here, please call me immediately as we are committed to working with all brokers in the area. In order to maintain a consistent approach to all offices, this policy can be modified only by me personally and no one else in my office. If you have questions, please call me.

Most sincerely,
The Orcas Island Company

by: Oliver E. Frascona, Broker

# Chapter Five
# The Contract
### *Drafting the Offer or Counteroffer*

## General Contract Drafting Tips

The contract will govern the entire transaction. After the contract is signed the terms are fixed. From this point forward the agreement is set in stone. The agreement should not be modified. Agency is no longer an issue. The real estate professional is charged with making sure that the terms of the contract are carried out. It is your job not to interfere with the contract to closing process. You are to expedite that process. Although this is not a complete forms manual for completing a sales contract, the authors have included multiple clauses that pertain to items discussed in this book.

**Closing Date.** The actual closing date, recordation date, or date that the property is conveyed should be one that is realistic for all parties. Allow time for mailing closing documents and mortgage documents if the entities are in different geographical locations. Unfortunately, you can not always rely upon the postal service to deliver in a timely manner. Also, ascertain early in the transaction if either the buyer or seller will require a power of attorney. Again, the title company, mortgage lender, and attorney must have the correct information in order to prepare documents properly for final closing.

**Contingencies or Conditions.** Remember the difference between promises and contingencies. Terms must be written to reflect the intent of the party who will benefit, provide a time limit for the term to be satisfied and a provision for the consequences in the event of non-compliance. By writing "Buyer to make loan application", the seller may have no recourse in the event of non-performance. "The obligation of the seller to sell is contingent upon the buyer making loan application within five days of acceptance" provides both an avenue for declaring the contract null and void as well as setting a deadline for satisfaction of the contingency.

Do not neglect to provide for the return of the buyer's deposits with deductions, if any, in the event a contingency is not met by a specific deadline. When a contingency depends upon an approval by either the buyer, seller, or third party, it is best to indicate that written disapproval must be provided within a specific time frame in order to declare the contract null and void or that approval will be deemed to be granted and the contingency thereby removed.

**Creative Financing.** More than any other aspect of a transaction, except possibly an undetectable defect in the condition of the property which was not discoverable and which does not show its ugly head until well after the closing, financing has become the hotbed of potential liability and loss. Much like latent defects, problems with financing can exist in a dormant state well into the future. The advent of complex arrangements and extensive television coverage of what some might consider "creative" methods of acquisition and financing that are not normally utilized has only partially educated the public and left them often worse off than before the process began. The misconceptions about financing that prevail among all segments of society and even in the ranks of attorneys and some real estate professionals never cease to amaze us.

The disclosure and explanation of the seller's involvement in the financing is best given at the time the listing contract is completed. Because the subject of financing alternatives may be lost in the multitude of other concerns during the initial marketing process, it may be appropriate to repeat the seller's financing involvement again at the time of the presentation of a contract. In any event, before the seller or buyer signs a contract that indicates seller involvement in the existing financing, a disclosure must be made.

The existing responsibility of the seller and/or the new obligation of the buyer to repay the existing loan can be altered dramatically in a transfer of property. With an assumption, the promise to pay the debt of another, the buyer is added to the list of obligors on the promissory note. If the transfer is subject to the existing promissory note, the seller remains solely responsible for the loan payment and the buyer is not personally liable to pay. With a novation the seller is released of any future obligation to repay the loan and the buyer is responsible for the loan's repayment. In addition, any of the foregoing alternatives can be coupled with a seller carry-back or owner-carry second mortgage.

Assumable financing may be the very factor that induces a buyer to purchase a particular house. However, the agent often fails to explain adequately the ramifications of the different alternatives until after the contract has been accepted or even after the closing. Even though assumable, the seller often remains liable for the payment of the debt. Assumable does not mean that the seller is released from liability.

**Caution.** *The "free living" effect. As a result of the slow economic conditions existing in some areas, the time-consuming and previously*

> *obscure foreclosure laws, the rules preventing or delaying the entry of deficiency judgments in some states and the delay imposed as a result of the modern Bankruptcy Code, some owners are realizing that they can stop making payments on the existing loan, whether they assumed it or took the property subject to the loan, and live in the residence from six to eighteen months rent free. The longest term Oliver knows was forty-two months--that's right, forty-two months--without the owner making a single payment.*
>
> *A family with any income can amass a good deal of money in that time period. Therefore, they have the down payment for the next home when they are finally removed from their current residence. You got it. This person now has the cash to assume another non-qualifying assumption (VA and FHA, subject to some restrictions, and some private and conventional financing) and could be looking at your current listing. Buyers with that kind of cash are rarely the subject of scrutiny, almost never trigger the request for a credit report, are hard to recognize and even harder for some brokers and sellers and other desperate people to turn down.*

**Default.** Draft the contract carefully so that you clearly indicate the responsibilities of each party. In the event of a default, as the drafter of the contract, you will immediately be on the hot seat to explain the term and the element of default. Write clearly. Use simple sentences. Avoid complex punctuation. One thought, one sentence.

Either the buyer or seller may be in default. Before you get carried away, remember that in almost all circumstances, it is difficult to demand specific performance from either party. Rarely is the seller forced to sell or the buyer compelled to purchase. Damages and/or attorney's fees may be the most realistic recourse for either party. In most circumstances the seller will not compel performance and will be relegated to retention of the earnest money. If the earnest money is substantial, litigation is almost assured.

**Fraud and the Government Loan.** With the tendency of the federal government agencies, especially the FHA and the VA, to be apparently unresponsive and unaware of what is happening in the world, some people have decided that the regulations that govern such loans are like the fifty-five mile speed limit. They believe that the regulations are ineffective, unrealistic, often unenforced, and carrying only a inconsequential penalty when adjudicated. You can be assured that although these giants appear to have a hard time getting anything accomplished and appear oblivious to the transgressions that are occurring, they have enlisted, in addition to their own in-house staff of overworked investigators, a cadre of FBI agents and the offices of the U.S. Attorney to assist in their search for, and prosecution of, those that are defrauding the government.

Some real estate licensees still are trying to have someone obtain an "owner occupant" loan when in fact the prospective borrower never intends to live in the property. Others have determined that a new FHA loan enhances the marketability of the property and are encouraging sellers to refinance and then sell the property. Yet another group is encouraging people to refinance and immediately sell to a buyer procured prior to the refinance.

The professional broker and agent, while never engaging in such activities, may be caught in the ever-expanding net thrown to capture the true offenders. Care needs to be taken in even the most routine transaction involving government loans to ensure that everything is properly completed. When the pressure starts, the buyer and seller point to the broker as being responsible.

The following case in point, while not exactly indicative of the foregoing, exemplifies the ramifications of what appears to be a normal transaction for a hectic agent.

**Case in Point.** *The hurried, experienced agent (ten years plus in the business) answers a call on an advertisement for the sale of a friend's property. A smooth showing results in a contract indicating a new VA loan. The agent takes the buyer to the lender who "does all my business." The loan goes through the normal process and is approved and ready to close. But a delay in funding forces the lender to reverify the employment of the purchaser. The call to the employer results in the reply: "He has never worked for my husband."*

*The lender contacts the agent who talks with the buyer who assures the agent that all is well; he just does not get along with the spouse of the boss. The agent, believing the buyer he barely knows, suggests to the lender that it is all a mistake. The lender calls the VA who comes to see the agent. Believing that the truth is a good defense and easily noticed by trained investigators, the real estate agent talks to the investigating agents, who include an FBI agent, and explains all he knows.*

*The result is that the agent is involved in a grand jury investigation which almost leads to his being indicted on several felony counts. The buyer, who never was employed by anyone, had sent the verification to himself. When confronted by the investigators, the buyer replied, "The agent thought up the entire scam."*

*Fortunately, the investigators also later talked with the friend-employer. The agent, poorer now from attorney's fees but still married, sane and alive pleads guilty to a misdemeanor and bargains for two years probation, not because he is guilty, but because he can not win. During that time the agent will not be allowed to be involved in any VA loans.*

The good news is that the prohibition against being involved in VA loans is reduced to only those transactions involving the agent. Formerly, it had been anyone associated with the agent. How could an office list property in good faith if VA financing was not an alternative for any buyer or seller?

The result was that a very good real estate professional almost lost it all. The lessons are clear and simple. Know at least a little about your buyer; maybe make a call to the place of work. Realize that due to the efforts of a terrible few, government loans are under attack and your reputation, a reputation made one deal at a time over a long period of time, may be the only thing that can save you when the going gets tough. In this case, a good reputation was one of the deciding factors.

**Names.** When working with multiple parties as buyers or sellers, use the entire name for each entity. Married couples should be addressed as Jonathan A. Goodman and Mimi Goodman instead of Jon and Mimi Goodman. Use the "and" and "or" as applicable and not "and/or" . And/or implies differing connotations to different people. Does it mean either? Does it mean both? It is best just to say "and" if you mean a group and "or" if you mean either.

**Party Designation.** Use the same designation for the players throughout the contract and all addenda. Once you refer to the buyers as "buyers", do not alter the designation to "purchasers". We find the easiest way to avoid the single party or multiple party designations is to use buyer(s).

**Price and Loan Adjustments.** Discount points and loan origination fees also need complete, timely, and adequate presentation prior to the seller or buyer becoming obligated to a contract. Does the seller have to pay the agreed-upon discount even if the buyer uses the money to obtain a lower interest rate? Is a discount point different from a loan origination fee? The payment of large sums to induce a lender to make a loan is being viewed by some regulators as a reduction in the effective purchase price and consequently a reduction of the amount upon which the commission is calculated. The use of zero coupon bonds, gems or questionable paper to offset the purchase price is receiving close scrutiny. Sometimes it can be very embarrassing when the broker can not explain the ramifications of using such items.

**Case in Point.** *At the direction and suggestion of the purchaser, a broker provides in the contract, that a seller accept a zero coupon bond as part payment of the listed price in order to obtain the full listed price, which both purchaser and seller have verbally agreed is in excess of the fair market value of the property. The bond had a current market value of about $2,000 and a future value, upon redemption in twenty years, of about $12,000. The seller is to give the purchaser a credit equal to the future value of the bond. The* *seller, an astute older woman, not only agrees to the proposal but counters lower, thus increasing the amount of the future value of the bond and also thereby changing the current value and cost of the bond that will be acquired.*

*The transaction closes pursuant to the terms of the contract, and the bond is purchased and delivered to the seller. The seller, now out of state and looking for a method to extract funds from the broker, files a complaint with the Real Estate Commission. They determine that there should have been no commission charged on the amount of the purchase price represented by the future value of the bond and "suggest" that the broker make an appropriate refund.*

*How lucky the broker was. In this particular case he did nothing wrong. However, with a little change in circumstances, he could have had a securities problem. He could have had a problem with the side agreement that was not available to the new lender who made the new loan. He could have gone to jail. Do not worry, he is still out there waiting to be your subagent.*

**Rough Draft.** The ease or "dis-ease" with which any transaction reaches final closing is primarily dependent upon how well the contract is written in the first place. Whether you represent the buyer submitting an offer or represent the seller in preparation of a counteroffer or simply are a real estate broker in a neutral position, draft the first contract in pencil. Yes, write the entire proposal in pencil or on the computer with "draft" written over the page to force you to re-look and rethink the terms. It is rare to be able to include all that is important on a first draft that will in fact be the final copy. Try not only to determine the conditions that must be addressed and the time periods within which these conditions must be satisfied, but also the default or waiver of rights in the event a particular action is not taken.

Of course, there are those times when you are writing the proposal on the hood of the car, in the airport before the buyer or seller catches the next flight and in the fast food booth with ketchup dripping on the papers. *Expediency should never become more important than accuracy.* In instances such as these, using a manual of clauses as a guideline is critical. It is much simpler to pick and chose the exact phraseology than rely on composing a complete clause when you may be too tired to think. Resist the temptation to "wing it" without prior approval from your broker. An incomplete or "open ended" condition will only lead to misconceptions and misunderstandings during the closing process. The key to a smooth transaction is to foresee any possible problems that may arise during the course of the escrow or closing process and address them in the proposal.

Whether representing the client in an agency capacity or assisting the customer when you have no agency status, you must be certain to present all the options to the buyer and/or seller. It is the salesperson's duty to provide information on all of the options that are available so that the buyer or seller may make their own decisions.

**Side Agreements.** The use of the term alone should trigger the conscience of most real estate professionals. Why is there an agreement that can not be a part of the contract? There can be no answer other than that the facts expressed in the side agreement are to be concealed from someone who, had they known all of the facts of the proposed transaction, would have reacted in a fashion different from what was intended--also often referred to as "Criminal Fraud on a Federally Chartered or Insured Lender."

With the exception of such obvious motivations such as keeping a relative or mother-in-law from knowing where you are moving or the purchasing of commercial property as an undisclosed agent, there are very few times when any side agreement is appropriate. This is a good area to avoid. The "If I do not see it, it does not exist" ostrich theory offers no safe haven. Once you know of an irregularity, you are under several often conflicting duties to report to the lender, the government, the seller, the buyer, your board and, always, your broker. Do not be a co-conspirator.

**Case in Point.** *The listing agent, who is a friend of the wife of a client-couple involved in a divorce, agrees to list the property for one commission and rebate a portion of the commission to the wife. The other seller, the husband, has no knowledge of this "side agreement." Is that not fraud? Are not both the sellers your clients?*

*The final straw is the agent's remark when questioned. He said, "I just wanted to help the wife. You know we have been friends for a long time."*

*Remember that the fiduciary duty is owed by an agent to all the principals.*

**Standard Forms.** Always use the standard forms proffered by your board or association, real estate commission, and/or by your real estate office. There is no excuse for not starting with these forms. Expediency in preparation is not a good defense. The judge will want to know why you did something different from the standard practice for this particular buyer or seller, especially if some protection is lost.

**The Standard Builder Contract.** Many builders, feeling for whatever reason that the forms offered by whatever agency of the government, a board or the bar association, are not as they would wish them, have developed a specific form for the use of all agents working through their listing broker. Although there is no prohibition indicating that a prospective buyer can not utilize any form that strikes his fancy, these sellers are so heavily regulated and concerned about litigation that they will generally insist that all offers be on their form. Only the pressure of the market can alter this firm stance. The broker needs to make his agents and subagents aware of the seller's requirements and at the same time indicate to all concerned that the broker is not responsible for the contents of or omissions in this or any other form.

**Transfers Without Prior Lender Consent, Silent Assumptions.** With rates being as low as they have been lately this form of financing is less prevalent than it was a few years ago. Still, many people decide to run the risk of a transfer without the prior consent of the lender, sometimes known as a "silent assumption." Since the advent of new FHA rules, this may become a more prevalent situation if notification of FHA is not desired by one or both of the parties. Such an assumption requires as a minimum an absolute disclaimer prior to contract acceptance. This is one instance where, no matter how firm the disclaimer, the parties will go ahead and do as they please anyway. Make your disclaimer very clear. When the trouble starts, everyone is going to try to point to the broker.

**Water and Ditch Rights.** Make sure that the property description includes all other rights, such as water and ditch rights. Check to ensure that these water or ditch rights are not separately encumbered.

**Letter - Contract Form**

Mr. Lawrence S. Schreder, President
Central Colorado Construction Company, Inc.
4th and Main Street
Colorado Springs, CO 80903

Re: Standard Form Contracts

Dear Larry:

I am happy to have the listing on the existing and "to-be-built" homes in your subdivision. I know that you understand that I need to write this letter to confirm what we have discussed in the past regarding your instructions for the use of your standard form contract that you have provided to our office.

Let me congratulate you on your efforts to select and draft a contract especially for your sales to be utilized instead of using the standard real estate commission approved form. As you know, I am a real estate broker and not an attorney. Therefore, I could not help with the drafting effort. It is nice to have legal counsel to write contracts so that all we have to do is fill in the blanks.

Neither this company nor any of its agents can possibly be responsible for the content of the contract. We will, however, complete it according to your direction. In addition, as you have indicated, we have been telling and continue to tell all potential buyers that all offers must be on your form. This may not stop someone from trying another form of an offer, but it should discourage all but a few. Whatever form is utilized by a buyer, we will present it to you for your consideration.

Sincerely,
The Orcas Island Company

by: Katherine E. Reece
Realtor®, CRS, GRI

**Letter - Use of Special Contract Form**

Ms. Linda Peterson, Broker
Peterson Properties, Ltd.
789 Westhaven Drive
Boulder, CO 80303

Re: Central Colorado Construction Company Homes

Dear Linda:

This will confirm that our office, as the listing agent for the above builder, has been instructed to utilize the contract form provided by our principal for the sales of properties in this development. I have enclosed copies of the desired form so that you will have them available for any sales you may make in this area.

Understand that this office is not responsible for the content of this contract. Should you need assistance in its completion, please do no hesitate to ask for a sample of a completed contract. I think that the seller has obtained this contract from his attorney and will not consider the use of other forms. However, I will be happy to present any offer that may be requested by one of your customers.

Finally, regardless of any other arrangement that we may have with respect to co-op fees on other properties, your office will receive a co-op fee equal to ___% of the total sales price, including extras, upon the actual closing and receipt of the purchase price by the seller. The only reservation is that you can not attempt to act as a subagent of the seller/builder.

I look forward to your selling one of these fine homes. Let me know if there is anything that I can do to help. We welcome your cooperation.

Sincerely,
The Orcas Island Company

by: Katherine E. Reece
Realtor®, CRS, GRI

## Financing Options, Clauses and Terminology

**Cash.** While a cash offer often sounds like the best financing alternative to the seller, that perception can crumble rapidly when it is determined that the cash is not available. The transaction may progress through to closing only for the seller to discover that there was no cash or that it was not available at the time of closing. When the contract indicates cash, a verification of the availability of the cash as well as its location and accessibility must be made. Specify the bank or financial institution when you can.

**Clause.**

1. Buyer shall, within ____ days of contract acceptance, provide listing broker with a verification from a state or federally chartered bank located within ____________ miles of the property indicating that the cash indicated in the contract is in fact on deposit and available for immediate withdrawal without restriction or limitation and shall remain so until the date of closing. Buyer's failure to provide this verification shall be considered as a default on the part of the buyer.

**New Financial Institution Loan.** This is the easiest way to go for a qualified buyer. Keep the time periods reasonable but short. There are many different things to think about

**Clause.**

1. $____________ as the net proceeds of a new first loan.

-or-

1. $____________ as the net proceeds of a new first loan to be obtained from a financial institution authorized to do business in this location.

-or-

1. $____________ as the net proceeds of a new first loan to be obtained from ______________________________________.

-or-

1. $____________ as the net proceeds of a new first loan to be obtained from ______________________________________.

-or-

1. $__________________ as a result of buyer seeking and obtaining a new first loan from _______________________ amortized over a period of _____ years at approximately $________________ per month including principal and interest not to exceed _____% per annum, plus, if required by Buyer's lender, a monthly deposit of 1/12 of the estimated annual real estate taxes, property insurance premium, and mortgage insurance premium. If the loan is an adjustable interest rate or graduated payment loan, the monthly payments and interest rate for the initial term of the loan shall not exceed the figures herein set forth.

2. Said loan shall be obtained at an interest rate of not less than _____ per cent per annum nor more than _______ percent per annum and for a term of not less than ___ years nor more than ____ years acceptable to buyer.

-or-

2. Said loan shall be obtained at an interest rate of not less than _____ per cent per annum nor more than _______ percent per annum and for a term of not less than ___ years nor more than ____ years acceptable to buyer. Provided however, buyer shall notify the listing broker in written form within ____ days of the acceptance of this contract of the exact loan terms. Failure to so notify the listing broker shall terminate this contract and all earnest money shall immediately be returned to Buyer.

3. $_______________ by Buyer obtaining a new first loan. The loan shall be of the following type: (Check applicable boxes.)

☐ Conventional __________ ☐ Fixed interest rate_______________

☐ FHA _________________ ☐ Adjustable interest rate ___________

☐ VA __________________ ☐ Graduated payment ______________

☐ Other ______________________________________________

4. The loan may be increased to add the cost of mortgage insurance, VA funding fee and other items for a total loan amount not in excess of $ _____________.

-or-

4. The loan shall be amortized over a period of _____ years at approximately $________________ per month including principal and interest not to exceed _____% per annum, plus, if required by Buyer's lender, a monthly deposit of 1/12 of the estimated annual real estate taxes, property insurance premium, and mortgage insurance premium.

5. Loan discount points, if any, shall be paid to lender at closing and shall not exceed ____% of the total loan amount. Notwithstanding the loan's interest rate, the first _____ loan discount points shall be paid by _____________________________________, and the balance, if any, shall be paid by ___________________________.

6. Buyer shall timely pay to the lender a loan origination fee not to exceed _____% of the loan amount and Buyer's loan costs.

7. Buyer reserves the right to designate an alternate loan on such other terms and conditions as are acceptable to buyer, for the indicated amount only, provided the lender issues an irrevocable commitment to provide said loan within the time period herein provided for loan approval.

8. Buyer shall promptly make application (within ____ days of contract acceptance) for and diligently comply with all requests made by lender to obtain loan approval.

-or-

8. Buyer shall promptly make application (within ____ days of contract acceptance) for and cooperate with lender to obtain loan approval, diligently and timely pursue the same in good faith, execute all documents and furnish all information and documents required by the lender and timely pay the costs of obtaining such loan or lender consent.

-or-

8. If Buyer is to pay all or part of the purchase price by obtaining a new loan, this contract is conditional upon lender's approval of the new loan on or before ________________, 19___. If not so approved by said date, this contract shall terminate.

**Assumption.** "The promise to pay the debt of another" is the definition of an assumption. You will note that the definition makes no mention of consent being sought or obtained by the lender. That issue is addressed later. Assumption agreements are two-party agreements between the person who is going to accept responsibility for the payment of the obligation and the individual to whom the promise is made. The recipient of the promise may or may not already have an obligation to discharge the debt. An example of the latter might be an astute broker who previously accepted the property as part of a guaranteed sale and wisely took the property subject to the loan and, therefore, is not personally obligated to repay the loan. The broker then requires the new purchaser to assume the obligation to pay the loan.

Assumption imposes a personal obligation and liability upon the individual making the promise to repay the debt according to its terms. It is important to note that there is no mention of a release of liability for the prior obligor, or borrower. A common misconception, even among some attorneys, is that an assumption releases the original obligor, usually the seller, from any ongoing personal obligation to repay the debt. The easy rule to remember is that no one is released from any obligation to pay unless the lender does so in writing. Therefore, the assumption of a debt merely adds another obligor for the lender to pursue. In some states there are laws that prohibit some lenders from obtaining personal deficiency judgments against borrowers thereby reducing this effect of an assumption.

If all or part of the purchase price is to be paid by an assumption, the contract needs to reflect the amount to be assumed and the extent to which the seller will remain liable for payment in the event of default. Remember that a release of liability requires a well qualified buyer--one that is most probably qualified to obtain a new loan. Check your state law to ensure that you understand any continuing seller liability for loans that are assumed.

**Clause.**

1. $________________ as a result of Buyer's assuming and agreeing to pay an existing __________ loan of record in this approximate amount, presently payable at $_______________ per month including principal, interest presently at _____% per annum, and an escrow for the following: ☐ real estate taxes, ☐ property hazard insurance premium, ☐ mortgage insurance premium, and __________________.

2. Buyer agrees to pay a loan transfer fee not to exceed $____________. At the time of assumption, the new interest rate shall not exceed _____% per annum and the new monthly payment shall not exceed $________________ principal and interest, plus escrow, if any.

3. Buyer shall apply for assumption with lender within ____ days of contract acceptance and shall cooperate with lender to obtain loan assumption approval, diligently and timely pursue the same in good faith, execute all documents and furnish all information and documents required by the lender and timely pay the costs of obtaining such loan or lender consent.

4. It shall be a condition precedent to performance by seller that seller ☐ shall ☐ shall not be released from liability on said loan.

-or-

4. It shall be a condition precedent to performance by seller that seller shall be released from liability on said loan. In the event lender approves the assumption without a release of liability for the seller, seller may, at seller's election, waive the requirement for release of liability.

5. Buyer and seller understand that broker has not done any independent investigation of buyer's ability to pay the indicated loan. Broker shall not be responsible to anyone in the event buyer does not pay the same according to its terms.

6. Seller understands that in the event of an assumption without release of liability, the seller remains liable for payment of the loan and the lender may enforce the note and mortgage against the seller as well as the buyer.

7. Seller shall provide copies of the loan documents (including note, mortgage and all modifications) to Buyer within _____ calendar days from acceptance

of this contract. This contract is conditional upon Buyer's review and approval of the provisions of such loan documents. Buyer consents to the provisions of such loan documents if no written objection is received by Seller from Buyer within _____ calendar days from Buyer's receipt of such documents.

8. If the lender's approval of a transfer of the Property is required, this contract is conditional upon Buyer's obtaining such approval without change in the terms of such loan, except as indicated herein. In the event lender's approval is not obtained on or before ________________, 19___ , this contract shall be terminated on such date.

**Subject To.** The key distinction in a "subject to" transaction is the lack of any personal obligation on the part of the buyer to retire the obligation, that is, it entails no personal liability to pay the loan. In event of either assumption or subject to financing, the property is transferred with the existing loan intact. In either instance, the buyer pays the lender because if s/he does not, the lender will foreclose on the property and the buyer's equity will probably be lost. The larger the down payment, the less the risk to the seller of eventual foreclosure because the buyer will have a lot to lose. A broker, doing a guaranteed sale, would want to take property subject to the existing financing so that he will not be personally liable for repayment indefinitely. In addition to disclosing to his client, the seller, that he would not be obligated on the loan and thus not responsible for its ultimate repayment, such a broker would want to ensure that his transferee assumed the loan.

**Tip.** *When the broker or salesperson guarantees that "if it does not sell we will buy it" the seller is thinking about an assumption. Maybe the broker wants to take the property subject to the existing loan and require an assumption on resale.*

**Clause.**

Broker is buying the property pursuant to a guaranteed sale. Broker shall not assume nor agree to pay the loan for the remainder of its term. Broker shall assume and agree to pay the loan for the period of time title is in the broker's name. Broker shall require the subsequent buyer to assume the loan as condition of the subsequent sale.

**Novation.** Novation is often confused and merged in some people's minds with the idea of an "approved" assumption. Be careful. When the lender accepts the new purchaser and qualifies that purchaser for the assumption, the lender may or may not grant a release of the old borrower. When the lender releases the old borrower, what is often referred to as "assumption with release of liability", a novation has occurred. The lender may, however, retain all parties on the debt in which event there is no novation. This is often referred to as "a qualifying assumption". A common misconception is that an assumption with a change in the rate or other terms becomes a novation and the original borrower, the seller, is automatically released. A written clarification of everyone's rights, duties, and obligations after an approved assumption is very important.

**Clause.**

1. Buyer shall immediately make application for an approved assumption of the existing loan and comply with all the reasonable requirements imposed by the existing lender . Approval of said assumption shall include a release of liability for the Seller.

2. Buyer shall apply for a novation wherein Buyer becomes a borrower and Seller is released from liability on the existing loan.

**Case in Point.** *The sellers, one of whom was a tax attorney and the other a chemical engineer, filed a complaint with a real estate licensing board requesting that the board revoke the license of a broker who failed to explain the difference between an assumption and a novation prior to listing the property and prior to the contract for sale being executed. Once the contract was executed the tax attorney did not want an assumption, he wanted a novation so that he would not remain liable for the continued payment of the loan. The attorney for the broker argued that the difference was surely in the knowledge bank of the tax attorney. The attorney general, representing the state, replied that "just being an attorney, even a tax attorney who did not deal with real estate on a regular basis, was not enough to let the broker off the hook for not explaining the difference."*

**Seller Financing--Purchase Money Mortgage.** This is probably the most dangerous area of the real estate transaction and yet an absolute necessity in many of today's transactions. Unfortunately for many sellers and buyers, all the ramifications of a particular seller-financed transaction are simply never explained let alone understood. Care should be taken to explain the entire transaction, not only orally but also in writing, and to indicate in advance all of the alternatives to, and ramifications of, the proposed financing. It is imperative to realize that the broker and salesperson are for all practical purposes practicing law in this area and therefore, their actions will be held to the standard of an attorney. Danger lurks because the documents written or completed by the broker will last longer than the memory of the even the most conscientious agent or other parties in the transaction.

There is no "standard" set of new loan documents upon which to rely. Whatever you write will be a condition of the owner carry back financing. If you have a standard form use it, period. Do not modify the mortgage, that is attorney work. The note terms are something that you can put in the contract. Some people, especially commercial brokers, attach a fully filled out note and mortgage to the contract as an addendum and dispense with describing the terms and conditions in the contract.

The perils of suggesting, drafting, structuring, or even allowing, as one regulator expressed it, a seller to accept some form of creative financing demand a similar detailed explanation and disclosure prior to placing such terms in a listing agreement or sales contract. Whenever the seller is going to remain involved with the financing of the real estate, that seller is going to have a tendency to look to the broker to "guarantee" the performance of the buyer.

**Terms and Conditions.** The Checklist may seem endless, but you should recognize that several items are imperative.

1. **Interest.** Double-check the normal ("face") interest rate and default interest rate that will accrue. Are the rates fixed or variable and if variable to which index are they tied?

2. **Late Charges.** Explain the existence, amount of, and effective date for a late charge. Remember, a late charge can be collected only once on each payment as opposed to once for each month the payment remains unpaid.

3. **Dates, Amount, Application.** Cover all the dates and payment application, spelling out the dates on which the payments will become due and the amount of each of the payments; the date and amount of non-periodic payments; the application or allocation between principal and interest--of all payments.

4. **Escrow.** Note the inclusion of an additional amount for an escrow for taxes and insurance. Note also the extent of the services and responsibilities of the escrow agent. Never become, or allow yourself to be coerced into becoming, an escrow agent. There is always a greater fool, a title company, a bank, a neighbor, or someone else for the job. Explain the rate of interest, if any, that will accrue upon the funds in escrow or the allocation of any escrow charges with regard to the escrow account. If no one is designated as being responsible for the monthly fee, we know who will get to pay it: the real estate broker. So share the fun and designate some other deserving party.

5. **Prepayment.** Detail the ability to prepay, the minimum amount of any prepayment and the timing of a prepayment. Some sellers may not be able to accept a prepayment for tax reasons. Unless specified in the note to the contrary, there is no right to prepay.

6. **Assumption.** Specify whether or not the loan is assumable and, if so, under what conditions. Unless specified otherwise, all loans are assumable. The word "assumability" is a misnomer. What one really means is: Does the loan contain a due-on-sale clause? Confusion here is to be avoided. Any method of qualifying a new borrower that calls for the subjective approval of the seller is to be avoided. Idea: Make the loan due-on-sale until the principal balance is reduced to a certain figure; thereafter, allow a transfer so long as the loan is

assumed. Consider the inclusion of a clause providing for the increase in the interest rate upon each transfer.

7. **Common Sense.** Can the seller really do without the money? Is this a good investment for the seller, especially given the current rates available in certificates of deposit? Although it is not your job to do financial planning for a seller, a thirty-year fixed rate loan comprising all of the assets of an elderly seller might cause one to pause and encourage the intervention of a trusted accountant, priest, or an attorney.

8. **Foreclosure.** Clearly explain the effect upon the seller if the buyer stops making the payments. Does the seller understand the foreclosure alternatives, the cost, the time delay, and the possible outcome? Many older sellers think that the buyer does not own the house until the debt is paid. They confuse a transaction which transfers title by deed with the seller retaining a security interest in the form of a mortgage with an installment land contract. (The law concerning Installment Land Contracts or Contracts for Deed vary so much from state to state that you need to seek local counsel before trying to explain this option.)

9. **Form Selection and Terms.** The best solution to avoid future misunderstandings is to annex the owner carry-back note and mortgage or other financing documents, completed in as much detail as possible, as an exhibit to the sales contract. That way there is no confusion about what was actually intended or which form will be utilized.

There are many clauses that you can use. Here are some options that you might consider. Remember the seller might not be able to take the money in a particular tax year without substantial hardship.

**Clause.**

1. $______________ as a result of Buyer executing a promissory note payable to Seller or his order with the following terms and conditions:

   a. The promissory note shall be amortized on the basis of ______ years, payable at $_________ per month including principal and interest at the rate of _____% per annum. Payments shall commence _______________, 19___ and shall be due on the _____ day of each succeeding month.

   c. If not sooner paid, the balance of principal and accrued interest shall be due and payable ____________________________________.

d. If any payment is not received within _____ calendar days after its due date, a late charge of _____% of such monthly payment, but in no event less than $_____, shall be due.

e. In the event of default the interest rate shall increase to _______% per annum.

f. Prepayments shall not relieve the maker of the obligation to make the agreed successive monthly payments.

e. All prepayments shall be in the minimum amount of $_______ or multiples thereof.

f. Buyer may prepay at any time and from time to time without a penalty or premium except _________________________.

g. The note shall be secured by a second mortgage, junior to the existing first loan or the loan indicated herein to be in the first position.

**All-Inclusive Financing.** The All-Inclusive Note and Mortgage, or Deed of Trust in some areas, allows the seller to carry back a note and mortgage that "wraps around" or includes another senior note and mortgage. In essence, there is an existing first loan of record. The seller desires to carry back a loan without regard for the existing loan or record. Example: The property sells for $100,000.00. There is an existing loan for $60,000.00. The buyer will put $20,000.00 cash down and owe the seller a balance of $80,000.00 on the purchase price. The seller will carry the entire $80,000.00 evidenced by an All-Inclusive Note and Mortgage. There will be no assumption. The buyer takes the property "subject to" the existing note and mortgage which the seller shall discharge according to it's terms. In short, the buyer owes the seller the full $80,000.00 and the seller is charged with paying the existing $60,000.00 first loan.

**Clause.**

1. The attached All-Inclusive Promissory Note and Mortgage are hereby made a part of this contract as Exhibits ___ and ___ respectively.

-or-

1. $__________ to be evidenced by buyer executing an all-inclusive note secured by an all-inclusive mortgage substantially in the form attached hereto as 'Exhibit A - All Inclusive Note and Mortgage' consisting of ___ pages.

**Buyer's Ability to Pay.** In the event of an assumption or an owner carried loan, the ability of the buyer becomes paramount. You do not want to become liable for the buyer's financial ability to pay. Add a clause that puts the obligation on the buyer and seller to make these determinations. The seller can not run a credit report on a buyer without his social security number and authorization. Anyone who runs a credit report without the express authorization of the buyer is in big trouble.

**Clause.**

1. Buyer hereby grants seller the right to obtain a credit report upon the buyer. Buyer's social security number is ____________________.

-or-

1. Should buyer be paying all or part of the purchase price by executing a promissory note in favor of Seller or if an existing loan is not to be released at closing, this contract is conditional upon Seller's approval of Buyer's financial ability and credit worthiness, which approval shall be at Seller's sole and absolute discretion.

-or-

1. Buyer shall supply to Seller on or before ________________, 19___, at Buyer's expense, information and documents concerning Buyer's financial, employment and credit condition and a current credit report.

-or-

1. Information and documents received by Seller shall be held by Seller in confidence, and not released to others except to protect Seller's interest in this transaction.

-or-

1. In the event Seller does not provide written notice of Seller's disapproval to Buyer on or before ________________, 19___, then Seller waives the condition providing for approval of Buyer's ability to pay. In the event Seller does provide written notice of disapproval to Buyer on or before said date, this contract shall terminate.

## Contract -- Special Terms

**Acceptance.** Contracts and offers are accepted only in written form signed by the party to be charged. This is often referred to as "the statute of frauds". When working with multiple parties in different geographical locations people may suggest that "the contract be accepted orally." Do not become involved in oral acceptances or counter proposals. Use either the overnight mail or provide for use of a facsimile.

**Clause.**

1. Acceptances may be evidenced by facsimile.

-or-

1. Acceptances may be evidenced by facsimile. In the event of acceptance by facsimile, an original shall be sent by way of overnight mail on the same date as the transmission of the facsimile.

**Acreage.** In the event the acreage has a material significance, its accuracy should be addressed. This is not applicable for a "lot" of approximately 20 acres where 19 acres to 21 acres has no significance. It is for a parcel where the exact acreage is critical. For example, to have horses you must have 1.5 acres per horse. The buyer wants to keep two horses. The acreage is critical. The price is reflective of the acreage. The buyer wants to buy the acreage for $1,000,000.00 only if there are 100 acres, otherwise the price is to be adjusted.

**Clause.**

1. Seller represents that the property consists of _____ acres. In the event that the property is discovered to contain less than that amount of acreage, the buyer may, at buyer's election, terminate this contract and all earnest money shall be returned to buyer immediately.

2. Seller represents that the property consists of _____ acres. In the event that the property is discovered to contain more or less acreage the price shall be adjusted proportionately to reflect the actual acreage.

-or-

2. Seller represents that the property consists of _____ acres. In the event that the property is discovered to contain more or less acreage, the buyer may, at buyer's election, either terminate this contract and all earnest money shall be returned to buyer immediately, or continue with the contract and the price shall be adjusted proportionately to reflect the actual acreage.

**Appraisal Condition.** Even though there is a new loan condition, an appraisal condition can be very important. Generally, the new loan condition is thought to cover the appraisal. You will hear salespeople say, "Do not worry, if the lender does not appraise it high enough, the lender will not make the loan". This is very true if the loan is 80% loan-to-value or greater. If the loan to value is less than 80% or the buyer is paying all or a large portion of the selling price in cash down, the lender may not be as interested in the appraisal. Now the buyer needs some protection.

**Clause.**

1. Buyer shall have the right to have the property appraised by an appraiser engaged by either buyer or lender at Buyer's election and expense. In the event the Property does not appraise for an amount at least equal to the purchase price and:

    a. written notice, signed by or on behalf of Buyer; and

    b. a copy of such appraisal or a written notice from the person or entity who engaged the appraiser which confirms the Property's valuation as less than the purchase price,

    is not received by Seller on or before ____________, 19 ____ (Appraisal Deadline), the Property's valuation shall be deemed to be satisfactory to Buyer. In the event said notice is received by Seller and if Buyer and Seller have not agreed, in writing, to a settlement thereof on or before ________, 19 ______ (Resolution Deadline), this contract shall terminate three calendar days following the Resolution Deadline unless, within the three calendar days, Seller receives written notice from Buyer waiving any objection to the Property's valuation.

-or-

1. Buyer shall have the right to have the property appraised by an appraiser engaged by buyer or lender at Buyer's election and expense. If the Property does not appraise for an amount at least equal to the purchase price and:

    a. written notice, signed by or on behalf of Buyer; and

    b. a copy of such appraisal or a written notice from the person or entity who engaged the appraiser which confirms the Property's valuation as less than the purchase price,

    is not received by Seller on or before ____________, 19 ____ (Appraisal Deadline), the Property's valuation shall be deemed to be satisfactory to Buyer. If such notice is received by Seller and if Buyer and Seller have not agreed, in writing, to a settlement thereof on or before ________, 19 ______ (Resolution Deadline), this contract shall terminate unless, on or before the Resolution Deadline, Seller receives written notice from Buyer waiving any objection to the Property's valuation.

**Buyer's Agency Fees.** Prior to discussing fees with anyone you must have your fee arrangement in place with your client, the buyer. If it is an oral agreement, a confirming cover letter is a good idea. That letter should restate your fee basis and the other critical aspects of your relationship with the buyer. Once you start to write the letter you will realize that it is the Buyer Agency Agreement in a letter format.

**Caution.** *You can not ask the other side, the seller, Realtor®, or listing broker, for a fee until it is agreed upon with your client. To attempt to negotiate your fee with the other side prior to making a fee agreement with your client is a violation of your fiduciary duties and the Code of Ethics.*

**The First Effort.** If possible work through the family. Work through the Multiple Listing Service, Board or Association of Realtors®. Real estate is a team sport. After making the fee agreement with your client, call the other side and determine how much of your agreed fee they will pay. In most circumstances, the listing broker recognizes that they are paying you to find the buyer and help on the buyer's side of the transaction. The listing broker sees you as the "cooperating broker" more that the buyer agent. In that event, all that is needed in the sale contract is a recital of the fee structure for disclosure purposes to everyone. If you are comfortable with your arrangement with your client and the other broker, you may not even need a clause in the contract. You could confirm your fee agreement by facsimile or letter. Consider using the *Agency and Compensation Card/Fax* discussed earlier.

**Caution.** *Do not become what you abhor in an attorney. Do not make the decisions for your client. Inform the client and let them make the decisions. This is especially true when it comes to the source of your fee.*

**Second Line of Defense.** If you have been unable to confirm with the seller (for sale by owner) or listing broker a satisfactory fee arrangement pursuant to your buyer's instructions, you must insert a clause into the contract that reflects your buyer's desires. The buyer may want to make sure that the listing broker is going to pay you. That can not be accomplished in the sale contract. The listing broker is not a party to the sale contract. Only the buyer and seller are parties to the sale contract. In this event, you will need to have the seller agree to pay you. In essence, the seller is agreeing to pay a buyer expense, your fee. This is similar to the payment of discount points.

**Multiple Sources of Payment.** Multiple sources of payment for a single broker, either a buyer's broker or a selling broker, are not frequent but are very possible. It is perfectly alright for a buyer to hire a broker to assist the buyer with the selection of a property and offer to pay that broker, in addition to the cooperative commission received from the other office, an additional fee. This could be in the form or a retainer or a success fee.

What disclosure needs to be made to the buyer or seller? The buyer already knows what is going on as it is part of the letter of confirmation or the buyer listing agreement. The seller needs only to know that the buyer is paying the selling broker an additional fee. Check your state to see if the amount of that fee must be disclosed.

The listing broker's fee is between the listing broker and the seller. The same should be true for the selling broker's fee.

**Clause.**

1. The parties acknowledge that the listing broker is paying the buyer broker, upon closing of the transaction, a fee equal to ______% of the final sales price.

-or-

1. The parties acknowledge that the listing broker is paying the buyer broker, upon closing of the transaction, a fee equal to $______________.

-or-

1. The parties acknowledge that the listing broker is paying the buyer broker, upon closing of the transaction, a fee equal to ______% of the final sales price. In addition, the buyer agent is collecting a separate fee from the buyer.

2. Buyer's obligation to buy is expressly conditional upon the seller paying the buyer agent, simultaneously with the closing of this transaction, a fee equal to ________% of the final sales price.

-or-

2. Buyer's obligation to buy is expressly conditional upon the seller paying the buyer agent, simultaneously with the closing of this transaction, a fee equal to ________% of the final sales price. Said fee is the sole compensation received by the buyer agent.

-or-

2. Seller shall pay or cause to be paid to the buyer agent, at the closing of this transaction, a fee equal to ________% of the final sales price.

-or-

2. Seller recognizes that the buyer agent procured the buyer and assisted the buyer with the purchase of the property. Buyer agent has sought a fee from the listing broker without satisfaction. In order for the buyer to buy, the buyer agent must be paid a fee. Therefore, the parties agree that the seller shall pay or cause to be paid to the buyer broker a fee equal to ____% of the final sales price upon the closing of the transaction. The price offered by the buyer takes this fee into account.

**Clause-Transaction Broker.**

1. The parties acknowledge that the listing broker is paying the selling broker, upon closing of the transaction, a fee equal to ______% of the final sales price.

-or-

1. The parties acknowledge that the listing broker is paying the selling broker, upon closing of the transaction, a fee equal to $______________.

-or-

1. The parties acknowledge that the listing broker is paying the selling broker, upon closing of the transaction, a fee equal to ______% of the final sales price. In addition, the selling broker is collecting a separate fee from the buyer.

2. Buyer's obligation to buy is expressly conditional upon the seller paying the selling broker, simultaneously with the closing of this transaction, a fee equal to ________% of the final sales price.

-or-

2. Buyer's obligation to buy is expressly conditional upon the seller paying the selling broker, simultaneously with the closing of this transaction, a fee equal to ________% of the final sales price. Said fee is the sole compensation received by the selling broker.

-or-

2. Seller shall pay or cause to be paid to the selling broker, at the closing of this transaction, a fee equal to _______% of the final sales price.

-or-

2. Seller recognizes that the selling broker procured the buyer and assisted the buyer with the purchase of the property. Selling broker has sought a fee from the listing broker without satisfaction. In order for the buyer to buy, the selling broker must be paid a fee. Therefore, the parties agree that the seller shall pay or cause to be paid to the buyer broker a fee equal to ____% of the final sales price upon the closing of the transaction. The price offered by the buyer takes this fee into account.

3. The selling broker is not acting as an agent for either the buyer or seller. The selling broker is a broker licensed to sell real estate in this state.

**Cash at Closing.** Designate what form of money will be acceptable at the final closing. If you use escrow agents, sometimes this is part of the instructions. Many escrow agents will not accept cash and will require a cashier's check to be drawn on a local clearing house bank. If in fact the "cash at closing" means real cash, remember that the Internal Revenue Service wants to know about cash transfers in excess of $10,000.00. Do not become involved in "laundering" the cash for your buyer or seller. Do not let them give you some cash in return for your check. The effect is to obviate the reporting requirement.

**Clause.**

> $______________, plus buyer's customary closing costs, to be paid by Buyer at closing by cash, electronic transfer funds, certified check, savings and loan teller's check, or cashier's check drawn on a ______________ clearing house bank.

**The Back Up Offer.** In times when the market is really hot and inventory is moving rapidly, it is possible to have multiple offers on one property. The seller may also decide to take back up offers when the initial accepted contract has some "shaky" contingencies, either planned or just developing.

Offering, presenting, and negotiating on a back up offer follows all the same rules as if it were being considered for first position. Most of the time the buyer will want to have the option to continue to search for other available homes and reserve the option to purchase another instead. You will need to provide an avenue to extract that buyer from the back up position. The key elements are the triggering method that allows the back up contract to assume first position. Use caution so as not to put the seller in jeopardy.

**Clause.**

1. Buyer is aware that Seller has an accepted previous offer on the Property ("Senior Contract"). This contract shall be junior to the Senior Contract.

2. In the event the Senior Contract does not close on or before __________ this contract shall become the Senior Contract.

-or-

2. In the event the Senior Contract shall terminate for any reason this shall become the Senior Contract.

-or-

2. This contract shall become the Senior Contract only in the event that the existing Senior Contract is terminated. In no event shall the Seller or Buyer

be obligated to close or otherwise perform under this contract so long as the Senior Contract is in existence.

-or-

2. In the event the previous Senior Contract is the subject of litigation or threatened litigation, Seller shall not be obligated to perform hereunder.

3. Seller reserves the right to extend, renegotiate or modify the Senior Contract.

4. Buyer reserves the right to terminate this contract at Buyer's election at any time prior to this contract becoming the Senior Contract. Such termination shall be effective upon receipt of written notification of the same given to the Seller or listing broker.

5. All performance dates shall be extended once by a number of days equal to the difference between the date of acceptance of the contract and the date this contract becomes the Senior Contract.

**Contingency Sale.** Buyer has to sell an existing home to qualify for the new home. This is a tough area. Use caution when drafting clauses that contemplate the parties being subject to another contract beyond the reach of the seller. Many buyers need to sell a current home in order to purchase the next. Depending on the market activity in the area, the buyer may lose negotiating power when needing to disclose this as a contingency. Now the seller not only worries about his property closing but the underlying contract and escrow also. However, in a slow seller's market the seller may welcome this type of an offer when the alternative choice is no offer at all.

Assuming you have a buyer and seller willing to negotiate under these terms, there are some critical issues related to the contingency sale. Will there be an early or late occupancy and possession to allow the two properties to close simultaneously? Keep in mind that you can close on two properties simultaneously on paper, but it is impossible to move furniture out, clean, and move in on the same day! You have not lived until you have the buyer's moving van sitting in the seller's driveway waiting to unload as the seller's movers are packing. There are better ways to be entertained in life.

Always compose your contract to allow for a review of any contract on the buyer's home. If possible, the seller most likely would prefer not to have a domino effect of that contract with a "contingency to sell" also. Consider if the seller wishes either take his home off the market until the buyer's home sells or if the seller will continue to market with a "bump" clause if another acceptable offer is received.

Remember that the removal of this "loan condition" will not solve the problem. As a practical matter the buyer will not be able to qualify for the new loan, and therefore the buyer is still protected. Meanwhile, the seller, thinking that there is no contingency believes he has a firm unconditional sale. Nothing could be further from the truth. Remind the seller that the buyer can not qualify for a new house until the old one is sold no matter what the contract says. If the contingency to sell is removed from the contract, the seller will need to verify that the funds to close are on deposit ready for immediate withdrawal without restriction.

**Clause.**

1. Seller is aware that Buyer must sell an existing home to be able to buy this property. A portion of the down payment and the ability to qualify for a new loan are conditional upon the sale of the Buyer's existing home located at ____________________________________. In the event buyer does not enter into a firm contract to sell his existing house and deliver a copy of the same to seller within _____ days of acceptance of this offer, Seller may declare this contract null and void and all deposits shall be returned to the buyer.

-or-

1. Seller is aware that a portion of the down payment will come from the proceeds of the sale of the buyer's home located at ___________________. In the event buyer does not enter into a firm contract to sell the above referenced property and deliver the contract to the Seller within _____ days of acceptance of this offer, Seller may declare this contract null and void and all deposits shall be returned to the buyer.

2. In addition, seller shall have ___ days from receipt of said contract for the sale of the buyer's property to approve the same in the sole discretion of seller and deliver evidence of approval to the buyer or the salesperson assisting the buyer.

3. In the event the buyer's property is unable to close pursuant to the terms of this contract within the time period provided, the buyer may once extend the closing date specified in this contract for a period not to exceed ____ calendar days.

**Earnest Money.** Although there is no substitute for a well drafted contract, it is money and the fear of its loss that motivates the average person. Try to collect an earnest money deposit that represents a significant amount of money for both the buyer and seller. For some that is $500.00 while for others it is $25,000.00. Most court systems have thresholds for the severity of cases. Make sure that the earnest money clearly fits the correct court.

Designate whether the earnest money was paid in cash, check (personal or corporate) or a promissory note. In the event the broker is the repository of the earnest money, the last clause (# 4 below) lets the broker relinquish the earnest money should things get a little hot.

To further show good faith on the buyer's behalf, an additional deposit may be made within a specified time after acceptance or when additional contingencies are satisfied. Do not let the earnest money come in on a monthly basis as some might claim the contract to purchase was in fact an installment sale.

Whomever holds the earnest money will be named in a suit to determine who gets it. To avoid being involved, you might not want to hold it. Think about letting someone else hold the earnest money. We recommend a reputable title company.

In addition, the question of interest on earnest money must be addressed. Think about how much interest will actually accrue before you decide that the earnest money should earn interest. The total interest is reflected by the amount held and the time it will be on deposit. If the amount of interest is anticipated to be less than $100.00, the time, effort and cost of setting up and maintaining an interest bearing account may not be warranted. Many companies raise that threshold to $500.00.

The following clause accomplishes several things. First, it designates that the interest will be additional earnest money. This makes the rest of the decisions simple. If the contract closes, the buyer gets the interest, pays tax on it and uses it toward the purchase. In the event that the transaction does not close and the earnest money is forfeited to the seller, the seller receives the entire amount of interest but the buyer pays tax on the interest. Other alternatives become a problem as the social security number for the account needs to be given to the bank when the account is set up. Changing the account number after interest is paid can be difficult. It is a nightmare if the interest is later credited to a different party.

**Clause.**

1. The earnest money shall be deposited in _____________ financial institution in the name of the entity designated herein as the holder of the earnest money. Interest shall be reported in the name of the buyer. Interest on the earnest money shall become additional earnest money.

2. The earnest money is in the form of _________________.

3. Broker is authorized to deliver the earnest money deposit to the closing or escrow agent, if any, at or before closing.

4. Notwithstanding any termination of this contract, Buyer and Seller agree that, in the event of any controversy regarding the earnest money, unless mutual written instructions are received by the holder of the earnest money, the party holding the earnest money shall not be required to take any action but may await any legal proceeding, or at their option and sole discretion, may interplead all parties and deposit any moneys into a court of competent jurisdiction and shall recover court costs and reasonable attorney fees.

**Home Warranty.** The buyer or seller has the property inspected by a home warranty company. That company, for a relatively small fee, issues a policy that guarantees those items that have a measured useful life. These include items such as the appliances, the furnace, the roof, etc. Each policy is a little different. Know what the policy that you sell or endorse covers. Buyer agents should be careful not to recommend a firm without an adequate disclosure of your interest in that firm, if any. This is not a structural warranty. The public is often confused about the exact coverage.

**Tip.** *It is the role of the salesperson to make sure that the buyer understands that a home warranty is or is not available. If it is not available, the buyer needs to know why it is not available. Often the salesperson will receive a commission as a result of the issuance of a home warranty. That fact needs to be clearly stated to everyone.*

**Clause.**

1. Buyer has been informed that a home warranty ☐ *is* ☐ *is not* available for this property. Buyers have elected ☐ *to* ☐ *not to* obtain a home warranty. The home warranty, if selected, shall be paid as a ☐ *Buyer's* ☐ *Seller's* expense. If seller's expense is selected, the Seller's expense shall be limited to $________ and the balance shall be paid by the Buyer.

2. The parties are aware that there are many home warranty insurers in the market place. In the event that ____________________ is selected as the home warranty company, ____________________, shall receive a commission of $____________ on the sale of the warranty.

-or-

2. The parties are aware that there are many home warranty insurers in the market place. In the event that ____________________ is selected as the home warranty company, ____________________, shall receive a commission of $____________ on the sale of the warranty which shall be credited to the Buyer.

**Inclusions and Exclusions.** When reviewing the proposal for final revisions, be certain you have adequately identified any personal property to be included in the contract. This includes appliances, light fixtures or chandeliers, window coverings, air conditioners, pool or spa equipment or furnishings designated on an inventory. It is just as important to note any specific exclusions. By specifically listing and deleting any item to be excluded, any misunderstandings will be eliminated about what actually is conveyed with the home. Hopefully this will prevent the salesperson from being obligated to purchase a replacement appliance. It takes buying only one appliance to learn this lesson!

If an item is being conveyed but its continuing operation is questionable, explain the exact status of that particular item. Explain not only the condition of the item, but also if it is to be repaired, replaced or accepted in its condition with no warranties expressed or implied.

In general, if an item is attached to the property such that tools would be required to remove it, that item is considered real property. Conversely, if the item is not so attached, it is not real property but personal property. Classic examples include a free standing range that is not hard wired and does not have tile in front of it. That is personal property. Once the range is hard wired or tile is placed in front of it, it becomes real property. Care should be taken to check television dishes *and the controls* to ascertain if they are real or personal property. Natural gas cylinders and burglar alarm systems may be leased by the seller and therefore are not owned by the seller.

Watch for expensive drapes and wall hangings. Carpet that "looks" wall to wall might be an area rug. The real estate salesperson needs to pay attention when viewing the property. Make a check list for each room in order to prepare a contract that accurately reflects the buyer's desires or is a true reflection of what the seller intends to convey. Always have the buyer or seller personally read and verify that the items checked are accurate.

**Clause.**

1. The purchase price includes the following items:

   (a) if attached to the Property on the date of this contract: lighting, heating, plumbing, ventilating, and air conditioning fixtures, TV antennas, water softeners, smoke/fire/burglar alarms, security devices, inside telephone wiring and connecting blocks/jacks, plants, mirrors, floor coverings, intercom systems, built-in kitchen appliances, sprinkler systems and controls, built-in vacuum systems (including accessories), and garage door openers including _____ remote controls; and

   (b) if on the Property whether attached or not on the date of this contract: storm windows, storm doors, window and porch shades, awnings, blinds, screens, curtain rods, drapery rods, fireplace inserts, fireplace screens, fireplace grates, heating stoves, storage sheds, all keys; and,

   (c) seller's interest in all the following leases for burglar, fire and intrusion detections systems, and all natural gas tanks and leases indicated herein:

   (d) The above-described included items (Inclusions) are to be conveyed to Buyer by Seller by bill of sale at the closing, free and clear of all taxes, liens and encumbrances, except as provided herein:

1. The following attached fixtures are excluded from this sale:

**Inspection.** Make sure that the buyer knows that not only are they entitled to an inspection but you recommend one. The largest single claim by buyers relates to the physical condition of the property. An inspection is a must. Do not select the inspector. We need a system to allow the parties to rectify the situation, agree on a closing and modification of the contract to correct defects on terms agreeable to both parties.

**Clause.**

1. Seller agrees to provide Buyer on or before ____________________, 19_____ with a Seller's Property Disclosure form completed by Seller to the best of Seller's current actual knowledge.

2. Buyer or any designee, shall have the right to enter upon the property at reasonable hours, with ____ hours prior notice, and have one or more inspection(s) of the physical condition of the Property and Inclusions, at Buyer's expense. In the event written notice of any unsatisfactory condition, signed by or on behalf of Buyer, is not received by Seller on or before ____________________, 19_____ (Objection Deadline), the physical condition of the Property and Inclusions shall be deemed to be satisfactory to Buyer. In the event such notice is received by Seller as set forth above, and Buyer and Seller have not agreed, in writing, to a settlement thereof on or before ____________________, 19_____ (Resolution Deadline), this contract shall terminate three calendar days following the Resolution Deadline; unless, within the three calendar days, Seller receives written notice from Buyer waiving objection to any unsatisfactory condition. Buyer is responsible for and shall pay for any damage which occurs to the Property and Inclusions as a result of such inspection.

**Legal Description.** Many contracts have a space for the insertion of the legal description. If the information will fit, that is the place for the legal description. If however, the space provided on the standard form is inadequate, then you must attach an addendum. Finally, there are times when you do not have the legal description and must provide that it be attached at a later date.

**Clause.**

1. The legal description on the attached addendum "legal description" is hereby made a part of this contract.

-or-

1. The legal description on the attached addendum is hereby made a part of this contract as if the same were set forth herein in full.

2. The legal description shall be provided to the buyer and attached to this offer by the seller within ___ days of contract acceptance. Thereafter the buyer shall have ten calendar days to approve the legal description by signing and dating the bottom of the same. Failure of the seller to provide the legal description or failure of the buyer to sign it shall make this contract void.

-or-

2. The legal description shall be provided to the buyer and attached to this offer by the seller within _____ days of contract acceptance. Thereafter the buyer shall have ten calendar days to approve of the legal description by signing and dating the bottom of the same. In the event that the seller does not provide the legal description within the specified time period, the buyer may, at the buyer's option, terminate the contract and the buyer shall be entitled to the immediate return of all earnest money. In the event that the buyer does not sign the legal description within the specified time period, the contract shall terminate and the buyer shall be entitled to the immediate return of all earnest money.

**Possession.** Two things need to occur to the broker. First, the insurable interest of the parties must be determined. If the seller owns the property and the buyer occupies the property prior to closing, the buyer is a tenant. If the buyer closes and the seller occupies the property, the seller is a tenant. Most homeowners policies do not cover tenants. The tenant needs a renter's policy.

Second, while everyone thinks things will go as planned the buyer may not close but remains in the property. Or, the seller may close and never vacate the property. The parties need a lease and not a "move in early" agreement. A comprehensive standard form lease can be attached to the contract.

**Clause.**

1. Possession of the Property shall be delivered to Buyer as follows:

   subject to the following lease(s) or tenancy(s):

2. In the event Seller, after closing, fails to deliver possession on the date herein specified, Seller shall be subject to eviction and shall be additionally liable to Buyer for payment of $_______________ per day from the date of agreed possession until possession is delivered.

3. Seller shall occupy the property for a period of ___ days after closing pursuant to the terms and conditions of the lease attached hereto as exhibit _____.

-or-

3. Buyer shall be permitted to occupy the property prior to closing for a period of ___ days pursuant to the terms and conditions of the lease attached hereto as exhibit _____.

4. Broker has advised both buyer and seller to consult with their respective insurance agents to determine the extent to which either needs additional insurance. Broker is not responsible for any loss sustained to the property at any time.

**Price (Consideration).** Many standard contracts have ample space here for clauses. However, there are often some different possibilities that arise. Care needs to be taken to ensure that the total numbers are, in fact, equal to the total price.

**Clause.**

1. The price shall be payable in U.S. Dollars.

2. The purchase price indicated was determined after making a careful inspection of the property. The buyer has not relied upon any information printed in the Multiple Listing Service or on any listing information sheets, which may contain errors, such as the total amount of square footage, the size of the lot, the school district, the availability of water, etc.

**Property Condition.** Standard in some contracts, this clause needs to be exact. Over 65% of all claims to the malpractice carrier are related to the condition of the property. Be specific about what is included and excluded so that there are no misunderstandings.

**Clause.**

1. Except as otherwise provided in this contract, the Property and Inclusions shall be delivered in the condition existing as of the date of this contract, ordinary wear and tear excepted. In the event the Property shall be damaged by fire or other casualty prior to time of closing, in an amount of not more than ten percent of the total purchase price, Seller shall be obligated to repair the same before the date of closing. In the event such damage is not repaired within said time or if the damage exceeds such sum, this contract may be terminated at the option of Buyer. Should Buyer elect to carry out this contract despite such damage, Buyer shall be entitled to credit for all the insurance proceeds resulting from such damage to the Property and Inclusions, not exceeding, however, the total purchase price. Should any Inclusion(s) or service(s) fail or be damaged between the date of this contract and the date of closing or the date of possession, whichever shall be earlier, then Seller shall be liable for the repair or replacement of such Inclusion(s) or service(s) with a unit of

similar size, age and quality, or an equivalent credit, less any insurance proceeds received by Buyer covering such repair or replacement.

2. Neither the seller, the listing or selling broker, nor any of their agents or employees is responsible for the condition of the property, the representations of the seller, as outlined on the Property Disclosure Sheet--attached hereto as Exhibit ______--or for other representations made directly to the buyer, or for the items outlined in the foregoing paragraph.

3. Buyer acknowledges that, prior to completing this offer, he has received a copy of the Property Condition Report and Soils Report completed by the seller which describes the condition of the property.

4. Neither the seller, the buyer, nor any of their agents is relying on any representation or omission of or by any real estate broker or salesperson associated with this transaction for any decision as to the value of the property, the condition of the property, the decision to purchase the property, or the terms and conditions of sale that are incorporated in this contract.

5. The parties acknowledge that none of the brokers or salespeople associated with this transaction has made an inspection of the property and none is responsible for any defect that such an inspection might have revealed.

6. Buyer understands that there is a HOW warranty currently covering the property. Buyer has made an independent investigation as to the term remaining, the extent of coverage, and the extent to which the available coverage has been utilized. Buyer realizes that the brokers and salespersons are not warranting the condition of the property and are not responsible for physical defects that might come to light after the sale.

7. Buyer is purchasing the property in AS IS condition without any warranty from the Seller or from any broker or salesperson working with the Seller or Buyer. There is no warranty that the property is fit for any particular purpose. Buyer understands and has been encouraged to have the property inspected by experts of Buyer's selection. Buyer realizes that the brokers and salespeople are not engineers and that they are not warranting the structural condition of the property nor the condition of any appliances or systems, or otherwise.

-or-

7. a. Purchaser understands and hereby agrees that Purchaser is purchasing the Property in an "AS IS" condition. Without limiting the foregoing, Purchaser understands that there are existing structural problems with the Property, the extent of which Seller is unaware. Purchaser acknowledges that the Purchase Price under this Contract reflects the uncertainty surrounding the condition of the Property. Seller makes no warranties, representations, or guarantees, either express or implied, of any kind, nature, or type whatsoever. Except as provided in the immediately preceding sentence and without in any way limiting the generality of the immediately preceding sentence,

Purchaser further acknowledges and agrees that in entering into this Contract and purchasing all or any part of the Property:

b. Neither Seller nor anyone acting for or on behalf of Seller has made, and does not and will not make, any statements, promises, warranties, or representations, either express or implied, with respect to the Property; the appurtenances, facilities, and improvements thereon; the grading, the soil condition, the geologic condition, and other physical aspects and conditions thereof; the value, profitability, marketability, feasibility, desirability, or adaptability thereof; or the projected income and expenses thereof. The engineering reports which may have been given to Purchaser are not intended to be relied upon by the Purchaser.

c. Neither Seller nor anyone acting for or on behalf of Seller has made, and does not and will not make, any warranties or representations, either EXPRESS OR IMPLIED, with respect to the Property's MERCHANTABILITY, TENANTABILITY, HABITABILITY, SUITABILITY, or FITNESS FOR A PARTICULAR PURPOSE or USE.

d. Purchaser has *not* relied on any statement, promise, warranty, or representation of Seller or anyone acting for or on behalf of Seller nor on any particular skill, knowledge, or expertise of Seller or anyone acting for or on behalf of Seller.

e. Purchaser has made all legal, factual, and other inquiries and investigations as Purchaser deems necessary, desirable, or appropriate with respect to the Property, the value, suitability, and marketability thereof, and the appurtenances, facilities, and improvements thereon and Purchaser is purchasing the Property based on Purchaser's own inspection and examination thereof. Such inquiries and investigations made by Purchaser shall be deemed to include, without limiting the generality thereof, (i) the availability of water, sewer, gas, electricity, telephone service, and all other public utility services necessary or desirable for any development of the Property contemplated by the Purchaser, (ii) the grading, the soil and geologic conditions of the Property, (iii) such state of facts as an accurate improvement survey plat prepared in accordance with state law would show, and (iv) the present and future subdivision and zoning ordinances, resolutions, and regulations of the city, county, and state where the Property is located and of any other governmental agency having jurisdiction over the Property.

f. Purchaser shall acquire the Property in an "AS IS" and "WITH ALL FAULTS" condition and state of repair.

g. PURCHASER DOES HEREBY WAIVE, and SELLER DOES HEREBY DISCLAIM, ALL REPRESENTATIONS and WARRANTIES, EXPRESS OR IMPLIED, of any kind, nature, or type whatsoever with respect to the Property (except as expressly contained in the deed contemplated hereby and the warranties provided herein), including, by way of description but not limitation, those of CONDITION, MERCHANTABILITY, TENANTABILITY, HABITABILITY, SUITABILITY, and FITNESS FOR A PARTICULAR PURPOSE or USE. In addition, Seller hereby specifically disclaims any representations or warranties regarding the accuracy of any materials delivered or to be delivered to Purchaser by Seller or contained in the files of Seller or prepared by agents of Seller, it being Purchaser's intent to purchase the Property without reliance on any materials prepared by Seller or its agents. Notwithstanding the foregoing, nothing herein shall relieve Seller from responsibility for any misrepresentations or omission of material facts known by Seller. Purchaser acknowledges that Seller has provided to it copies of preliminary soils reports and alerted Purchaser to potential soils problems with the Property. Seller shall not be liable or responsible for, and Purchaser assumes all risks related to, soils conditions.

h. The acknowledgements, agreements, and disclaimers contained in this shall be binding on Purchaser and its successors and assigns and shall run with the Property with respect to Seller.

8. **Release of Seller and Agents.** Without in any way limiting the generality of the preceding Paragraph a, Purchaser hereby specifically acknowledges and agrees that Purchaser waives, releases, and discharges all claims Purchaser now has, might have had, or may hereafter have against Seller and Seller's Agents with respect to the condition of the Property, either patent or latent; Purchaser's ability or inability to obtain preliminary approval or final approval of any zoning, subdivision plat, P.U.D., or any other development plan for the Property; Purchaser's ability or inability to obtain or maintain building permits, temporary or final certificates of occupancy, or other licenses for the development, use, or operation of the Property or any other improvements thereto, or certificates of compliance for the Property or any improvements thereto; the actual or potential income or profits to be derived from the Property; the real estate taxes now or hereafter payable thereon; and any other state of facts which exists with respect to the Property, provided.

**Right of First Refusal.** The buyer can not fully commit to the purchase. The buyer needs some time to try to eliminate a condition such as the need to sell an existing home that is prohibiting the buyer from being able to enter into a contract. Seller wants to accept the contract but reserve the right to market the property.

**Clause.**

1. This contract is subject to the sale of the Buyer's property located at ________________________. In the event Seller receives another acceptable offer, in Seller's sole discretion, Seller shall so notify Buyer. Buyer shall have __________ hours from receipt of said written notice to remove any condition upon the sale of the Buyer's existing property and to provide Seller

> with a firm unconditional loan commitment executed from the lender making the first loan indicating that Buyer's performance and new loan are not conditional upon any event including the sale of the Buyer's existing house. In the event such a commitment is received by Seller this contract shall be deemed in full force and effect as modified. In the event Seller does not receive such a commitment, Seller may declare this contract null and void.

**Short Payoff.** This guidelines for a short payoff vary from state to state. In some states the lender is prohibited from suing for a deficiency, the amount that remains due after the foreclosure sale is held. Others, called "deficiency states", allow lenders to sue on the note for the deficiency or short fall. In the event that the existing loan exceeds the market value the salesperson may try to assist the seller in obtaining a "short payoff". The lender consents to accepting the net proceeds in full satisfaction of the existing debt. In an area where troubled real estate is the watchword this can be the difference between the end of the nightmare and the second chapter.

**Clause.**

> Seller's obligations under this contract are expressly conditional upon the lender holding the note secured by the first mortgage upon the property agreeing in written form, on or before _______________, 19____, to accept the net proceeds (sales price less commission, new loan points, tax prorations and other contract obligations and customary closing costs) in full satisfaction of the indicated indebtedness.

**Tenancy.** *This is a very important part of the contract, and yet it is the most often overlooked. Think before you give advice on how an individual or individuals should assume tenancy. The tax implications, potential creditor remedies, flexibility of any future sale, and any other future ramifications of this selection can be very extreme.* The rules for holding title vary from state to state. There are a lot of people who think that joint tenancy is the best option. Keep in mind that people with two sets of kids from previous marriages might not have considered the disposition of their house in the event of their death. Maybe an attorney should help. If in doubt we prefer tenants in common. Then the portions can be designated in the will of each party.

**Case in Point.** *The buyers are a happily remarried couple. Mr. Buyer has two sons and Mrs. Buyer has two daughters. The children are young and everyone loves everyone else. The Buyers are putting all the money that they have into the new home since they need lots of space and a low payment. The real estate professional tells them that joint tenants is the best option for them. After the closing on the way to the airport there is a terrible traffic accident. Mrs. Buyer is killed instantly. Three days later after a rough time in intensive care Mr. Buyer dies. When Mrs. buyer died her property automatically went to Mr. Buyer. Now the property all goes to Mr. Buyer's children. The daughters of Mrs. Buyer get NOTHING.*

**Tenancy in Common.** The definition of tenancy in common varies from state to state. You will need to know the rules for your state. In general, tenancy in common means that each owns an undivided portion of the property. Each could transfer his/her portion to whomever he/she desired without the consent of the other. There is no right of survivorship, meaning that when one party dies, his/her portion does not automatically go to the remaining tenant. The grantee, buyer, can designate how much of the property they want each tenant to own. For example: "Jonathan A. Goodman and Mimi Goodman as tenants in common" would indicate that they own equal portions of the property. "Jonathan A. Goodman (75%) and Mimi Goodman (25%) as tenants in common" would indicate that they own their respective percentages. In most states tenants in common can designate the percentages that they desire.

**Joint Tenants.** The definition of joint tenancy varies from state to state. You will need to know the rules for your state. In general, joint tenancy means that each owns an *equal* undivided portion of the property. Generally, each party *can* transfer or encumber their portion without the consent or joinder of the other joint tenant. The grantee, buyer, *can not* designate how much of the property they want each tenant to own. For example: "Jonathan A. Goodman and Mimi Goodman as joint tenants" indicates that they own equal portions of the property as tenants in common. Jonathan A. Goodman (75%) and Mimi Goodman (25%) as joint tenants would not be proper. Joint tenancy has a right of survivorship. If either tenant dies the portion of the property titled in the dead tenant's name *automatically and immediately* transfers to the surviving tenants. *It does not pass through probate.*

**Tenancy by the Entirety.** This is a form of joint tenancy that is available for legally married people in most states. It has certain creditor protection aspects and is available only for the couple. Neither spouse can sell without the consent of the other. If additional parties are in title, they would hold title as tenants in common or joint tenants with the married couple who hold their portion of title as tenants by the entirety.

While it is best to designate the manner in which the buyers intend to take title *"______ Buyer(s), (as joint tenants, tenants in common, tenants by the entirety)"* you can leave it to a later designation when you are under less stress to get the contract signed.

**Clause.**

1. The buyers reserve the right to designate the tenancy at any time prior to the delivery of deed. In the event that they do not designate any tenancy then the title will reflect equal portions as tenants in common.

**Use of Professionals.** Encourage the use of professionals for areas outside the expertise of the broker. Stay in the real estate business and let the other professions run their own risks. You may save the buyer money by taking on the additional responsibility associated with a professional opinion. It is not worth it.

**Clause.**

1. Buyer is advised to seek, select and retain the professionals s/he desires to investigate the following: the presence and extent of radon gas or other hazardous materials or substances; the physical condition of the property, including the structural integrity; the condition of appliances, heating, plumbing, air conditioning, electrical and other mechanical and structural devices and systems; the condition of the soils and surrounding soils; the existence of, proximity to, adequacy and expense of utilizing or obtaining the services for water, sewer, natural gas, electrical, television and other services and utilities; the terms and conditions of all covenants and restrictions that affect the property; the condition and extent of the title and rights, duties and obligations that may exist as a result of existing documents of record and that may arise as a result of the obligations, duties, rights and privileges this transaction may impose or create, including the terms conditions and provisions of financing arrangements; and the character of allowed uses, zoning or other public or private regulations, codes, ordinances or the like that may affect the property.

-or-

1. This contract contemplates the purchase and sale of real property. All parties are hereby advised and have been advised to seek competent legal, accounting and such other advice as they in their own discretion determine to be advisable. All the brokers and salespeople do not and have not offered any legal, tax or accounting advice with regard to this or any other transaction involving these parties or otherwise.

-or-

1. The brokers and salespeople licensed in this state are not licensed as attorneys nor accountants. This is a legal contract. Seek competent legal or accounting assistance. Do not accept any statements made by any broker or salesperson as legal advice.

**1031 Exchanges.** Once a difficult transaction, these are now quite easy to complete. There is no need to locate the replacement property prior to sale of the relinquished property. The ability to defer some or all of the gain on a property makes understanding an exchange a must for the modern real estate salesperson. "Like kind" property essentially means that the property is not owner occupied. You will need access to a good CPA to make sure that you are up to date on any tax code changes. While no clause is required, the following two clauses will help if you need to insert a clause into a contract.

## Clause--Relinquished Property Contract.

Buyer shall cooperate in structuring this transaction as a like-kind exchange for the benefit of Seller; provided, however, that Buyer shall incur no additional cost or expense in connection therewith. Notwithstanding anything to the contrary contained herein, Seller shall have the right to assign Seller's rights and obligations hereunder to Frascona and Joiner Financial Services Corporation as Qualified Intermediary, for purposes of initiating the contemplated exchange; however, no such assignment shall have the effect of releasing Seller from continuing liability for performance of any of Seller's obligations. In the interest of convenience, however, Seller shall convey title to the Property directly to Buyer on behalf of the Qualified Intermediary. In no event shall Seller's structuring Seller's disposition of the Property as a like-kind exchange delay the closing of this transaction without Buyer's prior written consent.

## Clause--Replacement Property Contract.

Seller shall cooperate in structuring this transaction as a like-kind exchange under Section 1031 of the Internal Revenue Code as to Buyer; provided, however, that Seller shall incur no additional cost or expense in connection therewith. Notwithstanding anything to the contrary contained in this contract, Buyer shall have the right to assign Buyer's rights and obligations to Frascona and Joiner Financial Services Corporation as Qualified Intermediary, for the purpose of completing the contemplated exchange; however, no such assignment shall have the effect of releasing the Buyer from continuing liability for performance, however, Seller shall convey title to the Property directly to Buyer on behalf of the Qualified Intermediary. In no event shall Buyer's structuring Buyer's acquisition of the Property as a like-kind exchange delay the closing of this transaction without Seller's prior written consent.

**General "Boiler Plate" Clauses.** These are samples of various clauses. They can be used as a template for other clauses. If you get to a point where you may have forgotten what you said earlier and want to be sure that the clause that you are about to write will override other clauses use "*notwithstanding anything herein contained to the contrary*" which will put the new clause in a priority position.

## Clause.

1. Cost of any appraisal to be obtained after the date of this contract shall be timely paid to the appraiser by ______________________.

2. This contract shall not be assignable by Buyer without Seller's prior written consent which consent may be withheld for any reason.

3. Except as so restricted, this contract shall inure to the benefit of and be binding upon the heirs, personal representatives, successors and assigns of the parties.

4. Time is of the essence hereof. If any note or check received as earnest money hereunder or any other payment due hereunder is not paid, honored or tendered when due, or if any other obligation hereunder is not performed or waived as herein provided, there shall be the following remedies:

   a. In the event Buyer is in default Seller may elect to treat this contract as cancelled, in which case all payments and things of value received hereunder shall be forfeited and retained on behalf of Seller, and Seller may recover such damages as may be proper, or Seller may elect to treat this contract as being in full force and effect and Seller shall have the right to specific performance or damages, or both.

   b. In the event Seller is in default Buyer may elect to treat this contract as cancelled, in which case all payments and things of value received hereunder shall be returned and Buyer may recover such damages as may be proper, or Buyer may elect to treat this contract as being in full force and effect and Buyer shall have the right to specific performance or damages, or both.

4. Time is of the essence hereof. If any note or check received as earnest money hereunder or any other payment due hereunder is not paid, honored or tendered when due, or if any other obligation hereunder is not performed or waived as herein provided, there shall be the following remedies:

   a. In the event Buyer is in default, all payments and things of value received hereunder shall be forfeited by Buyer and retained on behalf of Seller and both parties shall thereafter be released from all obligations hereunder. It is agreed that such payments and things of value are liquidated damages and are seller's sole and only remedy for Buyer's failure to perform the obligations of this contract. Seller expressly waives the remedies of specific performance and additional damages.

   b. In the event Seller is in default Buyer may elect to treat this contract as cancelled, in which case all payments and things of value received hereunder shall be returned and Buyer may recover such damages as may be proper, or Buyer may elect to treat this contract as being in full force and effect and Buyer shall have the right to specific performance or damages, or both.

5. Anything to the contrary herein notwithstanding, in the event of any arbitration or litigation arising out of this contract, the arbitrator or court shall award to the prevailing party all reasonable costs and expenses, including attorney fees.

6. By signing this document, Buyer and Seller acknowledge that the Selling Company or the Listing Company has advised that this document has

important legal consequences and has recommended the examination of title and consultation with legal and tax or other counsel before signing this contract.

7. In the event this contract is terminated, all payments and things of value received hereunder shall be returned and the parties shall be relieved of all obligations hereunder.

8. The listing broker, ____________________________, and its salespersons have been engaged as ________________.

9. The selling broker, ____________________________, and its salespersons have been engaged as ________________.

10. Any notice to Buyer shall be effective when received by Buyer.

11. Any notice to Buyer shall be effective when received by either Buyer or the party indicated in paragraph ______ herein.

12. Any notice to Buyer shall be effective when received by either Buyer or the party indicated in paragraph ______ herein or three days after the same is deposited in the United States Mail properly addressed to Buyer at the address herein provided for notice.

13. Any notice to Seller shall be effective when received by Seller.

14. Any notice to Seller shall be effective when received by either Seller or the party indicated in paragraph ______ herein.

15. Any notice to Seller shall be effective when received by either Seller or the party indicated in paragraph ______ herein or three days after the same is deposited in the United States Mail properly addressed to Seller at the address herein provided for notice.

16. Any notices required under this Contract shall be personally delivered, or sent by regular or certified mail, postage prepaid, and addressed as follows:

If to Sellers: ____________________________

____________________________

____________________________

with a copy to: ____________________________

____________________________

____________________________

If to Buyer: ______________________________
______________________________
______________________________

with a copy to: ______________________________
______________________________
______________________________

Notice shall be deemed given when delivered, if personally delivered, or two business days after mailing, if mailed. Either party may change the address or addresses to which subsequent notices shall be sent, by notice given in accordance with this paragraph.

17. No subsequent modification of any of the terms of this contract shall be valid, binding upon the parties, or enforceable unless made in writing and signed by the parties.

18. This contract constitutes the entire contract between the parties relating to the subject hereof, and any prior agreements pertaining thereto, whether oral or written, have been merged and integrated into this contract.

19. A copy of this document may be executed by each party, separately, and when each party has executed a copy thereof, such copies taken together shall be deemed to be a full and complete contract between the parties.

20. This contract incorporates all the terms and conditions of all agreements between the parties. There are no promises, agreements, or representations, except as outlined herein. Neither the broker nor the sales agent has made any promises or representations to induce any party to enter into this contract.

## Once the Offer is Signed

**Contract Cover Letter.** Whether preparing the offer for the buyer or the counter offer for the seller, it is wise to provide the cooperating agent with a cover letter for the contract. This is useful especially when you will not be presenting your client's offer to the other party. The letter may certainly be the difference between an acceptance and/or counter proposal or an outright rejection. Do not rely upon the cooperating salesperson to favorably present all the terms. In addition, personal notes about the person made in the offer or complimentary phrases about the home itself will personalize the offer.

Introduce the buyer to the seller by giving some background information. Indicate if both spouses work if trying to reinforce qualification, if they have children, and any special amenities of the neighborhood that they anticipate they will enjoy.

Discuss the financing and any pre-qualification assurances from the lender. Continue with an explanation for the terms incorporated in the proposed contract. Disclosing the rationale behind specific terms will soften what may initially be perceived as an unreasonable request. Be careful that you do not compromise the buyer's or seller's negotiating position by overstating or making commitments not outlined in the actual proposal. Finish the letter on a complimentary note about the home, the terms, or the other party.

**Tip.** *Address the proposal cover letter to the cooperating salesperson with the knowledge that they must share it with their client.*

**Contract Letter to Seller.** This form of cover letter is used when sending an initial offer and when sending a counter proposal through another agent to the other party. During the frenzy and excitement of receiving an offer, the seller may not absorb all the details of the transaction regardless of how explicitly you review the terms. With the length of the standard contract in many states, just covering all the disclaimers would exhaust any seller. Primarily the seller is interested in two items: the purchase price and the bottom line net proceeds. It is the responsibility of the salesperson to explain, in a form that will hopefully reach the other party, the interrelationships between the remaining terms and the impact each may have on the final closing date. Stating the buyer's qualifications, the reasons for some of the terms included and the desire of the buyer to make this a hassle free transaction can make the difference. A letter serves to explain the offer and to make the buyer a real person.

**Letter - Offer Cover Letter**

Linda Peterson
Peterson Properties, Ltd
14 Your Street
Honolulu, HI 99999

Dear Linda:

Please extend my appreciation to your sellers for allowing us to view their home on such short notice today. It is easy to see that the Sellers maintain their home in "show condition" as a routine matter.

Bill and Betty Buyer have relocated to Hawaii from Boulder. Bill is a physician with Physician's Hospital and Betty has her degree in Business Administration with a concentration in finance. Betty is currently interviewing with several banks for employment opportunities. She already has offers for employment in a position in bank administration similar to the one she held in Boulder.

Bill and Betty will have no difficulty qualifying for the loan amount in the financing terms on Bill's income alone. They have no outstanding debt. They have already met with Joni Henderson of Honolulu Mortgage and will do their formal loan application immediately upon acceptance of their offer.

The buyers are aware of comparable sales in the neighborhood and are offering an exceptionally good price for the home. Their offer of $450,000.00 maximizes their available cash for down payment and closing costs. Certainly a benefit to the sellers would be to sell their home in today's market with no contingencies.

The Buyers are aware that the roof will most likely require replacement within the year as indicated in the Sellers' property disclosure and that the carpet will need to be replaced. They understand the seller wanted to leave this type of replacement items to the discretion and personal tastes of the new owner.

From their first drive through the neighborhood, Bill and Betty indicated they were attracted to the overall sense of community. They liked the open floor plan of your home as well as the yard size for their two children. A pool was not a requirement in their search for a home and actually somewhat of a concern with the two small children but it is acceptable.

Linda, I look forward to working together toward a mutually beneficial transaction for both the buyer and seller. Please call me directly if you or your clients have any particular questions. My cellular telephone is 226-0896 and my digital pager is 578-2649.

Sincerely,
The Orcas Island Company

by Katherine E. Reece
Realtor®, CRS, GRI

## Letter - Counter Offer Cover

Mary Begier
The Boulder Real Estate Connection
P. O. Box 3113
Boulder, Colorado 80307

Dear Mary:

Thank you for your time and effort in showing the sellers' home and preparing an offer on the home. It is obvious your buyers placed a great deal of thought in making their decision.

The sellers are in agreement with most of the terms and conditions of the offer. Only minor changes have been made and these are incorporated into the counter offer proposal.

The adjustment in selling price reflects the price the sellers feel is reasonable. They, too, are aware of the comparable sales in the neighborhood and feel that the addition of the pool and kitchen upgrades justify a higher price than the recent sold comparables without similar improvements. They do not anticipate any difficulty with a full price appraisal.

The sellers do recognize the benefit of a "clean" offer with no contingencies. Therefore, they are prepared to vacate the home earlier than planned in order to accommodate the buyers' proposed closing date.

The sellers were impressed with the thorough approach of the buyers in already meeting with their lender. It is always a pleasure to cooperate with such a professional. I look forward to hearing from you on the seller's counter proposal soon.

Sincerely,
Peterson Properties, Ltd.

by Linda Peterson, Broker

### Letter - Assumption, Subject To, and Novation

Mr. Sam Seller
Mrs. Sandy Seller
4750 Table Mesa Drive
Boulder, CO 80303

Re: 4750 Table Mesa Drive

Dear Sam and Sandy:

With the market in its current condition and the attractive terms already in place in the loan that you currently have on your property, there is a good possibility that we will receive an offer which requests that you allow the assumption of your existing loan. You indicated in your Listing Agreement that this was an acceptable alternative.

Because of the long-term nature of this arrangement, I would like to review the differences between the "Assumption" of the existing debt, the taking of the property "Subject To" the existing debt and a "Novation." Please review it now so that you will be familiar with the differences prior to receiving an offer that poses one of these alternatives. As the law is constantly changing in this area, you may wish to seek legal advice. This is a good topic to discuss with your real estate attorney.

First, let's review the process of "Assumption." Our attorney has advised us that when someone such as you allows your loan to be assumed, the buyer promises you that he will pay the lender, thereby promising to discharge the loan according to its terms. At this point, the buyer is personally liable to the lender and to you to complete that obligation. You remain liable for the repayment personally. Should the buyer not perform, you remain liable for the repayment of the obligation.

Should the lender commence a foreclosure, it could prove detrimental to your credit. This is a strange area since some lenders do not adversely reflect upon the credit of the original and intermediate borrowers, concentrating instead on the last person in line to formally, properly, assume the loan. Other lenders, however, do look to the original borrower. There seems to be no standard procedure. In the event of a foreclosure sale that is insufficient to fully retire the loan, some states allow the lender to commence a suit against all who are obligated on the note for the deficiency, while other states expressly prohibit such deficiency judgment actions. Colorado allows deficiency judgments and all lenders, with the notable current exception of FHA, are currently reviewing their loans to determine if such an action is justified.

When you allow your property to be transferred "Subject To" the loan, there is no personal obligation on the part of the buyer to pay the loan. The mortgage payments are made because the buyer knows that if they are not made, the lender will probably foreclose and take the property away from the buyer. You remain liable personally for the ultimate repayment, just as indicated in the assumption option. The buyer simply agrees to take title to the property with your existing loan in place.

A "Novation" occurs when the lender releases you from your personal obligation of, and liability for, the repayment of the loan and substitutes the new buyer. The original loan remains in place, just like the other alternatives. However, the lender, usually after qualifying the buyer, agrees that in the future the lender will look only to the new buyer and not to you for repayment. This may sound like the best solution, but it is not often a reality. The lender wants all the borrowers it can get to remain personally liable for the repayment of your loan. To require a novation will eliminate your liability in much the same manner as if the buyer had obtained a new loan. It will also greatly reduce your ability to sell your home since one of the attractive features of your existing financing is the fact that the loan can be assumed without any qualification or with the limited approval of the lender. The decision is a hard one and only you can make it.

In either event, your loan could go into foreclosure and you would be powerless, as a practical matter, to stop the foreclosure and recover the property from your buyer or from a subsequent purchaser. While you always have the opportunity to pay the lender, the ability to recover the property might involve a lawsuit and all the requisite delays and expenses associated therewith. This is simply a function of today's real estate market and the legal system. There is not an easy answer to this dilemma. Legal advice may help you understand everything a little better.

If you would like to discuss this matter further with either Kathy or me, please feel free to give one of us a call at any time. Financing is one of the more complicated aspects of modern real estate transactions and needs to be given careful consideration. We want to ensure that all our clients and customers have an ample opportunity to learn about, understand, and explore all the available options.

Most sincerely,
The Orcas Island Company

by: Oliver E. Frascona, Broker

### Letter to Seller - Obligation to Present All Offers

Mr. Sam Seller
Mrs. Sandy Seller
4750 Table Mesa Drive
Boulder, CO 80303

Re: 4750 Table Mesa Drive

Dear Sam and Sandy:

Please understand that we are obligated by law to present directly to you for consideration any and all offers that are delivered to us. Although it would be nice to empower us to make the initial determination, that is simply not the law, nor is it the policy of this office. You, and you alone, are the decision maker. Regardless of how far-fetched or unworkable the offer may seem at first, it is still a written indication that someone wants to find out if there is a possible avenue for the acquisition of your property.

Some of the offers will not be what you want to see. You may even ask us to tell you about them over the telephone. Unfortunately, we do not make telephone presentations unless you are out of the area. In that event, we first fax the proposed contract to you and then review it when we both have a copy.

Attempted telephone acceptance violates the statute of frauds. That means that a telephone agreement is not an enforceable agreement if the subject matter is the sale of real estate. In addition, when someone accepts a proposal over the telephone we have found that their willingness to sign that proposal changes rapidly. We present contracts only in person and request that salespeople from other offices do the same.

Thank you for your understanding. Now when one party signs the proposal we know that we will eventually have a firm enforceable contract.

Sincerely,
The Orcas Island Company

by: Katherine E. Reece
Realtor®, CRS, GRI

**Letter to Seller - Offer Proposes Owner Financing**

Mr. Sam Seller
Mrs. Sandy Seller
4750 Table Mesa Drive
Boulder, CO 80303

Re: 4750 Table Mesa Drive

Dear Sam and Sandy:

As you know by now, we are happy to have an offer on your home for your consideration. This particular offer, like all others, needs to be carefully reviewed to determine if it suits your needs. It is important that you fully understand the implications of the transaction as it is proposed, so feel free to contact me at any time to further explain the ramifications of the transaction as proposed by the buyer.

Please note that this offer proposes that you will lend the buyer some money as part of the purchase price in the form of a second note and mortgage. Your position will be junior to that of the existing first mortgage lender. Therefore, your rights will be subject to the senior lender's rights. A failure to make the payments on the senior mortgage may make it difficult for you to reclaim the property fast enough to realize on your security.

As I am sure you can understand, we are professionals in obtaining buyers but do not have the expertise to determine their current financial qualifications. Nor can we determine whether or not they will meet their obligations now or in the future. We simply can not be responsible for the credit-worthiness or the present or future performance of the buyer. I am amazed at the complex nature of the credit reporting system. Although we encourage you to obtain a financial statement and credit report, we must direct you to other professionals to interpret these documents. I have found that the use of your local banker or a trip to the credit bureau with the buyer will provide you with some insight into the qualifications of the buyer as well as which additional documents might be necessary to help determine the credit-worthy nature of the buyer.

Note that the proposed instruments to evidence the debt and secure its repayment have been attached and are included in the contract, should you decide to accept the buyer's offer and provide the requested financing. This is the time to review and understand these documents. I would be willing to explain them in general to you and also encourage you, if you so desire, to seek the advice of a real estate lawyer to assist you with the final decision. If you would like me to go along, I would be happy to help explain the transaction.

No home is ever sold until it closes. We realize that you are going to make some tentative commitments based on the contract as accepted. Therefore, we want to remind you that there are a lot of circumstances that must occur before the closing transpires. Be careful not to over commit your resources until we actually close.

We are on the way to closing, and I want to thank you for always having your home in such nice condition. I know the neat clean appearance took some extra time and effort, but I am sure it was a factor in attracting this buyer.

Sincerely,
The Orcas Island Company

by: Katherine E. Reece
Realtor®, CRS, GRI

**Letter to Seller - Offer Proposes an Assumption**

Mr. Sam Seller
Mrs. Sandy Seller
4750 Table Mesa Drive
Boulder, CO 80303

Re: 4750 Table Mesa Drive

Dear Sam and Sandy:

As you know by now, we are happy to have an offer on your home for your consideration. This particular offer, like all others, needs to be carefully reviewed to determine if it will suit your needs. Even though this offer is not exactly what you had requested, it deserves careful consideration. In a market such as this one, no reasonable offer should be dismissed. It is important that you fully understand the implications of the transaction as it is proposed. Please do not hesitate to call on me at any time to explain the ramifications of the proposal.

Please note that this offer proposes that your existing loan be assumed by the buyer. Assumption is a promise by the buyer to pay your note and mortgage according to its terms. Two items need your review:

First, the note and mortgage require that the buyer apply for, and be approved for, the assumption of the loan and the transfer of the property as proposed in the contract. This procedure keeps the lender from exercising its right to call the loan due and payable in full, or due-on-sale. Do not place too great a significance upon the lender's approval of the buyer for the assumption. Although we will request a novation or release of your personal obligation to repay the note, it is not currently a condition of the contract. Pressing too hard for one could undermine the transaction as proposed and is rarely given by this lender.

Second, since this is an assumption, both you and the buyer will be jointly and severally liable for the repayment of the loan unless the lender agrees to the contrary. In the event the buyer or his successor in interest does not make the payments, the lender has the option to seek payment in full from you. We do not know the effect that this might have on your credit. You will probably not be able to obtain a voluntary reconveyance of the property from the buyer or his successor in interest.

As we discussed when you listed your property, an assumption makes this property easier for a buyer to buy. Consider the offer carefully. I have asked the other salesperson to provide us with a financial statement and credit report so that you can better evaluate the offer. We do not review credit reports. We recommend that you contact your local banker and have him go over it with you. I will be glad to set up that appointment and go with you if it will help you evaluate this offer.

Sincerely,
The Orcas Island Company

by: Katherine E. Reece
Realtor®, CRS, GRI

**Letter to Seller - Offer Proposes "Silent" Assumption**

Mr. Sam Seller
Mrs. Sandy Seller
4750 Table Mesa Drive
Boulder, CO 80303

Re: 4750 Table Mesa Drive

Dear Sam and Sandy:

As you know by now, we are happy to have an offer on your home for your consideration. This particular offer, like all others, needs to be carefully reviewed to determine if it will suit your needs. Even though this offer is not exactly what you had requested, it deserves careful consideration. In a market such as this one, no reasonable offer needs to be summarily dismissed. It is important that you fully understand the implications of the transaction as it is proposed. Please do not hesitate to call on me at any time to explain the ramifications of the proposal.

Please note that this offer proposes that your existing loan be assumed by the buyer. Assumption is a promise by the buyer to pay your note and mortgage according to its terms. Two items need your review:

First, the note and mortgage require that the buyer apply for, and be approved for, the assumption of the loan and the transfer of the property as proposed in the contract. This procedure keeps the lender from exercising its right to call the loan due and payable in full, or due-on-sale. Do not place too great a significance upon the lender's approval of the buyer for the assumption. Although we will request a novation or release of your personal obligation to repay the note, it is not currently a condition of the contract. Pressing too hard for one could undermine the transaction as proposed and is rarely given by this lender.

Second, since this is an assumption, both you and the buyer will be jointly and severally liable for the repayment of the loan unless the lender agrees to the contrary. In the event the buyer or his successor in interest does not make the payments, the lender has the option to seek payment in full from you. We do not know the effect that this might have on your credit. You will probably not be able to obtain a voluntary reconveyance of the property from the buyer or his successor in interest.

As we discussed when you listed your property, an assumption makes this property easier for a buyer to buy. Consider the offer carefully. I have asked the other salesperson to provide us with a financial statement and credit report so that you can better evaluate the offer. We do not review credit reports. We recommend that you contact your local banker and have him go over it with you. I will be glad to set up that appointment and go with you if it will help you evaluate this offer.

You may be thinking about selling the property and not having the lender approve of the credit of the buyer. I certainly understand your feelings. This is your decision not mine. There is a substantial risk that the buyer may not perform and that the lender may not take the transfer lightly. In fact, the existing lender can call the entire loan due and payable in full should the lender discover the transfer to the buyer. We strongly advise you to consult with your attorney prior to deciding to complete such a transaction. Should you decide to proceed with such a transfer you will get a letter from my broker that indicates:

*You and the buyer have agreed, in spite of our advice to the contrary, that neither of you will seek the approval of the holder of the loan. That is, of course, your decision. Please understand that neither this office nor anyone associated with it, including but not limited to Katherine Reece and myself as broker, can be responsible or liable for any action taken by the holder of the loan or anyone else, or for any other ramifications of this transaction that may arise as a result of your following this course of action. These ramifications could include a foreclosure action and/or your being named in a lawsuit upon the note. You are advised to seek the advice of an attorney before embarking on such a course of action.*

Most sincerely,
The Orcas Island Company

by: Oliver E. Frascona, Broker

**Letter to Seller - Offer Proposes "Silent" FHA/VA Assumption**

Mr. Sam Seller
Mrs. Sandy Seller
4750 Table Mesa Drive
Boulder, CO 80303

Re: 4750 Table Mesa Drive

Dear Sam and Sandy:

As you know by now, we are happy to have an offer on your home for your consideration. This particular offer, like all others, needs to be carefully reviewed to determine if it will suit your needs. Even though this offer is not exactly what you had requested, it deserves careful consideration. In a market such as this one, no reasonable offer needs to be summarily dismissed. It is important that you fully understand the implications of the transaction as it is proposed. Please do not hesitate to call on me at any time to explain the ramifications of the proposal.

Please note that this offer proposes that your existing FHA or VA loan be assumed by the buyer. Assumption is a promise by the buyer to pay your note and mortgage according to its terms. Two items need your review:

First, the note and mortgage require that the buyer apply for, and be approved for, the assumption of the loan and the transfer of the property as proposed in the contract. This procedure keeps the lender from exercising its right to call the loan due and payable in full, or due-on-sale. The consent of the government through the lender is required for the transfer of FHA and VA loans lender, period. To do otherwise might cause a violation of the law.

Do not place too great a significance upon the lender's approval of the buyer for the assumption. Although we will request a novation or release of your personal obligation to repay the note, it is not currently a condition of the contract. Pressing too hard for one could undermine the transaction as proposed and is rarely given by this lender.

Second, since this is an assumption, both you and the buyer will be jointly and severally liable for the repayment of the loan unless the lender agrees to the contrary. In the event the buyer or his successor in interest does not make the payments, the lender has the option to seek payment in full from you. We do not know the effect that this might have on your credit. You will probably not be able to obtain a voluntary reconveyance of the property from the buyer or his successor in interest.

As we discussed when you listed your property, an assumption makes this property easier for a buyer to buy. Consider the offer carefully. I have asked the other salesperson to provide us with a financial statement and credit report so that you can better evaluate the offer. We do not review credit reports. We recommend that you contact your local banker and have him go over it with you. I will be glad to set up that appointment and go with you if it will help you evaluate this offer.

You may be thinking about selling the property and not having the lender approve of the credit of the buyer, forget it. It might violate the law. I certainly understand your feelings. However, in the event that you decide to do that we will not close the transaction. We strongly advise you to consult with your attorney prior to deciding to complete such a transaction.

Sincerely,
The Orcas Island Company

by: Katherine E. Reece
Realtor®, CRS, GRI

**Letter to Seller - All-Inclusive Financing**

Mr. Sam Seller
Mrs. Sandy Seller
4750 Table Mesa Drive
Boulder, CO 80303

Re: 4750 Table Mesa Drive

Dear Sam and Sandy:

As you know by now, we are happy to have an offer on your home for your consideration. This particular offer, like all others, needs to be carefully reviewed to determine if it will suit your needs. Even though this offer is not exactly what you had requested, it deserves careful consideration. In a market such as this one no reasonable offer needs to be dismissed. It is important that you fully understand the implications of the transaction as it is proposed. Please do not hesitate to call on me at any time to explain the ramifications of the proposal.

Please note that this offer proposes that you carry an All-Inclusive Note and Mortgage. Let me explain how such a note and mortgage works. First, your existing first loan stays of record. The buyer does not assume it nor agree to pay it. You remain totally responsible for payment of that loan.

The buyer executes a large note that includes the balances due on the existing first loan. This large or "All-Inclusive" note is payable to you in monthly installments as indicated in the proposal. It is secured by an All-Inclusive Mortgage showing you as the beneficiary. From each such installment you make the payments on the existing first note and mortgage.

This All-Inclusive Note and Mortgage allows you to reserve the right at your option to foreclose upon your All-Inclusive Mortgage and obtain the return to you of the property without disturbing the underlying loan. If this is interesting to you, we can explore it in more detail. It is an effective tool when the underlying financing does not have a due-on-sale clause such as your current first loan.

Should you elect to consider this option seriously, we will need to have you talk with your attorney to make sure that you understand the risks associated with the proposed transfer. We are real estate brokers and not attorneys.

Sincerely,
The Orcas Island Company
by: Katherine E. Reece
Realtor®, CRS, GRI

## Letter to Seller - Counterproposals

Mr. Sam Seller
Mrs. Sandy Seller
4750 Table Mesa Drive
Boulder, CO 80303

Re: 4750 Table Mesa Drive

Dear Sam and Sandy:

Thank you for talking with me on the telephone today. I want to be sure that you understand the effect of a counter proposal. This offer is capable of acceptance in its present condition. Any changes that are made, either by crossing out a term and initialing it or by executing a counter proposal, give the other party the opportunity to walk away from the transaction with impunity.

A counter proposal is a rejection of the initial offer and a return offer by you to the buyer. By definition, the initial offer is no longer capable of acceptance. Should you later change your mind and wish to accept the initial offer that will not be possible. You will have to wait for the buyer to make another offer or you will have to initiate such an offer.

With that in mind, let me encourage you to review each proposed change to determine if it is critical to the transaction before making any change to the offer. I know that we both want a sale that is as proper and correct as possible. However, I do not want to see you counter the offer for details that might give the buyer the ability to walk away. Thank you for your consideration.

As always, the advice of an attorney is recommended. If I can be of assistance in explaining the alternatives to you and/or your attorney, accountant, priest or other advisor, please do not hesitate to call. This is an important point in the sale and you need to feel comfortable in your understanding of the alternatives and in your ultimate decision.

It is a pleasure to be your listing agent for the sale of your property. If there is anything that I can do to assist you please do not hesitate to let me know.

Sincerely,
The Orcas Island Company

by: Katherine E. Reece
Realtor®, CRS, GRI

**Letter - Offer Proposing Questionable Deal**

Mr. Albert A. Desperate
Mrs. Martha B. Desperate
6990 Hopeless Avenue
Madison, MN 90303

Mr. Wilber C. Hungry
Mrs. Freda D. Hungry
Apartment 210 A
West End Apartments
999 Last Avenue
Madison, MN 80303

Re: 6990 Hopeless Avenue
Desperation City

Dear Mr. and Mrs. Desperate and Mr. and Mrs. Hungry:

I know that all of you are anticipating this letter, and I am sorry that I have to write it. I simply have no other option than to formally clarify my position and that of this office with regard to the transaction that you are proposing. Please understand our position and review this letter carefully.

As I indicated to all of you over the phone today and in person over the last two days, your joint decision to allow the sellers to apply for and utilize their credit to obtain a new FHA loan as owner occupants with the intention of immediately upon closing of said loan transferring the property to the buyers via assumption of the new FHA loan is a violation of the rules and regulations promulgated by the Department of Housing and Urban Development. Neither I nor this office can be a party to such a transaction.

We understand your respective desperate needs to sell and buy the home in question. We are not passing on the validity of the transaction, but only stating that it violates the regulations as we understand them. You are, of course, free to take whatever action you desire. We would advise you to seek the closing services of a title company or other suitable closing agent to ensure that the transaction's financial calculations are properly calculated. In addition, we again advise you to seek the services of a real estate attorney or to contact the FHA directly to fully understand the ramifications of the transaction you propose.

There is no doubt that the buyer was procured by the efforts of this office. Should the transaction close, we will be entitled to receive our commission, as indicated in the listing agreement. There is no requirement that we draft the contract or conduct the closing. We must only provide you with a buyer acceptable to you or that you transfer the property to a buyer that was procured by us.

I know that you understand our position, and we appreciate your respecting the fact that we can not be a part of the transaction as you propose it. Nevertheless, congratulations on the pending purchase and sale of this property.

As with any assumption, there is a potential for damage to be inflicted to the credit of both parties in the event that the loan payments are not timely made. Reference should be made to the pamphlet we have given you, "Assumption, Subject To and Novation, Your Liabilities and Rights".

Sincerely,
The Orcas Island Company

by: Katherine E. Reece
Realtor®, CRS, GRI

**Letter - Offer Matching the Listing**

Mr. Sam Seller
Mrs. Sandy Seller
4750 Table Mesa Drive
Boulder, CO 80303

Re: 4750 Table Mesa Drive

Dear Sam and Sandy:

With this letter, we are happy to include an offer that exactly meets the terms and conditions you requested in your Listing Agreement. It is always a pleasure to present this kind of offer. It is important that you fully understand the implications of the transaction as proposed by the offer so feel free to contact me immediately to explain to you the ramifications of the proposed transaction. As always, should you feel you need it, the advice of an attorney is recommended.

Few people are capable of paying all cash, so I have insisted that the earnest money be equal to five percent of the total sales price. It is rare to obtain such a substantial amount of earnest money. Although all indications are that it will be a quick closing within the next few weeks, I never consider a property sold until the actual closing, the funds having been paid and having cleared the bank. [Contrary to popular opinion, even certified funds must clear and are subject to stop payment orders.] I would advise you not to obligate yourselves irrevocably based upon this contract until it actually closes.

Sincerely,
The Orcas Island Company

by: Katherine E. Reece
Realtor®, CRS, GRI

## Letter - Offer Proposing New Financing

Mr. Sam Seller
Mrs. Sandy Seller
4750 Table Mesa Drive
Boulder, CO 80303

Re: 4750 Table Mesa Drive

Dear Sam and Sandy:

The news we have all been waiting for has arrived. This letter contains an offer from Jon and Mimi Goodman. They are both attorneys but that is no cause for alarm. The terms are not exactly what you wanted but they are very close. Review the offer as quickly as possible because it expires tomorrow at midnight. While it is always possible for a buyer to withdraw an offer before it is accepted, I think the Goodmans want you to consider their offer very seriously. They have already met with a lender and a letter indicating their pre-qualification for the proposed financing has been submitted with the offer.

This offer indicates that the buyers' obligations are conditional upon their being able to obtain a new first loan in the amount of $256,000.00 which represents a 77% loan-to-value ratio of their proposed contract price. While there is a risk that they cannot qualify for the financing, there are very few buyers who can either pay cash or enter into a contract without such a loan condition. You will note that the application must be made by Tuesday of next week and the loan approved on or before fifteen days of closing. Thereafter, the earnest money could be in jeopardy.

It is impossible for us to determine if any buyer will qualify for the proposed loan. For purposes of this offer, I have asked that the buyer present a financial statement and work history with the offer to assist you in determining if they are a good risk.

Your home will be effectively off the market while the loan application is in process. Although we can continue to solicit back-up offers, the news that a house is under contract discourages other potential buyers from trying to purchase it.

Sincerely,
The Orcas Island Company

by: Katherine E. Reece
Realtor®, CRS, GRI

## Letter - Offer Proposing New Financing

Mr. Sam Seller
Mrs. Sandy Seller
4750 Table Mesa Drive
Boulder, CO 80303

Re: 4750 Table Mesa Drive

Dear Sam and Sandy:

The news we have all been waiting for has arrived. This letter contains an offer from Jon and Mimi Goodman. They are both attorneys but that is no cause for alarm. The terms are not exactly what you wanted but they are very close. Review the offer as quickly as possible because it expires tomorrow at midnight. While it is always possible for a buyer to withdraw an offer before it is accepted, I think the Goodmans want you to consider their offer very seriously. They have already met with a lender and a letter indicating their pre-qualification for the proposed financing has been submitted with the offer.

This offer indicates that the buyers' obligations are conditional upon their being able to obtain a new first loan in the amount of $256,000.00 which represents a 77% loan-to-value ratio of their proposed contract price. While there is a risk that they can not qualify for the financing, there are very few buyers who can either pay cash or enter into a contract without such a loan condition. You will note that the application must be made by Tuesday of next week and the loan approved on or before fifteen days of closing. Thereafter, the earnest money could be in jeopardy.

It is impossible for us to determine if any buyer will qualify for the proposed loan. For purposes of this offer, I have asked that the buyer present a financial statement and work history with the offer to assist you in determining if they are a good risk.

Your home will be effectively off the market while the loan application is in process. Although we can continue to solicit back-up offers, the news that a house is under contract discourages other potential buyers from trying to purchase it.

A new loan will cause your old loan to be paid off in full which may trigger the payoff penalty that we discussed earlier. One good aspect of such a payoff is the termination of your personal liability for the repayment of that loan.

If you wish to require that the buyer first try to get a loan from the holder of your mortgage in order to possibly avoid that penalty, a provision will need to be inserted in a counter proposal before the contract can become a firm and final deal. The buyer then has the following options: accepting the counter proposal, rejecting the entire transaction, or making another offer.

Since the offer is within the limits that you initially set when we first listed your house, I think that you should seriously consider accepting it as written. I will try to encourage the buyer to use your existing lender. However, it would seem that you would hate to loose this buyer who looks quite qualified and is paying a reasonable price over the payoff penalty. Please advise me.

Sincerely,
The Orcas Island Company

by: Katherine E. Reece
Realtor®, CRS, GRI

## Letter - Offer Conditional Upon Sale of Current Home

Mr. Sam Seller
Mrs. Sandy Seller
4750 Table Mesa Drive
Boulder, CO 80303

Re: 4750 Table Mesa Drive

Dear Sam and Sandy:

As you are aware by now, we are happy to have an offer on your home for your consideration. It has been a difficult job to market your home due to the large inventory of other homes in your price range on the market. There are just too many from which to choose. We really appreciate your efforts to have the home always ready to show even on a few moments' notice. I believe the purchasers selected your home because of the superb condition of the property, and you deserve credit for your efforts.

This offer indicates that the buyer will have to sell and close upon the buyer's present home before he can be obligated to purchase your home. This imposes some degree of risk because the contract for the sale of the buyer's current home has its own potential problems. I have insisted that a copy of the buyer's contract for the sale of the buyer's home be attached to this offer so that you can review it in detail.

In addition, I have contacted the agent who is assisting the buyer in the purchase of the buyer's house and indicated that I will probably be calling to discuss the status of that transaction. The buyers have indicated that you are more than welcome to speak with their salesperson if it will help you decide to accept their offer. Their office and home telephones follow:

Agent for the buyer of the buyers' house:
James E. Rodenbeek
The Rodenbeek Agency
Scott City, Kansas (316) 872-5134

Most people who will be able to afford your home are the owners of an existing house. The sale of their current residence, although sometimes not indicated in the contract, is going to be the deciding factor in the approval process of the new lender. The lender also then will probably make the closing of the current home a condition of loan approval.

As with any offer, even ones that have no indicated conditions, there is a degree of uncertainty until the deal actually closes. It is with this in mind that we caution you not to rely too heavily on this particular sale until it is final. We can not be responsible for actions or inactions that are not within our control, and the abilities and intentions of a buyer are definitely outside of our control. Although we will try hard to keep ourselves abreast of the events as they unfold, we can not make the decisions for any of the parties.

This particular offer, like any other legally binding contract, needs to be carefully reviewed to determine if it suits your needs. It is important that you fully understand the implications of the transaction as it is proposed, so please feel free to ask me at any time to explain further the ramifications of the proposed transaction. We can not give legal advice, and, therefore, you may wish to use an attorney for that purpose. We can, however, explain the contract in detail so that you can make an informed decision.

I know I speak for the entire staff when I say that we have enjoyed having your home in our inventory. I think the buyers are excited to be buying your house and that good feeling is certainly a nice help in keeping them interested through the rigorous loan application, qualification, and closing processes.

Sincerely,
The Orcas Island Company

by: Katherine E. Reece
Realtor®, CRS, GRI

## Letter - *Just for Fun* - Practice of Law

Mr. Sam Seller
Mrs. Sandy Seller
4750 Table Mesa Drive
Boulder, CO 80303

Re: 4750 Table Mesa Drive

Dear Sam and Sandy:

As you are aware by now, we are happy to have an offer on your home for your consideration. It has been a difficult job to market your home due to the large inventory of other homes in your price range on the market. There are just too many from which to choose. We really appreciate your efforts to have the home always ready to show even on a few moments' notice. I believe the purchasers selected your home because of the superb condition of the property, and you deserve the credit for your efforts.

We would be happy to accompany you to your attorney's office to help review the contract if you wish. If you decide not to select an attorney, we will just do his job without compensation; and, in the event we do not meet your expectations, you can feel free to sue us. Our contracts are so poorly drafted that we are nervous about having you take them to an attorney.

*In addition, since you never really agreed to anything in the contract and are so unsure of the transaction we are very suspect of your taking the contract to anyone to review it. If you are such a simple-minded fool to let some lawyer talk you out of the deal, there is really no need to go see one. I can just take care of the details such as reviewing the title commitment he would normally do, only to find that you do not really own the property, and only finding that out now because I was too lazy to order a commitment before I listed your property. Plus, I can also give you erroneous financial and tax advice.*

I know I speak for the entire staff when I say that we have enjoyed having your home in our inventory. I think the buyers are excited to be buying your house and that good feeling is certainly a nice help in keeping them interested through the rigorous loan application, qualification, and closing processes.

Sincerely,
The Orcas Island Company

by: Katherine E. Reece
Realtor®, CRS, GRI

## Standard Home Warranty Election/Waiver

The broker wants all buyers and sellers to be aware of the availability of a home warranty policy for this property. This firm is an authorized representative of the indicated home warranty company. As such we will receive a commission in the event you select a home warranty from that company. A copy of the policy is attached for your review. There are other home warranty companies in the market place. We will be happy to locate one that suits your needs.

We encourage all buyers and sellers to take advantage of the home warranty program. The real estate brokers and salesperson are not liable for defects in the property unknown to us. We will tell you everything that we know about the physical condition of the property. This policy covers repair or replacement of the following items:

Read the policy to make sure that you understand the exact coverage that is included. *This is not a structural policy.* It will not cover repair or replacement of the sidewalk, driveway, foundation wall,

Buyers, please complete the following so that we may properly insert a clause in to the contract.

Buyer(s) has been informed that a home warranty ☐ *is* ☐ *is not* available for this property. Buyers have elected ☐ *to* ☐ *not to* obtain a home warranty. The home warranty, if selected, shall be paid as a ☐ *Buyer's* ☐ *Seller's* expense. If Seller's expense is selected, the Seller's expense shall be limited to $________ and the balance shall be paid by the Buyer(s).

Broker ☐ *will* ☐ *will not* credit Buyer(s) with the commission received by Broker as a result of the selection of a home warranty policy sold through this company.

Property:______________________________________________________

Home Warranty Company:__________________________________________

Commission to Real Estate Broker: $_______________

Buyer Buyer

________________________________ date ________________________________ date

# Chapter Six
# After The Contract Is Signed
### *The Road to a Successful Closing*

## Contract Progress

**Contract is Signed.** At some point, whether after the initial offer or after one or more counteroffers, the final document is signed and the real estate professional feels that there is a contract. Communicating the fact that the final document has been signed, rather than that there is a contract, is necessary to the transaction. *Presenting the facts and allowing the parties to draw their own conclusions is the best way to be professional.*

**Performance Deadlines for Conditions.** The complexity of today's real estate transaction necessitates that many contingencies are often incorporated into the contract with specific deadlines for performance or removal by either the seller or the buyer. Failure to do so may render the contract null and void or waive the benefitting party's right to make the specific item a contract issue at any future date. It becomes imperative that all parties to the contract--buyer, seller, real estate brokers, lenders, escrow officers and attorneys--be in full agreement on the performance deadlines for all contingencies in the accepted contract. For this reason a form that itemizes these dates in chronological sequence that is circulated and signed by all will facilitate timely compliance as well as eliminate any misunderstandings in the future.

The performance deadline form can be used both in the beginning for the initial concurrence of specific performance deadlines required as well as for periodic updates as each deadline is met. It is a simple matter then to fill in the date completed, highlight the item addressed, perhaps write a short confirming note and mail it. Copies to your clients, the cooperating broker, the lender, the escrow or title company or other third parties keeps everyone aware of the progress being made.

Katherine has found that there is little misunderstanding from any of the parties in a transaction when the form is used. As an additional benefit she has found that the client or customer will track the events more carefully and assume more of the responsibility for their own actions or inactions without expecting her to carry the full responsibility for any delay or problem that arises during the escrow closing process. Usually she is informed well in advance if any performance deadline may need to be modified or extended and a solution can be negotiated between all the parties before tempers flare over last minute changes.

Oliver has also been faced with the situation where a contract is falling apart because people have not completed their assigned tasks. He finds that simply assigning the tasks in a letter goes a long way to eliminating confusion. It has the advantage of assigning tasks and also of relieving the sender of the implied responsibility for a task that in fact belongs to someone else. His letter appears first followed by the forms that Katherine uses.

## Letter - Assignment of Tasks

Mr. Sam Seller
Mrs. Sandy Seller
4750 Table Mesa Drive
Boulder, CO 80303

Re: 4750 Table Mesa Drive

Dear Sam and Sandy:

Now that we have a contract there are a number of tasks that must be accomplished to ensure a prompt and proper closing. Some tasks we accept responsibility for, some are the buyer's obligation, some are the seller's obligation, and some are the obligation of the other salesperson.

To assist everyone in determining who has the responsibility for each item, I have enclosed a list showing the tasks, the party that needs to complete each item, and, in parenthesis, the completion date for each item. Please consult the list and advise me if you need additional help with any of your responsibilities. Although we can not guarantee the performance of the other parties, we will endeavor to assist them in every reasonable way possible to complete their tasks in a timely fashion.

*Seller*:

*Buyer*:

1. Apply for the loan at (April 1, 2010):
   Colorado National Mortgage (Valerie Simpson)
   Arapahoe and 28th Street
   Boulder, CO 80303
   (303) 444-1234

2.

*Listing Broker*:

*Selling Broker*:

Sincerely,
The Orcas Island Company

by: Katherine E. Reece
Realtor®, CRS, GRI

## CONTRACT DEADLINES

PROPERTY ADDRESS: ______________________________

SELLER: ______________________________

BUYER: ______________________________

CONTRACT DATED: ______________________________

ESCROW OFFICER: ______________________________

TELEPHONE: ______________________________

| Deadline date: | Completion date: | Contingency: |
|---|---|---|
| | | |

This is to confirm all the dates necessary to achieve a smooth closing. Please verify the dates with either the buyer or seller, sign the form, keep a copy, mail a copy to either the buyer or seller and return a copy to me.

Realtor® assisting Buyer:______________________ Date:______________

Realtor® assisting Seller:______________________ Date:______________

cc: Mr. and Mrs. Seller
Mr. and Mrs. Buyer
Escrow officer
Lender

## Letter - Broker to Buyer After Offer Accepted

Mr. and Mrs. Jonathan A. Goodman
Apartment 610 A
12th and Main Street
Denver, CO 80303

Re: 909 East First Street

Dear Mr. and Mrs. Goodman:

As you have probably heard, your offer on 909 East First Street was accepted and signed by the seller this Tuesday at 10:00 P.M. Congratulations on the purchase of your new home! There are many things that need to be done to get ready for the closing and possession of the home. In order to let everyone know who has what responsibility, let me outline the various assignments for all concerned.

First, you will need to apply within the next five days for a loan fitting the minimum parameters of the contract, i.e., a loan amount of $45,000.00, an interest rate of 10% per annum amortized over thirty years. I have provided you with a partial list of lenders who have elected to have their rates and other information included in the list and who are currently doing business in this area. Although not exhaustive, it should give you a good place to start. As always, the ultimate selection of a lender is yours. We recommend that you call a few lenders for rate quotations and then select one or two for your initial application. Each has its own programs and alternatives in addition to the standard government (VA and FHA) loans.

It has been our experience that purchasers like to discuss their finances with a loan officer of their choice and let that lender assist them in making the personal determination of the exact type, terms, and amount of loan that will suit their needs. For this reason, we do not attempt to counsel anyone concerning the best loan for his needs. When you have selected a lender and made a loan appointment, please let us know so that we can assist you and that lender in gathering the information and documentation that the lender requires. To assist you in preparing for the initial interview, I have enclosed a partial list of information often requested so that you can gather as much of it as possible in advance and expedite the application process.

Second, you will need to select a home inspection service and termite inspection service, as well as a moving company. While many home inspection services are available, we have included a list of services used by previous customers for your review. Each should be happy to provide you with a list of past customers to assist you in making your decision.

Third, you will need to decide on the educational alternatives available. A list of the public and private schools within a reasonable distance from your new home is included. It has been so long since any of the salespeople in the office attended school that an opinion on the quality or availability of various educational services would not be reliable. Each person evaluates the needs of their children and the various offerings of each school system differently. It is a personal choice. Please note the phone number of the school board. They are available to assist you and can provide answers to your questions in the future.

You will need to complete the first item by Monday, the 20th, and the others within the next two weeks. Remember, the closing date is set for Friday, the 15th of March, and you will need to have your funds available. To expedite obtaining the balance of the down payment for the closing, I would suggest opening a local bank account at your earliest convenience. I am sure that whomever you initially select will be able to get you started with an account and provide you with certified funds for closing.

Thank you for letting me serve you in viewing and selecting the home of your choice. It has been fun helping you to locate a home you are happy with.

Sincerely,
The Orcas Island Company

by: Katherine E. Reece
Realtor®, CRS, GRI

enclosures:

## Letter - HOW Home Warranty Program

Mr. and Mrs. Jonathan A. Goodman
c/o Martha Douglas
Douglas and Company Real Estate
12th and Main Street
Longmont, CO 80000

Re: 909 First Street

Dear Mr and Mrs. Goodman:

In response to your recent inquiry about the extent of the Home Owners Warranty (HOW) on the property, I contacted ________________ at __________ and s/he indicated that there is a policy, #____________________, currently in effect. I would suggest that you talk with Janine directly so that she can answer your questions. That way there will be nothing lost in the transmission, and you can ask follow-up questions without having to contact me.

Since our firm has a policy that prohibits us from making any guarantees with regard to any property, I always encourage interested buyers to talk directly with the insurance agency to avoid confusion. I would encourage you to inquire about the extent of the coverage, the term remaining, the balance of the unexpired limits which remains available. Thank you for your understanding. If you reach an impasse with HOW, please do not hesitate to let me know and I will try to find the person over there who can assist you.

Sincerely,
The Orcas Island Company

by: Katherine E. Reece
Realtor®, CRS, GRI

**Escrow Instructions.** Every area of the country calls them something different. Some states do not have escrow instructions and simply use the contract as the basis for the closing entity to prepare for closing. Many brokers do the closing themselves as a service to both buyer and seller.

Some states utilize a third party escrow service to receive and distribute the funds and ensure that all conveyance documents are properly prepared, executed and recorded in a timely fashion. Sometime this party is an attorney.

Instructions to the responsible entity providing all the information and at the same time delivering a duplicate original of the contract and earnest money deposit will facilitate the process. In the event the earnest money is held by other than the escrow agent, a copy of the receipt showing the depository of the earnest money will suffice. By sending copies to all entities at the same time you will ensure that each of the entities starts with an identical set of copies.

Memos or a letter with deadlines indicated to the escrow agent with a copy to the cooperating salesperson and the proposed lender will keep all the parties to the transaction well informed of the progress.

One salesperson sends a copy of the documents with a cover letter indicating that these are copies of the originals with instructions to inform him immediately if any corrections are necessary. He also attaches a blue backing sheet similar to the ones that attorneys use for wills so that the package will remain intact. Yes, the backing sheet does have his company name, address and telephone number.

Escrow Checklist. A checklist of activities necessary to close your transaction is invaluable when attempting to track multiple escrows. At one quick glance at the checklist you can ascertain what has been accomplished and what yet needs to be done. If you are working with an assistant, the checklist can eliminate duplicate efforts and keep you both informed about what has been done. Your communication with your buyer or seller will be both concise and precise.

## Letter - Contract Review and Assignment of Tasks

Mr. Sam Seller
Mrs. Sandy Seller
4750 Table Mesa Drive
Boulder, CO 80303

Re: 4750 Table Mesa Drive

Dear Sam and Sandy:

Enclosed you will find an exact copy of the contract as it was finally signed and initialed. Please review it immediately to verify that in fact it represents the transaction as you think it should be. You will note that I have sent an identical copy to your designated lender, the title insurance company (closing or escrow agent), the Buyer and all Realtors® involved.

Now that we have a contract there are a number of tasks that must be accomplished to ensure a prompt and proper closing. Some tasks we accept responsibility for, some are the buyer's obligation, some are the seller's obligation, and some are the obligation of the cooperating salesperson.

To assist everyone in determining who has the responsibility for each item, I have enclosed a list showing the tasks, the party that needs to complete each item, and, in parenthesis, the completion date for each item. Please consult the list and advise me if you need additional help with any of your responsibilities. Although we cannot guarantee the performance of the other parties, we will endeavor to assist them in every reasonable way possible to complete their tasks in a timely fashion.

*Seller*:
*Buyer*:
*Listing Broker*:
*Selling Broker*:
*Lender:*

Sincerely,
The Orcas Island Company

by: Katherine E. Reece
Realtor®, CRS, GRI

cc: Listing Broker or Selling Broker
Seller or Buyer
Lender
Escrow (title) Agent

## Escrow Instructions

TO:______________________________ ESCROW OFFICER:____________________

______________________________ ESCROW PHONE:____________________

______________________________ ESCROW FAX:____________________

CONTRACT DATE:____________ ESCROW NO:____________________

ACCEPTANCE DATE:__________ ESCROW OPENED:____________________

---

Please open escrow for the following:

PROPERTY ADDRESS:

---

CLOSING DATE:______________ EARLY

OCCUPANCY:______________

INITIAL DEPOSIT:______________ LEASE FORM:____________________

ADD'L DEPOSIT:______________ LOAN TYPE:____________________

DOWN PAYMENT:______________ LOAN AMT:____________________

PURCHASE PRICE:______________

---

SELLERS:______________________ BUYERS:______________________

ADDRESS: ADDRESS:

Phone:(w)____________(h)__________ Phone:(w)____________(h)__________

---

BROKER INFORMATION

SELLER'S:______________________ BUYER'S:______________________

S'PERSON:______________________ S'PERSON:______________________

ADDRESS: ADDRESS:

Phone:(w)____________(h)__________ Phone:(w)____________(h)__________

EXISTING LENDER:____________ NEW LENDER:____________________
LOAN AMOUNT:_______________ LOAN OFFICER:__________________
ADDRESS: ADDRESS:

LOAN TYPE:(FHA)(VA)(CONV) PROCESSOR:__________________
Phone:(o)____________(f)_________

ATTY FOR LEGAL DOCUMENTS:______________________________
Phone:(office)____________(fax)_________

COMMISSION DIVISION FROM ESCROW:

COMPANY:______________________ AMT:________________
COMPANY:______________________ AMT:________________

ENCLOSURES

____ORIGINAL CONTRACT DATED:___________________
____CHECK IN THE AMOUNT OF $_______________ DATED:____________
____COUNTER PROPOSAL DATED:_______________________
____OTHER_____________________________________________
____OTHER_____________________________________________

Thank you for your attention to this matter. We appreciate your efforts. Please keep everyone informed regarding the status of this escrow. Call me at any time if you have any questions.

Sincerely,
The Orcas Island Company

by: Katherine E. Reece
Realtor®, CRS, GRI

cc: Cooperating Broker
Lender

## Escrow Checklist

Client NAME:______________________________

Property ADDRESS:______________________________

Sales PRICE:__________Contract DATE:__________Accept DATE:__________

Loam AMOUNT:____________________Loan CO:____________________

Loan OFFICER:________________PHONE:______________FAX:____________

COOPERATING BROKER:__________________ S'PERSON:______________

OFFICE PHONE:_________________FAX:______________PHONE:___________

ESCROW CO:______________________OFFICER:____________________

FAX:________________PHONE:____________FILE NO:________________

MONEY
____Earnest money deposited
____Add'l Earnest money deposited
____Tasks letter sent

APPRAISAL
____Ordered on____________
____Company__________________
____Comps prepared
____Appraiser met
____Appraisal in

DOCUMENTS
____Preparer__________________
____Deed ordered
____Lease ordered
____Mortgage ordered

EXISTING LOAN
____Lender____________________
____Payoff ordered
____Payoff received

PROPERTY DISCLOSURE
____Rec'd from seller
____Del'd to buyer
____Accepted

CONDO/ASSN DOCUMENTS
____Ordered
____Delivered to buyer
____Accepted by buyer
____Objections
____Turned over to______________

LOAN
____Application made with________
____Commitment date___________
____Interest lock in date__________
____Rate locked in by____________
____Points locked in by__________
____Appraisal ordered
____Appraisal in
____Property appraised
____Loan amount fixed
____Loan confirm letter sent

INSPECTIONS
____Pool Ordered from__________
____Done
____Accepted
____Appliances w/buyer
____Done
____Accepted
____Home Warranty_____________
____Policy commitment received
____Repair items noted

____Repairs ordered
____Termite inspection ordered
____Company________________
____Key to company
____Lock box combo to company
____Completed
____Inspection letter sent

INSURANCE
____New policy ordered from______
____Old policy proration ordered
____Buyer advised
____Escrow notified

EARLY OCCUPANCY
____Lease to buyer
____Lease to seller
____Insurance notification
____Buyer policy issued
____Seller policy issued
____Utilities switched over

CLOSING
____Date scheduled
____Informed buyer
____Informed seller
____Power of attorney for _________
____Lender approve Power of Attorney
____Escrow/Title co approved POA
____Confirmed with other s'person
____Obtained amount for buyer
____Gave amount to buyer
____Confirmed buyer has the money
____It closed

KEYS FOR BUYER
____Rec'd from seller
____Del'd to buyer
____Letter sent

GIFTS
____Arranged
____Delivered

MARKETING LETTERS
____Prepared
____Sent

**Telephone Log.** The importance of maintaining a telephone log and continuous correspondence during the contract closing process can not be overstated. Adopt a system that works for you. Just do it. Indicate in the log if the calls made are incoming or outgoing, the party with whom you actually speak (name), the context of the conversation and even the time of day. Indicate when calls are made but not answered or when a message is left on a recording machine. Follow either with a memo that states "*sorry I missed you by telephone, but I would like to discuss...*" Be as detailed as you possibly can. At times when memories are failing your telephone log will prod even the most confused mind to recall explicit events clearly. The person with the telephone log is the credible witness. The consistency of a standard of practice employed on all transactions is the best defense in time of trouble.

| DATE | IN/OUT | PARTY | COMMENTS: |
|---|---|---|---|
| | | | |
| | | | |

**Removal of Conditions Precedent.** As each of the conditions listed in the contract is satisfied, it is important to notify the parties of this progress. Notification of the fact that an item has been removed or satisfied is better than drawing a conclusion as to the effect of the removal. This is a good stage at which to send copies of a letter addressed to one party to the other parties. Careful structure here can be an adroit way to accomplish your objectives.

**Title Insurance Commitment Arrival.** In most contracts it is important to ensure that the buyer receives and receipts for the title insurance commitment prior to the date specified in the contract. Once this has occurred, everyone needs to be notified. There have been successful attempts by supreme courts to make the selling agent, even if a subagent, an agent of the buyer for the purposes of receipt of the title commitment. In those cases the buyer can not claim he did not receive the title commitment if it was delivered to a subagent assisting him in the purchase.

Notification serves two purposes. First, it confirms that the commitment was actually delivered. Second, it puts the recipient on notice that in the event the notification is defective, he must speak up or there or will arise a presumption that the notification was correct as delivered. In other words, notification gives the recipient notice that he must address any discrepancy or waive any future right to do so.

## Letter - Title Insurance Commitment

Ms. Sharon Reichman
Reichman Title and Abstract Company
1600 Fairview Lane
Boulder, CO 80303

Re: Commitment Number 56-89234-890

Dear Sharon:

Thank you for moving fast to obtain the title insurance commitment for this transaction. I appreciate your delivering a copy of it to the buyers at their address in the contract, as well as the copy that you left at this office. As usual I have told the buyers that you are the person to contact if they have any questions about the specifics of the commitment.

As you know, I like copies of all documents that relate to any typed exceptions and any covenants and restrictions that effect the property attached to each copy of the commitment. The copy of the commitment I received did not contain all of the covenants and restrictions, and I am concerned that the buyer's copy may also have been short. If you would deliver a full set of the indicated copies I would appreciate it.

Please excuse my nagging. I am a detail oriented person who must know that the parties have all the information they require to arrive at their own decisions. I know that we both want a perfect closing and an informed buyer. I have indicated to the buyers that as long as we close in your office, you will update the commitment to the latest possible date and provide gap protection for any items that do not appear on the commitment or the update which goes of record prior to the recording of the deed. Although I am sure that the buyers desire this coverage, I am ordering it in my own right if necessary to ensure that it is in effect. I have assured the buyers that you will take care of obtaining the endorsement and gap protection.

You have my standard closing instruction sheet, and I would appreciate it if you would deliver a set of the closing papers to both attorneys indicated thereon for their review at least three days prior to the closing. Again, it is a delight to do business with such a professional title company. I am aware that it is your efforts that make the transaction close properly. I am proud to be able to send you this additional business. If there is anything that I can do to expedite this transaction, please let me know right away.

Sincerely,
The Orcas Island Company
by: Katherine E. Reece

cc: Charles A. Reasoner

**Loan Application and Commitment.** Communicate the information firmly to the other party when the buyer has commenced a loan application or when she has been approved for the loan. Often this is first done by telephone. However, a follow up letter will avoid potential problems with the timing and content of the telephone conversation.

Cover letters to lenders are an integral part of any transaction. The market changes quickly. There is intense competition in the mortgage lending business. The pressure on the loan officers to make deals and attract business, while at the same time ensuring that the business is profitable, is extreme. The memories of all parties in a transaction are taxed to the maximum. A simple cover letter with the appropriate copies can help to redefine the deal, keep good business friends happy, and protect yourself, as well as informing the other parties of the exact contents of the quotation or commitment. Think for a minute: Who can lock in the rate? The buyer, the seller, someone's agent?

It is always a good idea to ask for the specific terms of any loan commitment notice when you represent the seller. Do not rely on the mortgage knowledge of the cooperating broker when he informs you verbally that his client has a final loan commitment. Many times the lender will give "conditional approval" and you may learn that the "condition" is the buyer securing a new job! There are no "conditional approvals"—only loan approvals which are unconditional.

**Case in Point.** *Katherine represented a seller who had already moved out of state prior to closing and was anxiously awaiting recordation on the vacant home. Two weeks prior to closing, loan commitment was obtained and the buyer requested an early occupancy. Further inquiries to the loan officer revealed that the loan commitment was conditional upon the buyer securing a new job similar to his previous one in the military. The lender had processed the loan as if the buyer would be maintaining his active duty status when in fact his verification of employment actually indicated he would be separating from the military service within a month. (New lender with "bargain" rates who was unfamiliar with his own forms!)*

*What appeared to be a "dead deal" to the buyer, lender, and buyer's broker was successfully closed with a delayed closing, an early occupancy with non-refundable deposit sufficient to cover re-marketing the home if necessary, a seller who had funds to continue making mortgage payments, and Katherine working directly with the buyer and lender to acquire the new job position that met all the requirements within the new deadlines accepted by all.*

**Caution.** *When you tackle early occupancy make sure that you have a lease, not just an "early occupancy agreement". In addition consult with a local attorney to make sure that "non-refundable deposits" are not possibly characterized as down payment on an installment sale instead of a lease.*

### Letter - Lender--Confirming Quotation

Ms. Rosie Leino, Loan Officer
Howard and Howard Mortgage, Inc.
1900 West Chambers Drive
Denver, CO 80007

Re: Loan Quotation

Dear Rosie:

Thank you for taking the time to give me an oral quotation yesterday. With the market as hectic as it appears, I know you have a lot to do and I appreciate your stopping to help me. I have passed to my buyer the information you gave me. I just wanted to make a little note so that I will remember the specifics of the quotation.

I understand that any quotation pre-supposes that the buyer/borrower can qualify. This is to confirm that the quotation is as follows:

| | |
|---|---|
| Purchase price: | Loan amount: |
| Loan type: | Discount points: |
| Quotation firm until: | Loan origination fees: |

This quotation is open for the period indicated. You will honor it regardless of the market conditions at that time of application so long as the application is within the above time period. I have explained to the buyers that the loan origination fee will be payable when the rate is locked and is a non-refundable fee.

Since this is a conventional loan, I understand that, depending on the loan-to-value ratio, you may require private mortgage insurance (PMI). If this is the case, the loan will have to be approved not only by your loan committee but also by your PMI underwriter, which you think usually takes an extra three days.

If I have made an error, please call me at the above telephone number and follow that call up with a letter. I hope the buyers' contract is accepted and they select you for the new loan. I know you can get the processing done on time in a professional manner and will get the loan closed on the scheduled date. You know I enjoy working with you and your company and I look forward to another successful contract, loan and closing.

Sincerely,
The Orcas Island Company

by: Katherine E. Reece

## Letter - Loan Approval--Other Broker

Mrs. Sandy Miller
SanVern Realty and Investment
Boulder, CO. 80303

Re: 4750 Table Mesa Drive

Dear Sandy:

Thank you for the news that the loan requested by the buyers was approved by Howard Mortgage yesterday. I knew Rosie Leino would be able to help them determine the best financing and process the application to a commitment. I know you have conveyed the news to the buyers. I have told the seller the good news. It is also nice to have the commitment before the deadline in the contract. Thank you for your efforts.

There are still a few items to be completed and I wanted to outline them here so that we may each know the extent of our tasks:

I look forward to another smooth closing. It has been nice to have you as the buyers' agent on this particular transaction. I enjoy working with you. Please let me know if there is anything that either I or the seller can do to assist you in your transition.

Sincerely,
The Orcas Island Company

by: Katherine E. Reece
Realtor®, CRS, GRI

cc: Sam and Sandy Seller
Rosie Leino, Howard Mortgage
Escrow officer

**Letter - Loan Approval--Lender**

Ms. Joni Henderson, Loan Officer
Honolulu Mortgage
4510 Salt Lake Boulevard
Honolulu. HI 96818

Re: Loan Commitment/Bob and Betty Buyer

Dear Joni:

I was so happy to get your call today indicating that the loan you helped these borrowers select for their new home has been approved. I know how much you like to help buyers select the loan best suited for their needs. Thank you for helping them and taking the time to call.

I have told the buyers that you indicated that their loan approval was on the terms listed below. Please take a minute to check my understanding and let me know by telephone and certified mail if this is not the case.

1. Loan Amount:$______________________________
2. Fixed interest rate of:_____% per annum.
3. Thirty-year term.
4. Loan origination fee of:____%
5. Loan discount fees of ______%
6. The loan is "locked" through:________________________.

I knew you could get this loan approved, and I appreciate the opportunity to be involved with a loan that you are handling. I know that you were of great assistance in helping the buyers review their personal finances and in selecting this particular loan as the best one for their needs. Good loan counselors such as you are hard to find. I look forward to seeing you at closing.

Sincerely,
The Orcas Island Company

by: Katherine E. Reece
Realtor®, CRS, GRI

cc: Sam and Sandy Seller
c/o The Listing Office
The Listing Office
Bob and Betty Buyer

## Letter - Loan Approval--Buyer

Mr. Jon Goodman and
Mrs. Mimi Goodman
Room 24 Lookout Motel and Casino
Grand Forks, WA 99876

Re: 4750 Table Mesa Drive

Dear Jon and Mimi:

This letter has good news, and I am glad to bring it to you. Enclosed is a copy of the letter I just sent to the mortgage company confirming my conversation with them today wherein they indicated that your loan has been approved on the terms you requested.

I never really believe it until the mortgage company actually writes the check, but I have scheduled the closing for the date indicated in the contract. I will be contacting you as soon as I have the exact figures so that we can arrange for the actual closing time and I can provide you with directions.

Just a last reminder, please review the title insurance commitment that I dropped off yesterday. Just call the title company if you have questions. They are ready to answer any questions that you may have. If I do not hear to the contrary, I will assume that the document meets with your approval.

There are only a few items left on the checklist to be completed. Remember, you need to:

1. Contact Public Service to arrange for the power to be turned on.

2. Make your final inspection on ________________________. I will be picking you both up at the motel at 2:45 p.m.

If there is anything else that I can do, please do not hesitate to call me immediately. Looks like you are on the way into your new home. Congratulations.

Sincerely,
The Orcas Island Company

by: Katherine E. Reece
Realtor®, CRS, GRI

**Letter - Document Delivery to Lender**

Ms. Joni Henderson, Loan Officer
Honolulu Mortgage
4510 Salt Lake Boulevard
Honolulu. HI 96818

Re: Charles A. Reasoner's Application

Dear Joni:

I hope all is going well with this loan application. The approval deadline is coming up fast. The seller's agent reminds me that there are other contracts just waiting for this one to collapse so please let me know if there is anything else that I can do to help you. The proper, timely completion of this loan application and the closing of the contract are the most important things to me.

Here is the copy of the Planned Unit Development that you asked me to pick up for you. I just asked for the documents that you indicated. If it is not what you need, please let me know today.

Again, I want to thank you for working with the buyers and helping them with their selection of their loan program. I know how to sell real estate but I like leaving the selection of the proper and adequate financing to you and the buyers privately. I know they value your professional assistance.

Sincerely,
The Orcas Island Company

by: Katherine E. Reece
Realtor®, CRS, GRI

cc: Charles A. Reasoner, Buyer

**Final Inspection.** Prior to final recordation most contracts allow a final walk through or inspection of the premises by the buyer to ensure that the home is in the same condition and working order as it was at the date of contract acceptance. An item in the contract that indicates that the "buyer will be entitled to a walk-through prior to closing" but which, by implication, leaves open the options--other than total satisfaction--until the day of the walk-through can put you on in a tough position. There is often no mention of what will happen if the buyer disapproves of anything, major or minor, regarding the condition of the house. You may have created a monster. Use precise wording about walk-throughs. Do not let your deal walk through the door. A well written contract would have already addressed any special conditions in "as-is" clauses or specific items to be repaired or replaced at the seller's expense prior to recordation.

Sellers are held more and more accountable for the condition of their homes, especially in a resale. Keep in the mind that the seller expects to convey the home just as he received it (often times years and years earlier), and the buyer most often is expecting a "resale" in "new" condition. It is difficult to explain to the seller that contractual expectations of the consumer have changed dramatically since the time he purchased the home and that new guidelines may exist that depict the common standard of practice for the area as well as compliance with state and federal law. At the same time it is important to help the buyer understand that a resale will be conveyed in working order "consistent with its age".

It is best to "pave the way" with potential objections and expectations of both the buyer and the seller in order that frustrations can be avoided later. It is silly to lose a transaction over a minor item such as a leaking faucet at the end of the transaction, but deals have been lost over even less significant issues. A disclosure to the seller early in the listing period of potential problems that may be identified during a final inspection can facilitate a smooth conveyance.

A "standard" pre-closing walk-through inspection sheet with "standard" wording printed at the bottom can be a useful tool. This is a good opportunity to avoid responsibility for items that were never your responsibility in the first place. Have the seller and buyer check off the condition of the house as they go through it together.

## Appliance Check

All appliances, electrical and plumbing, have been checked by the buyer and are in good working order.

Pool/Spa equipment:

Boundary markers checked:

Discrepancies:____________________________________________________

______________________________________________________________

______________________________________________________________

______________________________________________________________

______________________________________________________________

We have conducted a walk-through inspection of the property, and it is in the condition indicated on the contract, except as noted on this form. We understand that, excluding any attempt to conceal a defect known only to the broker, the broker and his agents are not responsible for the condition of the property. We accept the property in the condition indicated on this form on this date.

______________________________ ______________________________

Buyer date Buyer date

## Problems Frequently Identified During a Final Walk Through

The purpose of this list is to identify problems that often arise during a buyer's final walk-through. It is normally much easier and far less costly to fix problems prior to the walk-through than during the frequently hectic days immediately prior to closing.

1. General Comments.

   a. It is important to operate all equipment on all cycles or setting prior to the walk-through. Frequent offenders are dishwashers, washing machines and dryers.

   b. All equipment features are expected to operate unless identified otherwise in the contract. For example, a refrigerator with an ice maker is expected to keep food cold and make ice.

   c. A condition that existed when you bought the home does not relieve you from the responsibility of correcting the problem when it is your turn to sell. "It has always been that way" is usually not an acceptable reason not to fix a problem. Common offenders are missing keys for locks, sliding glass doors that are locked by way of a wooden rod in the track and electric outlets/switches that are inoperable.

   d. Older, non-digital, built-in clocks and oven timing devises are frequently a problem. Over a period of time the heat from the oven will dry out the lubricating oil causing a built-in clock to malfunction.

   e. Expect the buyer to operate window cranks for all windows including those that may have been untouched for years. Prior to the inspection operate them all yourself. Ensure that there are no broken or chipped panes. Also ensure that all sliding glass doors and screen doors operate and lock properly.

   f. Expect a buyer to try the heating and air conditioning systems to ensure that they not only blow air but that the air is hot or cool.

2. Water Problems.

   a. When a dishwasher is seldom used, grease will frequently build-up in the drainage line causing water to come out of the anti-syphon device.

   b. Check under all sinks (bathroom and kitchen) with a flashlight while the water is running for leaks and drips.

   c. Ensure that all water cutoff valves are fully operational. Some of them are seldom operated and will tend to freeze in the open position over a period of time. Common offenders are sink and toilet cutoff valves.

d. All tub, shower and sink faucets and diverters need to be operated to ensure that there are no leaks or drips.

e. Tub and sink stoppers need to be operational and able to hold water.

f. Toilets need to operate properly and flush without leaking.

g. If you have a sprinkler system for your lawn, ensure that it is operating properly. Expect buyers to test the system and inspect each outlet for proper spray and flow.

h. Know where your main water shut-off is.

3. Electrical Problems.

a. Know what each switch operates. Expect the buyer to test the sockets to ensure that electricity reaches each outlet.

b. All three prong outlets must be grounded.

c. Prior to the walk-through, replace any burned out light bulbs. Pay particular attention to outside garage lights.

d. Inoperable door bells are a frequent problem.

e. Test your smoke detectors and fire alarms to ensure proper operation. Replace batteries if necessary.

f. Expect the buyer to operate all exhaust fans. They should operate without any excessive noise. The range exhaust fan should attract and hold a piece of paper.

p. 389

Seller's Broker: Buyer's Broker:

p. 391

Seller: $_________

## Letter - Broker to Buyer--Checklist for Closing

Mr. Scott Plum
12th and Main Street
Denver, CO 80303

Re: 909 East First Street

Dear Mr. Plum:

The time is fast approaching when you will make the final walk-through of your new home. Keep in mind that while it is new to you, the home has been around for some time. I have included a list that I provide to sellers when I am assisting them for your review.

In addition, the contract calls for you to review the title insurance commitment. I have enclosed your copy. The contract provides that unless you register some objection to the title commitment by __________ it will be deemed accepted. You have only a few days so please give this your prompt attention.

Questions about the commitment? Contact the title officer indicated at the top of the commitment. In the event that it is not satisfactory let me know, and I will deliver a copy to the attorney of your choice. Of course we do not review title commitment as that would be the unauthorized practice of law.

The lender will also probably review it for their own purposes to assure that they are happy with the condition of title. You should not allow the lender's acceptance of the commitment to influence your determination of its sufficiency since the lender has no obligation to you with regard to their determination of the adequacy of the commitment.

Sincerely,
The Orcas Island Company

by: Katherine E. Reece
Realtor®, CRS, GRI

## Letter - Broker to Buyer--Checklist for Closing

Mr. and Mrs. Jonathan A. Goodman
12th and Main Street
Denver, CO 80303

Re: 909 East First Street

Dear Mr. and Mrs. Goodman:

The time is fast approaching when you will make the final walk-through of your new home. Keep in mind that while it is new to you, the home has been around for some time. I have included a list that I provide to sellers when I am assisting them for your review.

The lender has ordered and completed the appraisal that the lender requires to determine whether they will make the loan you have requested. Although you pay for the appraisal, it is the property of the lender. They will however indicate the amount of the appraisal since we made that a condition of the contract.

The survey required by the lender is not really a survey at all, it is an Improvement Location Certificate. It merely indicates that the house is on the lot and roughly in the proper position. It is not intended to be relied upon for any other uses, such as the exact location of any of the improvements or easements in reference to other items. There is no substitute for a boundary survey if you are going to build additions or want an accurate determination of the physical condition of the property. As we discussed, that is not a requirement for the loan and is not included in the expenses of the seller as outlined in the contract.

This would be a good time to verify that your mover has the correct date and time of your anticipated move and that your bank has on deposit ready and available for closing the balance of the amount of your funds needed to complete the transaction. The title company will require that the funds be in the form of a certified check to the order of the title company. I have requested that the title insurance company provide us with the exact amount as soon as possible to facilitate this process.

I'm sure you are happy and excited to be getting close to moving day. It is a real project, but when it's over you will be settled in your nice new home. We are glad you selected us to assist you. Please let me know if there is anything I can do to help with the move or in further preparing for the closing.

Sincerely,
The Orcas Island Company

by: Katherine E. Reece
Realtor®, CRS, GRI

## Letter - Broker to Buyer FHA Appraisal Low

Mr. and Mrs. Jonathan A. Goodman
Apartment 610 A
12th and Main Street
Denver, CO 80303

Re: 909 East First Street

Dear Mr. and Mrs. Goodman:

The time is fast approaching when you will make the final walk-through of your new home. Keep in mind that while it is new to you, the home has been around for some time. I have included a list that I provide to sellers when I am assisting them for your review.

The lender has ordered and completed the appraisal that the lender requires to determine whether they will make the loan you have requested. The FHA appraisal has come back a few thousand dollars lower than anticipated. Therefore, you are in a position to either proceed with the purchase as proposed, making up the loan proceeds shortage with additional down payment, or consider the contract as void, and allow someone else to purchase the home. Please let me know of your decision so that I can advise the seller immediately and prepare the necessary addendum or release form.

The survey required by the lender is not really a survey at all, it is an Improvement Location Certificate. It merely indicates that the house is on the lot and roughly in the proper position. It is not intended to be relied upon for any other uses, such as the exact location of any of the improvements or easements in reference to other items. There is no substitute for a boundary survey if you are going to build additions or want an accurate determination of the physical condition of the property. As we discussed, that is not a requirement for the loan and is not included in the expenses of the seller as outlined in the contract.

I'm sure you are happy and excited to be getting close to moving day. It is a real project but when it's over you will be settled in your nice new home. We are glad you selected us to assist you. Please let me know if there is anything I can do to help with the move or in further preparing for the closing.

Sincerely,
The Orcas Island Company

by: Katherine E. Reece
Realtor®, CRS, GRI

## Letter - Removal of Conditions

Mr. Sam Seller
Mrs. Sandy Seller
4750 Table Mesa Drive
Boulder, CO 80303

Re: 4750 Table Mesa Drive

Dear Sam and Sandy:

I am happy to be able to tell you that the purchaser and his engineer went through the property yesterday for their second inspection. As of this date, I have not heard any complaints. The contract provided the following:

> "Purchaser, accompanied by such professionals as he alone shall select, shall have the right to inspect the property at the purchaser's expense to determine if the property, in the opinion of the purchaser, is structurally sound. In the event that the purchaser does not indicate to the contrary, the property shall be deemed to be of sound character acceptable to the purchaser. Notice to the contrary must be written, specify the exact details of the deficiency and be delivered to the listing broker prior to the 28th of June, 2007."

At this time I am assuming that this condition is no longer a factor. It looks as though we are one step closer to the closing. The property shows so nicely, and I know it is the result of your efforts. I appreciate being selected to help you sell your house.

Sincerely,
The Orcas Island Company

by: Katherine E. Reece
Realtor®, CRS, GRI

cc: Buyer

## The Contract Changes

**Consideration, The Key.** Somewhere along the line, the original contractual agreement as proposed by the buyer and accepted by the seller may change. Consideration is the key to unlocking this puzzle. Always ensure that each side has altered its obligation in some manner.

**Case in Point.** *The classic case is the one where the builder and owner sign a contract for the construction of a building. Halfway through the construction, the builder announces that there is not enough money to finish the project and that he will quit if the contract can not be renegotiated. The parties then agree to a new contract for more money. The builder goes back to work and completes the building. When asked to pay the additional amount, the owner refuses and the case goes to court.*

*The decision: There was no consideration for the revision. The owner was entitled to exactly what he received as outlined in the first contract, and the builder provided nothing new in return for the increased price. Lacking additional consideration, the new contract was not enforceable.*

**Extension and Modification Agreements.** Great care should be exercised to recite the additional consideration, if it exists, for the modification or extension of the contract. Generally, if the obligations of both sides are altered, that is enough. The use of the words "this contract supersedes and replaces all previous contracts between the parties for this property" should be used only when that is the intent of the parties. Be careful that all the desired clauses from the first contract make it into the subsequent modified contract. Often it is better to draft a modification agreement, keeping all unchanged parts of the contract intact and only changing some of the terms.

**Use of a Contract Modification and Mutual Release Agreement.** When the modifications are negotiated in return for some performance or when the parties have made concessions, whether through threat of nonperformance or to settle claims, it is very nice to obtain a final settlement agreement. This is a good place to try to limit the recourse against the broker.

**Release Agreements - General Comments and Format.** The following is a formal agreement structure. It will look very much like an agreement drafted by a lawyer. If you want to make it more low-key but still effective, leave out the lawyer words such as "Witnesseth"," Whereas"," Now Therefore", etc. Although it has no legal effect, the title of the document is always a helpful hint for the person who expects a certain document; the content controls.

These agreements contain many provisions that are not needed in the average simple agreement. In addition, there are some appropriate little clauses for general contract preparation that could be taken from this agreement.

"WHEREAS" paragraphs report what has occurred. These are descriptive paragraphs to orient the reader with regard to which transaction is the subject of the release, the things that led up to the settlement, and a little about the dispute. Be concise. Use as many as you need to use.

"Word" is a way to label or identify the appropriate word. From then on it can be used with an initial capital letter. John and Mary Buyer "Buyers" for example.

**Sample Release Agreement**

THIS AGREEMENT, made and entered into this___ day of ___, by and between ______________________________ and______________________________, collectively the "Parties";

WITNESSETH:

WHEREAS, the Parties______________ entered into a contract for the purchase and sale of the property known as:

"Property";

NOW, THEREFORE, each of the parties hereby agrees with the understanding that the other parties are relying upon the representations herein contained, or, for and in consideration of the following promises and conditions, the parties hereby agree as follows:

1.
2.

IN WITNESS WHEREOF, we have executed this Sample Release Agreement on the day and date immediately following our respective signatures and hereby receipt for a copy of the same.

______________________________ date

______________________________ date

## Contract Modification and Mutual Release Agreement

THIS AGREEMENT, entered into this ____ day of ____________, by and between ________________________________________________________________ ("Seller");
and ______________________________________________________________ ("Buyer");
and ________________________________________________________ ("Seller's Broker"),
and ________________________________________________________ ("Buyer's Broker"),
all of whom shall constitute the parties ("Parties");

WITNESSETH:

WHEREAS, Seller and Buyer entered into a certain Contract for the Purchase and Sale of Real Estate ("Contract") regarding the "Property" commonly known as: ________________________________________________________________________; and,

WHEREAS, there is a dispute between the parties with regard to the total square footage of the Property, its value, the items that are to be transferred with the Property, the possession date and the liability for the condition of the Property on and after this date; and,

WHEREAS, a new loan has been obtained by the Buyer, the Property has been inspected by the Buyer and/or the Buyer's authorized agent; and,

WHEREAS, the Parties wish to resolve their disputes as they relate to this Contract, specifically but not by way of limitation as they relate to the aforementioned items, and to forever fully release and discharge each other from any and all liability of any nature which may have arisen as a result of the indicated Contract, and the events that followed and provide for the closing and transfer of a proper deed as contemplated in the Contract;

NOW, THEREFORE, each of the Parties hereby irrevocably covenants, promises and agrees as follows, with the knowledge and intent that the other parties rely on these promises, covenants, agreements and representations:

1. That the Gross Sales Price indicated in the Contract is hereby reduced by the amount of $__________________; and,

2. That the actual square footage is unknown and not a material part of the transaction; and,

3. That the date for possession shall be ______________________; and,

4. The items contained in the Bill of Sale are the only items that are being transferred as a part of the Contract, that they have a relative value of $__________ and are hereby receipted for by the Buyer in their present condition; and,

5. That the Buyer has had ample time and opportunity to inspect the Property, and hereby accepts the Property in its present condition, AS

IS, WITHOUT ANY WARRANTY, EXPRESS OR IMPLIED, INCLUDING ANY WARRANTY OF FITNESS FOR A PARTICULAR PURPOSE; and,

6. Except with respect to the enforcement of this Mutual Release, the Parties, for themselves, their heirs, successors and assigns, do hereby remise, release and forever discharge each other, their representatives and agents, servants, officers, directors, heirs, successors, and assigns, of and from any and all claims, actions, causes of action, demands, agreements, damages, costs, promises, expenses and compensation, in law or in equity, known or unknown, which the undersigned Parties, their respective, heirs, successors or assigns, or any of them, may have against one another or which may hereafter accrue or occur, in connection with, on account of, or in any way stemming from any transaction, matter, thing or occurrence the source of which is the Contract, including but not limited to, any and all claims of breach of any contract or agreement whether written or oral, any claims for money had and received, fraud, misrepresentation, negligence, breach of a fiduciary duty, specific performance, and any other claims based on any and all legal or equitable theories upon which a claim for relief or recovery can or could be based; and,

7. That the Parties have each had an opportunity to seek legal counsel and have done so or elected not to do so as their sole and independent act and have not relied in any fashion on any representation made by any party or any agent or employee of any party, for any advice or direction as to the advisability of entering into this Mutual Release; and,

8. That all Parties understand that after this release is executed there will be no opportunity to reevaluate or reopen the matters herein indicated. It being the express purpose of this Mutual Release for everyone to forever completely release the other from any and all claims arising out of the Contract; and,

9. That in the event any party commences any legal action as a result of this release, whether to enforce it, defend an action based on it or otherwise, the non-defaulting party shall be entitled to a judgment in addition to all other sums, equal to the non-defaulting party's actual reasonable attorney's fees.

10. This agreement contains the full and complete agreements of the Parties. There are no promises, agreements or representations between any of the Parties except as set forth in this Agreement.

11. This agreement shall be construed under the laws of the State of ____________________, and the Parties agree the venue shall be proper in the _________ Court located in _________________________.

12. The singular shall include the plural and the plural the singular. Any references in this Agreement to gender shall include all genders.

13. This Agreement may be executed in counterparts and, in that event, the counterparts, taken together, shall constitute a single instrument.

IN WITNESS WHEREOF, we the undersigned, after having fully read this agreement, hereby execute the same and acknowledge receipt of a duplicate original of the same on the day and date first above indicated.

| Seller: | Buyer: |
|---|---|
| ______________________ | ______________________ |
| ______________________ | ______________________ |
| Seller's Broker: | Buyer's Broker: |
| By:____________________ | By:____________________ |

## Release of Earnest Money

When earnest money has been deposited with the broker and a dispute arises as to the application of the funds, the only way to insure that the broker will be able to distribute the money without the possibility of a future suit is to call for the mutual release by all parties and specify the directions to be followed for the disbursement of the funds.

There is no doubt that the pressure will be increasing from either or both parties, as well as from the cooperating broker, to have the broker make a determination regarding who is entitled to the money based on a subjective look at the actions or inactions of either or both parties. To allow yourself to get caught here, no matter what you believe is correct, is an error in judgment and a good time to fall back on "company policy," that is, a mutual release.

Do not let the threat of litigation or the assurance that "everything will be all right" or the promise, no matter how tempting, that one party, usually the seller, will "indemnify you against loss" lull you into a false sense of security. Sure, everybody is going to sue you because you have the money. Get it settled now while you have it. When you have had enough, you can ask the court to take the money and decide who gets how much of it. In addition, you may still reserve your claim to a portion of the money. This is addressed in many of the standard forms. To be effective, the form should indicate that the court "shall," not "may," award attorney's fees to the prevailing party. Courts are wary of having to determine attorney's fees and they avoid the imposition of an award for fees unless the contract is specific.

The Mutual Release that follows contains very comprehensive release language, but you should be able to pare your own form down a bit. For a legal appearance it is good to give it a format similar to the one presented; however, a letter format is just as binding. The "Whereas" clauses simply state facts already agreed to and lay the foundation for the solution. You can do this in a letter in any fashion you wish. The "Now, Therefore" clause sets forth the action agreed to and to be taken. Note some of the boiler plate language about reliance. This is nice to have in a release letter.

A form like this can be set up for any mix of parties and agents and is best in a printed and standard-appearing format. Even if it is a special form, title it with a standard label, type the form right margin justified, and then copy it so that it does not appear to be special. People sign "standard" forms much more easily than ragged-right, double-spaced letters because there is a sense of correctness about a "standard" form. Use this to your advantage.

**Mutual Release and Distribution Agreement**

THIS AGREEMENT, entered into this ____ day of ____________, by and between ______________________________________________ ("Seller"); and ______________________________________________ ("Buyer"); and ______________________________________________ ("Seller's Broker"), and ______________________________________________ ("Buyer's Broker"), all of whom shall constitute the parties ("Parties");

WITNESSETH:

WHEREAS, Seller and Buyer on ________________________, entered into a certain Contract for the Purchase and Sale of Real Estate ("Contract") for the purchase and sale of the property located at ________________________________, ("Property"); and,

WHEREAS, pursuant to said Contract, Buyer deposited with the Seller's Broker as Earnest Money ("Earnest Money") the amount of $__________________ in the form of a personal check; and,

WHEREAS, there is a dispute between the parties and they wish to resolve their disputes as they relate to this contract and to forever fully release and discharge each other from any and all liability which may have arisen as a result of the indicated contract and the events that followed and provide for the disbursement of the Earnest Money;

NOW, THEREFORE, each of the Parties hereby irrevocably covenants, promises and agrees as follows, with the knowledge and intent that the other Parties rely on these promises, covenants, agreements and representations:

1. That the Earnest Money, as soon as the funds are considered collected funds, are available for withdrawal without limitation, and have cleared the banking system, be distributed as follows:

   Seller: $__________ Buyer: $__________
   Seller's Agent: $__________ Buyer's Agent: $__________
   Other:____________________________ $__________

2. Except with respect to the enforcement of this Mutual Release, the Parties, for themselves, their heirs, successors and assigns, do hereby remise, release and forever discharge each other, their representatives and agents, servants, officers, directors, heirs, successors, and assigns, of and from any and all claims, actions, causes of action, demands, agreements, damages, costs, promises, expenses and compensation, in law or in equity, known or unknown, which the undersigned Parties, their respective heirs, successors or assigns, or any of them, may have against one another or which may hereafter accrue or occur, in connection with, on account of, or in any way stemming from any transaction, matter, thing or occurrence the

source of which is the Contract, including but not limited to, any and all claims of breach of any contract or agreement whether written or oral, any claims for money had and received, fraud, misrepresentation, negligence, breach of a fiduciary duty, specific performance, and any other claims based on any and all legal or equitable theories upon which a claim for relief or recovery can or could be based; and,

3. That the Parties have each had an opportunity to seek legal counsel and have done so or elected not to do so as their sole and independent act and have not relied in any fashion on any representation made by any party or any agent or employee of any party for any advice or direction as to the advisability of entering into this Mutual Release; and,

4. That all Parties understand that after this release is executed there will be no opportunity to reevaluate or reopen the matters herein indicated. It being the express purpose of this Mutual Release for everyone to forever completely release the other from any and all claims arising out of the Contract; and,

5. That in the event any party commences any legal action as a result of this release, whether to enforce it, defend an action based on it or otherwise, the non-defaulting party shall be entitled to a judgment in addition to all other sums, equal to the non-defaulting party's actual reasonable attorney's fees.

6. This Agreement may be executed in counterparts and, in that event, the counterparts, taken together, shall constitute a single instrument.

IN WITNESS WHEREOF, we the undersigned, after having fully read this agreement, hereby execute the same and acknowledge receipt of a duplicate original of the same and of our respective checks in the amount indicated as being payable to each of us, on the day and date first above indicated.

| Seller: | Buyer: |
|---|---|
| ______________________ | ______________________ |
| ______________________ | ______________________ |
| Seller's Broker: | Buyer's Broker: |
| By:____________________ | By:____________________ |

**Letter - Earnest Money Dispute**

Mr. Sam Seller
Mrs. Sandy Seller
4750 Table Mesa Drive
Boulder, CO 80303

Mr. Bob Buyer
Mrs. Betty Buyer
25 Temporary Housing Square
Boulder, CO 80303

Re: 4750 Table Mesa Drive

Dear Sam, Sandy, Bob and Betty:

It is unfortunate that there has been an impasse as to the disposition and distribution of the earnest money deposit held by this company. There is currently on deposit in our trust account the sum of $_____________. According to state law, we are prohibited from assessing the merits of competing claims to the earnest money or whether there is or is not a contract or a breach of contract. That is the job assigned to the court system, and we as real estate professionals are simply not licensed by this state to make that determination.

We will continue to hold the earnest money in our trustee or escrow account, segregated from our general operating funds, as provided by law, until either the court directs us as to how much to distribute and to whom or we receive the enclosed Mutual Release and Distribution Agreement signed by everyone.

In the event that neither of those alternatives seems to be forthcoming, we will interplead the money into the court, name each of you as having an interest in the funds, and ask the court to make a determination. You will note that your contract provides that we are entitled to recover our attorney's fees out of the earnest money in the event we are involved in any action dealing with the disposition of the earnest money. For that reason, we will endeavor to wait for what we feel is a reasonable time before taking any legal action to resolve the dispute.

I encourage you to seek competent legal counsel and decide amongst yourselves how you want the money to be distributed. I am sorry that I can not make this determination for us all; it is simply illegal for me to attempt a determination on the merits. I am a real estate broker and have no desire to be an attorney or a judge in this matter.

Thank you for your cooperation, understanding, and assistance in this matter. Please let me know if there is anything that I can do to assist either of you or your attorneys. Since we also have an attorney, we are sure that you will understand that we would like all communication to go through this office before our attorney is contacted so that we too can keep our attorney's fees from exceeding the earnest money.

I await your response.

Sincerely,
The Orcas Island Company

by: Oliver E. Frascona, Broker

cc: ORIGINALS SENT CERTIFIED
Copies sent Regular Mail
Other parties

**Letter - Earnest Money Dispute/Title Company**

Mr. Sam Seller
Mrs. Sandy Seller
4750 Table Mesa Drive
Boulder, CO 80303

Mr. Bob Buyer
Mrs. Betty Buyer
25 Temporary Housing Square
Boulder, CO 80303

Re: 4750 Table Mesa Drive

Dear Sam, Sandy, Bob and Betty:

It is unfortunate that everyone can not agree on the distribution of the earnest money deposit, currently in the amount of $_______________, held by the title or escrow company in their trust account. According to state law, this firm and the title company are prohibited from determining the merits of competing claims to the earnest money or whether or not there is a valid contract dealing with the property or the earnest money or whether that contract has been breached. That is the job assigned to the court system, and we as real estate professionals are simply not licensed by this state to make that determination.

My conversations with the title company indicate that they will need a Mutual Release and Distribution Agreement executed by everyone before they will take any action to disburse the earnest money. A sample of their standard agreement is attached for your review. The title company has the option of interpleading the money into the court, naming each of us as someone they feel may have an interest in the funds, and asking the court to make a determination. You will note that your contract provides that we are entitled to recover our attorney's fees out of the earnest money in the event we are involved in any action dealing with the disposition of the earnest money other than as claimants for our portion of the earnest money retained by the seller.

In the event that neither of those alternatives seems to be forthcoming, we will interplead the money into the court, name each of you as having an interest in the funds, and ask the court to make a determination. You will note that your contract provides that we are entitled to recover our attorney's fees out of the earnest money in the event we are involved in any action dealing with the disposition of the earnest money. For that reason, we will endeavor to wait for what we feel is a reasonable time before taking any legal action to resolve the dispute.

I encourage you to seek competent legal counsel and decide amongst yourselves how you want the money to be distributed. I am sorry that I can not make this determination for us all; it is simply illegal for me to attempt a determination on the merits. I am a real estate broker and have no desire to be an attorney or a judge in this matter.

Thank you for your cooperation, understanding, and assistance in this matter. Please let me know if there is anything that I can do to assist either of you or your attorneys. Since we also have an attorney, we are sure that you will understand that we would like all communication to go through this office before our attorney is contacted so that we too can keep our attorney's fees from exceeding the earnest money.

I await your response.

Sincerely,
The Orcas Island Company

by: Oliver E. Frascona, Broker

cc: ORIGINALS SENT CERTIFIED
Copies sent Regular Mail
Other parties

enclosure:

## Returning Earnest Money to a Trusted Client

**Basic Guidelines.** There are those occasions when, for whatever reasons, you decide to deliver either all or part of the earnest money to one of the parties. Sometimes it is apparent that one party does not intend to take any action or employ an attorney but is simply stalling and refusing to execute a release. Other times, for whatever reason, the amount in question simply does not lend itself to litigation.

**General Rule.** As a general rule, it is best never to transfer the money to anyone other than your client. Cooperation, testimony, interest, and pressure are easier to control if you keep the money.

**Broker Portion.** You may be entitled to a portion of forfeited earnest money. Retention of your portion may help to offset your potential loss and make the matter less risky. Care should be exercised prior to distributing any money to a subagent as its recovery may be more difficult when the action starts. As a general rule, never pay anyone, especially subagents, buyers' brokers, or independent contractors until the matter is resolved. Obtaining a return of the money delivered, no matter what agreement has been reached, will never be cost effective.

**Notice.** Prior to distribution of the earnest money, it might be a good idea to put everyone on notice that you intend to distribute it and to specify the basis for your determination. The longer you have had the money, the greater the need to notify people. The failure to receive any formal or timely requests for its delivery does not eliminate the need to provide everyone with some form of notice. Certified Mail, Return Receipt Requested, Addressee Only, is obviously the best of the options.

**Indemnification.** There is no need to give anyone any money without an Indemnification Agreement holding the broker, agent, subagent, or other parties, harmless against any and all loss that the broker may sustain, including attorney's fees, in the defense or ultimate payment of a claim to the money. The broker should reserve the right to settle any claim by paying the claim in full and receiving recovery from the seller.

**Collected Funds.** Many brokers have written checks on uncollected funds in their hurry to resolve an earnest money problem. Be sure that the check that you received for the earnest money has cleared both your bank and the bank it was drawn on before you hand over the money. A good general rule is ten days, but make two simple phone calls and confirm it.

**Letter - Aggressive Position--Earnest Money**

Certified Mail

Mr. Sam Seller
Mrs. Sandy Seller
4750 Table Mesa Drive
Boulder, CO 80303

Mr. Bob Buyer
Mrs. Betty Buyer
25 Temporary Housing Square
Boulder, CO 80303

Re: 4750 Table Mesa Drive

Dear Sam, Sandy, Bob and Betty:

This firm has been holding the earnest money in the amount of $__________ for over a year since the transaction was scheduled to close. This is a small amount of money and it does not seem appropriate for us to retain it indefinitely. Although we have the right to pay the money into the registry of the court and give you both the ability to enter your appearances and fight over the money, we have decided to take an alternate action.

After careful consideration and review of the matter with our attorneys, our feelings are as follows: The purchaser will never willingly allow the earnest money to be distributed under any terms to anyone; there is not enough money for anyone to hire an attorney and fight the matter; there has been no claim for the money in the form of litigation; the purchaser has never presented us with a substantiated claim to the money; therefore, feeling confident as we do in our relationship with the seller, and after receiving from the seller an assurance of indemnification in a form acceptable to us, we are going to distribute the money to the seller. If, however, the buyers can, prior to noon on ________________________, present and substantiate their claim to the earnest money, specifically itemizing the facts that support the buyers' position in a manner that, in our opinion, is sufficient to warrant continued retention of the monies, we will continue to retain the money.

Sincerely,
The Orcas Island Company

by: Oliver E. Frascona, Broker

cc: Copies sent Regular Mail

# Chapter Seven
# Closing Matters
### *Finishing The Job*

## Professional Details

As closing approaches and passes, there are a lot of little items that will need your attention. This is a good time to mend strained relationships, confirm forever the strong ones, and have a last attempt at protecting yourself from the potential problems that lurk out there after closing. This is the time to reconfirm oral representations, attempt to bootstrap disclaimers that should have been made but were not, and to try to make everyone feel that they will never have a claim against you in the future. Most litigation, with the exception of earnest money actions, comes after closing.

**The Late Disclaimer.** Closing is upon you and there are a few problems you would like to put to bed. Disclaimers, to be effective, must have taken place before the decision to purchase or sell was made. The theory is that the party had all the information, including the disclaimers, before he obligated himself on the contract. Once a party has changed his position, he will claim that had he known the facts you revealed in the disclaimer he would not have changed his position. In other words, he relied upon your silence or what he thought you indicated and you are now prevented from making an effective disclaimer since he can not reverse the transaction, absent rescission. Do not let that deter you. "Better late than never" definitely applies here. It is how the parties feel that is most important. If they feel that they have released you, that may be enough to remove from there minds an action against you.

**Memorandum of Previous Oral Disclaimer.** If you are placed in the above position, you should structure all disclaimers and other attempts to limit your liability in the form of memoranda of what was previously, timely, and orally indicated to the proper party. Just start the statement with "This is a memorandum of our previous oral understanding", and then state whatever you feel you need.

**Protective Language Placement at Closing.** The best place to add the necessary statements is directly on the closing statement. The front page is appropriate but the back will suffice. Statements in your handwriting are not as good as typed ones and can raise some questions, but they are better than none at all. If you can get the person from whom you are trying to protect yourself to write it in their handwriting, you are doing very well indeed.

**Hazard and Fire Insurance.** This is an area very few people spend much time considering. It is a place in the transaction where a disaster can strike. It is something for which you will probably be held responsible. You will only have to have one fire while you are at closing, or one fire in the post closing pre-occupancy period, to become a devout insurance fanatic. Regardless of the form of financing, always check for the existence of insurance.

For an assumption, the insurance premium is often prorated and the policy is transferred to the new buyer. Care needs to be exercised to ensure that there is in fact a policy in force and that, effective with the closing date, the buyer will be a named insured. There is no substitute for a written letter or endorsement from the insurance company or the insurance agent. The principal, the insurance company, is bound to uphold what the insurance agent writes.

For a new loan you need to verify, in addition to the verification done by the new lender, that the insurance premium is paid and the insurance is in force as of the date of the transfer of deed. The buyer will elect to buy a homeowner's policy or a fire and extended insurance policy. The first is for owner occupants and the latter for a rental house. Do not give advice on the type of policy that is selected. Never give advice regarding the company to select nor the extent of coverage.

Nothing takes the place of a paid policy. Everything else is open for interpretation. Insurance companies make money by collecting premiums, not by paying claims. They know that.

**Homeowner vs. Rental Policy.** Different coverage exists for owner occupied and rental, or nonowner-occupied, property. If there is a change in the character, even for a few days, make sure the insurance reflects the actual use of the property. This loss is so rare that we tend to ignore the potential problem; yet the insurance to cover a potential disaster is so easy to obtain.

If the seller remains in possession of the property after the closing, he most probably has either canceled or transferred his policy to the buyer. Therefore, he is not covered since he is now a tenant. He is not insured and neither is his property. He needed a tenant's policy for this limited period.

Likewise, the buyer, not yet the occupant, may have obtained, either by assignment from the seller or independently, a homeowners policy, although he technically is not a homeowner occupant. His new insurance will not cover the loss of the possessions of the old owner occupant. He needed coverage similar to that of a landlord for this short period.

**Case in Point.** *Oliver will never forget sitting at the closing table with the buyer and seller. The property had just transferred, when the call came in that his buyer's, his customer's, new home was on fire. He was in his rookie year and knew nothing about insurance. The seller's policy was not in effect and the buyer's policy covered an owner occupied home. The seller had forgotten to turn off a burner on the stove, and the buyer had put down a newspaper. Fortunately the loss was a little less than Oliver's commission. A hard lesson to learn.*

**Title Insurance.** Some companies never issue the Title Insurance Policy. Without the actual policy, no one can make a claim. A tickler for about two weeks after closing can avoid latent problems. This also gives you the chance for additional contact with the purchaser and an opportunity to show how professional and detail oriented you are.

**Security.** There is no excuse for failing to give a new buyer a written suggestion to get the property re-keyed immediately. Do not suggest anyone nor take this as a job that you will be responsible for arranging. It is simply a task for the buyer. So simply remind him.

**Payment History.** In the event that there is owner financing, the chances are good that no one will ever keep an accurate record of the payments made, the dates, the amounts, etc. Even new lenders make mistakes on occasion. The recommendation of a ledger system for each party to track the payments serves two purposes. First, it gives them both the same form on which to make their entries. This alone will help simplify any potential problem should one arise. Second, for the life of the loan your name will be printed on the sample ledger card!

These items should be included as a minimum:

| Date Paid | Check Number | Total Paid | Interest | Principal | Balance Due |
|---|---|---|---|---|---|
| | | | | | |
| | | | | | |

**Document Retention.** Few people have a grasp on the nature and value of important documents. Most people have not suffered a major casualty or loss by fire or theft. Advise the use of a safe deposit box for the Deed, the Title Insurance Policy, and especially for the owner-carry Note and Mortgage. If none is available, maybe you, under the right circumstances, could offer that service. It might be a nice way to keep in contact with the parties. Make sure you retain documents under a specific agreement.

**Homeowner's Exemption.** In order to qualify for the homeowner's property tax exemption available in some states, it is necessary to complete a form prior to the end of the year that the home was purchased. The buyer who occupies his home is then eligible for a reduction in his property taxes for the next tax year and each year thereafter. Most buyers forget to do this after all the documentation is signed and they are busy with their move and transition into the new neighborhood. A reminder to complete this task is another useful method of keeping in contact with the new buyer.

**Tip.** *Research the tax department to ascertain if homeowners in your farm area are entitled to or are already registered for their tax exemption. This is always guaranteed to generate calls.*

## FORMAL NOTICE
## OF
## CONTRACT CLOSING AND SETTLEMENT

**YOU ARE HEREBY FORMALLY INFORMED THAT** on the day and date below indicated, the indicated closing agent will, after preparing all the required legal documents and calculating the amounts due and payable, be present, pursuant to the terms of the contract for the purchase and sale of real property indicated herein, to conduct the closing of that certain contract dated _______________, 19_____, entered into by and between ____________________________________________, as buyer(s) and ____________________________________________, as seller(s) for the purchase and sale of the following described real property, to-wit:

**CLOSING AGENT/LOCATION:**

**CLOSING DATE:**_______________________________________, 19__________.
**CLOSING TIME:**_____________________________________ (a.m.)(p.m.)

**WHEN AND WHERE YOU MAY APPEAR** prepared to close according to the terms of said contract.

**FAILURE TO APPEAR** may subject you, the defaulting party, to the following legal action indicated in the contract:

**FUNDS REQUIRED:** The buyer and/or seller must be present a cashier's check or certified check drawn on a local clearing house bank payable to the order of the indicated closing agent, or cash in the final settlement amount herein below indicated. The basis for, and the calculation of, said amount shall be made available to all parties for inspection at the date, place and time of closing.

Seller:$_____________________________ Buyer:$_____________________________

**IN WITNESS WHEREOF, AFTER BEING DULY SWORN UPON OATH,** the undersigned has executed this Formal Notice of Contract Closing and Settlement this ____________ day of ____________________, 19____.

**SELLER/BUYER:**____________________________________________
by:____________________________________, as authorized agent.

**WITNESS MY HAND AND OFFICIAL SEAL** this _____ day of __________, 19______

(Notary Seal/Court Clerk) ________________________________________

My commission expires:________________________________

## Letter - Document Retention

Mr. Sam Seller and Mrs. Sandy Seller
25 Temporary Housing Square
Boulder, CO 80303

Mr. Bob Buyer and Mrs. Betty Buyer
4750 Table Mesa Drive
Boulder, CO 80303

Re: 4750 Table Mesa Drive/Document Retention

Dear Mr. and Mrs. Seller and Mr. and Mrs. Buyer:

Congratulations on the successful conveyance of this exceptional property. All of us at The Orcas Island Company were glad to have been able to assist all of you with this transaction. After closing there are a few administrative details that remain. Although we indicated them to each of you at the closing, we like to follow up with a letter to confirm what is yet to be done for your records. As you have surely surmised by now, we are detail-oriented letter writers.

The transaction provided for a loan to be carried by the seller for the buyer. Since neither of you is in the lending business, we would suggest a simple record-keeping procedure for you. Of course, this is just our idea and your accountant, or tax adviser, may require different standards and records to be kept. Our suggestions are for the practical and not the legal or accounting record-keeping rules.

| Date Paid | Check Number | Total Paid | Interest | Principal | Balance Due |
|---|---|---|---|---|---|
| | | | | | |
| | | | | | |

In addition, save all checks and receipts that relate to the expenses related to the loan, the insurance, any improvements that you might make or the taxes and assessments. The holders of the note and mortgage need to keep these in a very safe place since they will be required to present them for the release of the mortgage and receipt of the final payment.

If we can assist you in any way, please do not hesitate to call.

Sincerely,
The Orcas Island Company
by: Katherine E. Reece, CRS, GRI

**Letter - Buyer Broker to Buyer--Title Policy and Deed**

Mr. Bob Buyer and
Mrs. Betty Buyer
4750 Table Mesa Drive
Boulder, CO 80303

Re: 4750 Table Mesa Drive

Dear Bob and Betty:

I am so glad that we could help you with the purchase of your new house. Nothing is as rewarding as knowing that I have been able to help a nice family like yours acquire this home. I know you will enjoy the home, and I am glad that we have become friends. You made a good selection.

There are a couple of items to which you need to be alert in the near future. First, after the deed has been recorded, it will be returned to your current address. If you do not get it in three weeks, please let me know. When it arrives, you should be prepared to put it in a safe place. The act of recording the deed evidences your acceptance of it and puts the world on notice that you own the property. A deed is not transferred by endorsement. Therefore no one could obtain the physical deed and endorse it over to another purchaser in the way one might endorse a check. Still, I like to recommend that the deed be retained in a safe place.

Similarly, the title insurance policy will arrive in the mail in about four weeks. This is a different matter. The actual title insurance policy needs to be retained in a safe place since it will have to be surrendered in the event of a problem or in the event that you want a reissue rate on a subsequent sale. If you do not receive this in the allotted time, contact me or the title company directly. It is very important that you obtain the policy and that it be reviewed to ensure that it reflects exactly the terms of the commitment.

If you need someone to assist you in obtaining these documents, please let me know. There is no charge for this service, and I want to make sure the transaction is completed properly. I look forward to seeing you both as soon as you are settled.

Sincerely,
The Orcas Island Company

by: Katherine E. Reece
Realtor®, CRS, GRI

# JUST A REMINDER!

Mr. Bob Buyer and
Mrs. Betty Buyer
4750 Table Mesa Drive
Boulder, CO 80303

Re: 4750 Table Mesa Drive

Dear Bob and Betty:

Do you have your receipt for having filed the Homeowners Tax Exemption Form? In order to qualify for the homeowners exemption for next year as the new owner for you home, you must file with the Tax Office no later than the last day of this year. You may recall we discussed the form just prior to the closing of your new home.

If you are uncertain whether or not you are registered at the Tax Office or need information for filing now, please call me at my home or office number immediately. I can not file this for you. You must do it yourself. I want to make sure that you obtain all the tax relief to which you are entitled.

Sincerely,
The Orcas Island Company

by: Katherine E. Reece
Realtor®, CRS, GRI

**Letter - Buyer--New Keys**

Mr. Bob Buyer and
Mrs. Betty Buyer
4750 Table Mesa Drive
Boulder, CO 80303

Re: 4750 Table Mesa Drive

Dear Bob and Betty:

Congratulations on your new home! I know you are excited to have completed what may have seemed like an ordeal at times. It took work and lots of decisions on your part to find it, contract for it, finance it and close the transaction. Although we were the agents for the seller, we enjoyed assisting you in the transaction.

I know I mentioned this at closing, but I want to remind you again that the key to your home has passed through many hands during the showing and sale procedure. While we do not know of any unaccounted-for keys, we always recommend that new owners have the property re-keyed as soon as possible. We can not possibly be responsible for the security of the home or represent that you are the only people with keys.

If I can help you with a locksmith, just let me know. I look forward to seeing the house after you finish all that you indicated you were going to do to the house. A new house is a lot of work and a lot of fun. Thank you again.

Sincerely,
The Orcas Island Company

by: Katherine E. Reece
Realtor®, CRS, GRI

## Letter - Buyer--New Keys #2

Mr. Bob Buyer and
Mrs. Betty Buyer
4750 Table Mesa Drive
Boulder, CO 80303

Re: 4750 Table Mesa Drive

Dear Bob and Betty:

Congratulations on your new home! I know you are excited to have completed what may have seemed like an ordeal at times. It took work and lots of decisions on your part to find it, contract for it, finance it and close the transaction. Although we were the agents for the seller, we enjoyed assisting you in the transaction.

I know I mentioned this at closing, but I want to remind you again that the key to your home has passed through many hands during the showing and sale procedure. While we do not know of any keys that are unaccounted for, we always recommend that new owners have the property re-keyed as soon as possible. We can not be responsible for the security of the home or represent that you are the only people with keys. We have made arrangements with the locksmith indicated below to re-key your home at our expense. All you need to do is call them.

Thank you for selecting a property listed with this office. I am glad that we have met. I hope your son is enjoying the swing set and the tree house. I will look forward to seeing you at the pool this summer.

Sincerely,
The Orcas Island Company

by: Katherine E. Reece
Realtor®, CRS, GRI

cc: Fast Action Locksmiths
Phone:

**Letter - Cooperating Salesperson**

Thomas A. Gill
The Other Real Estate Company
400 Way
AcrossTown, CO 00001

Re: Property located at 4750 Table Mesa Drive

Dear Tom:

Congratulations on your successful sale. I don't know about you but closings are the best part of this business to me. Any delays or exasperation experienced by either or both of our clients are now mostly forgotten by all, and we finally can measure the value of our work by the paycheck we receive.

It has truly been a pleasure to work with you in the successful closing of this property. Your dedication and professionalism in the negotiations both before and during the escrow process certainly helped to reduce potential tension and stress. I look forward to many more transactions together in the months ahead.

Let's do it again soon!

Sincerely,
The Orcas Island Company

by: Katherine E. Reece
Realtor®, CRS, GRI

# Goodbye and Good Luck!

We have had a good time compiling and writing this book. We hope that it will help you attract and retain buyers and sellers. We wish you the best of prosperity, clarity, and the resulting happiness that comes from the inner knowledge that you are doing a professional job of assisting people with their most basic of needs, shelter. If you have questions or comments, please feel free to drop us a letter. We want to continue making this guide as useful a tool as we possibly can, and I would value your thoughts as you modify and apply these ideas and methods in the course of your own work.

It has been our desire to create a comprehensive manual for all real estate professionals, both the inexperienced and seasoned, salespeople and brokers. Not all the letters and forms will work for you. Take the ones that do and ignore the others. Modify the terms and conditions as you need to reflect the particularities of your marketplace.

The way the consumer views you as a professional is determined by the way conduct yourself. They see you first and last in your written communication. Consumers today expect the latest in technology to help them acquire or convey that most basic of needs, shelter. However, you can not ignore the most important expectation of the customer or client--that she will receive service. That service includes not only the personal rapport necessary to identify individual needs but also the clarity and business acumen to negotiate successfully and close the transaction on the consumer's behalf.

If you have questions or comments, please do not hesitate to drop us a letter. It is our desire to continue making this guide as useful a tool as we possibly can. We would appreciate your thoughts as you modify and apply these ideas and methods in the course of your work.

## The Authors

**Oliver E. Frascona** is a Colorado native, born and raised in Boulder, Colorado. He did his undergraduate work at the University of Colorado, graduating as a Bachelor of Science in Business with an emphasis in finance and real estate.

Mr. Frascona's mother, Jean Ezard Frascona, an English barrister, and his father, Joseph L. Frascona, a professor, author and attorney, instilled in him a strong desire to become an attorney. After serving as an officer in the United States Navy Reserve, he returned to Colorado, became a licensed real estate salesperson, a Realtor®, and subsequently a broker, listing, selling and building single family homes. He attended law school at night while working as a residential real estate salesman during the day, and graduated with a Doctor of Jurisprudence degree from the University of Denver School of Law in 1974. He began his legal career by practicing real estate and business law. He maintains his real estate broker's license, having been licensed since 1972.

A shareholder in the law firm of Frascona, Joiner and Goodman, P.C., Mr. Frascona limits his personal practice to real estate, business and association law. He is currently a Certified Advanced Law, Contracts, Agency and Risk Reduction Instructor for the Colorado Association of Realtors®, of which he is a member, the attorney for fifteen local boards/associations of Realtors®., a member of Certified Closers and the attorney for many real estate companies, large and small.

His wide experience and insight have given him the opportunity to lecture frequently to the national and state associations of Realtors®, the memberships of large and small brokerage concerns, and various other groups on topics relating to real estate and other timely matters of business and association law throughout the United States.

As an active investor for his personal account, Mr. Frascona has the opportunity to, and regularly does, utilize the services of Realtors® to assist him with the purchase, sale, and management of real estate on behalf of his clients and himself. He is the author of other manuals for the real estate professional and considers his mission as a lawyer to be that of a deal maker rather than a deal breaker. In this regard, he appreciates, recommends, and frequently utilizes the services of Realtors®.

**Katherine E. Reece** is a native of Georgia who has lived in Germany, Florida, Texas, Washington, Hawaii and now Colorado. She began her real estate career as a sales associate when she moved to Oahu, Hawaii in 1985. Katherine consistently maintained a multi-million production and was recognized in both the state and nation for her outstanding production. One such honor ranked her tenth among thirty-five thousand agents in a national franchise. Her ongoing commitment to provide professional services to relocating families earned her a recognition as a national relocation specialist.

Katherine obtained her Broker's license in 1988, earned her Graduate Realtor® Institute designation in 1989 and completed all requirements for accreditation as a Certified Residential Specialist in 1991. In 1992 Katherine was co-founder and President of her own real estate company.

As a real estate professional, Katherine has been proud to be a member of the National Association of Realtors®. Her involvement with both the Hawaii Association of Realtors® and the Honolulu Board of Realtors® has placed her as a director on both boards as well as a participant for membership, legislative, convention, and standard forms committees. She has often testified before city, county and state governments on important housing issues.

Katherine brings the special talents of a practitioner, someone who lists and sells real estate, to this publication.

# Index

## Professional Discounts

As we wrote this book we were aware that there were many products available to assist the professional Realtor®. We asked two vendors if they would offer to those real estate professionals who have purchased this publication a discount toward the purchase of those vendors' products. They kindly agreed.

While we can not guarantee the products, we are proud to be able to bring you the discount. We do have the highest admiration for the two companies represented here.

**Mr. Pat Zaby.** Pat has been kind enough to allow those real estate professionals who have purchased this book a discount on selected products produced by Programs by Pat Zaby, Inc. 4125 Keller Springs Road, Suite 120, Dallas TX 75244. Pat will honor discounts by telephone at 1-214-407-1310. In order to collect your discount tell the operator *"I'd like the miracle of Pat Zaby with the Oliver Frascona discount."*

**Howard and Sandy Sanderson** of Sanderson Data Systems, Inc., 155 West Cedar, Ste. 181, Sequim, WA 98382, producers of "Howard and Friends" and many other computer programs have also kindly allowed us to indicate that they will grant a discount to owners of this publication. You can call Howard and Sandy at 206-452-4100. In order to collect your discount you will need to tell the Sanderson Data Systems' operator *"I'd like the gnomes of Sanderson Data with the Oliver Frascona discount."*

Ask Howard if he has the forms and/or letters integrated into Howard and Friends. It is possible that you can obtain the forms and letters as a part of Howard and Friends.

# *REAL LAW BOOKS, INC.*

Post Office Box 3113 Boulder, Colorado 80307-3113 Telephone 303-494-6661

**ORDER FORM**

## THE *REAL ESTATE* BOOK Forms, Letters and Clauses

by *Oliver E. Frascona, Esq. and Katherine E. Reece*

_____ **Books,** *THE Real Estate BOOK* **49.95** $__________

_____ **Computer Disks,**
containing all the ***Forms, Letters & Clauses***
from *THE Real Estate BOOK* **99.95** $__________

_____ **Forms,** photo ready 8.5" x 11" format
from *The Real Estate BOOK* **49.95** $__________

_____ **Audio Cassette Libraries,** **99.95** $__________

Colorado residents add 6.66% sales tax $__________
Mail order postage and handling 4.00

*Please print or attach business card* **Total Order:** $__________

Name: ____________________________________________

Company: __________________________________________

Address: ___________________________________________

City: ______________________ State:________ Zip:__________

Charge my credit card__________-__________-__________-__________

MC ____ Visa ____ Amex ____ Exp Date:____/____

**Signature:**___________________________________________

Phone: (________) _________-__________________

*For faster service* ***Call: 800-688-1555*** or *FAX 303-494-6309*

Thank You!

**Real** Help for **Real** People in **Real** Estate®